# Principles
# of Language
# Learning
# and Teaching

# Principles of Language Learning and Teaching

## Third Edition

## H. Douglas Brown

San Francisco State University

Prentice Hall Regents
Englewood Cliffs, NJ 07632

**Library of Congress Cataloging-in-Publication Data**

Brown, H. Douglas H., (date)
    Principles of language learning and teaching/H. Douglas Brown.-
-3rd ed.
        p. cm.
    Includes bibliographical references and index.
    ISBN 0-13-191966-0
    1. Language and languages—Study and teaching.  2. Language
acquisition.  I. Title.
P51.B775  1993                              93-26090
418'.007—dc20                               CIP

Publisher: Tina Carver
Project Management: J. Carey Publishing Service
Interior Design: Shirley Hinkamp
Cover Design: YES Graphics
Cover Photo: Servizio Editorale Fotografico
Buyer: Raymond Keating

Printed in the United States of America

10 9 8 7 6 5 4 3 2 1

Printed on Recycled Paper

ISBN 0-13-191966-0

Prentice-Hall International (UK) Limited, *London*
Prentice-Hall of Australia Pty. Limited, *Sydney*
Prentice-Hall Canada Inc., *Toronto*
Prentice-Hall Hispanoamericana, S.A., *Mexico*
Prentice-Hall of India Private Limited, *New Delhi*
Prentice-Hall of Japan, Inc., *Tokyo*
Prentice-Hall of Southeast Asia Pte. Ltd., *Singapore*
Editora Prentice-Hall do Brasil, Ltda., *Rio de Janeiro*

# Contents

**8  Contrastive Analysis, Interlanguage, and**
**Error Analysis**                                                    **192**

*[handwritten: 8 Communicative Competence]*

**9  Communicative Competence**                                       **226**

*[handwritten: 9. Cross-Linguistic Influence & Learner Language]*

**10  Language Testing**                                              **251**

**11  Theories of Second Language Acquisition**                                **275**

# Preface to the Third Edition

In the previous edition I commented that we were in "the best of times and the worst of times" in the language teaching profession. The best, because of a mushrooming of our knowledge about the process of second language acquisition; the worst, because of the many questions about that process that still remain unanswered. As this book goes into its third edition, "worst of times" may have too much of a pessimistic ring to it. Oh, yes, we still have plenty of mysteries left to challenge the minds of second language sleuths. But as we speed toward and into the twenty-first century, the helter-skelter nature of our research of just two to three decades ago has been replaced by a coordinated, systematic stockpile of information. Subfields have been defined and explored. Researchers around the world are meeting, talking, exchanging findings, comparing data, and arriving at some mutually acceptable explanations. A remarkably increased number of respectable, refereed journals are printing the best and most interesting of this research. Our research miscarriages are fewer as we have collectively learned how to conceive the right questions.

At the same time, we should not be too smug. The wonderful intricacy of any aspect of human behavior will be very much with us for some time. Roger Brown's (1966:326) wry remark three decades ago still applies:

> Psychologists find it exciting when a complex mental phenomenon—something intelligent and slippery—seems about to be captured by a mechanical model. We yearn to see the model succeed. But when, at the last minute, the phenomenon proves too much for the model and darts off on some uncapturable tangent there is something in us that rejoices at the defeat.

We can rejoice in our defeats because we know that it is the very elusiveness of this phenomenon of second language acquisition that makes the quest for answers so exciting. Second language acquisition is no simple, unidimensional reality. It is "slippery" in every way.

*Principles of Language Learning and Teaching* is designed to give you a picture of both the slipperiness of second language acquisition and the systematic storehouse of reliable knowledge that is now available to us. As you consider the issues, chapter by chapter, you are led on a quest: a search for your own personal, integrated understanding of how people learn—and sometimes fail to learn—a second language. That quest is eclectic. No single theory or hypothesis will provide a magic formula for all learners in all contexts. Therefore, several disciplinary perspectives are involved in looking at second language acquisition—principally, linguistics, psychology, and education. And the quest is cautious: you will be urged to be as critical as you can in considering the merit of various models and theories and research findings. By the end of the final chapter, you will no doubt surprise yourself on how many pieces of this giant puzzle you can actually put together!

A spiraling approach is used for presenting material. A concept may be introduced in one chapter but not dealt with substantially until a later chapter. Or a concept may be defined at one point but its significance and implications discussed at a later point. For example, behaviorism is defined in Chapter One, related to first language learning in Chapter Two, then treated technically in Chapter Four in reference to learning theories and used as a reference point throughout the rest of the book. The importance of the distinction between rote and meaningful learning is noted in the discussion of first language acquisition in Chapter Two but is not substantively defined until Chapter Four. Learning theories are summarized in Chapter Four, but the implications of learning theories are evident throughout the volume in almost every chapter. The interrelated nature of aspects of second language acquisition make such spiraling a necessity.

At the end of each chapter are three sections.

1. *"In-the-classroom" vignettes* provide some information on various pedagogical applications and implications of second language research. The vignettes in the first nine chapters (except Chapter Five) describe a historical progression of specific language teaching methods that have been popular at one time or another; other chapters deal simply with some classroom suggestions that follow from the information in the chapter itself.

2. *Suggested readings* offer brief notations on possible further reading which could enhance one's understanding of the material in the chapter. The readings consist of a number of key articles and books in relevant subfields of second language acquisition, providing a means of fruitful exploration beyond and beneath the words of this volume.

3. *Topics and questions* serve two purposes. One is to capsulize and review some of the important topics and issues presented in the chapter. The other purpose is to lead one into a consideration of further issues related to those presented in the chapter and into a refining of concepts whose groundwork has been laid in the chapter. This exploring and refining sometimes takes the form of making practical

applications of some of the more abstract or theoretical material presented in the chapter.

To that end it is strongly recommended that the user of this book maintain regular contact with a group—however small—of second language learners. That group may be a class in a foreign language or it may be a conversation or tutorial group that meets, say, once a week. That regular contact with second language learners will provide the opportunity to observe persons engaged in the process of second language learning in a real situation and to put certain principles into practice. Without this regular exposure to second language learners one runs the risk of placing the material in this book into abstract compartments which may not square with reality. The feedback of the real world is an important if not essential facet of building a viable understanding of the second language acquisition process.

This book is designed to serve as a textbook for graduates or advanced undergraduates who are seeking training in language teaching. It can also serve as a handbook for teachers wishing to get an overview of current theoretical issues in the field. Prior technical knowledge of linguistics or psychology is not necessary. An attempt has been made to build, from the beginning, on what an educated person knows about the world, life, people, and communication. And the book can be used in programs for educating teachers of any foreign language, even though many illustrative examples here are in English since that is the language common to all readers.

This book has grown out of graduate courses in the theoretical foundations of language teaching that I have taught at San Francisco State University, the University of Illinois, and the University of Michigan. My first debt of gratitude is therefore to my students—for their insights, enthusiasm, and support. They offered invaluable comments on the first (1980) and second (1987) editions of the book, and I have attempted to incorporate those insights into this third edition. I am also grateful to faculty colleagues both here at San Francisco State University and around the world for offering verbal commentary, informal written opinion, and formal published reviews, all of which were useful in fashioning this third edition. I also wish to acknowledge the staff and the resources of the American Language Institute for support in this revision and in other research and writing projects. Finally, hugs and kisses to Mary for once again putting up with papers and journals and books strewn all over the house.

H. Douglas Brown
San Francisco, California

# Acknowledgments

Grateful acknowledgment is made to the following publishers for permission to reprint copyrighted material:

Educational Testing Service, for material from: Guidelines for the Use of TOEFL Scores. 1985. Page 3.

Madeline Ehrman, for material from: Ehrman, Madeline. 1989. Ants and grasshoppers, badgers and butterflies: Qualitative and quantitative investigation of adult language learning styles and strategies. Doctoral dissertation. Table IX.

English Language Teaching Journal, for material from: Jack C. Richards. 1973. A noncontrastive approach to error analysis. Volume 25:187.

Georgetown University Press, for material from: H. Douglas Brown. 1983. From ivory tower to real world: A search for relevance. In J. Alatis, H.H. Stern, and P. Strevens (Editors). Applied Linguistics and the Preparation of Second Language Teachers: Toward a Rationale. Pages 53–58; Swain, Merrill. 1990. The language of French immersion students: Implications for theory and practice. In J. Alatis (Editor), Georgetown University Round Table on Languages and Linguistics. Page 403.

Gnosology Books, Ltd. for material from: D. Keirsey and M. Bates. 1984. Please Understand Me. Pages 25–26.

International Review of Applied Linguistics, for material from: S. Pit Corder. 1971. Idiosyncratic dialects and error analysis. Volume 9:167.

Language Learning: A Journal of Applied Linguistics, for the following material: H. Douglas Brown. 1973. Affective variables in second language acquisition. Volume 23; Barry P. Taylor. 1975. The use of overgeneralization and transfer learning strategies by elementary and intermediate students in ESL. Volume 25:95; Carlos A. Yorio. 1976. Discussion of 'Explaining sequence and variation in second language acquisition'. Special Issue Number 4:61; Ellen Bialystok. 1978. A theoretical model of second language learning. Volume

28:71; B. McLaughlin, T. Rossman, and B. McLeod, 1983. Second language learning: An Information processing perspective. Volume 33:143.

The Modern Language Journal, for the following material: H. Douglas Brown. 1972. Cognitive pruning and second language acquisition. Volume 56; Ehrman, Madeline E. and Oxford, Rebecca. 1990. Adult language learning styles and strategies in an intensive training setting. Volume 74:313–314.

Oxford University Press, for material from: R. and K. Chesterfield. 1985. Natural order in children's use of second language learning strategies. Applied Linguistics Volume 6:49–50; Bachman, Lyle F. 1990. Fundamental Considerations in Language Testing. Pages 85 and 87.

Pergamon Press, for material from: Hofstede, Geert. 1986. Cultural differences in teaching and learning. International Journal of Intercultural Relations Volume 10:312.

Prentice-Hall, Inc., for material from John Carroll. 1964. Language and Thought. Page 96.

Teachers of English to Speakers of Other Languages, for the following material: Elaine Tarone. 1981. Some thoughts on the notion of communication strategy. TESOL Quarterly Volume 15:3; J. O'Malley, A. Chamot, G. Stewner-Manzanares, R. Russo, an9 L. Kupper. 1985. Learning strategy applications with students of English as a second language. TESOL Quarterly Volume 19:582–584.

University of Michigan Press, for material from: H. Douglas Brown. 1976. What is applied linguistics? In Ronald Wardhaugh and H. Douglas Brown (Editors). A Survey of Applied Linguistics.

# Principles
# of Language
# Learning
# and Teaching

# Chapter 1

# LANGUAGE, LEARNING, AND TEACHING

Becoming bilingual is a way of life. Your whole person is affected as you struggle to reach beyond the confines of your first language and into a new language, a new culture, a new way of thinking, feeling, and acting. Total commitment, total involvement, a total physical, intellectual, and emotional response is necessary to successfully send and receive messages in a second language. Second language learning is not a set of easy steps that can be programmed in a quick do-it-yourself kit. No one can tell you "how to learn a foreign language without really trying." The learning of a second language is a complex process, involving a seemingly infinite number of variables. So much is at stake that academic courses in foreign languages are often inadequate training grounds, in and of themselves, for the successful learning of a second language. Few if any people achieve fluency in a foreign language solely within the confines of the classroom.

It may appear contradictory, then, that this book is about both learning and *teaching*. But some of the contradiction is removed if you look at the teaching process as the facilitation of learning, in which you can "teach" a foreign language successfully if, among other things, you know something about that intricate web of variables that are spun together to affect how and why one learns or fails to learn a second language. Where does a teacher begin the quest for an understanding of the principles of foreign language learning and teaching? By first asking some questions.

*Who?* Who does the learning and teaching? Obviously, learners and teachers. But who are these learners? Where do they come from? What are their native languages? levels of education? socioeconomic levels? Who are their parents? What are their intellectual capacities? What sort of personalities do they have? There are many other questions that could be asked, but these will do for starters. These questions, if addressed carefully, focus attention on some of the crucial variables affecting both the learner's success in acquiring a foreign language and the teacher's capacity to enable the learner to achieve that acquisition. The chapters that follow will help to tease out those variables.

In the case of the teacher, another set of questions emerges. What is the teacher's native language? experience and/or training? knowledge of the second language and its culture? philosophy of education? personality characteristics? Most importantly, how do the teacher and the student interact with each other as human beings engaged in linguistic communion?

*What?* No simpler a question is one that probes the nature of the subject matter itself. What is it that the learner must learn and the teacher teach? What is communication? What is language? What does it mean when you say someone knows how to *use* a language? How can both the first and the second language be described adequately? What are the linguistic differences between the first and the second language? These profound questions are of course central to the discipline of linguistics. The language teacher needs to understand the system and functioning of the second language and differences between the first and second language of the learner. It is one thing for a teacher to speak and understand a language and yet another matter to consciously understand and explain the system of that language—its phonemes and morphemes and words and sentences and discourse structures.

*How?* How does learning take place? How can a person ensure success in language learning? What cognitive processes are utilized in second language learning? What kinds of strategies and styles does the learner use? What is the optimal interrelationship of cognitive, affective, and physical domains for successful language learning?

*When?* When does second language learning take place? One of the key issues in second language research and teaching is the differential success of children and adults in learning a second language. Common observation tells us that children are "better" language learners than adults. Is this true? If so, why does the age of learning make a difference? How is a second language learned by preschool children still very much involved in the acquisition of their first language? Or by preadolescents who have virtually mastered their first language and are now embarking on the second? Or by teenagers with the insecurities and ego identification dynamics involved in that period of life? Or adults who are affectively and cognitively mature? Other *when* questions center around the amount of time spent in the activity of learning the second language. Is the learner exposed to 3 or 5 or 10 hours a week in the classroom? Or a 7-hour day in an immersion program? Or 24 hours a day totally submerged in the culture?

*Where?* Are the learners attempting to acquire the second language within the cultural and linguistic milieu of the second language—that is, in a "second" language situation in the technical sense of the term? Or are they focusing on a "foreign" language context in which the second language is heard and spoken only in an artificial environment, such as the modern language classroom in an American university or high school? How might the sociopolitical conditions of a particular country affect the outcome of a learner's mastery of the language? How do general intercultural contrasts and similarities affect the learning process?

*Why?* Finally, the most encompassing of all questions: Why are learners attempting to acquire the second language? What are their purposes? Are they motivated by the achievement of a successful career? by passing a foreign language requirement? or by wishing to identify closely with the culture and people of the target language? Beyond these categories, what other affective, emotional, personal, or intellectual reasons do learners have for pursuing this gigantic task of learning another language?

These questions have been asked, in very global terms, to give you an inkling of the diversity of issues involved in the quest for understanding the principles of language learning and teaching. And while you cannot hope to find final answers to all the questions, you can begin to achieve some tentative answers as you move through the chapters of this book. Or you can hone the global questions into finer, subtler questions, which in itself is an important task, for often being able to ask the right questions is more valuable than possessing storehouses of knowledge.

Thomas Kuhn (1970) referred to "normal science" as a process of puzzle solving in which part of the task of the scientist, in this case the teacher, is to discover the pieces, and then to fit the pieces together. Many of the pieces of the language learning puzzle are not yet discovered, and the careful defining of questions will lead to finding those pieces. We can then undertake the task of fitting the pieces together into a "paradigm"—an interlocking design, a theory of second language acquisition.

That theory, like a jigsaw puzzle, needs to be coherent and unified. If only one point of view is taken, if you look at only one facet of second language learning and teaching, you will derive an incomplete, jaundiced theory. The second language teacher, with eyes wide open to the total picture, needs to form an integrated understanding of the many aspects of the process of second language learning.

In order to begin to define further questions and to find answers to some of those questions, this first chapter addresses some fundamental issues that form essential foundations of an integrated understanding of second language acquisition. These issues are: what is *language,* and how do persons *learn* and *teach* language?

# Language

To presume to define *language* adequately would be folly. Linguists and philologists have been trying for centuries to define the term. A definition is really a condensed version of a theory, and a theory is simply—or not so simply—an extended definition. Yet second language teachers clearly need to know generally what sort of entity they are dealing with and how the particular language they are teaching fits into that entity.

Suppose you were stopped by a reporter on the street and in the course of an interview about your vocational choice you were asked: "Well, since you are a foreign *language* teacher, would you define *language* in a sentence or two?" Nonplused, you would no doubt dig deep into your memory for a typical dictionary-type definition of language. Such definitions, if pursued seriously, could lead to a lexicographer's wild-goose chase, but they also can reflect a reasonably coherent synopsis of current understanding of just what it is that linguists are trying to study. Consider the following definitions of *language* found in dictionaries and introductory textbooks:

> Language is a system of arbitrary, vocal symbols which permit all people in a given culture, or other people who have learned the system of that culture, to communicate or to interact (Finocchiaro 1964:8).

> Language is a system of communication by sound, operating through the organs of speech and hearing, among members of a given community, and using vocal symbols possessing arbitrary conventional meanings (Pei 1966:141).

> Language is any set or system of linguistic symbols as used in a more or less uniform fashion by a number of people who are thus enabled to communicate intelligibly with one another (*Random House Dictionary of the English Language* 1966:806).

> Language is a system of arbitrary vocal symbols used for human communication (Wardhaugh 1972:3).

> [Language is] any means, vocal or other, of expressing or communicating feeling or thought . . . a system of conventionalized signs, especially words, or gestures having fixed meanings (*Webster's New International Dictionary of the English Language* 1934:1390).

> [Language is] a systematic means of communicating ideas or feelings by the use of conventionalized signs, sounds, gestures, or marks having understood meanings (*Webster's Third New International Dictionary of the English Language* 1961:1270).

Still other common definitions found in introductory textbooks on linguistics include the concepts of (1) the generativity or creativity of language, (2) the presumed primacy of speech over writing, and (3) the universality of language among human beings.

Many of the significant characteristics of language are capsulized in these definitions. Some of the controversies about the nature of language are also illustrated through the limitations that are implied in certain definitions. Finocchiaro, Pei, and Wardhaugh, for example, restrict themselves to the notion of vocal symbols, while both of the *Webster's* definitions include more than merely vocal symbols as the proper domain of language. Finocchiaro, *Random House,* and Wardhaugh limit their definitions to human language, thereby implying that animal communication and language are essentially different.

A consolidation of the definitions of language yields the following composite definition.

1. Language is systematic and generative.
2. Language is a set of arbitrary symbols.
3. Those symbols are primarily vocal, but may also be visual.
4. The symbols have conventionalized meanings to which they refer.
5. Language is used for communication.
6. Language operates in a speech community or culture.
7. Language is essentially human, although possibly not limited to humans.
8. Language is acquired by all people in much the same way—language and language learning both have universal characteristics.

These eight statements provide a reasonably concise "twenty-five-words-or-less" definition of language. But the simplicity of the eightfold definition should not be allowed to mask the sophistication of linguistic endeavor underlying each concept. Enormous fields and subfields, year-long university courses, are suggested in each of the eight categories. Consider some of these possible areas:

1. Explicit and formal accounts of the system of language on several possible levels (most commonly syntactic, semantic, and phonological).
2. The symbolic nature of language; the relationship between language and reality; the philosophy of language; the history of language.
3. Phonetics; phonology; writing systems; kinesics, proxemics, and other "paralinguistic" features of language.
4. Semantics; language and cognition; psycholinguistics.

5.  Communication systems; speaker-hearer interaction; sentence processing.

6.  Dialectology; sociolinguistics; language and culture; bilingualism and second language acquisition.

7.  Human language and nonhuman communication; the physiology of language.

8.  Language universals; first language acquisition.

Serious and extensive thinking about these eight topics involves a mind-boggling journey through a labyrinth of linguistic science—a maze that has yet to be mastered. Yet the language teacher needs to know something about this system of communication which we call language. Can foreign language teachers effectively teach a language if they do not know, even generally, something about the relationship between language and cognition, writing systems, nonverbal communication, sociolinguistics, and first language acquisition, just to name a few items at random? Teachers need not be master linguists, but they cannot hope to teach a part (the particular language) of reality without knowing how that part fits into the whole (language in general).

The TESOL (Teachers of English to Speakers of Other Languages) organization, in its *Guidelines for the Certification and Preparation of Teachers of English to Speakers of Other Languages in the United States* (1975), cited the necessity for the teacher to "understand the nature of language, the fact of language varieties—social, regional, and functional, the structure and development of the English language systems. . . ." Surely if the second language learner is being asked to be successful in acquiring a system of communication of such vast complexity, it is only reasonable that the teacher have awareness of what the components of that system are.

Your understanding of the components of language will determine to a large extent how you teach a language. If, for example, you believe that nonverbal communication is a key to successful second language learning, you will center attention on nonverbal systems and cues. If you perceive language as a phenomenon that can be dismantled into thousands of discrete pieces and those pieces programmatically taught one by one, you will attend carefully to an understanding of the separability of the forms of language. There are few right and wrong answers to questions about language. Truth is multifaceted and is usually surrounded by undecipherable gray areas.

This book touches on some of the general aspects of language as defined above. More specific aspects will have to be understood in the context of the teacher's training program in a particular language, in which specialized study of linguistics is obviously recommended along with a careful analysis of the foreign language itself.

# Learning and Teaching

What is *learning* and what is *teaching* and how do they interact? Consider again some traditional definitions. A search in contemporary dictionaries reveals that learning is "acquiring or getting of knowledge of a subject or a skill by study, experience, or instruction." A more specialized definition might read as follows: "Learning is a relatively permanent change in a behavioral tendency and is the result of reinforced practice" (Kimble and Garmezy 1963:133). Similarly, teaching, which is implied in the first definition of learning, may be defined as "showing or helping someone to learn how to do something, giving instructions, guiding in the study of something, providing with knowledge, causing to know or understand." How awkward these definitions are! Isn't it rather curious that professional lexicographers cannot devise more precise scientific definitions? More than perhaps anything else, such definitions reflect the difficulty of defining complex concepts like learning and teaching.

Breaking down the components of the definition of learning, we can extract, as we did with language, domains of research and inquiry:

1. Learning is acquisition or "getting."
2. Learning is retention of information or skill.
3. Retention implies storage systems, memory, cognitive organization.
4. Learning involves active, conscious focus on and acting upon events outside or inside the organism.
5. Learning is relatively permanent but subject to forgetting.
6. Learning involves some form of practice, perhaps reinforced practice.
7. Learning is a change in behavior.

These concepts can also give way to a number of subfields within the discipline of psychology: acquisition processes, perception, memory (storage) systems, recall, conscious and subconscious learning styles and strategies, theories of forgetting, reinforcement, the role of practice. Very quickly the concept of learning becomes every bit as complex as the concept of language. Yet the second language learner brings all these and more variables into play in the learning of a second language.

Teaching cannot be defined apart from learning. Nathan Gage (1964:269) noted that "to satisfy the practical demands of education, theories of learning must be 'stood on their head' so as to yield theories of teaching." Teaching is guiding and facilitating learning, enabling the learner to learn, setting the conditions for learning. Your understanding of how the learner learns will determine your philosophy of education, your teaching style, your approach, methods, and classroom techniques. If, like B.F. Skinner, you look at learning as a process of operant conditioning through a carefully paced program of rein- forcement, you will teach accordingly. If you view second language learning basically as a deductive rather than an inductive process, you will probably choose to present copious rules and paradigms to your students rather than let them "discover" those rules inductively. An extended definition—or theory— of teaching will spell out governing principles for choosing certain methods and techniques. A theory of teaching, in harmony with your integrated under- standing of the learner and of the subject matter to be learned, will point the way to successful procedures on a given day for given learners under the vari- ous constraints of the particular context of learning.

The chapters of this book are intended to serve not as a theory of teaching or instruction, but rather as an essential component underlying the subsequent formulation of a theory of instruction. Jerome Bruner (1966b:40-41) noted that a theory of instruction should specify the following features:

1. The experiences which most effectively implant in the individual a predisposition toward learning
2. The ways in which a body of knowledge should be structured so that it can be most readily grasped by the learner
3. The most effective sequences in which to present the materials to be learned
4. The nature and pacing of rewards and punishments in the process of learning and teaching

At least the first three features refer quite pointedly to the subject matter itself and to the learner, implying that one needs an understanding of the subject matter and a practical theory of learning before a theory of instruction can be formed. The purpose of this volume is to focus on the general nature of the subject matter, *language,* and upon the process of *learning* as essential founda- tion stones for building a theory of teaching.

# Trends in Linguistics and Psychology

While the general definitions of language, learning, and teaching offered here might meet with the approval of most linguists, psychologists, and educa- tors, you can find points of vast disagreement upon a little probing of the com- ponents of each definition. For example, is language a "set of habits" or a "system of internalized rules"? Differing viewpoints emerge from equally knowledgeable linguists and psychologists.

Yet with all the possible disagreements among linguists and among psy- chologists, the two disciplines themselves are not that far apart. A historical glance back through the last few decades of linguistic and psychological research reveals some rather striking parallels in the philosophies and approaches of the two disciplines. In linguistics the *structural* school, in its heyday in the 1940s and 50s, gave way to the *generative* school with its beginnings in the early 60s and continuing in various manifestations to the present day. Similarly, psychologists in the 1940s and 1950s were predominantly committed to a *behavioristic* mode of thinking—or even "neo-behavioristic"—while more recent decades have brought increasing attention to *cognitive* psychology. The respective revolutions in thinking are important for the second language teacher to understand, because they highlight contrastive ways of thinking within disciplines yet parallel approaches across disciplines.

An understanding of the varied philosophies can serve as "cognitive pegs" on which to hang further information specialized to second language learning and teaching. The polarization of thought presented in the following explanations may not so much depict reality as act as a means of providing a contrastive description. Just as any population is, in statistical terms, normally distributed between two end points, so too each individual's philosophy falls somewhere in between two contrasting poles. You may never find a really "hardnosed" behaviorist in all the possible extremes, or a cognitivist who recognizes absolutely no legitimacy in the constructs of behaviorism. You too will in all likelihood fall somewhere in between the poles described here, but you, and only you, by fitting various pieces of the puzzle together, can fashion your own personal theory of learning or theory of language.

What then, in a nutshell, are these theories whose popularity has fallen and risen in parallel chronology? In the 1940s and 1950s the *structural,* or *descriptive* school of linguistics, with its advocates—Leonard Bloomfield, Edward Sapir, Charles Hockett, Charles Fries, and others—prided itself in a rigorous application of the scientific principle of *observation* of human languages. Only the "publicly observable responses" could be subject to investigation. The linguist's task, according to the structuralist, was to describe human languages and to identify the structural characteristics of those languages. This led to the unchecked rush of linguists to the far reaches of the earth to write the grammars of exotic languages. An important axiom of structural linguistics, however, was that "languages can differ from each other without limit," and that no preconceptions must be taken to the field. Freeman Twaddell (1935:57) stated this principle in perhaps its most extreme terms. "Whatever our attitude toward mind, spirit, soul, etc., as realities, we must agree that the scientist proceeds as though there were no such things, as though all his information were acquired through processes of his physiological nervous system. Insofar as he occupies himself with psychical, nonmaterial forces, the scientist is not a scientist. The scientific method is quite simply the convention that mind does not exist. . . . " The structural linguist examined only the overtly observable data with no assumption that another human being might have cognitive processes that resembled his own. Such attitudes prevail in Skinner's thought, particularly in *Verbal Behavior* (1957), in which he says that any notion of "idea" or "meaning" is explanatory fiction, and that the speaker is merely the locus of verbal behavior, not the cause. Charles Osgood reinstated meaning in verbal behavior, explaining it as a "representational mediation process," but still did not depart from a generally nonmentalistic view of language.

Of further importance to the structural or descriptive linguist was the notion that language could be dismantled into small pieces or units and that these units could be described scientifically, contrasted, and added up again to form the whole.

In the 1960s the generative-transformational school of linguistics emerged through the influence of Noam Chomsky. What Chomsky was trying to show is that language (not languages) cannot be scrutinized simply in terms of observable stimuli and responses or the volumes of raw data gathered by field linguists. The generative linguist is interested not only in describing language or achieving the level of *descriptive* adequacy but also in arriving at an *explanatory* level of adequacy in the study of language—that is, a "principled basis, independent of any particular language, for the selection of the descriptively adequate grammar of each language" (Chomsky 1964:63).

Over 70 years ago, Ferdinand de Saussure (1916) said that there was a difference between *parole* (what Skinner "observes," and what Chomsky calls "performance") and *langue* (akin to the "competence" that generative theory seeks to account for), but descriptive linguistics chose largely to ignore *langue* and to study *parole.* The revolution brought about by generative linguistics broke with the descriptivists' penchant for studying performance—the outward manifestation of language—and capitalized on the important distinction between the overtly observable *surface* level of language and the *deep* structure of language, that hidden level of meaning and thought that gives birth to and generates observable surface linguistic performance.

On the psychological side, a similar revolution came about with the scrutiny of the adequacy of behavioral theories to account for human behavior. Like the structural linguistic position, the behavioristic view focused on publicly observable responses—those that can be objectively perceived, recorded, and measured. The "scientific method" was rigorously adhered to, and therefore such concepts as consciousness and intuition were regarded as "mentalistic," illegitimate domains of inquiry. The unreliability of observation of states of consciousness, thinking, concept formation, or the acquisition of knowledge made such topics impossible to examine in a behavioristic framework. Typical behavioristic models were classical and operant conditioning, rote verbal learning, instrumental learning, and discrimination learning. You are familiar with the classical experiments with Pavlov's dog and Skinner's boxes—these too typify the position that organisms can be conditioned to respond in desired ways, given the correct degree and scheduling of reinforcement.

Cognitive psychologists, on the other hand, take a contrasting theoretical stance. Meaning, understanding, and knowing are significant data for psychological study. Instead of focusing rather mechanistically on stimulus-response connections, cognitivists try to discover psychological *principles* of organization and functioning. David Ausubel (1965:4) noted: "From the standpoint of cognitive theorists, the attempt to ignore conscious states or to reduce cognition to mediational processes reflective of implicit behavior not only removes from the field of psychology what is most worth studying but also dangerously oversimplifies highly complex psychological phenomena." By using a *rationalistic* approach instead of a strictly *empirical* approach, cognitive psychologists, like generative linguists, have sought to discover underlying motivations and deeper structures of human behavior; going beyond descriptive to explanatory power has taken on utmost importance.

Both the structural linguist and the behavioral psychologist are interested in description, in answering *what* questions about human behavior: objective measurement of behavior in controlled circumstances. The generative linguist and cognitive psychologist are, to be sure, interested in the *what* question; but they are far more interested in a more ultimate question, *why*: what underlying reasons, thinking, and circumstances caused a particular event? If you were to observe someone walk into your house, pick up a chair and fling it through your window, and then walk out, different kinds of questions could be asked. One set of questions would relate to what happened: the physical description of the person, the time of day, the size of the chair, the impact of the chair, and so forth. Another set of questions would ask why the person did what he did: what were his motives, what was his psychological state, was he agitated, was he a political enemy of yours, and so on. The first set of questions is very rigorous and exacting; it allows no flaw, no mistake in measurement, but does it give you ultimate answers? The second set of questions is richer, but obviously riskier. By risking asking some difficult questions about the unobserved, we may lose some ground but gain more profound insight about human behavior.

Table 1–1 summarizes concepts and approaches germane to each of the two polarized theories that have been presented here. The table may help to pinpoint certain broad ideas that are associated with the respective positions.

The parallel between the two disciplines is not really surprising when one considers the fact that the disciplines of psychology and linguistics are closely related. Both disciplines focus on human behavior, with linguistics representing a somewhat more specialized aspect of human behavior. A number of psychologists have made a lasting impact on linguistic theories, not the least of them B.F. Skinner, Charles Osgood, George Miller, and more recently, Barry McLaughlin. And linguists of the caliber of Ferdinand de Saussure, Benjamin Whorf, Noam Chomsky, and George Lakoff have influenced psychological thinking. And so, as Kuhn (1970) points out in his treatise on the structure of scientific revolutions, all "normal" sciences go through a revolutionary

### TABLE 1-1    Linguistic-Psychological Parallels

| SCHOOLS OF PSYCHOLOGY | SCHOOLS OF LINGUISTICS | CHARACTERISTICS |
|---|---|---|
| Behavioristic | Structural<br><br>Descriptive | Repetition and reinforcement<br>Learning, conditioning<br>Stimulus-response<br>Publicly observable responses<br>Empiricism<br>Scientific method<br>Performance<br>Surface structure<br>Description—"what" |
| Cognitive | Generative<br><br>Transformational | Analysis and insight<br>Acquisition, innateness<br>States of consciousness<br>Rationalism<br>Process<br>Mentalism, intuition<br>Competence<br>Deep structure<br>Explanation—"why" |

pattern that begins with a successful paradigm within which to work, followed by a period of anomaly (doubt, uncertainty, questioning of prevailing theory), then crisis (the fall of the existing paradigm) with all the professional insecurity that comes therewith, and then finally a new paradigm, a novel theory, is put together. This cycle is evident in both psychology and linguistics, though the limits and bounds are not always easily perceived—perhaps less easily perceived in psychology, in which both paradigms currently operate somewhat in tandem. The cyclical nature of theories underscores the fact that no single theory or paradigm is either right or wrong. It is impossible to refute with any finality one theory with another. Some truth can be found in virtually every theory.

# Applied Linguistics

Earlier in this chapter, you saw that a simple definition of *language* suggested many issues and concerns within the discipline of linguistics, all of which relate directly to the central goal of linguistic study: discovering what language is. However, among the concerns listed were a number that are typically grouped into "applied" rather than "theoretical" linguistics. Applied linguistics has been considered a subset of linguistics for several decades, and it has been interpreted to mean the applications of linguistics principles or theories to certain more or less practical matters (Brown 1976b, Kaplan, et al. 1981). Second language teaching and teaching of reading, composition, and language arts in the native language are typical areas of practical application.

The applications of linguistic theory extend well beyond pedagogical concerns, even to the point of drawing very fuzzy lines between what is applied and what is theoretical. In studies of phonetics, nonverbal communication, semantics, dialectology, first language acquisition, the psychology of language, and second language acquisition, there is much that is theoretical—that is, much that bears on seeking an extended definition of language. Some might argue that the devising of explicit and formal accounts of linguistic systems is surely theoretical; however, semantics, speaker-hearer interaction, and communication systems are important in any consideration of the nature of the linguistic system. Perhaps, then, every question about language—from devising lessons on the subjunctive in French to formulating universal syntactic rules—is theoretical in that the answers to those questions both derive from and contribute to an understanding of just what language is.

Must we conclude, therefore, that there is really no such thing as applied linguistics? This is indeed too simplistic and too easy a solution. Every discipline has its theoretical and its applied aspects. The theoretical and applied areas simply must not be thought of as necessarily mutually exclusive. An area of inquiry may evidence certain applications of theory to practice and at the same time contribute to a better theoretical understanding of the particular phenomenon.

Reacting to the common British usage of the term "applied linguistics" (in which case the term is almost synonymous with "language teaching"), Corder (1973:10) differentiated applied linguistics and language teaching, and went on to note that "the applied linguist is a consumer, or user, not a producer, of theories." Many important components of a theory have been influenced and changed by "consumer feedback." In first language acquisition, for example, researchers discovered that the purely syntactic, rational linguistic theories of the 1960s held explanatory power for only a small portion of the actual data. Neither the semantic/cognitive aspect of language nor the social aspect could be accounted for adequately. Partly as a result of the "demands" of first language researchers, and partly through other forces, theoretical linguists quickly began to focus on the semantic component of language, which brought a renewed interest in psycholinguistic topics in general. Along with this focus has emerged a revived interest in the social aspects of language, formerly considered to be irrelevant to theoretical linguistics. Psycholinguistics and sociolinguistics, once very clearly considered to be "applied" areas, now just as clearly overlap both the applied and theoretical domains.

The purity of so-called pure linguistics is impossible to maintain, as Robin Lakoff (1976:222) noted:

> Linguistics is heading in the direction of practicality. There will be in the ensuing years an ever-greater emphasis on application of theoretical discoveries; and application will be considered as valuable in its own right as pure theoretical contributions to knowledge have been. In fact, it will be increasingly recognized that theory severed from applications is suspect, that data generated in the rocking chair, tested at the blackboard, and described in learned jargon are probably ridden with errors and inaccuracies.

# Theories and Methods

A glance through the past century or so of language teaching gives us an interesting picture of how varied the interpretations have been of the best way to teach a foreign language. As schools of thought have come and gone, so have language teaching methods waxed and waned in popularity. Teaching methods are the application of theoretical findings and positions. They may be thought of as "theories in practice." It is no surprise that in a field as young and dynamic as second language teaching there have been a variety of such applications, some in total philosophical opposition to others.

Albert Marckwardt (1972:5) saw these "changing winds and shifting sands" as a cyclical pattern in which a new paradigm (to use Kuhn's term) of teaching methodology emerged about every quarter of a century, with each new method breaking from the old but at the same time taking with it some of the positive aspects of the previous paradigm. One of the best examples of the cyclical nature of methods is seen in the revolutionary Audiolingual Method (ALM) of the late 1940s and 1950s. The ALM borrowed tenets from its predecessor by almost half a century, the Direct Method, while breaking away entirely from the Grammar-Translation paradigm. Within a short time, however, ALM critics were advocating more attention to rules and to the "cognitive code" of language, which, to some, smacked of a return to Grammar Translation! Shifting sands indeed.

Since the early 1970s, the relationship of theoretical disciplines to teaching methodology has been especially evident. The field of psychology has witnessed a growing interest in interpersonal relationships, in the value of group work, and in the use of numerous self-help strategies for coping with the stresses of daily living. The same era has seen linguists searching ever more deeply for answers to the nature of communication and communicative competence and for explanations of the interactive process of language. The language teaching profession has responded to these theoretical trends with methods that stress the importance of self-esteem, of students cooperatively learning together, of developing individual strategies for success, and above all of focusing on the *communicative* process in language learning. Today the term "communicative language teaching" is a byword for language teachers. Indeed, the single greatest challenge in the profession is to move significantly beyond the teaching of rules, patterns, definitions, and other knowledge "about" language to the point that we are teaching our students to *communicate* genuinely, spontaneously, and meaningfully in the second language.

This book is intended to give you a comprehensive picture of the theoretical foundations of language learning and teaching. But that theory remains abstract and relatively powerless without its application to the practical concerns of pedagogy in the classroom. In an attempt to help to build bridges between theory and practice, I have provided at the end of each of the chapters of this book a brief "vignette" on classroom considerations. These vignettes are designed to acquaint you progressively with some of the major methodological trends and issues in the profession. The vignettes are obviously not intended to be exhaustive (you will need to refer to such books as Brown [1994], Nunan [1991b], Richards and Rodgers [1986], Larsen-Freeman [1986], and Blair [1983] for a more specific treatment of the nature of methods), but they should begin to give you a bit of history and a picture of the practical consequences of developing the theoretical principles of language learning and teaching.

A word of advice. However appealing a particular method might be to you as you first encounter it, however sensible and practical it might seem, the *best* method is one which you have derived through your very own careful process of formulation, try-out, revision, and refinement. You cannot teach effectively without understanding varied theoretical positions. This understanding forms a principled basis upon which you can choose particular methods for teaching a foreign language. And unless that principled basis is your own carefully and thoughtfully devised theory, you become a slave to one way of thinking, a puppet without self-control. Your task in the formulation of an integrated understanding of the principles of language learning and teaching is to find those points of compromise or tension between two poles of possibilities that will best fit a global theory of second language acquisition. Rather than yielding to the temptation of making a quick, haphazard choice of a stance, it is imperative first to sift through the many variables that come to bear on learning and teaching a second language.

Such a prospect may seem formidable. There are no instant recipes. No quick and easy method is guaranteed to provide success. Every learner is unique. Every teacher is unique. And every learner-teacher relationship is unique. Your task is to understand the properties of those relationships. Using a cautious, enlightened, eclectic approach, you can build a theory—an understanding of the principles of second language learning and teaching. The chapters that follow are designed to help you formulate that understanding.

# In the Classroom:
# The Grammar Translation Method

We begin our series of vignettes on classroom applications with a language teaching "tradition" that, in various manifestations and adaptations, has been practiced in language classrooms worldwide for centuries. A glance back in history reveals few if any research-based language teaching methods prior to the twentieth century. In the Western world, "foreign" language learning in schools was synonymous with the learning of Latin or Greek. Latin, thought to promote intellectuality through "mental gymnastics," was only until relatively recently held to be indispensable to an adequate higher education. Latin was taught by means of what has been called the Classical Method: focus on grammatical rules, memorization of vocabulary and of various declensions and conjugations, translation of texts, doing written exercises. As other languages began to be taught in educational institutions in the eighteenth and nineteenth centuries, the Classical Method was adopted as the chief means for teaching foreign languages. Little thought was given at the time to teaching oral use of languages; after all, languages were not being taught primarily to learn oral/aural communication but to learn for the sake of being "scholarly" or, in some instances, for gaining a reading proficiency in a foreign language. Since there was little if any theoretical research on second language acquisition in general, or on the acquisition of reading proficiency, foreign languages were taught as any other skill was taught.

In the nineteenth century the Classical Method came to be known as the Grammar Translation Method. There was little to distinguish Grammar Translation from what had gone on in foreign language classrooms for centuries, beyond a focus on grammatical rules as the basis for translating from the second to the native language. But the Grammar Translation Method remarkably withstood attempts at the turn of the twentieth century to "reform" language teaching methodology, and to this day it remains a standard methodology for language teaching in educational institutions. Prator and Celce-Murcia (1979:3) list the major characteristics of Grammar Translation:

1.  Classes are taught in the mother tongue, with little active use of the target language.
2.  Much vocabulary is taught in the form of lists of isolated words.
3.  Long elaborate explanations of the intricacies of grammar are given.
4.  Grammar provides the rules for putting words together, and instruction often focuses on the form and inflection of words.
5.  Reading of difficult classical texts is begun early.
6.  Little attention is paid to the content of texts, which are treated as exercises in grammatical analysis.
7.  Often the only drills are exercises in translating disconnected sentences from the target language into the mother tongue.
8.  Little or no attention is given to pronunciation.

It is remarkable, in one sense, that this method has been so stalwart among many competing models. It does virtually nothing to enhance a student's communicative ability in the language. It is "remembered with distaste by thousands of school learners, for whom foreign language learning meant a tedious experience of memorizing endless lists of unusable grammar rules and vocabulary and attempting to produce perfect translations of stilted or literary prose" (Richards and Rodgers 1986:4). However, in another sense, one can understand why Grammar Translation is so popular. It requires few specialized skills on the part of teachers. Tests of grammar rules and of translations are easy to construct and can be objectively scored. Many standardized tests of foreign languages still do not attempt to tap into communicative abilities, so students have little motivation to go beyond grammar analogies, translations, and rote exercises. And it is sometimes successful in leading a student toward a *reading* knowledge of a second language. But, as Richards and Rodgers (1986:5) point out, "it has no advocates. It is a method for which there is no theory. There is no literature that offers a rationale or justification for it or that attempts to relate it to issues in linguistics, psychology, or educational theory." As we continue to examine theoretical principles in this book, I think we will understand more fully the "theory-lessness" of the Grammar Translation Method.

## Suggested Readings

A number of references were made in this chapter to general linguistics, generative-transformational grammar, structural linguistics, and applied linguistics. For some background on such topics, consult an introduction to linguistics. Highly recommended are *O'Grady, Dobrovolsky, and Aronoff* (1989) and *Ohio State University* (1991). Other similar textbooks may also be useful.

*Kuhn* (1970) will give you a comprehensive understanding of the cyclical nature of theories and models in all disciplines. Language teaching methods and approaches can be more perceptively understood when they are placed within Kuhn's model.

The four components of a theory of instruction as outlined by *Bruner* (1966b:40f.) help to put a theory of learning into the perspective of teaching in the classroom. You may wish to specify the particular second language features of each of Bruner's four components.

For a rather concise—if somewhat biased—comparison between behavioral and cognitive psychology, read *Anderson and Ausubel* (1965:3–17). Other accounts of differing psychological perspectives can usually be found in introductory psychology textbooks. Such material may also be appropriate to read in conjunction with the material in Chapter Four of this book. *Hammerly* (1985) provided a good summary of differences between behavioristic and cognitive approaches to teaching a foreign language.

The most comprehensive and current information on various subfields of interest within what is broadly termed applied linguistics is available through the *Annual Review of Applied Linguistics,* a series that has continued to be edited by Robert Kaplan, the first of which is referenced under *Kaplan, Jones, and Tucker* (1981). For an early overview of such subfields, see *Wardhaugh and Brown* (1976).

Recent books surveying and offering critical analysis of language teaching methods include *Brown* (1994), *Nunan* (1991b), and *Richards and Rodgers* (1986).

## Topics and Questions for Study and Discussion

1.  In the first part of the chapter a number of "who, what . . ." questions were posed. What other possible questions occur to you? Attempt some tentative answers to at least a few of the questions, and write them down for referral as you progress through the chapters of this book.

2.  Look at the definitions of language on page 4. How are they different from each other? Why are there differences in such definitions? What assumptions or biases do they reflect on the part of the writer?

3.  Write your *own* "twenty-five-word-or-less" definitions of *language, learning,* and *teaching.* What would you add to or delete from the definitions given in this chapter? Save your definitions and when you finish the book determine if you would revise those definitions in any way.

4.  Look up some abstract words in a dictionary. Try words like *love, good, evil, emotion, peace,* and other such terms. In what way might those definitions fall short of being adequate? Do they reveal certain theoretical biases on the part of the definer?

5.  What kind of *teaching* emphases would emerge in the second language classroom by keying the *exclusive* importance of any *one* of the eight subfields of linguistics listed on pages 5–6. Take several subfields and discuss the type of approach to second language teaching that might emerge.

6.  What did Twaddell (1935:57) mean when he said, "The scientific method is quite simply the convention that mind does not exist. . . ."? Discuss the advantages and disadvantages of attending only to "publicly observable responses" in studying human behavior. Don't limit yourself just to language teaching in considering the ramifications of behavioristic principles.

7.  Define *rationalism* and *empiricism.* You should consult an encyclopedia or other reference for some details. Why are generative grammar and cognitive psychology classified as rationalistic approaches?

8. Linguistics isn't the only discipline with its theoretical and applied aspects. How would you describe similar distinctions in psychology, sociology, or other disciplines with which you are familiar?

9. What did Robin Lakoff mean by "data generated in the rocking chair . . . ?"

10. If a "method" is, in one sense, a "theory in practice," does that mean that theories always have to come first? In what way do you suppose theory and practice are interactive? How do theories get changed?

11. Referring to the Grammar Translation Method, Richards and Rodgers (1986:5), said, "It is a method for which there is no theory." Why did they make that statement? Do you agree with them?

# Chapter 2

# FIRST LANGUAGE ACQUISITION

That marvelous capacity for acquiring competence in one's native language within the first few years of life has been a subject of interest for many centuries. "Modern" research on child language acquisition dates back to the late eighteenth century when the German philosopher Dietrich Tiedemann recorded his observations of the psychological and linguistic development of his young son. For a century and a half, few if any significant advances were made in the study of child language; for the most part research was limited to diarylike recordings of observed speech with some attempts to classify word types. Only in the second half of the twentieth century did researchers begin to analyze child language systematically and to try to discover the nature of the psycholinguistic process that enables every human being to gain fluent control of an exceedingly complex system of communication. In a matter of a few decades some giant strides were taken, especially in the generative and cognitive models of language, in describing the acquisition of particular languages, and in probing universal aspects of acquisition. Today literally hundreds of linguists and psychologists are studying linguistic, psychological, sociological, and physiological aspects of first language acquisition.

This wave of research in child language acquisition led foreign language teachers and teacher trainers to study some of the general findings of such research with a view to drawing analogies between first and second language acquisition, and even to justifying certain teaching methods and techniques on the basis of first language learning principles. On the surface, it is entirely reasonable to make the analogy. After all, all children, given a normal developmental environment, acquire their native languages fluently and efficiently; moreover, they acquire them "naturally," without special instruction, though not without notable conscious effort and attention to language. However, the direct comparisons such as those that have been made must be treated with caution. There are dozens of salient differences between first and second language learning; the most obvious difference, in the case of adult second language learning, is the tremendous cognitive and affective contrast between adults and children. A detailed examination of these differences is made in Chapter Three.

This chapter is designed to outline issues in first language learning as a foundation on which you can build an understanding of principles of second language learning. A coherent grasp of the nature of first language learning is an invaluable aid, if not an essential component, in the construction of a theory of second language acquisition. This chapter provides an overview of various theoretical positions—positions that can be related to the paradigms discussed in Chapter One—in first language acquisition, and a discussion of some key issues that are particularly significant for an understanding of second language learning. Information on first language acquisition beyond that which is presented here should be sought in the suggested readings at the end of this chapter.

# Theories of First Language Acquisition

There is no one who has not at some time witnessed the remarkable ability of children to communicate. As small babies, children babble and coo and cry and vocally or nonvocally send an extraordinary number of messages and receive even more messages. As they reach the end of their first year, specific attempts are made to imitate words and speech sounds heard around them, and about this time they utter their first "words." By about 18 months of age these words have multiplied considerably and are beginning to appear in combination with each other to form two-word and three-word "sentences"—commonly referred to as "telegraphic" utterances—such as "allgone milk," "bye-bye Daddy," "gimme toy," and so forth. The production tempo now begins to increase as more and more words are spoken every day and more and more combinations of two- and three-word sentences are uttered. By about age 3, children can comprehend an incredible quantity of linguistic behavior; their speech capacity mushrooms as they become the generator of nonstop chattering and incessant conversation, language thus becoming a mixed blessing for those around them! This fluency continues into school age as children internalize increasingly complex structures, expand their vocabulary, and sharpen communicative skills. At school age, children not only learn what to say but what *not* to say as they learn the social functions of their language.

How can we explain this fantastic journey from that first anguished cry at birth to adult competence in a language? From the first word to tens of thousands? From telegraphese at 18 months to the compound-complex, cognitively precise, socioculturally appropriate sentences just a few short years later? It is these sorts of questions that theories of language acquisition attempt to answer.

In principle you can adopt one of two polarized positions in the study of first language acquisition. The extreme behavioristic position would be that children come into the world with a *tabula rasa,* a clean slate bearing no preconceived notions about the world or about language, and these children are then shaped by their environment, slowly conditioned through various schedules of reinforcement. At the other extreme, you would find a position that claims that children come into this world with very specific innate knowledge, knowledge that includes not only general predispositions and tendencies but also knowledge of the nature of language and of the world. Then, through their own volition, they act upon their environment by developing these bodies of knowledge.

Both of the extreme positions represent opposites on a continuum with many possible positions in between. Three such points are elucidated in this chapter. The first (behavioristic) position is set in contrast to the second (nativist) and third (functional) positions, which are more clearly on the generative/cognitive side of the continuum.

# Behavioristic Approaches

Language is a fundamental part of total human behavior, and behaviorists have examined it as such and sought to formulate consistent theories of first language acquisition. The behavioristic approach focuses on the immediately perceptible aspects of linguistic behavior—the publicly observable responses—and the relationships or associations between those responses and events in the world surrounding them. A behaviorist might consider effective language behavior to be the production of correct responses to stimuli. If a particular response is reinforced, it then becomes habitual, or conditioned. Thus children produce linguistic responses that are reinforced. This is true of their comprehension as well as production responses, though to consider comprehension is to wander just a bit out of the publicly observable realm. One learns to comprehend an utterance by reacting appropriately to it and by being reinforced for that reaction.

One of the best-known attempts to construct a behavioristic model of linguistic behavior is embodied in B.F. Skinner's (1957) classic, *Verbal Behavior.* Skinner was commonly known for his experiments with animal behavior in "Skinner's boxes," but he also gained recognition for his contributions to education through teaching machines and programmed learning (Skinner 1968). Skinner's theory of verbal behavior was an extension of his general theory of learning by *operant conditioning.* Operant conditioning refers to conditioning in which the organism (in this case, a human being) emits a response, or *operant* (a sentence or utterance), without necessarily observable stimuli; that operant is maintained (learned) by reinforcement (for example, a positive verbal or nonverbal response for another person). If a child says "want milk" and a parent gives the child some milk, the operant is reinforced and, over repeated instances, is conditioned. According to Skinner, verbal behavior, like other behavior, is controlled by its *consequences.* When consequences are rewarding, behavior is maintained and is increased in strength and perhaps frequency. When consequences are punishing, or when there is lack of reinforcement entirely, the behavior is weakened and eventually extinguished.

Skinner's theories attracted a number of critics, not the least among them Noam Chomsky (1959), who penned a highly critical review of *Verbal Behavior.* Some years later, however, Kenneth MacCorquodale (1970) published a reply to Chomsky's review in which he eloquently and quite convincingly defended Skinner's points of view. And so the battle raged on. Today few linguists and psychologists would agree that Skinner's model of verbal behavior adequately accounts for the capacity to acquire language, for language development itself, for the abstract nature of language, and for a theory of meaning. A theory based on conditioning and reinforcement is hard-pressed to explain the fact that every sentence you speak or write—with a few trivial exceptions—is novel, never before uttered either by you or by anyone else! These novel utterances are nevertheless created by the speaker and processed by the hearer.

In an attempt to broaden the base of behavioristic theory, some psychologists proposed modified theoretical positions. One of these positions was *mediation* theory, in which meaning was accounted for by the claim that the linguistic stimulus (a word or sentences) elicits a *"mediating"* response that is self-stimulating. Charles Osgood (1953, 1957) called this self-stimulation a "representational mediation process," a process that is really covert and invisible, acting within the learner. Interestingly, mediation theory thus attempted to account for abstraction by a notion that reeked of "mentalism"—a cardinal sin for dyed-in-the-wool behaviorists! In fact, in some ways mediation theory was really a cognitive-rational theory masquerading as behavioristic.

Mediation theories still left many questions about language unanswered. The abstract nature of language and the integral relationship between meaning and utterance were unresolved. All sentences have deep structures—the level of underlying meaning that is only manifested overtly by surface structures. These deep structures are intricately bound up in a person's total cognitive and affective experience. Such depths of language were scarcely plumbed by mediational theory.

Yet another attempt to account for first language acquisition within a behavioristic framework was made by Jenkins and Palermo (1964). While admitting that their conjectures were "speculative" and "premature" (p. 143), the authors attempted to synthesize notions of generative linguistics and mediational approaches to child language. They claimed that the child may acquire frames of a phrase-structure grammar and learn the stimulus-response equivalences that can be substituted within each frame; imitation was an important if not essential aspect of establishing stimulus-response associations. But this theory, too, fails to account for the abstract nature of language, nor does it account satisfactorily for the generalization process that is inferred in the theory. Also, it does not account for the creativity evident in even a young child's ability to comprehend and produce novel utterances. David McNeill (1968:408–409) further pointed out that it is mathematically impossible for a child to acquire all the frames and items implied by Jenkins and Palermo's theory.

> The difficulties with finite-state grammars are simple and arithmetical. In order to acquire grammar through mediation paradigms, a child must learn all the transitions among grammatical classes that are allowable in English. The number of these, however, is astronomical. Take, for example, the sentence, "The people who called and wanted to rent your house when you go away next year are from California" (Miller and Chomsky 1963). There is a dependency between the second word (people) and the seventeenth word (are). If this intuition was learned through mediation, then each of us has learned a unique set of transitions covering a sequence of 15 grammatical categories. Assuming (conservatively) that an average of four grammatical categories might occur at any point in the development of an English sentence, detection of the dependency between "people" and "are" signifies that we have learned at least $4^{15} = 10^9$ different transitions, which means, as Miller and Chomsky point out, that we learned " . . . the value of $10^9$ parameters in a childhood lasting only $10^8$ seconds" (p. 430). Evidently, mediation paradigms yield the wrong kind of structure. At the very least, we need a theory which avoids assuming that sentences consist of nothing more than simple left-to-right transitions.

It would appear that the rigor of behavioristic psychology, with its emphasis on empirical observation and the scientific method, can only begin to explain the miracle of language acquisition. It leaves untouched a vast domain that can be explored only by an approach that probes deeper.

# The Nativist Approach

On the other end of the theoretical continuum we find generative theories of child language, with their typical rationalistic approach—asking deeper questions, looking for clearer explanations of the mystery of language acquisition. The failure, or at least the shortcomings, of behavioristic views of child language caused researchers to ask more ultimate questions—questions that probed beneath and beyond scientific investigation.

One such set of questions was found in a generative approach to child language known as the *nativist* approach. The term *nativist* is derived from the fundamental assertion that language acquisition is innately determined, that we are born with a built-in device of some kind that predisposes us to language acquisition—to a systematic perception of language around us, resulting in the construction of an internalized system of language. Innateness hypotheses gained support from several sides. Eric Lenneberg (1967) proposed that language is a "species-specific" behavior and that certain modes of perception, categorizing abilities, and other language-related mechanisms are biologically determined. Chomsky (1965) similarly claimed the existence of innate properties of language to explain the child's mastery of his native language in such a short time despite the highly abstract nature of the rules of language. This innate knowledge, according to Chomsky, is embodied in a "little black box" of sorts, a *language acquisition device* (LAD). McNeill (1966) described LAD as consisting of four innate linguistic properties: (1) the ability to distinguish speech sounds from other sounds in the environment, (2) the ability to organize linguistic events into various classes which can later be refined, (3) knowledge that only a certain kind of linguistic system is possible and that other kinds are not, (4) the ability to engage in constant evaluation of the developing linguistic system so as to construct the simplest possible system out of the linguistic data that are encountered.

McNeill and other Chomskyan disciples composed eloquent arguments for the appropriateness of the LAD proposition, especially in contrast to behavioristic, stimulus-response (S-R) theory which was so limited in accounting for the generativity of child language. Aspects of meaning, abstractness, and creativity were accounted for more adequately. Even though it was readily recognized that the LAD was not literally a cluster of brain cells that could be isolated and neurologically located, such inquiry on the rationalistic side of the linguistic-psychological continuum stimulated a great deal of fruitful research.

In recent years, researchers in the nativist tradition have continued this line of inquiry through a new genre of child language acquisition research (see Bley-Vroman 1988, Horstein & Lightfoot 1981) that focuses on what has come to be known as *Universal Grammar* (UG). Positing that all human beings are genetically equipped with language-specific abilities, researchers are now expanding the LAD notion into a system of universal linguistic rules that go well beyond what was originally proposed for the LAD. UG research is attempting to discover what it is that all children, regardless of their environmental stimuli (the language(s) they hear around them) bring to the language acquisition process. Such studies have looked at question formation, negation, word order, discontinuity of embedded clauses (The ball that's on the table is blue), subject deletion (Es mi hermano), and a host of other grammatical phenomena.

One of the more practical contributions of nativist theories is evident if you look at the kinds of discoveries that have been made about how the *system* of child language works. Research has revealed that the child's language, at any given point, is a legitimate system in its own right. The child's linguistic development is not a process of developing fewer and fewer "incorrect" structures, not a language in which earlier stages have more "mistakes" than later stages. Rather, the child's language at any stage is *systematic* in that the child is constantly forming hypotheses on the basis of the input received and then testing those hypotheses in speech (and comprehension). As the child's language develops, those hypotheses get continually revised, reshaped, or sometimes abandoned.

Of course, the notion of the child as hypothesis tester is not new. Fifteen centuries ago St. Augustine provided in his *Confessions* a self-analysis of his own language learning process:

> For I was no longer a speechless infant, but a speaking boy. This I remember; and have since observed how I learned to speak. It was not that my elders taught me words . . . in any set method; but I, longing by cries and broken accents and various motions of my limbs to express my thoughts, that so I might have my will, and yet unable to express all that I willed, or to whom I willed, did myself, by the understanding which Thou, my God, gavest me, practise the sounds in my memory. . . . And thus by constantly hearing words, as they occurred in various sentences, I collected gradually for what they stood; and having broken in my mouth to these signs, I thereby gave utterance to my will. Thus I exchanged with those about me these current signs of our wills, and so launched deeper into the stormy intercourse of human life.

Before generative linguistics came into vogue, Jean Berko (1958) demonstrated that children learn language not as a series of separate discrete items, but as an integrated system. Using a simple nonsense-word test, Berko discovered that English-speaking children as young as 4 years of age applied rules for the formation of plural, present progressive, past tense, third singular, and possessives. She found, for example, that if a child saw one "wug" he could easily talk about two wugs, or if he were presented with a person who knows how to "gling," the child could talk about a person who gling*ed* yesterday, or sometimes who gl*ang*.

Nativists carried out a rash of studies on the systematic nature of child language acquisition. Having thrown off the shackles of behavioristic constraints, researchers were free to construct hypothetical "grammars" of child language, although such grammars were still solidly based on empirical data. These grammars were largely formal representations of the deep structure—the abstract rules underlying surface output, the structure not overtly manifest in speech. Linguists began to examine child language from early forms of "telegraphese" to the complex language of 5- to 10-year-olds. Borrowing one tenet of structural and behavioristic paradigms, they approached the data with few preconceived notions about what the child's language *ought* to be, and probed the data for internally consistent systems, in much the same way that a linguist describes a language in the "field." The use of a generative framework was, of course, a departure from structural methodology.

The generative model has enabled researchers to take some giant steps toward understanding the process of first language acquisition. The early grammars of child language were referred to as *pivot grammars.* It was commonly observed that the child's first two-word utterances seemed to manifest two separate word classes, and not simply two words thrown together at random. Consider the following utterances:

> *My cap*
> *That horsie*
> *Allgone milk*
> *Mommy sock*

Linguists noted that the words on the left-hand side seemed to belong to a class that words on the right-hand side generally did not belong to. That is, *my* could co-occur with *cap, horsie, milk,* or *sock,* but not with *that* or *allgone. Mommy* is, in this case, a word that belongs in both classes. The first class of words was called *pivot,* since they could pivot around a number of words in the second, *open* class. Thus the first rule of the generative grammar of the child was described as follows:

> Sentence → Pivot word + Open word

Reams of research data have been gathered in the generative framework, yielding a multitude of such rules. Some of these rules appear to be grounded in the UG of the child. As the child's language matures and finally becomes adult-like, the number and complexity of generative rules accounting for language competence simply boggles the mind.

In recent years the generative "rule-governed" model in the Chomskyan tradition has been challenged. The assumption underlying this tradition is that those generative rules, or "items" in a linguistic sense, are connected *serially,* with one connection between each pair of neurons in the brain. A new "messier but more fruitful picture" (Spolsky 1989:149) is provided by what has come to be known as the *parallel distributed processing* (PDP) model (also called *connectionism*) in which neurons in the brain are said to form multiple connections: each of the 100 billion nerve cells in the brain may be linked to as many as 10,000 of its counterparts. Thus, a child's (or adult's) linguistic performance may be the consequence of many levels of *simultaneous* neural interconnections and not a serial process of one rule being applied, then another, then another, and so forth.

A simple analogy to music might illustrate this complex notion. Think of an orchestra playing a symphony. The score for the symphony may have, let's say, twelve separate parts that are performed simultaneously. The "symphony" of the human brain enables us to process many segments and levels of language, cognition, affect, and perception all at once—in a parallel configuration. And so, according to the PDP model, a sentence—which has phonological, morphological, syntactic, lexical, semantic, discourse, sociolinguistic, and strategic properties—is not "generated" by a series of rules (Sokolik 1990; Ney and Pearson 1990). Rather, sentences are the result of the simultaneous interconnection of a multitude of brain cells.

All of these approaches within the nativist framework have made at least three important contributions to our understanding of the first language acquisition process: (1) freedom from the restrictions of the so-called "scientific method" to explore the unseen, unobservable, underlying, abstract linguistic structures being developed in the child; (2) systematic description of the child's linguistic repertoire as either rule-governed or operating out of a parallel distributed processing capacities; and (3) the construction of a number of potential properties of Universal Grammar.

## Functional Approaches

As liberating as the nativist framework was, it still possessed some glaring inadequacies. The late 1960s witnessed a shift in patterns of research, not away from the generative/cognitive side of the continuum, but perhaps better described as a move "deeper" into the essence of language. The generative rules that were proposed under the nativistic framework were abstract, formal, explicit, and quite logical, yet they dealt specifically with the forms of language and not with the very deepest level of language, that level where memory, perception, thought, meaning, and emotion are all interdependently organized in the superstructure of the human mind. Linguists began to see that language was one manifestation of general development, one aspect of the cognitive and affective ability to deal with the world and with self. Linguists also began to see that language was hardly something you could extract and detach from your cognitive and affective framework and consider separately, and that linguistic rules written as mathematical equations failed to capture that ever-elusive facet of language: meaning. The generative rules of nativists were failing to account for the *functions* of language.

Lois Bloom (1971) cogently illustrated the issue in her criticism of pivot grammar when she pointed out that the relationships in which words occur in telegraphic utterances are only superficially similar. For example, in the utterance "Mommy sock," which nativists would describe as a sentence consisting of a pivot word and an open word, Bloom found at least *three* possible underlying relations: agent-action (Mommy is putting the sock on), agent-object (Mommy sees the sock), and possessor-possessed (Mommy's sock . . . ). By examining data in reference to contexts, Bloom concluded that children learn underlying structures, and not superficial word order. Thus, depending on the context, "Mommy sock" could mean a number of different things to the child. Those varied meanings were inadequately captured in a pivot grammar approach.

Lewis Carroll aptly captures this characteristic of language in *Through the Looking Glass* (1872), where Alice argues with Humpty Dumpty about the meanings of words:

> "When I use a word," Humpty Dumpty said, in a rather scornful tone, "it means just what I choose it to mean—neither more nor less."
> "The question is," said Alice, "whether you can make words mean so many different things."
> "The question is," said Humpty Dumpty, "which is to be master—that's all."

Bloom's research, along with that of Jean Piaget, Dan Slobin, and others, paved the way for a new wave of child language study, this time centering on the cognitive prerequisites of linguistic behavior. Piaget described overall development as the result of children's interaction with their environment, with a complementary interaction between their developing perceptual cognitive capacities and their linguistic experience. What children learn about language is determined by what they already know about the world. As Gleitman and Wanner (1982:13) noted in their review of the state of the art in child language research, "children appear to approach language learning equipped with conceptual interpretive abilities for categorizing the world. . . . Learners are biased to map each semantic idea on the linguistic unit *word*."

Lois Bloom (1976:37) summarized the shift in emphasis:

> There have been two main thrusts in attempts to explain how children learn to talk. On the one hand, it was proposed that the course of language development depends directly on the nature of the linguistic system and, more specifically, on the nature of those aspects of language that might be universal and represented in an innate, predetermined program for language learning. On the other hand, evidence began to accrue to support a different hypothesis which emphasized the interaction of the child's perceptual and cognitive development with linguistic and nonlinguistic events in his environment.

Dan Slobin (1971, 1986), among others, demonstrated that in all languages, semantic learning depends on cognitive development and that sequences of development are determined more by semantic complexity than by structural complexity: "There are two major pacesetters to language development, involved with the poles of function and of form: (1) on the functional level, development is paced by the growth of conceptual and communicative capacities, operating in conjunction with innate schemas of cognition; and (2) on the formal level, development is paced by the growth of perceptual and information-processing capacities, operating in conjunction with innate schemas of grammar" (Slobin 1986:2). Bloom (1976:37) noted that "an explanation of language development depends upon an explanation of the cognitive underpinnings of language: what children know will determine what they learn about the code for both speaking and understanding messages." So child language researchers are now tackling the formulation of the rules of the *functions* of language, and the relationships of the *forms* of language to those functions.

In recent years it has become quite clear that language functioning extends well beyond cognitive thought and memory structure. Holzman (1984:119), in her "reciprocal model" of language development, proposes that "a reciprocal behavioral system operates between the language-developing infant-child and the competent [adult] language user in a socializing-teaching-nuturing role." Some recent research (Berko-Gleason 1988, Lock 1991) is looking at the interaction between the child's *language* acquisition and the learning of how *social systems* operate in human behavior. Other investigations (see Kuczaj 1984, for example) of child language have centered on one of the thorniest areas of linguistic research: the function of language in *discourse.* Since language is used for communication, it is only fitting that one study the communicative functions of language: what do children know and learn about talking with others? about connected pieces of discourse (relations between sentences)? the interaction between hearer and speaker? conversational cues? This newest wave is revolutionizing research on first language acquisition. The very heart of language—its communicative function—is being tackled in all its variability.

But even more revolutionary is the almost paradoxical fact that the most current research on the generative side of the theoretical continuum has focused once again on the *performance* level of language. All those overt responses that were so carefully observed by structuralists and hastily weeded out as "performance variables" by generative linguists in their zeal to get at competence have now returned to the forefront. Hesitations, pauses, backtracking, and the like are indeed significant conversational cues. Even some of the contextual categories described by—of all people—Skinner, in *Verbal Behavior,* turn out to be relevant! The linguist can no longer deal with abstract, formal rules without dealing with all those minutiae of day-to-day performance which were previously ignored.

Several theoretical positions have been sketched out here. Perhaps we will never realize a complete, consistent, unified theory of first language acquisition, but even in its infancy, child language research has manifested some enormous strides toward that ultimate goal. And even if all the answers are far from evident, maybe we are asking more of the right questions.

We turn now to a look at a number of "issues" in first language acquisition—key questions and problems that have been and are being addressed by researchers in the field. A study of these issues will help you to round out your understanding of the nature of child language acquisition.

# Competence and Performance

For centuries scientists and philosophers have operated with the basic distinction between competence and performance. *Competence* refers to one's underlying knowledge of a system, event, or fact. It is the nonobservable ability to do something, to perform something. *Performance* is the overtly observable and concrete manifestation or realization of competence. It is the actual doing of something: walking, singing, dancing, speaking. In Western society we have used the competence-performance distinction in all walks of life. In our schools, for example, we have assumed that children possess certain competence in given areas and that this competence can be measured and assessed by means of the observation of elicited samples of performance called "tests" and "examinations."

In reference to language, competence is your underlying knowledge of the system of a language—its rules of grammar, its vocabulary, all the pieces of a language and how those pieces fit together. Performance is actual production (speaking, writing) or the comprehension (listening, reading) of linguistic events. You will recall in Chapter One of reference to Ferdinand de Saussure's (1916) version of the competence/performance construct: a distinction between *langue* and *parole* as two separate phenomena, independent of each other. "*Langue* exists in the form of a sum of impressions deposited in the brain of each member of the community. . . . *Parole* [is] . . . an individual, . . . willful phonational acts" (Saussure 1916:14–19).

Chomsky (1965) likened competence to an "idealized" speaker-hearer who does not display such performance variables as memory limitations, distractions, shifts of attention and interest, errors, and hesitation phenomena such as repeats, false starts, pauses, omissions, and additions. (Maclay and Osgood [1959:24] outline a diverse number of hesitation types.) Chomsky's point was that a theory of language had to be a theory of competence lest the linguist vainly try to categorize an infinite number of performance variables which are not reflective of the underlying linguistic ability of the speaker-hearer.

The distinction is one that linguists and psychologists in the generative/cognitive framework have been operating under for some time, a mentalistic construct that structuralists and behaviorists do not deal with. Just *how* does one infer this unobservable, underlying level? How can one be sure that an accurate assessment has been made?

Brown and Bellugi (1964) give us a rather delightful example of the difficulty of attempting to extract underlying grammatical knowledge from children. Unlike adults, who can be asked, for example, whether it is better to say "two foots" or "two feet," children exhibit what is called the "pop-go-weasel" effect, as witnessed in the following dialogue between an adult and a two-year-old child:

> ADULT:  Now Adam, listen to what I say. Tell me which is better to say . . . *some* water, or a water.
>
> ADAM:  Pop go weasel.

The child obviously has no interest in—or cognizance of—the adult's grammatical interrogation and therefore says whatever he wants to! The researcher is thus forced to devise indirect methods of inferring competence. Among those methods are the tape recording and transcription of countless hours of speech followed by studious analysis, or the direct admission of certain imitation, production, or comprehension tests, all with numerous disadvantages. How is one, for example, to infer some general competence about the linguistic system of a 5-year-old, monolingual, English-speaking girl whose recounting of an incident viewed on television is transcribed below:

> . . . they heared 'em underground ca-cause they went through a hoyle—a hole— and they pulled a rock from underground and then they saw a wave going in— that the hole—and-they brought a table and the wave brought 'em out the k—tunnel and then the—they went away and then—uh—m—ah—back on top and it was—uh—going under a bridge and they went—then the braves hit the— the bridge—they—all of it—th-then they looked there—then they—then they were safe.

On the surface it might appear that this child is severely impaired in her attempts to communicate. In fact, this same transcript was presented without identification of the speaker to a group of speech therapists several years ago and I asked them to analyze the various possible "disorders" manifested in the data. After they cited quite a number of technical manifestations of aphasia, I gleefully informed them of the real source of the data! The point is that every day in our processing of linguistic data we comprehend such strings of speech and comprehend them rather well by attending to the underlying meaning of the utterance and by not allowing ourselves to be distracted by a number of performance variables. Adult talk is often no less fraught with monstrosities, as we can see in the following verbatim transcription of comments made on a talk show by golfer Tony Jacklin:

> Concentration is important. But uh—I also—to go with this of course if you're playing well—if you're playing well then you get up tight about your game. You get keyed up and it's easy to concentrate. You know you're playing well and you know . . . in with a chance than it's easier, much easier to—to you know get in there and—and start to . . . you don't have to think about it. I mean it's got to be automatic.

Perhaps Mr. Jacklin would have been better off if he had simply uttered the very last sentence and omitted all the previous verbiage!

If we were to record many more samples of the 5-year-old's speech we would still be faced with the problem of inferring her competence. What is her knowledge of the verb system? of the concept of a "sentence"? Even if we administer rather carefully designed tests of comprehension or production to a child, we are still left with the problem of inferring, as accurately as possible, the child's underlying competence. Often these inferences are mere guesses, and what research is all about is converting the guesswork to accurate measurement.

The competence-performance model has not met with universal acceptance. Major criticisms of the model focus on the notion that competence, as defined by Chomsky, consists of the abilities of an "idealized" hearer-speaker, devoid of any so-called performance variables. As Tarone (1988) points out, such views disclaim responsibility for a number of linguistic goofs and slips of the tongue that may well arise from the *context* within which a person is communicating. In other words, every single one of a child's (or adult's) slips and hesitations and self-corrections are potentially connected to what Tarone calls *heterogeneous* competence—abilities that are in the process of being formed. So, while we may be tempted to claim that the five-year-old quoted above knows the difference, say, between a "hole" and a "hoyle," we must not too quickly pass off the latter as an irrelevant slip of the tongue.

What are you to conclude, therefore, about language acquisition theory based on a competence-performance model? I think it is clear that a *cautious* approach to inferring someone's competence will allow you to draw some conclusions about overall ability while still leaving the door open for some significance to be attributed to those linguistic tidbits that you might initially be tempted to discount.

# Comprehension and Production

Not to be confused with the competence/performance distinction, *comprehension* and *production* can be aspects of *both* performance *and* competence. One of the myths that has crept into some foreign language teaching materials is that comprehension (listening, reading) can be equated with competence, while production (speaking, writing) is performance. It is important to recognize that this is not the case: production is of course more directly observable, but comprehension is as much performance—a "willful act," to use Saussure's term—as production is.

In child language, most observational and research evidence points to the general superiority of comprehension over production: children seem to understand "more" than they actually produce. For instance, a child may

understand a sentence with an embedded relative in it, but not be able to produce one. W.R. Miller (1963:863) gave us a good example of this phenomenon
in phonological development: "Recently a three-year-old child told me her
name was Litha. I answered 'Li*th*a?' 'No, Litha.' 'Oh, Lisa.' 'Yes, Litha.'" The
child clearly perceived the contrast between English *s* and *th,* even though she
could not produce the contrast herself.

How are we to explain this difference, this apparent "lag" between comprehension and production? We know that even adults understand more
vocabulary than they ever use in speech, and also perceive more syntactic variation than they actually produce. Could it be that the same competence
accounts for both modes of performance? Or can we speak of comprehension
competence as something that is somewhat separately identified from production competence? Because comprehension for the most part runs ahead of production, is it more completely indicative of our overall competence? Is
production indicative of a smaller portion of competence? Surely not. It is
therefore necessary to make a distinction between production competence and
comprehension competence. A theory of language must include some accounting of the separation of two types of competence. In fact, linguistic competence
no doubt has several modes or levels, at least as many as four, since speaking,
listening, reading, and writing are all separate modes of performance.

Perhaps an even more compelling argument for the separation of competencies comes from research that appears to support the superiority of production over comprehension. Gathercole (1988) reported on a number of studies
in which children were able to produce certain aspects of language they could
not comprehend. For example, Rice (1980) found that children who did not
previously know terms for color were able to respond verbally to such questions as "What color is this?" But they were not able to respond correctly (by
giving the correct colored object) to "Give me the [color] one." While lexical
and grammatical instances of production-before-comprehension seem to be
few in number, it still behooves us to be wary in concluding that *all* aspects of
linguistic comprehension precede, or facilitate, linguistic production.

# Nature or Nurture?

Chomsky contended that the child is born with an innate knowledge of or
predisposition toward language, and that this innate property (the LAD or UG)
is universal in all human beings. The innateness hypothesis was a possible resolution of contradiction between the behavioristic notion that language is a set
of habits that can be acquired by a process of conditioning and the fact that
such conditioning is much too slow and inefficient a process to account for the
acquisition of a phenomenon as complex as language. But the innateness
hypothesis presented a number of problems itself. One of the difficulties has
already been discussed in this chapter: the LAD proposition simply postpones

facing the central issue of the nature of the human being's capacity for language acquisition. Having thus "explained" language acquisition, one must now explain LAD. Ambrose Bierce summed it up wryly in *The Devil's Dictionary:* "The doctrine of innate ideas is one of the most admirable faiths of philosophy, being itself an innate idea and therefore inaccessible to disproof" (in Clark and Clark 1977:517).

What, exactly, are the innate properties and predispositions embodied in LAD? How are they genetically transmitted? What has so far been discovered in research on *universals* of language points toward answers, but the discovery of universals does not necessarily imply innateness. Furthermore, research has been an inadequate testing ground in support of the LAD hypothesis; researchers have too often merely assumed the hypothesis to be true when accounting for their data.

Another problem emerges if you consider the complement of innateness: learning. For years psychologists and educators have been embroiled in the "nature-nurture" controversy: What are those behaviors that "nature" provides either innately, in some sort of predetermined biological timetable, and what are those behaviors that are, by environmental exposure—by "nurture," by teaching—learned and internalized? We do observe that language acquisition is universal, that every child acquires language. But how is the efficiency and success of that learning determined by the environment the child is in? Can children be "taught" their first language? The waters of the innateness hypothesis are considerably muddied by such questions, whose answers are yet to be found.

An interesting line of research on innateness was pursued by Derek Bickerton (1981), who found evidence, across a number of languages, of common patterns of linguistic and cognitive development. He proposed that human beings are "bio-programmed" to proceed from stage to stage. Like flowering plants, people are innately programmed to "release" certain properties of language at certain developmental ages. Just as you can not make a geranium bloom before its "time," so human beings will "bloom" in predetermined, pre-programmed steps.

# Universals

Closely related to the innateness controversy is the claim that language is universally acquired in the same manner, and moreover, that the deep structure of language at its deepest level may be common to all languages. Years ago Werner Leopold (1949) who, incidentally, was far ahead of his time, made a rather eloquent case for certain phonological as well as grammatical universals in language. Leopold inspired later work by Greenberg (1963, 1966), Bickerton (1981), and Slobin (1986, 1992). Currently, as noted earlier in this chapter, research in Universal Grammar continues this quest. One of the keys to such inquiry lies in research on child language acquisition across many different languages in order to determine the commonalities. Slobin (1986, 1992) and his colleagues have gathered some data on language acquisition in Japanese, French, Spanish, German, Polish, Hebrew, and Turkish, among others. Interesting universals of pivot grammar and other telegraphese are emerging. Maratsos (1988) enumerates some of current universal linguistic categories under investigation by a number of different researchers:

word order

morphological marking

tone

agreement (e.g., of subject and verb)

reduced reference (e.g., pronouns, elipsis)

nouns and noun classes

verbs and verb classes

predication

negation

question formation

## Systematicity and Variability

One of the assumptions of a good deal of current research on child language is the *systematicity* of the process of acquisition. Indeed, most of the data gathered so far point to the systematic nature of the learning process. From pivot grammar to three- and four-word utterances, and to full sentences of almost indeterminate length, children exhibit a remarkable ability to infer the phonological, structural, lexical, and semantic system of language. Ever since Berko's (1958) ground-breaking "wug" study, we have been discovering more and more about the systematicity of the acquisition process.

But in the midst of all this systematicity, there is an equally remarkable amount of *variability* in the process of learning! Even in English, researchers are not agreed on how to define various "stages" of language acquisition. Certain "typical" patterns appear in child language. For example, it has been found that young children who have not yet mastered the past-tense morpheme tend first to learn past tenses as separate items ("walked," "broke," "drank") without knowledge of the difference between regular and irregular verbs. Then, around the age of 4 or 5, they begin to perceive a system in which the *-ed* morpheme is added to a verb, and at this point all verbs become regularized ("breaked," "drinked," "goed"). Finally, after school age, children perceive that there are two classes of verbs, regular and irregular, and begin to sort out verbs into the two classes, a process that goes on for many years and in some cases persists into young adulthood.

Even after acquisition has been more or less completed, the native language of adults is full of variability. Consider the variations in regional and social dialects and styles, as stated by Saussure (1916:9):

> But what is language? . . . It is both a social product of the faculty of speech and a collection of necessary conventions that have been adopted by a social body to permit individuals to exercise that faculty. Taken as a whole, speech is many-sided and heterogeneous; straddling several areas simultaneously—physical, physiological, and psychological—it belongs both to the individual and to society; we cannot put it into any category of human facts, for we cannot discover its unity.

In both first and second language acquisition, the problem of variability is being carefully addressed by researchers (see Tarone 1988). One of the major current research problems is to account for all this variability: to determine if what is now variable in our present point of view can some day be deemed systematic through such careful accounting.

## Language and Thought

The relationship between language and thought poses thorny issues and questions. For years researchers have probed the relationship between language and cognition. The behavioristic view that cognition is too mentalistic to be studied by the scientific method is diametrically opposed to such positions as that of Piaget, who claimed that cognitive development is at the very center of the human organism and that language is dependent upon and springs from cognitive development. Others choose to emphasize the influence of language on cognitive development. Jerome Bruner (Bruner, Olver, and Greenfield 1966), for example, singled out sources of language-influenced intellectual development: words shaping concepts, dialogues between parent and child or teacher and child serving to orient and educate, and other sources. It is clear that the research of the past decade has pointed to the fact that cognitive and linguistic development are inextricably intertwined with dependencies in both directions.

One of the champions of the position that language affects thought was Benjamin Whorf, who with Edward Sapir formed the well-known Sapir-Whorf hypothesis of linguistic relativity—namely, that each language imposes on its speaker a particular "world view." (See Chapter Seven for more discussion of the Sapir-Whorf hypothesis.)

The issue at stake in child language acquisition is to determine *how* thought affects language, *how* language affects thought, and *how* linguists can best describe and account for the interaction of the two. Once again we probe the issue of how best to explain both the forms *and* the function of a language. And again we do not have complete answers. But we do know that language is a way of life, is at the foundation of our being, and interacts simultaneously with thoughts and feelings.

# Imitation

It is a common, informal observation that children are "good imitators." We think of children typically as imitators and mimics, and then conclude that imitation is one of the important strategies a child uses in the acquisition of language. That conclusion is not inaccurate on a global level. Indeed, research has shown that *echoing* is a particularly salient strategy in early language learning and an important aspect of early phonological acquisition. Moreover, imitation is consonant with behavioristic principles of language acquisition— principles relevant, at least, to the earliest stages.

But it is important to ask what type of imitation is implied. Behaviorists assume one type of imitation, but there is a deeper level of imitation that is far more important in the process of language acquisition. The first type is sur- face-structure imitation, where a person repeats or mimics the surface strings, attending to a phonological code rather than a semantic code. It is this level of imitation that enables an adult to repeat random numbers or nonsense sylla- bles, or even to mimic unknown languages. The semantic data, if any, underly- ing the surface output are neither internalized nor attended to. In foreign language classes, rote pattern drills often evoke surface imitation: a repetition of sounds by the student without the vaguest understanding of what the sounds might possibly mean. The earliest stages of child language acquisition may manifest a good deal of surface imitation since the baby may not possess the necessary semantic categories to assign "meaning" to utterances. But as children perceive the importance of the semantic level of language, they attend primarily if not exclusively to that meaningful semantic level—the deep struc- ture of language. They engage in deep-structure imitation. In fact, the imitation of the deep structure of language can literally block their attention to the sur- face structure so that they become, on the face of it, poor imitators. Consider the following conversation as recorded by McNeill (1966:69):

CHILD:   Nobody don't like me.
MOTHER:   No, say "nobody likes me."
CHILD:   Nobody don't like me.
          (eight repetitions of this dialogue)

.
.
.

MOTHER:   No, now listen carefully; say "nobody likes me."

CHILD:    Oh! Nobody don't likes me.

You can imagine the frustration of both mother and child, for the mother was attending to a rather technical, surface grammatical distinction, and yet the child sought to derive some meaning value. Finally the child perceived some sort of surface distinction between what she was saying and what her mother was saying and made what she thought was an appropriate change.

A similar case in point occurred one day when the teacher of an elementary-school class asked her pupils to write a few sentences on a piece of paper, to which one rather shy pupil responded, "Ain't got no pencil." Disturbed at this nonstandard response the teacher embarked on a barrage of corrective models for the child: "I don't have *any* pencils, you don't have a pencil, they don't have pencils, . . ." When the teacher finally ended her monologue of patterns, the intimidated and bewildered child said, "Ain't *nobody* got no pencils?" The teacher's purpose was lost on this child because he too was attending to language as a meaningful and communicative tool and not to the question of whether certain forms were "correct" and others were not. The child, like all children, was attending to the *truth value* of the utterance.

Research has also shown that children, when explicitly asked to repeat a sentence in a test situation, will often repeat the correct underlying deep structure with a change in the surface rendition. For example, sentences like "The ball that is rolling down the hill is black" and "The boy who's in the sandbox is wearing a red shirt" tend to be repeated back by preschool children as "The black ball is rolling down the hill" and "The red boy is in the sandbox" (Brown 1970). Children are excellent imitators. It is simply a matter of understanding exactly what it is that they are imitating.

# Practice

Closely related to the notion of imitation is a somewhat broader question, the nature of *practice* in child language. Do children practice their language? If so, how? What is the role of the *frequency* of hearing and producing items in the acquisition of those items? It is common to observe children and conclude that they "practice" language constantly, especially in the early stages of single-word and two-word utterances. A behavioristic model of first language acquisition would claim that practice—repetition and association—is the key to the formation of habits by operant conditioning.

One unique form of practice by a child is recorded by Ruth Weir (1962). She found that her children produced rather long monologues in bed at night before going to sleep. Here is one example: "What color . . . What color blanket . . . What color mop . . . What color glass . . . Mommy's home sick . . . Mommy's home sick . . . Where's Mommy home sick . . . Where's Mikey sick . . . Mikey sick." Such monologues are not uncommon among children, whose inclination it is to "play" with language just as they do with all objects and events around them. Weir's data show far more structural patterning than has commonly been found in other data. Nevertheless, children's practice seems to be a key to language acquisition.

Practice is usually thought of as referring to speaking only. But one can also think in terms of comprehension practice, which is often considered under the rubric of the *frequency* of linguistic input to the child. Is the acquisition of particular words or structures directly attributable to their frequency in the child's linguistic environment? There is evidence that certain highly frequent forms are acquired first: *what* questions, irregular past-tense forms, certain common household items and persons. Brown and Hanlon (1970), for example, found that the frequency of occurrence of a linguistic item in the speech of mothers was an overwhelmingly strong predictor of the order of emergence of those items in their children's speech.

There are some conflicting data, however. Telegraphic speech is one case in point. Some of the most frequently occurring words in the language are omitted in such two- and three-word utterances. And McNeill (1968:416) found that a Japanese child produced the Japanese postposition *ga* far more frequently and more correctly than another contrasting postposition *wa,* even though her mother was recorded as using *wa* twice as often as *ga*. McNeill attributed this finding to the fact that *ga* as a subject marker is of more importance, grammatically, to the child, and she therefore acquired the use of that item since it was more meaningful on a deep-structure level. Another feasible explanation, however, for that finding might lie in the easier pronunciation of *ga.*

The jury is still out on the frequency issue. Nativists who claim that "the relative frequency of stimuli is of little importance in language acquisition" (Wardhaugh 1971:12) might, in the face of evidence thus far, be more cautious in their claims. It would appear that frequency of *meaningful* occurrence may well be a more precise refinement of the notion of frequency.

# Input

The role of input in the child's acquisition of language is undeniably crucial. Whatever one's position is on the innateness of language, the speech that young children hear is primarily the speech heard in the home, and much of that speech is parental speech or the speech of older siblings. Linguists once claimed that most adult speech is basically semigrammatical (full of performance variables), and that children are exposed to a chaotic sample of language and only their innate capacities can account for their successful acquisition of language. McNeill, for example, wrote: "The speech of adults from which a child discovers the locally appropriate manifestation of the linguistic universals is a completely random, haphazard sample, in no way contrived to instruct the child on grammar" (1966:73). However, Labov (1970:42) noted that on the basis of his studies the presumed ungrammaticality of everyday speech appears to be a myth, really. Bellugi and Brown (1964) and Drach (1969) found that the speech addressed to children was carefully grammatical and lacked the usual hesitations and false starts common in adult-to-adult speech. Landes's (1975) summary of a wide range of research on parental input supported their conclusions. More recent studies of parents' speech in the home (Hladik and Edwards 1984; Moerk 1985) confirm earlier evidence demonstrating the selectivity of parental linguistic input to their children.

At the same time, it will be remembered that children react very consistently to the deep structure and the communicative function of language, and they do not react overtly to expansions and grammatical corrections as in the "nobody likes me" dialogue quoted above. Such input is largely ignored unless there is some *truth* or *falsity* that the child can attend to. Thus, if a child says "Dat Harry" and the parent says "No, that's *John,*" the child might readily self-correct and say "Oh, dat *John.*" But what Landes and others showed is that in the long run children will, after consistent, repeated models in meaningful contexts, eventually transfer correct forms to their own speech and thus correct "dat" to "that's."

The importance of the issue lies in the fact that it is clear from more recent research that adult and peer input to the child is far more important than nativists earlier might have believed. Adult input seems to shape the child's acquisition, and the interaction patterns between child and parent change according to the increasing language skill of the child. Nurture and environment in this case are tremendously important, though it remains to be seen just how important parental input is as a proportion of total input.

# Discourse

A subfield of research that is occupying the attention of an increasing number of child language researchers is the area of *conversational* or *discourse* analysis. While parental input is a significant part of the child's development of conversational rules, it is only one aspect, as the child also interacts with peers and, of course, with other adults. Berko-Gleason (1982:20) described the new trend: "While it used to be generally held that mere *exposure* to language is sufficient to set the child's language generating machinery in motion, it is now clear that, in order for successful first language acquisition to take place, *interaction,* rather than exposure, is required; children do not learn language from overhearing the conversations of others or from listening to the radio, and must, instead, acquire it in the context of being spoken to."

While conversation is a universal human activity performed routinely in the course of daily living, the means by which children learn to take part in conversation appear to be very complex. Sinclair and Coulthard (1975) proposed that conversations be examined in terms of *initiations* and *responses*. What might in a grammatical sentence-based model of language be described as sentences, clauses, words, and morphemes, are viewed as transactions, exchanges, moves, and acts. The child learns not only how to initiate a conversation but how to respond to another's initiating utterance. Questions are not simply questions but are recognized functionally as requests for information, for action, or for help. At a relatively young age, children learn subtle differences between, say, assertions and challenges. They learn that utterances have both a literal and an intended or functional meaning. Thus, in the case of a question "Can you go to the movies tonight?," the response "I'm busy," is understood correctly as a negative response ("I can't go to the movies"). How do children manifest the development of discourse rules? What are the key features the child attends to? These and other questions about the acquisition of discourse ability are being researched.

Much remains to be studied in the area of the child's development of conversational knowledge (see Shatz and McCloskey 1984, and McTear 1984 for a good summary). Nevertheless, such development is perhaps the next frontier to be mastered in the quest for answers to the mystery of language acquisition. Clearly there are important implications here, as we shall see in the next chapter, for second language learners. The barrier of discourse is one of the most difficult for second language learners to break through.

A number of theories and issues in child language have been explored in this chapter with the purpose of briefly characterizing both the current state of child language research and of highlighting a few of the key concepts that emerge in the formation of an understanding of how babies learn to talk and eventually become sophisticated linguistic beings. There is much to be learned in such an understanding. Every human being who attempts to learn a *second* language has already learned a *first* language. It is said that the second time around on something is always easier. In the case of language this is not necessarily true. But in order to understand why it is not, you need to understand the nature of that initial acquisition process, for it may be that some of the keys to the mystery are found therein. That search is continued in the next chapter as we compare and contrast first and second language acquisition.

## In The Classroom:
## Gouin and Berlitz—The First Reformers

In the second of our series of vignettes on classroom applications of theory, we turn the clock back about a hundred years to look in on the first two reformers in the history of "modern" language teaching, François Gouin and Charles Berlitz. Their perceptive observations about language teaching help us to set the stage for the development of language teaching methodologies for the century following.

In his *The Art of Learning and Studying Foreign Languages* (1880), François Gouin described a painful set of experiences that finally led to his insights about language teaching. Having decided in his midlife to learn German, he took up residency in Hamburg for one year. But rather than attempting to converse with the natives he engaged in a rather bizarre sequence of attempts to "master" the language. Upon arrival in Hamburg he felt he should *memorize* a German grammar book and a table of the 248 irregular German verbs! He did this in a matter of only 10 days and then hurried to "the academy" (the university) to test his new knowledge. "But alas!" he wrote, "I could not understand a single word, not a single word!" Gouin was undaunted. He returned to the isolation of his room, this time to memorize the German roots and to rememorize the grammar book and irregular verbs. Again he emerged with expectations of success. "But alas!"—the result was the same as before. In the course of the year in Germany Gouin memorized books, translated Goethe and Schiller, and even memorized 30,000 words in a German dictionary—all in the isolation of his room, only to be crushed by his failure to understand German afterwards. Only once did he try to "make conversation" as a method, but this caused people to laugh at him and he was too embarrassed to continue that method. At the end of the year, Gouin, having reduced the classical method to absurdity, was forced to return home, a failure.

But there is a happy ending. Upon returning home Gouin discovered that his 3-year-old nephew had, during that year, gone through that wonderful stage of child language acquisition in which he went from saying virtually nothing at all to become a veritable chatterbox of French. How was it that this little child succeeded so easily in a task, mastering a first language, that Gouin, in a second language, had found impossible? The child must hold the secret to learning a language! So Gouin spent a great deal of time observing his nephew and other children and came to the following conclusions: Language learning is primarily a matter of transforming perceptions into conceptions. Children use language to represent their conceptions. Language is a means of thinking, of representing the world to oneself. (These insights, remember, are being formed by a language teacher over a century ago!)

So Gouin set about devising a teaching method that would follow from these insights. And thus the Series Method was created, a method that taught learners *directly* (without translation) and conceptually (without grammatical rules and explanations) a "series" of connected sentences that are easy to perceive. The first lesson of a foreign language would thus teach the following series of 15 sentences:

I walk toward the door. I draw near to the door. I draw nearer to the door. I get to the door. I stop at the door.

I stretch out my arm. I take hold of the handle. I turn the handle. I open the door. I pull the door.

The door moves. The door turns on its hinges. The door turns and turns. I open the door wide. I let go of the handle.

The 15 sentences have an unconventionally large number of grammatical properties, vocabulary items, word orders, and complexity. This is no simple "Voici la table" lesson! Yet Gouin was successful with such lessons because the language was so easily understood, stored, recalled, and related to reality.

The "naturalistic"—simulating the "natural" way in which children learn first languages—approaches of Gouin and a few of his contemporaries did not take hold immediately. A generation later, largely through the efforts of Charles Berlitz, applied linguists finally established the credibility of such approaches in what became known as the Direct Method.

The basic premise of Berlitz's method was that second language learning should be more like first language learning: lots of active oral interaction, spontaneous use of the language, no translation between first and second languages, and little or no analysis of grammatical rules. Richards and Rodgers (1986:9–10) summarize the principles of the Direct Method:

1. Classroom instruction was conducted exclusively in the target language.
2. Only everyday vocabulary and sentences were taught.
3. Oral communication skills were built up in a carefully graded progression organized around question-and-answer exchanges between teachers and students in small, intensive classes.
4. Grammar was taught inductively.
5. New teaching points were introduced orally.
6. Concrete vocabulary was taught through demonstration, objects, and pictures; abstract vocabulary was taught by association of ideas.
7. Both speech and listening comprehension were taught.
8. Correct pronunciation and grammar were emphasized.

The Direct Method enjoyed considerable popularity through the end of the nineteenth century and well into the twentieth. It was most widely accepted in private language schools where students were highly motivated and where native-speaking teachers could be employed. To this day "Berlitz" is a household word; Berlitz language schools are thriving in every country of the world. But almost any "method" can succeed when clients are willing to pay high prices for small classes, individual attention, and intensive study. The Direct Method did not take well in public education where the constraints of budget, classroom size, time, and teacher background made such a method difficult to use. Moreover, the Direct Method was criticized for its weak theoretical foundations. The methodology was not so much to be credited for its success as the general skill and personality of the teacher.

By the end of the first quarter of this century the use of the Direct Method had declined both in Europe and in the United States. Most language curricula returned to the Grammar Translation Method or to a "reading approach" that emphasized reading skills in foreign languages. But interestingly enough, by the middle of the 20th century the Direct Method was revived and redirected into what was probably the most visible of all language teaching "revolutions" in the modern era, the Audiolingual Method (see Chapter Three). So even this somewhat short-lived movement in language teaching would reappear in the changing winds and shifting sands of history.

## Suggested Readings

Most of the first language acquisition issues dealt with in this chapter are treated in textbooks on child language. A comprehensive treatment of child language acquisition was provided by *Berko-Gleason* (1985), *Wanner and Gleitman* (1982), and *Clark and Clark* (1977).

Theoretical positions and research issues in child language acquisition are the subject of three anthologies that you might wish to consult: *Krasegnor et al.* (1991), *Weissenborn et al.* (1991), and *Kessel* (1988).

It would be valuable to read a synopsis of *Skinner*'s (1957) classic work (the whole volume itself is interesting but time-consuming reading). *Chomsky*'s (1959) review of Skinner, followed by *MacCorquodale*'s (1970) belated response to Chomsky are both heavy reading, but they are eloquent defenses of two contrasting points of view.

*Bickerton*'s (1981) fascinating book on creolization contains his explanation of the notion of bioprogramming.

*Taylor* (1988) provides a good review of theories of competence.

Much of the research on Universal Grammar is difficult to comprehend without a substantive background in linguistic theory, but you might want to try reading *Larsen-Freeman and Long* (1991:227f) or *Bley-Vroman* (1988) for readable descriptions of research in this area.

For further information on Parallel Distributed Processing and its relationship to first and second language issues, look at *Sokolik* (1990), *Spolsky* (1989), and *Ney and Pearson* (1990).

For a good discussion of Chomsky's "homogeneous" competence model and Tarone's "heterogeneous" competence model, consult *Tarone* (1988).

*Diller* (1978) provides a summary of Francois Gouin's language learning experiences and his Series Method.

## Topics and Questions for Study and Discussion

1.  Why is it that behavioristic theories can account sufficiently well for the earliest utterances of the child, but not for utterances at the sentence and discourse level? Do nativistic and functional approaches provide the necessary tools for accounting for those later, more complex utterances?

2. If you can, try to record samples of young children's speech. A child of about 3 is an ideal subject for you to observe in the study of a human being's growing competence in a language. Transcribe a segment of your recording and see if, inductively, you can determine some of the rules the child is using.

3. Briefly describe the continuum of behavioristic, nativistic, and functional approaches to the study of child language acquisition. In what way do functional approaches cycle back, in part, to behavioristic approaches?

4. What is Universal Grammar? Is it something different from the nativists' concept of LAD?

5. Why do you think Chomsky insisted on weeding out "performance variables" in analyzing language? What do theorists gain from examining only the "idealized" speaker-hearer? What do they lose? How might Tarone's notion of "heterogeneous" competence go beyond the limitations of Chomsky's understanding of competence?

6. Competence and performance are difficult to define. In what sense are they interdependent? Suppose, for example, that an accomplished pianist suffers an accident in which her hands are cut off: does the pianist still possess the *competence* to play her favorite Mozart concerto? If a person suffers brain damage and can no longer talk, does that person still have the competence to talk?

7. Do you think comprehension and production are two separate modes of competence? In what way are they distinctly related? Cite examples supporting their possible unrelatedness.

8. Explain the essential difference between what is referred to as the *forms* of language and the *functions* of language. To which aspect does the child give more conscious attention?

9. Do you think that theories of the *variability* in child language are simply a researcher's way of saying there are many utterances that children produce that we just can't account for in terms of a possible *system*?

10. The frequency of a linguistic item in the child's input may or may not be an important factor in determining acquisition. What is meant, though, by saying that "frequency of *meaningful* occurrence may well be a more precise refinement of the notion of frequency" (p. 40)?

11. Listen to the conversation of a 3- or 4-year-old child, either with parents or with peers. Try to notice the subtleties of language that the child processes: understanding intended meaning, seeking clarification, turn-taking, nonverbal communication, and so on. Then try to

make subtle grammatical corrections of his childlike forms. How does the child respond to the corrections?

12. In what way do you think Gouin reflected some ideas about language and about language acquisition that are now current over a hundred years later? Would the Series Method or the Direct Method work for you as a teacher? Discuss pros and cons.

# Chapter 3

# COMPARING AND CONTRASTING FIRST AND SECOND LANGUAGE ACQUISITION

The increased pace of research on first language acquisition in the 60s and 70s attracted the attention not only of linguists of all kinds but also of educators in various language-related fields. Today the applications of research findings in first language acquisition are widespread. In language arts education, for example, it is not uncommon to find teacher trainees studying first language acquisition, particularly acquisition after age 5, in order to improve their understanding of the task of teaching language skills to native speakers. In foreign language education most standard texts and curricula now include some introductory material in first language acquisition. The reasons for this are clear: We have all observed children acquiring their first language easily and well, yet the learning of a second language, particularly in an educational setting, often meets with great difficulty and sometimes failure. We should therefore be able to learn something from a systematic study of that first language learning experience.

What may not be quite as obvious, though, is how the second language teacher should interpret the hundreds of facets of first language research and theory. It would be conceivable at this point simply to ask you to make your own interpretations and draw your own conclusions about the implications of theories and research in first language acquisition. But that very process of interpretation invokes so many thorny issues that it is easy to draw false analogies. The purpose of this chapter is to set forth explicitly some of the parameters for comparing and contrasting the two types of language acquisition.

The first step in that interpretation process might be to dispel some myths about the relationship between first and second language acquisition. H.H. Stern (1970:57–58) summarized some common arguments that cropped up from time to time to recommend a second language teaching method or procedure on the basis of first language acquisition:

1.  In language teaching, we must practice and practice, again and again. Just watch a small child learning his mother tongue. He repeats things over and over again. During the language-learning stage he practices all the time. This is what we must also do when we learn a foreign language.

2.  Language learning is mainly a matter of imitation. You must be a mimic. Just like a small child. He imitates everything.

3.  First, we practice the separate sounds, then words, then sentences. That is the natural order and is therefore right for learning a foreign language.

4.  Watch a small child's speech development. First he listens, then he speaks. Understanding always precedes speaking. Therefore, this must be the right order of presenting the skills in a foreign language.

5.  A small child listens and speaks and no one would dream of making him read or write. Reading and writing are advanced stages of language development. The natural order for first and second language learning is listening, speaking, reading, writing.

6.  You did not have to translate when you were small. If you were able to learn your own language without translation, you should be able to learn a foreign language in the same way.

7.  A small child simply uses language. He does not learn formal grammar. You don't tell him about verbs and nouns. Yet he learns the language perfectly. It is equally unnecessary to use grammatical conceptualization in teaching a foreign language.

These statements represent the views of those who felt that "the first language learner was looked upon as the foreign language teacher's dream: a pupil who mysteriously laps up his vocabulary, whose pronunciation, in spite of occasional lapses, is impeccable, while morphology and syntax, instead of being a constant headache, come to him like a dream" (Stern 1970:58). The statements also tend to represent the views of those who were dominated by a behavioristic theory of language in which the first language acquisition process is viewed as consisting of rote practice, habit formation, shaping, overlearning, reinforcement, conditioning, association, stimulus and response, and who therefore assumed that the second language learning process involves the same constructs.

There are flaws in each view. Sometimes the flaw is in the assumption behind the statement about first language learning and sometimes it is in the analogy or implication that is drawn; sometimes it is in both. The flaws represent some of the misunderstandings that need to be demythologized for the second language teacher. The process of demythologizing requires a broad understanding of first language theory and issues, as well as a keen awareness of the variables that come into play in drawing analogies to second language learning. By characterizing and classifying those variables in this chapter I hope that you will be able, on the one hand, to avoid the pitfalls of these and other false assumptions and analogies, and on the other hand, to draw enlightened, plausible analogies wherever possible, thereby enriching your understanding of the second language learning process itself.

As generative and cognitive research on first language acquisition gathered momentum, second language researchers and foreign language teachers began to recognize the mistakes in drawing direct global analogies between first and second language acquisition. Some of the first warning signals were sent up by the cognitive psychologist David Ausubel (1964). In foreboding terms, Ausubel outlined a number of glaring problems with the then popular Audiolingual Method, some of whose procedures were derived from notions of "natural" (first) language learning. He warned that the rote learning practice of audiolingual drills lacked the meaningfulness necessary for successful first and second language acquisition, that adults learning a foreign language could, with their full cognitive capacities, benefit from deductive presentations of grammar, that the native language of the learner is not just an interfering factor—it can *facilitate* learning a second language, that the written form of the language could be beneficial, that students could be overwhelmed by language spoken at its "natural speed" and that they, like children, could benefit from more deliberative speech from the teacher. These warnings were derived from Ausubel's cognitive perspective, which ran counter to prevailing behavioristic paradigms on which the Audiolingual Method was based. But Ausubel's criticism may have been too far ahead of its time, for in 1964 few teachers were ready to entertain doubts about the widely accepted method. (See the vignette at the end of this chapter for a further discussion of the Audiolingual Method.)

By the late 1960s and early 1970s generative linguistics was becoming the accepted theoretical mode of thinking, and criticism of earlier direct analogies between first and second language acquisition was mounting. Stern's (1970) article, along with articles by Jakobovits (1968), Cook (1969, 1973), Macnamara (1975), and more recently, Schachter (1988) addressed the inconsistencies of direct analogies between first and second language learning but at the same time recognized the legitimate similarities that, if viewed cautiously, allowed one to draw some constructive conclusions about second language learning.

# Types of Comparison and Contrast

All too often the comparison of first and second language acquisition has been quite carelessly treated. At the very least, one needs to approach the comparison procedure by first considering the differences between *children* and *adults.* It is, in one sense, rather illogical to compare the first language acquisition of a child with the second language acquisition of an adult (see Schachter 1988). This involves trying to draw analogies not only between first and second language learning situations but also between children and adults. It is much more logical to compare first and second language learning in children or to compare second language learning in children and adults. Nevertheless, child first language acquisition and adult second language acquisition are common and important categories of acquisition to compare. It is reasonable, therefore, to view the latter type of comparison within a matrix of possible comparisons. Figure 3–1 represents four possible categories to compare, defined by age and type of acquisition. Note that the vertical shaded line between the "child" and "adult" is "fuzzy" to allow for varying definitions of adulthood. It is generally understood, however, that an adult is one who has reached the age of puberty.

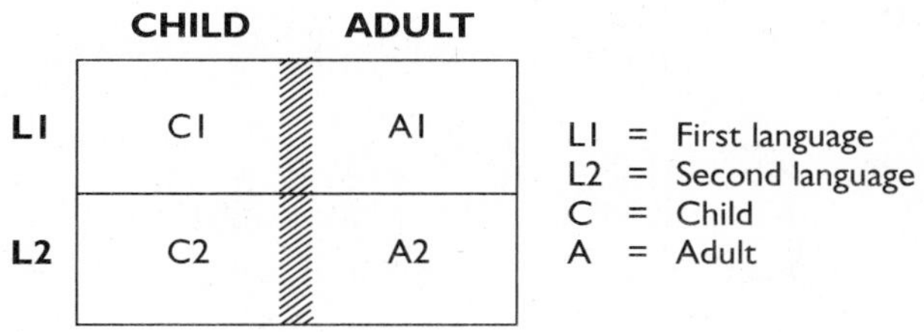

|  | **CHILD** | **ADULT** |
|---|---|---|
| **L1** | C1 | A1 |
| **L2** | C2 | A2 |

L1 = First language
L2 = Second language
C = Child
A = Adult

FIGURE 3–1.    First and second language acquisition in adults and children

Cell A1 is clearly representative of an abnormal situation. There have been few recorded instances of an adult acquiring a first language. Curtiss (1977) wrote about Genie, a 13-year-old girl who had been socially isolated all her life until she was discovered, and who was faced with the task of acquiring a first language. Accounts of "wolf children" and other instances of severe retardation fall into this category. Since it is not imperative at this time to deal with abnormal or pathological cases of language acquisition, we can ignore category A1.

That leaves three possible comparisons: C1-C2, C2-A2, and C1-A2. For the sake of considering issues in this chapter the three comparisons will be referred to by type:

1.  first and second language acquisition in children (C1-C2), holding age constant
2.  second language acquisition in children and adults (C2-A2), holding second language constant
3.  first language acquisition in children and second language acquisition in adults (C1-A2)

In the first type of comparison, holding age constant, one is manipulating the language variable. It is important to remember, however, that a 3-year-old and a 9-year-old—both children by definition—exhibit vast cognitive, affective, and physical differences, and that comparisons of all three types must be treated with caution when varying ages of children are being considered. In the second type of comparison one is manipulating the differences between children and adults. Such comparisons are, for obvious reasons, the most fruitful in yielding analogies for adult second language classroom instruction. In the third type of comparison, of course, both variables are being manipulated. Most of the traditional comparisons have been of Type 3, and such comparisons are difficult to make because of the enormous cognitive, affective, and physical differences between children and adults. That is not to say that Type 3 comparisons ought to be avoided entirely; some valuable insights are to be gained from such comparisons.

One way to approach the various comparisons of children and adults and of first and second language acquisition might be to examine directly the three types of comparison outlined above. A potentially more fruitful approach is taken here, however, and that is to consider all three possible types of comparison within a number of key theoretical issues and considerations. In so doing, such issues form the central focus, with types of comparison serving as subcategories within each issue.

# The Critical Period Hypothesis

Most discussions on first and second language acquisition differences center on the question of whether there is a "critical period" for language acquisition—a biologically determined period of life when language can be acquired more easily and beyond which time language is increasingly difficult to acquire. The *critical period hypothesis* claims that there is such a biological timetable. Initially the notion of a critical period was connected only to first language acquisition. Pathological studies of children who failed to acquire their first language, or aspects thereof, became fuel for arguments of biologically determined predispositions, timed for release, which would wane if the correct environmental stimuli were not present at the crucial stage. We have already seen, in the last chapter, that researchers like Lenneberg (1967) and, more recently, Bickerton (1981) made strong statements in favor of a critical period before which and after which certain abilities do not develop.

Second language researchers have outlined the possibilities of extrapolating the critical period hypothesis to second language contexts (see Scovel 1988; Long 1990b; Johnson 1992; Flege 1981, 1987; Morris *et al.* 1986; Patkowski 1982, 1990; Walsh and Diller 1981; Jacobs 1988; Cummins 1980; Thompson 1991). The "classic" argument is that a critical point for second language acquisition occurs around puberty, beyond which people seem to be relatively incapable of acquiring a nativelike accent of the second language. This has led some to assume, incorrectly, that by the age of 12 or 13 you are "over the hill" when it comes to the possibility of successful second language learning. Such an assumption must be viewed in the light of what it really means to be "successful" in learning a second language, and particularly the role of "accent" as a component of success. In order to examine these issues we will look at *neurological* and *psychomotor* considerations first; these will then be followed by an examination of cognitive, affective, and linguistic considerations.

# Neurological Considerations

One of the most interesting areas of inquiry in second language acquisition has been the study of the function of the *brain* in the process of acquisition (see Jacobs and Schumann 1992 for an excellent synopsis). How might neurological (brain) development affect second language success? Does the maturation of the brain at some point spell the doom of language acquisition ability? Some scholars have singled out the *lateralization* of the brain as the key to answering such a question. There is evidence in neurological research that as the human brain matures certain functions are assigned—or "lateralized"—to the left hemisphere of the brain and certain other functions to the right hemisphere. Intellectual, logical, and analytic functions appear to be largely located in the left hemisphere while the right hemisphere controls functions related to emotional and social needs. (See Chapter Five for more discussion of left-right-brain functioning.) Language functions appear to be controlled mainly in the left hemisphere, though there is a good deal of conflicting evidence. For example, patients who have had left hemispherectomies have been capable of comprehending and producing an amazing amount of language (see Zangwill 1971:220). But generally speaking, a stroke or accident victim who suffers a lesion in the left hemisphere will manifest some language impairment, and such is not as often the case with right-hemisphere lesions.

While questions about how language is lateralized in the brain are interesting indeed, a more crucial question for second language researchers has centered on *when* lateralization takes place, and how that lateralization process affects language acquisition. Eric Lenneberg (1967) and others suggested that lateralization is a slow process that begins around the age of 2 and is completed around puberty. During this time the child is neurologically assigning functions little by little to one side of the brain or the other; included in these functions, of course, is language. And it has been found that children up to the age of puberty who suffer injury to the left hemisphere are able to relocalize linguistic functions to the right hemisphere, to "relearn" their first language with relatively little impairment. Thomas Scovel (1969) extended these findings to propose a relationship between lateralization and *second* language acquisition. He suggested that the plasticity of the brain prior to puberty enables children to acquire not only their first language but also a second language, and that possibly it is the very accomplishment of lateralization that makes it difficult for people to be able ever again to easily acquire fluent control of a second language, or at least to acquire it with what Alexander Guiora et al. (1972a) call "authentic" (nativelike) pronunciation.

While Scovel's (1969) suggestion had only marginal experimental basis, it was a suggestion that prompted him (Scovel 1988) and other researchers to take a careful look at neurological factors in first and second language acquisition with respect to all three types of comparisons. This research has considered the possibility that there is a critical period not only for first language acquisition but also, by extension, for second language acquisition. Much of the neurological argument centers on the *time* of lateralization. While Lenneberg (1967) contended that lateralization is complete around puberty, Norman Geschwind (1970), among others, suggested a much earlier age. Stephen Krashen (1973) believed that the development of lateralization may be complete around age 5. Krashen's suggestion does not grossly conflict with research on first language acquisition if one considers "fluency" in the first language to be achieved by age 5. Scovel (1984:1) cautioned against assuming, with Krashen, that lateralization is *complete* by age 5. "One must be careful to distinguish between 'emergence' of lateralization (at birth, but quite evident at 5) and 'completion' (only evident at about puberty)." If lateralization is not completed until puberty, then one can still construct arguments for a critical period based on lateralization.

One of the most compelling arguments for an accent-related critical period came from Thomas Scovel's (1988) fascinating multidisciplinary review of the evidence that has been amassed. Among other points of focus, Scovel cited evidence for a *sociobiological* critical period in various species of mammals and birds. (Others, e.g., Neapolitan *et al.* 1988, have drawn analogies between the acquisition of birdsong and human language acquisition.) The development of a socially bonding accent at puberty enables species (a) to form an identity with their own community as they anticipate roles of parenting and leadership, and (b) to attract mates of "their own kind" in an instinctive drive to maintain their own species.

If the stabilization of an accepted, authentic accent is biologically prepro-grammed for baboons and birds, why not for human beings? The sociobiologi-cal evidence that Scovel cites persuades us to conclude that native accents, and therefore "foreign" accents after puberty, may be a genetic leftover which, in our widespread human practice of mating across dialectal, linguistic, and racial barriers, is no longer necessary for the preservation of the human species. "In other words," explains Scovel (1988:80), "an accent emerging after puberty is the price we pay for our preordained ability to be articulate apes."

Following another line of research efforts, Walsh and Diller (1981:18) con-cluded that different aspects of a second language are learned optimally at dif-ferent ages:

> Lower-order processes such as pronunciation are dependent on early maturing and less adaptive macroneural circuits, which makes foreign accents difficult to overcome after childhood. Higher-order language functions, such as semantic relations, are more dependent on late maturing neural circuits, which may explain why college students can learn many times the amount of grammar and vocabulary that elementary school students can learn in a given period of time.

This conclusion lends support for a neurologically based critical period, but principally for the acquisition of an authentic (nativelike) *accent,* and not very strongly at all for the acquisition of *communicative* fluency and other "higher-order" processes. We return to this issue in the next section.

Yet another branch of neurolinguistic research focused on the role of the right hemisphere in the acquisition of a second language. Obler (1981:58) notes that in second language learning there is significant right hemisphere participation and that "this participation is particularly active during the early stages of learning the second language." But this "participation" to some extent consists of what we will later (Chapter Five) define as "strategies" of acquisition. Obler (1981) cites the strategy of guessing at meanings, and of using formulaic utterances, as examples of right-hemisphere activity. Others (Genesee 1982, Seliger 1982) also found support for right-hemisphere involve-ment in the form of complex language *processing* as opposed to early language *acquisition.* Genesee (1982:321) concluded that "there may be greater right hemisphere involvement in language processing in bilinguals who acquire their second language *late* relative to their first language and in bilinguals who learn it in informal contexts." While this conclusion may appear to contradict Obler's statement, it does not. Obler found support for more right-hemisphere activity during the early *stages* of second language acquisition, but her conclu-sions were drawn from a study of seventh-, ninth-, and eleventh-grade sub-jects—all postpubescent. Such studies seem to suggest that second language learners, particularly adult learners, might benefit from more encouragement of right-brain activity in the classroom context. But, as Scovel (1982:324–325) noted, that sort of conclusion needs to be cautious, since the research provides a good deal of conflicting evidence, some of which has been grossly misinterpreted in "an unhappy marriage of single-minded neuropsychologists and double-minded educationalists. . . . Brain research . . . will not provide a quick fix to our teaching problems."

Some adults have been known to acquire an authentic accent in a second language after the age of puberty, but such individuals are few and far between. Anthropologist Jane Hill (1970) provided an intriguing response to Scovel's (1969) study by citing anthropological research on non-Western societies yielding evidence that adults can, in the normal course of their lives, acquire second languages perfectly. One unique instance of second language acquisition in adulthood was reported by Sorenson (1967), who studies the Tukano tribes of South America. At least two dozen languages are spoken among these peoples, and each tribal group, identified by the language it speaks, is an exogamous unit—people must marry outside their group, and hence almost always marry someone who speaks another language. Sorenson reported that during adolescence individuals actively and almost suddenly begin to speak two or three other languages to which they have been exposed at some point. Moreover, "in adulthood [a person] may acquire more languages; as he approaches old age, field observation indicates, he will go on to perfect his knowledge of all the languages at his disposal" (Sorenson 1967:678). In conclusion Hill (1970:247–248) suggests that

> the language acquisition situation seen in adult language learners in the largely monolingual American English middle class speech communities . . . may have been inappropriately taken to be a universal situation in proposing an innatist explanation for adult foreign accents. Multilingual speech communities of various types deserve careful study. . . . We will have to explore the influence of social and cultural roles which language and phonation play, and the role which attitudes about language play, as an alternative or a supplement to the cerebral dominance theory as an explanation of adult foreign accents.

Hill's suggestion has been followed in more recent years. Today researchers are continuing the quest for answers to child-adult differences by looking beyond neurological factors. Flege (1987) and Morris *et al.* (1986), for example, cited motivation, affective variables, social factors, and the quality of input as important in explaining the apparent advantage of the child. Both Long (1990b) and Patkowski (1990) disputed such conclusions and sided with Scovel in their relatively strong interpretation of an age-related critical period for first and second language acquisition.

# Psychomotor Considerations

An issue closely related to strictly neurological considerations is the role of the psychomotor coordination of the "speech muscles" in second language acquisition, or, more commonly, *accent.* We all know that great athletes, great musicians, and others who have become accomplished in a set of skills requiring muscular dexterity have almost always begun to develop that skill in childhood, probably before the age of puberty. We can also appreciate the fact that given the existence of several hundred muscles that are used in the articulation of human speech (throat, larynx, mouth, lips, tongue, and other muscles), a tremendous degree of muscular control is required to achieve the fluency of a native speaker of a language. The physical development of the child must be considered carefully in Type 1 comparisons. At birth the speech muscles are developed only to the extent that the larynx can control sustained cries. These speech muscles gradually develop, and control of some complex sounds in certain languages (in English the *r* and *l* are typical) sometimes is not achieved until after age 5, though virtually complete phonemic control is present in most 5-year-old children. Children who acquire a second language after the age of 5 may have a physical advantage in that phonemic control of a second language is physically possible yet that mysterious plasticity is still present.

Comparisons of Types 2 and 3 may be more significant than Type 1 comparisons in considering the role of muscular coordination. If it is indeed true, and it appears to be so, that starting a physical skill at a young age is advantageous, the same should clearly be true of language with respect to pronunciation of a language. It is no wonder that children acquire authentic pronunciation while adults generally do not, since pronunciation involves the control of so many muscles.

Research on the acquisition of authentic control of the *phonology* of a foreign language supports the notion of a critical period. The evidence thus far indicates that persons beyond the age of puberty do not generally acquire authentic pronunciation of the second language. Such a critical period may have little to do with the lateralization of the brain, though, and much to do with the child's neuromuscular plasticity. Of course, you can cite immediate exceptions to this rule—adults who, well after puberty, learned a second language and now speak it flawlessly. (You can also cite cases of athletes or musicians who started developing their skill relatively late in life and became very proficient.) These, however, appear to be isolated instances. But what is tantalizingly interesting about the isolated instances is that those special people possess somewhere within their competence the ability to override and overcome the general tendency to be less than perfect in the pronunciation of a foreign language. If we could only discover what those unique properties are!

A curious set of studies was undertaken by Neufeld (1977, 1979, 1980) to determine to what extent adults could approximate native-speaker accents in a second language never before encountered. In the earliest experiment 20 adult native English speakers were taught to imitate 10 utterances, each from 1 to 16 syllables in length, in Japanese and in Chinese. Native-speaking Japanese and Chinese judges listened to the taped imitations. The results indicated that 11 of the Japanese and 9 of the Chinese imitations were judged to have been produced by "native speakers." While Neufeld recognizes the limitations of his own studies, he does suggest that "older students have neither lost their sensitivity to subtle differences in sounds, rhythm, and pitch nor the ability to reproduce these sounds and contours" (1979:234). A number of critics (including Scovel 1984) are quick to point out, however, that glaring experimental flaws mitigate against using Neufeld's studies to draw any significant conclusions about the critical period hypothesis.

It is important to remember in all these considerations that pronunciation of a language is not by any means the sole criterion for acquisition, nor is it really the most important one. We all know people who have less than perfect pronunciation but who also have magnificent and fluent control of a second language, control that can even exceed that of many native speakers. I like to call this the "Henry Kissinger effect" in honor of the former U.S. Secretary of State whose German accent was so noticeable yet who was clearly more eloquent than the large majority of native speakers of American English. So, muscular coordination may be of minimal significance in establishing criteria for overall successful acquisition of a second language. The acquisition of the communicative and functional purposes of language is far more important. Scovel (1988:186) captures the spirit of this way of looking at second language acquisition:

> For me, the acquisition of a new language will remain a phenomenon of natural fascination and mystery, not simply because it is a special skill of such incredible complexity that it remains one of the greatest achievements of the human mind, but because it also is a testimony of how much we can accomplish within the limitations that nature has placed upon us. We among all animals possess the gift of tongues because we have a time to speak.

## Cognitive Considerations

All three types of adult-child comparisons cited earlier relate to the cognitive domain of human behavior. Human cognition develops rapidly throughout the first 16 years of life and less rapidly after adulthood. Some of these changes are critical, others are more gradual and difficult to detect. Jean Piaget outlines the course of intellectual development in a child through various stages: the sensorimotor stage from ages 0 to 2, the preoperational stage from ages 2 to 7, and the operational stage from ages 7 to 16, with a crucial change from the concrete operational stage to the formal operational stage around the age of 11. The most critical stage for a consideration of first and second language acquisition appears to occur, in Piaget's outline, at puberty. It is here that a person becomes capable of abstraction, of formal thinking which transcends concrete experience and direct perception. Cognitively, then, you can make a strong argument for a critical period of language acquisition by connecting language acquisition and the concrete/formal stage transition.

Ausubel (1964) hinted at the relevance of such a connection in noting that adults learning a second language could profit from certain grammatical explanations and deductive thinking that obviously would be pointless for a child. Whether adults do in fact profit from such explanations depends, of course, on the suitability and efficiency of the explanation, the teacher, the context, and other pedagogical variables. We have observed, though, that children do learn second languages well *without* the benefit—or hindrance—of formal operational thought. Adults, possessing superior cognitive capacity, often do not successfully learn a second language. Is this capacity, then, a facilitating or inhibiting effect on language acquisition? Ellen Rosansky (1975:96) offers an explanation noting that initial language acquisition takes place when the child is highly "centered": "He is not only egocentric at this time, but when faced with a problem he can focus (and then only fleetingly) on one dimension at a time. This lack of flexibility and lack of decentration may well be a necessity for language acquisition." Young children are generally not "aware" that they are acquiring a language, nor are they aware of societal values and attitudes placed on one language or another. It is said that "a watched pot never boils"; is it possible that a language learner who is too consciously aware of what he or she is doing will have difficulty in learning the second language?

You may be tempted to answer that question affirmatively, but there is both logical and anecdotal counterevidence. Logically, a superior intellect should facilitate what is in one sense an intellectual activity. Anecdotal evidence shows that some adults who have been successful language learners have been very much aware of the process they were going through, even to the point of utilizing self-made paradigms and other fabricated linguistic devices to facilitate the learning process. So, if it is true that mature cognition is a liability to successful second language acquisition, clearly some intervening variables are allowing some persons to be quite successful second language learners after puberty. These variables may in most cases lie outside the cognitive domain entirely, perhaps more centrally in the affective—or emotional—domain.

The lateralization hypothesis may provide another key to cognitive differences between child and adult language acquisition. As the child matures into adulthood, the left hemisphere (which controls the analytical and intellectual functions) becomes more dominant than the right hemisphere (which controls the emotional functions). It is possible that the dominance of the left hemisphere contributes to a tendency to overanalyze and to be too intellectually centered on the task of second language learning.

Another construct that should be considered in examining the cognitive domain is the Piagetian notion of *equilibration.* Equilibration is defined as "progressive interior organization of knowledge in a stepwise fashion" (Sullivan 1967:12), and is related to the concept of equilibrium. That is, cognition develops as a process of moving from states of doubt and uncertainty (disequilibrium) to stages of resolution and certainty (equilibrium) and then back to further doubt that is, in time, also resolved. And so the cycle continues. Piaget claimed that conceptual development is a process of progressively moving from states of disequilibrium to equilibrium and that periods of disequilibrium mark virtually all cognitive development up through age 14 or 15, when formal operations finally are firmly organized and equilibrium is reached.

It is conceivable that disequilibrium may provide the key motivation for language acquisition: language interacts with cognition to achieve equilibrium. Perhaps until that state of final equilibrium is reached, the child is cognitively ready and eager to acquire the language necessary for achieving the cognitive equilibrium of adulthood. That same child is, until that time, decreasingly tolerant of cognitive ambiguities. Children are amazingly indifferent to contradictions, but intellectual growth produces an awareness of ambiguities about them and heightens the need for resolution. Perhaps a general intolerance of contradictions produces an acute awareness of the myriad of differences between two languages and thus perhaps around the age of 14 or 15, the prospect of learning a second language suddenly becomes overwhelming, discouraging the learner from proceeding a step at a time as a younger child would do.

The final consideration in the cognitive domain is the distinction that Ausubel makes between *rote* and *meaningful* learning. Ausubel notes that people of all ages have little need for rote, mechanistic learning that is not related to existing knowledge and experience. Rather, most items are acquired by meaningful learning, by anchoring and relating new items and experiences to knowledge that exists in the cognitive framework. It is a myth to contend that children are good rote learners, that they make good use of meaningless repetition and mimicking. We have already seen in Chapter Two that children's practice and imitation is a very meaningful activity that is contextualized and purposeful. Adults, actually, have developed greater concentration and so have greater ability for rote learning; but rote learning is usually used only for short-term memory or for somewhat artificial purposes. Here, then, one can make a legitimate Type 3 comparison: both adults and children utilize primarily meaningful learning operations. By inference, we may conclude that the foreign language classroom should not become the locus of excessive rote activity—rote drills, pattern practice without context, reciting rules, and other activities that are not in the context of meaningful communication. It is interesting to note that Type 3 comparisons almost always refer in the case of adults (A2), to the *classroom* learning of a second language, but many foreign language classrooms utilize an excessive number of rote-learning procedures. So, naturally if you compare adults learning a foreign language by rote methods with children learning their first language in a natural, meaningful context, you will claim the superiority of the child's learning! The cause of such superiority may not be in the *age* of the person but in the *context* of learning. The child happens to be learning language meaningfully and the adult is not.

The cognitive domain holds yet other areas of interest for comparing first and second language acquisition. These areas will be treated more fully in Chapters Four and Five. We turn now to what may be the most complex, yet the most illuminating of the four domains: the affective domain.

# Affective Considerations

Human beings are emotional creatures. At the heart of all thought and meaning and action is emotion. As "intellectual" as we would like to think we are, we are influenced by our emotions. It is only logical, then, to look at the affective (emotional) domain for some of the most significant answers to the problems of contrasting the differences between first and second language acquisition.

Research on the affective domain in second language acquisition has been mounting steadily for a number of years. This research has been inspired by a number of factors. Not the least of these is the fact that linguistic theory is now asking the deepest possible questions about human language, with some linguists and applied linguists examining the inner being of the person to discover if in the affective side of human behavior there lies an explanation to the mysteries of language. A lengthy treatment of affective variables in second language acquisition is provided in Chapters Six and Seven; in this chapter it is important to take a brief look at selected affective factors as they relate to the first and second language issue.

The affective domain includes many factors: empathy, self-esteem, extroversion, inhibition, imitation, anxiety, attitudes—the list could go on for some time. Some of these may seem at first rather far removed from language learning, but when you consider the pervasive nature of language, any affective factor can conceivably be relevant to second language learning.

A case in point is the role of egocentricity in human development. Very young children are totally egocentric. The world revolves about them, and they see all events as focusing on themselves. Small babies at first do not even distinguish a separation between themselves and the world around them. A rattle held in a baby's hand, for example, is simply an inseparable extension of the baby as long as it is grasped; when the baby drops it or loses sight of it, it ceases to exist. As children grow older they become more aware of themselves, more self-conscious as they seek both to define and understand their self-identity. In preadolescence children develop an acute consciousness of themselves as separate and identifiable entities but ones which, in their still-wavering insecurity, need protecting. They therefore develop *inhibitions* about this self-identity, fearing to expose too much self-doubt. At puberty these inhibitions are heightened in the trauma of undergoing critical physical, cognitive, and emotional changes. Adolescents must acquire a totally new physical, cognitive, and emotional identity. Their egos are affected not only in how they understand themselves but also in how they reach out beyond themselves, how they relate to others socially, and how they use the communicative process to bring on affective equilibrium.

Alexander Guiora, a researcher in the study of personality variables in second language learning, proposed what he called the *language ego* (Guiora et al. 1972b) to account for the identity a person develops in reference to the language he or she speaks. For any monolingual person the language ego involves the interaction of the native language and ego development. Your self-identity is inextricably bound up with your language and ego development. Your self-identity is inextricably bound up with your language, for it is in the communicative process—the process of sending out messages and having them "bounced" back—that such identities are confirmed, shaped, and reshaped. Guiora suggested that the language ego may account for the difficulties that adults have in learning a second language. The child's ego is dynamic and growing and flexible through the age of puberty, and thus a new language at this stage does not pose a substantial "threat" or inhibition to the ego and adaptation is made relatively easily as long as there are not undue confounding sociocultural factors such as, for example, a damaging attitude toward a language or language group at a young age. However, the simultaneous physical, emotional, and cognitive changes of puberty give rise to a defensive mechanism in which the language ego becomes protective and defensive. The language ego clings to the security of the native language to protect the fragile ego of the young adult. The language ego, which has now become part and parcel of self-identity, is threatened, and thus a context develops in which you must be willing literally to make a fool of yourself in the trial-and-error struggle of speaking and understanding a foreign language. Younger children are less frightened because they are less aware of language *forms,* and the possibility of making mistakes in those forms—mistakes that one really must make in an attempt to communicate spontaneously—does not concern them greatly.

It is no wonder, then, that the acquisition of a new language ego is an enormous undertaking, not only for young adolescents but also for an adult who has grown comfortable and secure in his or her own identity and who possesses inhibitions that serve as a wall of defensive protection around the ego. Making the leap to a new or second identity is no simple matter; it can be successful only when one musters the necessary ego strength to overcome inhibitions. It is possible that the successful adult language learner is someone who can bridge this affective gap. Some of the seeds of success might be sown early in life. In a bilingual setting, for example, if a child has already learned one second language in childhood, then affectively, learning a third language might represent much less of a threat. Or such seeds may be independent of a bilingual setting; they may simply arise out of whatever combination of nature and nurture makes for the development of a strong ego.

In Type 1 comparisons of first and second language acquisition, ego development and identification may be relevant factors. Preadolescent children of 9 or 10, for example, are beginning to develop inhibitions, and it is conceivable, though little research evidence is available, that children of this age have a good deal of affective dissonance to overcome as they attempt to learn a second language. Type 2 and 3 comparisons are of course highly relevant. We know from both observational and research evidence that even mature adults are highly inhibited organisms, particularly in Western society. Again, cross-cultural research such as that reported by Hill (1970) is important to consider. These inhibitions surface in modern language classes where the learner's attempts to speak in the foreign language are often fraught with embarrassment. We have also observed the same inhibition in the "natural" setting (a nonclassroom setting, such as a learner living in a foreign culture), though in such instances there is the likelihood that the necessity to communicate will soon override the inhibitions.

Other affective factors seem to hinge on the basic notion of ego identification. It would appear that the study of second language learning as the acquisition of a *second identity* might pose a fruitful and important issue in understanding not only some differences between child and adult first and second language learning but second language learning in general (see Chapter Seven).

Another affectively related variable deserves mention here even though it will be given fuller consideration in Chapter Six: the role of *attitudes* in language learning. From the growing body of literature on attitudes, it seems clear that negative attitudes can affect success in learning a language. Very young children, however, who are not developed enough cognitively to possess "attitudes" toward races, cultures, ethnic groups, classes of people, and languages, are unaffected. Macnamara (1975:79) notes that "a child suddenly transported from Montreal to Berlin will rapidly learn German no matter what he thinks of the Germans." But as a child reaches school age, he also begins to acquire certain attitudes toward types and stereotypes of people. Most of these attitudes are "taught," consciously or unconsciously, by parents, other adults, and peers. The learning of negative attitudes toward the people who speak the second language or toward the second language itself has been shown to affect the success of language learning in persons from school age on up.

Finally, *peer pressure* is a particularly important variable in Type 2 and Type 3 comparisons. The peer pressure children encounter in language learning is quite unlike what the adult experiences. Children usually have strong constraints upon them to conform. They are told in words, thoughts, and actions that they had better "be like the rest of the kids." Such peer pressure extends to language. Adults experience some peer pressure but of a different kind. Adults tend to tolerate linguistic differences more than children, and therefore errors in speech are more easily excused. If adults can *understand* a second language speaker, for example, they will usually provide positive cognitive and affective feedback, a level of tolerance that might encourage some adult learners to "get by." Children are harsher critics of one another's actions and words and may thus provide a necessary and sufficient degree of pressure to learn the second language.

## Linguistic Considerations

We have so far looked at the *organism* and considered a number of different types of comparison. Now we turn to the subject matter itself. What are some of the *linguistic* considerations in first and second language learning? A growing number of research studies are now available to shed some light on the linguistic processes of second language learning and how those processes differ between children and adults. A good deal of this research will be treated in Chapters Eight, Nine, and Ten, but at this point we can look briefly at some of the linguistic findings, particularly in the child's acquisition of a second language (Type 1 comparison).

It is clear that children learning two languages simultaneously acquire them by the use of similar strategies. They are, in essence, learning two first languages, and the key to success is in distinguishing separate contexts for the two languages. (People who learn a second language in such separate contexts are referred to as *coordinate bilinguals*; they have two meaning systems, as opposed to *compound bilinguals* who have one meaning system from which both languages operate.) Children generally do not have problems with "mixing up languages," regardless of the separateness of contexts for use of the languages. In some cases the acquisition of both languages in bilingual children is slightly slower than the normal schedule for first language acquisition. However, a respectable stockpile of research (see Schinke-Llano 1989, Reynolds 1991) shows a considerable cognitive *benefit* of early childhood bilingualism, supporting Lambert's (1962) contention that bilingual children are more facile at concept formation and have a greater mental flexibility.

Nonsimultaneous second language acquisition is difficult to define within the limits of childhood. One could refer to children who are acquiring a second language soon after they have begun to learn their first language (say at age 3 or 4), or as late as age 10. For the most part, research confirms that the linguistic and cognitive processes of second language learning in children are in general similar to first language processes. Ravem (1968), Milon (1974), Natalicio and Natalicio (1971), Dulay and Burt (1974a), Ervin-Tripp (1974), and Hansen-Bede (1975), among others, concluded that similar strategies and linguistic features are present in both first and second language learning in children. Dulay and Burt (1974a) found, for example, that in an examination of over 500 errors made by Spanish-speaking children learning English, 86 percent of the errors reflected normal developmental characteristics—that is, expected intralingual strategies, not interference errors from the first language. Hansen-Bede (1975) examined such linguistic structures as possession, gender, word order, verb forms, questions, and negation in an English-speaking 3-year-old child who learned Urdu upon moving to Pakistan. In spite of some marked linguistic contrasts between English and Urdu, the child's acquisition did not appear to show first language interference and, except for negation, showed similar strategies and rules for both the first and the second language.

Adult second language linguistic processes are more difficult to pin down. Only a few detailed studies have been carried out on the natural, untutored acquisition of a second language by adults (see Schmidt 1983 for an example). So much of adult second language acquisition in Western culture is tempered and shaped by classroom variables—textbooks, methods, and the like—that it is difficult to conclude much about the natural process. While other chapters in this book will touch on this issue, what can be said here is that adults do approach a second language systematically and attempt to formulate linguistic rules on the basis of whatever linguistic information is available to them—information from both the native language and from the second language itself. The nature and sequencing of these systems is the subject of a good deal of second language research today. What we have learned above all else from this research is that the saliency of interference from the first language does not imply that interference is the most relevant or most crucial factor in adult second language acquisition. Adults learning a second language manifest some of the same types of errors found in children learning their first language.

One of the first steps demonstrating the importance of factors other than first language interference was taken in a series of research studies by Heidi Dulay and Marina Burt (1972, 1974a, 1974b, 1976). They even went so far at one point as to claim that "transfer of L1 syntactic patterns *rarely* occurs" (italics mine) in child second language acquisition (1976:72). They claimed that children learning a second language use a *creative construction* process, just as they do in their first language. This conclusion was supported by some massive research data collected on the acquisition order of 11 English morphemes in children learning English as a second language. Dulay and Burt found a common order of acquisition among children of several native language backgrounds, an order very similar to that found by Roger Brown (1973) using the same morphemes but for children acquiring English as their first language.

There are logical and methodological arguments about the validity of Dulay and Burt's findings. Rosansky (1976) argued that the statistical procedures used were suspect, and others (Larsen-Freeman 1976, Andersen 1978) noted that 11 English morphemes constitute only a minute portion of English syntax. Nevertheless, the assertion that children do not appear to be as distracted by the first language as do adults is upheld by other research on children's second language acquisition, though the assertion that first language interference is "rare" is an overstatement. It may be more prudent to assert that the first language, for cognitive and affective reasons already discussed, does not pose the same degree of interference in children learning a second language as it does in adults.

Adults, more cognitively secure, appear to operate from the solid foundation of the first language and thus manifest more interference. But it was pointed out earlier that adults, too, manifest errors not unlike some of the errors children make, the result of creative perception of the second language and an attempt to discover its rules apart from the rules of the first language. The first language, however, may be more readily used to bridge gaps that the adult learner cannot fill by generalization within the second language. In this case we do well to remember that the first language can be a facilitating factor, and not just an interfering factor.

We have touched on four domains that hold significant factors for the comparison of first and second language acquisition. In all four, though, it is important to maintain the distinction among the three types of comparisons between first and second language acquisition. Beware of the pitfalls of merely comparing "first" and "second" language acquisition! By considering the three logically possible comparisons, unnecessary loopholes in logic should be minimized. Once again, final answers have not been provided, but parameters for considering the comparisons have been set forth. By operating on them you can construct your own personal integrated understanding of what the relationship is between the first and second language acquisition, and how that relationship might hold fruitful implications for second language teaching.

# Issues in First Language Acquisition Revisited

Having examined the comparison of first and second language acquisition in four general domains of human behavior, we turn in this final section to a brief consideration of the eight issues in first language acquisition that were presented in Chapter Two. In most cases the implications of these issues are already clear, from the comments in the previous chapter, from your own logical thinking, or from comments in this chapter. Therefore what follows is a way of highlighting the implications of the issues for second language learning.

## Competence and Performance

It is difficult to "get at" linguistic competence in a second language as it is in a first. For children, judgments of grammaticality may elicit a second language "pop-go-weasel" effect. For adults you can be a little more direct in inferring competence; adults can make choices between two alternative forms and sometimes they manifest an awareness of grammaticality in a second language. But you must remember that adults are not generally able to verbalize "rules" and paradigms consciously even in their native language. Furthermore, in judging utterances in the modern language classroom and responses on various tests, teachers need to be cautiously attentive to the discrepancy between performance on a given day or in a given context and competence in a second language in general. Remember that one isolated sample of second language speech may on the surface appear to be rather malformed until you consider that sample in comparison with the everyday mistakes and errors of native speakers.

## Comprehension and Production

Whether comprehension is derived from a separate level of competence or not, there is a universal distinction between comprehension and production. Learning a second language usually means learning to speak it *and* to comprehend it! When we say "Do you speak English?" or "Parlez-vous français?" we usually mean "...and do you *understand* it too?" Learning involves both modes (unless you are interested only in, say, learning to read in the second language). So teaching involves attending to both comprehension and production and the full consideration of the gaps and differences between the two. Adult second language learners will, like children, often *hear* a distinction and not be able to produce it. The inability to produce an item, therefore, should not be taken to mean that the learner cannot comprehend the item.

## Nature or Nurture?

What happens to the magic "little black box" called LAD after puberty? Does the adult suffer from linguistic "hardening of the arteries"? Does LAD "grow up" somehow? Does lateralization signal the death of LAD? We do not have the answers to these questions, but there have been some hints in the discussion of physical, cognitive, and affective factors. What we do know is that adults and children alike appear to have the capacity to acquire a second language at any age. If a person does not acquire a second language successfully, it is probably because of intervening cognitive or affective variables and not the absence of innate capacities. Defining those intervening variables appears to be more relevant than probing the properties of innateness.

## Universals

Is there a universal deep structure, common to all languages? If so, then second language learning is merely the learning of a new surface structure, a new set of forms for the basic meanings already established. However, there seems to be little evidence that deep structures are all so universal. Meaning and thought seem to be as culturally determined as surface structures are. The complexity of the professional literature in a field like Universal Grammar is overwhelming for most language teachers and Masters-level graduate students. So, one practical way to adhere to the spirit of linguistic universals may be (a) simply to look for commonalities between the first and second languages in question, and (b) to consider a few possible universally applicable cognitive processes of acquisition. Learners may all use similar strategies at similar stages in their acquisition process. If there is a universally successful way to learn a second language, detailed studies of the characteristics of "good language learners" around the world may begin to open up some new vistas.

## Systematicity and Variability

Clearly second language acquisition, both child and adult, is characterized by both systematicity and variability. Second language linguistic development appears in many instances to mirror the first language acquisition process: learners induce rules, generalize across a category, overgeneralize, and proceed in stages of development (more on this in Chapter Nine). The variability of second language data poses thorny problems which have been addressed by people like Tarone (1988) and Ellis (1987, 1989). The variability of second language acquisition is exacerbated by a host of cognitive, affective, cultural, and contextual variables that are sometimes not applicable to a first language learning situation.

## Language and Thought

Another mind-boggling issue in both first and second language acquisition is the precise relationship between language and thought. We can see that surely language helps to shape thinking and that thinking helps to shape language. What happens to this interdependence when a second language is acquired? Does the bilingual person's memory consist of one storage system (compound bilingualism) or two (coordinate bilingualism)? The second language learner is clearly presented with a tremendous task in sorting out new meanings from old, distinguishing thoughts and concepts in one language that are similar but not quite parallel to the second language, perhaps really acquiring a whole new system of conceptualization. The second language teacher needs to be acutely aware of cultural thought patterns that may be as interfering as the linguistic patterns themselves.

## Imitation

While children are good deep-structure imitators, adults can fare much better in imitating surface structure if they are explicitly directed either internally or externally to do so. Sometimes their ability to center on surface distinctions is a distracting factor; at other times it is helpful. Adults learning a second language might do well to attend consciously to truth value and to be less aware of surface structure as they communicate. The implication is that *meaningful* contexts for language learning are necessary; second language learners ought not to become too preoccupied with form lest they lose sight of the function and purpose of language.

## Practice

Too many language classes are filled with rote practice that centers on surface forms. If Ausubel is correct in his theory of learning, the *frequency* of stimuli and the number of times spent practicing a form are not highly important in learning an item. What is important is meaningfulness. Contextualized, appropriate, meaningful communication in the second language seems to be the best possible practice the second language learner could engage in.

## Input

In the case of adult second language learning, parental input is replaced by teacher input. Teachers might do well to be as deliberate, but meaningful, in their communications with students as the parent is to the child since input is as important to the second language learner as it is to the first language learner. And that input should foster meaningful communicative use of the language.

## Discourse

We have only begun to scratch the surface of possibilities of second language discourse analysis (for further discussion, see Chapter Ten and such references as Larsen-Freeman 1980 and Hatch 1978b). As we search for better ways of teaching communicative competence to second language learners, research on the acquisition of discourse becomes more and more important. Perhaps a study of children's amazing dexterity in acquiring rules of conversation and in perceiving intended meaning will help us to find ways of teaching such capacities to second language learners. We will look more at these issues in Chapter Ten.

Can you now more adequately dispel the myths represented in the statements cited by H.H. Stern at the beginning of the chapter? It is probably apparent why you cannot, in simple statements, compare first and second language acquisition. The fallacies of many of such statements should be more clearly perceived with carefully integrated considerations of the several types and domains of comparison and some of the implications of the issues of first language acquisition.

# In the Classroom:
# The Audiolingual Method

In the first half of this century, the Direct Method did not take hold in the United States the way it did in Europe. While one could easily find native-speaking teachers of modern foreign languages in Europe, such was not the case in the United States. Also, European high school and university students did not have to travel far to find opportunities to put the oral skills of another language to actual, practical use. Moreover, U.S. educational institutions had become firmly convinced that a reading approach to foreign languages was more useful than an oral approach, given the perceived linguistic isolation of the United States at the time. The highly influential Coleman Report of 1929 (Coleman 1929) had persuaded foreign language teachers that it was impractical to teach oral skills, and that reading should become the focus. Thus schools returned in the 1930s and 1940s to Grammar Translation, "the handmaiden of reading" (Bowen et al. 1985).

Then World War II broke out and suddenly the United States was thrust into a worldwide conflict, heightening the need for Americans to become orally proficient in the languages of both their allies and their enemies. The time was ripe for a language teaching revolution. The U.S. military provided the impetus with funding for special, intensive language courses that focused on the aural/oral skills; these courses came to be known as the Army Specialized Training Program (ASTP), or, more colloquially, the "Army Method." Characteristic of these courses was a great deal of oral activity—pronunciation and pattern drills and conversation practice—with virtually none of the grammar and translation found in traditional classes. Ironically, numerous foundation stones of the discarded Direct Method were borrowed and injected into this new approach. Soon, the success of the Army Method and the revived national interest in foreign languages spurred educational institutions to adopt the new methodology. In all its variations and adaptations, the Army Method came to be known in the 1950s as the Audiolingual Method.

The Audiolingual Method (ALM) was firmly grounded in linguistic and psychological theory. Structural linguists of the 1940s and 1950s were engaged in what they claimed was a "scientific descriptive analysis" of various languages; teaching methodologists saw a direct application of such analysis to teaching linguistic patterns (Fries 1945). (We will return to this particular theory-practice issue in Chapter Eight.) At the same time, behavioristic psychologists advocated conditioning and habit-formation models of learning which were perfectly married with the mimicry drills and pattern practices of audiolingual methodology.

The characteristics of the ALM may be summed up in the following list (adapted from Prator and Celce-Murcia 1979):

1.  New material is presented in dialog form.

2.  There is dependence on mimicry, memorization of set phrases, and overlearning.

3.  Structures are sequenced by means of contrastive analysis and taught one at a time.

4.  Structural patterns are taught using repetitive drills.

5.  There is little or no grammatical explanation: Grammar is taught by inductive analogy rather than deductive explanation.

6.  Vocabulary is strictly limited and learned in context.

7.  There is much use of tapes, language labs, and visual aids.

8.  Great importance is attached to pronunciation.

9.  Very little use of the mother tongue by teachers is permitted.

10.  Successful responses are immediately reinforced.

11.  There is a great effort to get students to produce error-free utterances.

12.  There is a tendency to manipulate language and disregard content.

For a number of reasons the ALM enjoyed many years of popularity, and even to this day, adaptations of the ALM are found in contemporary methodologies. The ALM was firmly rooted in respectable theoretical perspectives at the time. Materials were carefully prepared, tested out, and disseminated to educational institutions. "Success" could be more overtly experienced by students as they practiced their dialogs in off-hours. But the popularity was not to last forever. Led by Wilga Rivers' (1964) eloquent criticism of the misconceptions of the ALM, and by its ultimate failure to teach long-term communicative proficiency, its popularity waned. We discovered that language was not really acquired through a process of habit formation and overlearning, that errors were not necessarily to be avoided at all costs, and that structural linguistics did not tell us everything about language that we needed to know. While the ALM was a valiant attempt to reap the fruits of language teaching methodologies that had preceded it, in the end it still fell short, as all methods do. But we learned something from the very failure of the ALM to do everything it had promised, and we moved forward.

## Suggested Readings

There were several well-known articles that compared first and second language acquisition. *Ausubel* (1964), *Cook* (1969), and *Stern* (1970) were some of the first to deal with the issue. *Dulay and Burt* (1972), *Macnamara* (1975) and *Schacter* (1988) added some important arguments to the comparison.

One of the most intriguing books available on the Critical Period Hypothesis is *Scovel*'s (1988) summary and critique of a host of related studies, all serving to support a "sociobiological" interpretation of the Critical Period Hypothesis.

The discussion of the effects of lateralization on first and second language acquisition is an interesting topic of debate. *Lenneberg* (1967) gave the classic position, then *Scovel*'s (1969) article related lateralization to foreign accents. *Krashen*'s (1973) work on the notion of a critical period for language acquisition extended the argument further. *Hill*'s (1970) response to Scovel was an intriguing account of language learning in non-Western contexts.

The issue of left-right-brain differences in second language acquisition is covered in two readily available sources: *Diller*'s (1981) volume has several articles on the topic, and the September 1982 issue of the *TESOL Quarterly* has three articles that summarize the state of the art.

The series of studies by *Dulay and Burt* (1972, 1974a, 1974b, 1976) are widely known as being among the first few attempts to demonstrate empirically that children learning a second language do not manifest the same degree of interference attributed to adults. *Larsen-Freeman*'s (1976) study provided an important commentary on Dulay and Burt's data.

*Long* (1990b) gives an excellent summary of age-related differences in language acquisition.

## Topics and Questions for Study and Discussion

1. Read over each of the common arguments (p. 7) cited by Stern (1970) which have been used to justify analogies between first language learning and second language teaching. For each statement determine what is assumed or presupposed. Then decide whether the analogy is correct or not. If so, why? If not, why not?

2. What are the implications of including cell A1 in the possible comparisons on page 52? You might speculate a little on what speech therapists have to face in getting persons to relearn a first language.

3. Restate in your own words what the critical period hypothesis is. Can you cite some anecdotal evidence for a critical period? Can you think of anyone whom you have met who started learning a second language after puberty and who nevertheless has an almost "perfect" accent? Why do you suppose such a person has been able to be so successful?

4. Try to explain Scovel's claim that the acquisition of a native accent around the age of puberty is an evolutionary left-over of sociobiological critical periods evident in many species of animals and birds.

5. What is the significance of left- and right-brain differences in learning to draw? To play a musical instrument? To play a sport? How are these activities analogous to second language learning? How might classroom teaching techniques take into account students' variation in left-right-brain preferences?

6. It was noted on page 65 that "the *saliency* of interference . . . from the first language does not imply that interference is the most rele-

vant . . . factor in adult language acquisition." Explain what is meant by that statement.

7. Summarize the ten "revisited" issues in your own words. How does your understanding of those issues, as they apply to second language learning, help you to formulate a better understanding of the total process of second language acquisition? Cite what you think might be some practical classroom implications of the ten issues.

8. Do you think it is worthwhile at all to *teach* children a second language in the classroom? If so, how might approaches and methods differ between a class of children and a class of adults?

# Chapter 4

# HUMAN LEARNING

Thus far in outlining a theory of second language acquisition we have discovered that the cognitive domain of human behavior is of key importance in the acquisition of both a first and a second language. The processes of perceiving, judging, knowing, and remembering are central to the task of internalizing a language. In this chapter we continue to look at cognitive processes by examining the general nature of human learning. In the first part of the chapter, four different learning *theories* are outlined: (a) classical behaviorism (Pavlov, among others); (b) operant conditioning (Skinner); (c) meaningful learning (Ausubel); (d) humanistic approaches (Rogers). Then, we deal with some other universal learning *principles,* namely Gagné's taxonomy of learning types, followed by a consideration of the processes of transfer, interference, overgeneralization, induction, and deduction. Finally, some current thoughts about *intelligence* are presented.

## Of Mice and Men

How do human beings learn? Are there certain basic principles of learning that apply to all learning acts? Is one theory of learning "better" than another? If so, how can you evaluate the usefulness of a theory? These and other important questions need to be answered in order to achieve an integrated understanding of second language acquisition.

Before tackling theories of human learning directly, consider for a moment the following situation as an illustration of the awesome task of sorting out cognitive considerations in any task in which you are trying to determine what it means to conclude that an organism has *learned* something. Suppose you have been asked to train a mouse to walk backward in a circle in an open space (without barriers or guiding markers). Overwhelming? Yes indeed, unless you are an expert mouse trainer. Nevertheless, you might be able to begin to identify some of the pertinent questions you would need to have answered before you attempt the training program. What would those questions be?

First, you will need to specify *entry behavior*: what the organism already "knows." What abilities does it possess upon which you, the trainer, can build? What are its drives, needs, motivations, limitations? Next, the *goals* of the task would need to be formulated explicitly. You have a general directive; what are the specific objectives? How many times and how fast must the mouse walk backward in the circle? With what percentage of regularity? In what differing environments or contexts? You would also need to devise some *methods of training*. Based on what you know about entry behavior and goals of the task, how would you go about the training program? Where would you begin? Would you use some external stimuli—some goading or pushing? Would you construct a circular guide as a beginning stimulus—to be removed later when behavior is "achieved"? Would you use rewards? Punishment? What alternatives would you have ready if the mouse failed to learn? Finally, you would need some sort of *evaluation procedure.* How would you determine whether or not the mouse had indeed learned what you set out to teach? You would need to determine short-term and long-term evaluation measures. If it performs correctly within one day of training, what will happen one month from your training session? That is, how will the organism *maintain* what it has learned?

Already a somewhat simple task has become quite complex with technical questions that require considerable expertise to answer. But we are talking only about a mouse! If we talk about human beings learning a second language, the task is clearly mind-boggling! Not only is the task itself anything but simple; the organism is a highly complex cognitive being. Nevertheless, the questions and procedures that apply to you, the language teacher, are akin to those that applied to the mouse trainer. You must have a comprehensive knowledge of the entry behavior of a person, of objectives you wish to reach, of possible methods that follow from your understanding of the first two factors, and of an evaluation procedure. All this hinges on your conception of how human beings learn, and that is what this chapter is all about.

In turning now to varied theories of how human beings learn, consider once again the definition of learning given in Chapter One: "acquiring or getting of knowledge of a subject or a skill by study, experience, or instruction," or "a relatively permanent change in a behavioral tendency, . . . the result of reinforced practice." When we consider such definitions it is clear that one can understand learning in many different ways, which is why there are so many different theories—extended definitions—of learning. The polarized distinction between cognitive and behavioristic theories of human behavior has become apparent in the topics covered in the first three chapters. We now focus on how psychologists have defined *learning*, and I have chosen to look at these theories through the eyes of four psychologists, representing *classical behaviorism, neobehaviorism, meaningful learning theory*, and *humanistic psychology*. The first two views represent theories on the behavioristic side of the continuum described in Chapter One and the latter two the cognitive side. The four positions should enable you to catch a glimpse not only of the history of learning theory, but of the diverse perspectives that form the foundations of varying language teaching approaches and methods.

## Classical Behaviorism

Certainly the best-known classical behaviorist is the Russian psychologist Ivan Pavlov, who at the turn of the century conducted a series of experiments in which he trained a dog to salivate to the tone of a tuning fork through a procedure that has come to be labeled *classical conditioning*. For Pavlov the learning process consisted of the formation of associations between stimuli and reflexive responses. All of us are aware that certain stimuli automatically produce or elicit rather specific responses or reflexes, and we have also observed that sometimes that reflex occurs in response to stimuli that appear to be indirectly related to the reflex. Pavlov used the salivation response to the sight or smell of food (an unconditioned response) in many of his pioneering experiments. In the classical experiment he trained a dog, by repeated occurrences, to associate the sound of a tuning-fork tone with salivation until the dog acquired a *conditioned response*: salivation at the sound of the tuning fork. A previously neutral stimulus (the sound of the tuning fork) had acquired the power to elicit a response (salivation) that was originally elicited by another stimulus (the smell of meat).

Drawing on Pavlov's findings, John B. Watson (1913) coined the term *behaviorism*. In the empirical tradition of John Locke, Watson contended that human behavior should be studied *objectively*, rejecting mentalistic notions of innateness and instinct. Taking an "environmentalist" position, following Pavlov, he adopted classical conditioning theory as the explanation for all learning: by the process of conditioning, we build an array of stimulus-response connections, and more complex behaviors are learned by building up series or chains of responses. Watson's emphasis on the study of overt behavior and his rigorous adherence to the scientific method had a tremendous influence on learning theories for decades. Language teaching methods likewise for many years followed a behavioristic tradition.

# Skinner's Operant Conditioning

In 1938 B.F. Skinner published his *Behavior of Organisms* and in so doing established himself as one of the leading behaviorists in the United States. He followed the tradition of Watson, but other psychologists (see Anderson and Ausubel 1965:5) have called Skinner a *neo*behaviorist because he added a unique dimension to behavioristic psychology. The classical conditioning of Pavlov was, according to Skinner, a highly specialized form of learning utilized mainly by animals and playing little part in human conditioning. Skinner called Pavlovian conditioning *respondent conditioning* since it was concerned with respondent behavior—that is, behavior that is *elicited* by a preceding stimulus. Skinner's *operant conditioning* attempts to account for most of human learning and behavior. Operant behavior is behavior in which one "operates" on the environment; within this model the importance of stimuli is deemphasized. For example, we cannot identify a specific stimulus leading a small baby to pull himself to a standing position or to take his first step; we therefore need not be concerned about that stimulus, but we should be concerned about the *consequences*—the stimuli that follow the response. Skinner, stressing Thorndike's Law of Effect, demonstrated the importance of those events that follow a response. Suppose that another baby accidentally touches an object near her in her crib and a tinkling bell-sound occurs. The infant may look in the direction from which the sound came, become curious about it, and after several such "accidental" responses discover exactly which toy it is that makes the sound and how to produce that sound. The baby operated on her environment. Her responses were *reinforced* until finally a particular concept or behavior was learned.

According to Skinner, the events or stimuli—the reinforcers—that follow a response and that tend to strengthen behavior or increase the probability of a recurrence of that response constitute a powerful force in the control of human behavior. Reinforcers are far stronger aspects of learning than mere association of a prior stimulus with a following response, as in the classical conditioning model. We are governed by the consequences of our behavior, and therefore Skinner felt we ought, in studying human behavior, to study the effect of those consequences. And if we wish to control behavior, say, to teach someone something, we ought to attend carefully to reinforcers.

*Operants* are classes of responses. Crying, sitting down, walking, and batting a baseball are operants. They are sets of responses that are *emitted* and governed by the consequences they produce. In contrast, *respondents* are sets of responses that are *elicited* by identifiable stimuli. Certain physical reflex actions are respondents. Crying can be respondent or operant behavior. Sometimes crying is elicited in direct reaction to a hurt. Often, however, it is an *emitted* response that produces the consequences of getting fed, cuddled, played with, comforted, and so forth. Such operant crying can be controlled. If

parents wait until a child's crying reaches a certain intensity before responding, loud crying is more likely to appear in the future. If parents ignore crying
(when they are certain that it is operant crying), eventually the absence of reinforcers will extinguish the behavior. Operant crying depends on its *effect* on
the parents and is maintained or changed according to their response to it.

Skinner believed that, in keeping with the above principle, punishment
"works to the disadvantage of both the punished organism and the punishing
agency" (1953:183). Punishment can be both the withdrawal of a positive reinforcer or the presentation of an aversive stimulus. More commonly we think of
punishment as the latter—a spanking, a harsh reprimand—but the removal of
certain positive reinforcers, a privilege, for example, can also be considered a
form of punishment. Skinner felt that in the long run punishment does not
actually eliminate behavior, but that mild punishment may be necessary for
temporary suppression of an undesired response, although no punishment of
such a kind should be meted out without positively reinforcing *alternate*
responses. The best method of extinction, said Skinner, is the absence of reinforcement entirely; however, the active reinforcement of alternate responses
hastens that extinction. So if a parent wishes the children would not kick a
football in the living room, Skinner would maintain that instead of punishing
them adversively for such behavior when it occurs, the parent should refrain
from any negative reaction and should provide positive reinforcement for kick-
ing footballs outside instead; in this way the undesired behavior will be effectively extinguished. Such a procedure is, of course, easier said than done,
especially if the children break your best table lamp in the absence of any punishment!

Skinner, as you can see, was extremely methodical and empirical in his
theory of learning, to the point of being preoccupied with scientific controls.
While many of his experiments were performed on lower animals, his theories
had an impact on our understanding of human learning and on education. His
book *The Technology of Teaching* (1968) was a classic in the field of programmed instruction. Following Skinner's model, one is led to believe that virtually any subject matter can be taught effectively and successfully by a
carefully designed program of step-by-step reinforcement. Programmed
instruction had its impact on foreign language teaching, though language is
such complex behavior, penetrating so deeply into both cognitive and affective
domains of persons, that programmed instruction in languages was limited to
very specialized subsets of language.

The impact of Skinnerian psychology on foreign language teaching has
extended well beyond programmed instruction. Skinner's *Verbal Behavior*
(1957) described language as a system of verbal operants, and his understanding of the role of conditioning led to a whole new era in language teaching
around the middle of the century. A Skinnerian view of both language and language learning dominated foreign language teaching methodology for several

decades, leading to a heavy reliance in the classroom on the controlled practice of verbal operants under carefully designed schedules of reinforcement. A discussion of the popular audiolingual method in Chapter Five will elucidate Skinner's impact on American language teaching practices in the decades of the 1950s, 1960s, and early 1970s.

There is no doubt that behavioristic and Skinnerian learning theory have had a lasting impact on our understanding of the process of human learning. There is much in the theory that is true and valuable. There is another side to the coin, however. We have looked at the side that claims that human behavior can be predicted and controlled and scientifically studied and validated. We have not looked at the side that views human behavior as essentially abstract in nature, as being composed of such a complex of variables that behavior, except in its extreme abnormality, simply cannot be predicted or easily controlled. That is not to say, though, that lack of prediction means that the behavior of people cannot be nevertheless lawful and dependable, with abiding characteristics and tendencies that can indeed be studied. We turn now to two representatives of this other side of the coin—David Ausubel's meaningful learning theory and Carl Rogers' humanistic psychology.

# Ausubel's Meaningful Learning Theory

David Ausubel contends that learning takes place in the human organism through a meaningful process of relating new events or items to already existing cognitive concepts or propositions—hanging new items on existing cognitive pegs. Meaning is not an implicit *response,* but a "clearly articulated and precisely differentiated conscious *experience* [my italics] that emerges when potentially meaningful signs, symbols, concepts, or propositions are related to and incorporated within a given individual's cognitive structure on a nonarbitrary and substantive basis" (Anderson and Ausubel 1965:8). It is this relatability that, according to Ausubel, accounts for a number of phenomena: the acquisition of new meanings (knowledge), retention, the psychological organization of knowledge as a hierarchical structure, and the eventual occurrence of forgetting.

The cognitive theory of learning as put forth by Ausubel is perhaps best understood by contrasting *rote* and *meaningful* learning. In the perspective of rote learning the concept of meaningful learning takes on new significance. Ausubel described rote learning as the process of acquiring material as "discrete and relatively isolated entities that are relatable to cognitive structure only in an arbitrary and verbatim fashion, not permitting the establishment of [meaningful] relationships" (1968:108). That is, rote learning involves the mental storage of items having little or no association with existing cognitive structure. Most of us, for example, can learn a few necessary phone numbers and zip codes by rote without reference to cognitive hierarchical organization.

Meaningful learning, on the other hand, may be described as a process of relating and anchoring new material to relevant established entities in cognitive structure. As new material enters the cognitive field, it interacts with, and is appropriately *subsumed* under, a more inclusive conceptual system. The very fact that material is subsumable, that is, relatable to stable elements in cognitive structure, accounts for its meaningfulness. If we think of cognitive structure as a system of building blocks, then rote learning is the process of acquiring isolated blocks with no particular function in the building of a structure, and therefore with no relationship to other blocks. Meaningful learning is the process whereby blocks become an integral part of already established categories or systematic clusters of blocks. For the sake of a visual picture of the distinction, consider the graphic representation that I have depicted in Figures 4–1 and 4–2.

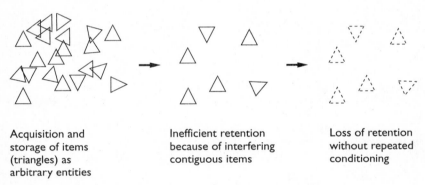

Acquisition and storage of items (triangles) as arbitrary entities

Inefficient retention because of interfering contiguous items

Loss of retention without repeated conditioning

FIGURE 4–1.   Schematic representation of rote learning and retention

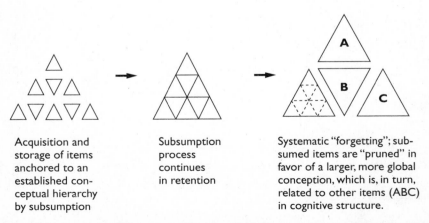

Acquisition and storage of items anchored to an established conceptual hierarchy by subsumption

Subsumption process continues in retention

Systematic "forgetting"; subsumed items are "pruned" in favor of a larger, more global conception, which is, in turn, related to other items (ABC) in cognitive structure.

FIGURE 4–2.   Schematic representation of meaningful learning and retention (subsumption)

Any learning situation can be meaningful if (1) learners have a meaningful learning set—that is, a disposition to relate the new learning task to what they already know; and (2) the learning task itself is potentially meaningful to the learners—that is, relatable to the learners' structure of knowledge. The second method of establishing meaningfulness—one that Frank Smith (1975:162) called "manufacturing meaningfulness"—is a potentially powerful factor in human learning. We can make things meaningful if necessary and if we are strongly motivated to do so. Common among students cramming for an examination is the invention of a mnemonic device for remembering a list of items; the meaningful retention of the device successfully retrieves the whole list of items. Frank Smith (1975) also noted that similar strategies can be used in parlor games in which, for example, you are called upon to remember for a few moments several items presented to you. By associating items either in groups or with some external stimuli, retention is enhanced. Imagine "putting" each object in a different location on your person: a safety pin in your pocket, a toothpick in your mouth, a marble in your shoe. By later "taking a tour around your person" you can "feel" the objects there in your imagination. Nearly a century ago William James (1890:662) described meaningful learning:

> In mental terms, the more other facts a fact is associated with in the mind, the better possession of it our memory retains. Each of its associates becomes a hook to which it hangs, a means to fish it up by when sunk beneath the surface. Together, they form a network of attachments by which it is woven into the entire issue of our thought. The "secret of good memory" is thus the secret of forming diverse and multiple associations with every fact we care to retain. . . . Briefly, then, of two men with the same outward experiences and the same amount of mere native tenacity, the one who thinks over his experiences most, and weaves them into systematic relation with each other, will be the one with the best memory.

The distinction between rote and meaningful learning may not at first appear to be important since in either case material can be learned. But the significance of the distinction becomes clear when we consider the relative efficiency of the two kinds of learning in terms of retention, or long-term memory. We are often tempted to examine learning from the perspective of input alone, failing to consider the uselessness of a learned item that is not retained. Human beings are capable of learning almost any given item within the so-called "magic seven, plus or minus two" (Miller 1956) units for perhaps a few seconds, but long-term memory is a different matter. We can remember an unfamiliar phone number, for example, long enough to dial the number, after which point it is usually extinguished by interfering factors. But a meaningfully learned, subsumed item has far greater potential for retention. Try, for example, to recall all your previous phone numbers (assuming you have moved a number of times in your life). It is doubtful you will be very successful; a phone number is quite arbitrary, bearing little meaningful relationship to reality (other than perhaps area codes and other such numerical systematization). But previous street addresses, for example, are sometimes more efficiently retained since they bear some meaningful relationship to the reality of physical images, directions, streets, houses, and the rest of the town, and are therefore more suitable for long-term retention without concerted reinforcement.

# Systematic Forgetting

Ausubel provides a plausible explanation for the universal nature of forgetting. Since rotely learned materials do not interact with cognitive structure in a substantive fashion, they are learned in conformity with the laws of association, and their retention is influenced primarily by the interfering effects of similar rote materials learned immediately before or after the learning task (commonly referred to as *proactive* and *retroactive inhibition*). In the case of meaningfully learned material, retention is influenced primarily by the properties of "relevant and cumulatively established ideational systems in cognitive structure with which the learning task interacts" (Ausubel 1968:108). Compared to this kind of extended interaction, concurrent interfering effects have relatively little influence on meaningful learning, and retention is highly efficient. Hence, addresses are retained as part of a meaningful set, while phone numbers, as self-contained, isolated entities, are easily forgotten.

We cannot say, of course, that meaningfully learned material is never forgotten. However, in the case of such learning, forgetting takes place in a much more intentional and purposeful manner because it is a continuation of the very process of subsumption by which one learns; forgetting is really a second or "obliterative" stage of subsumption, characterized as "memorial reduction to the least common denominator" (Ausubel 1963:218). Because it is more economical and less burdensome to retain a single inclusive concept than to remember a large number of more specific items, the importance of a specific item tends to be incorporated into the generalized meaning of the larger item. In this obliterative stage of subsumption the specific items become progressively less identifiable as entities in their own right until they are finally no longer available and are said to be forgotten (see Figure 4–2). It is this second stage of subsumption that operates through what I have called "cognitive pruning" procedures (Brown 1972). Pruning is the elimination of unnecessary clutter and a clearing of the way for more material to enter the cognitive field, in the same way that pruning a tree ultimately allows greater and fuller growth. Using the building-block analogy, you might say that, at the outset, a structure made of blocks is seen as a few individual blocks, but as "nucleation" begins to give the structure a perceived shape, some of the single blocks achieve less and less identity in their own right and become subsumed into the larger structure.

Finally, the single blocks are lost to perception, or "pruned" out, to use the metaphor, and the total structure is perceived as a single whole without clearly defined parts.

An example of such pruning may be found in a child's learning of the concept of "hot"—that is, excessive heat capable of burning someone. A small child's first exposure to such heat may be either direct contact with or verbally mediated exposure to hot coffee, a pan of boiling water, a stove, an iron, a candle. That first exposure may be readily recalled for some time as the child maintains a meaningful association between a parent's hot coffee and hurting. After a number of exposures to things that are very hot, children begin to form a concept of "hotness" by clustering their experiences together and forming a generalization. In so doing the bits and pieces of experience that actually built the concept are slowly forgotten—"pruned"—in favor of the general concept which, in the years that follow, enable children to extrapolate to future experiences and to avoid burning fingers on hot objects.

An important aspect of the pruning stage of learning is that subsumptive forgetting, or pruning, is not haphazard or chance—it is systematic. Thus by promoting optimal pruning procedures, we have a potential learning situation that will produce retention beyond that normally expected under more traditional theories of forgetting.

In recent years the process of language *attrition* has garnered some attention. There are a variety of possible causes of the loss of second language skills (see Cohen and Weltens 1989; Weltens 1987; Lambert and Freed 1982). Some of the more common reasons center on the strength and conditions of initial learning, on the kind of use that a second language has been put to, and on the motivational factors contributing to forgetting. Gardner (1982) noted that in some contexts a lack of an "integrative" orientation (see Chapter Six) toward the target culture could contribute to forgetting. Native language forgetting occurs in some cases of "subtractive" bilingualism (members of a minority group learn the language of the majority group, and the latter group downgrades speakers of the minority language). Some researchers have suggested that "neurolinguistic blocking" and left-/right-brain functioning could contribute to forgetting (Obler 1982). And it appears that long-term forgetting can apply to certain linguistic features (lexical, phonological, syntactic, and so on) and not to others (Andersen 1982). Finally, Olshtain (1989) suggested that some aspects of attrition can be explained as a reversal of the acquisition process.

Language attrition research generally focuses on long-term loss and not on those minute-by-minute or day-by-day losses of material that learners experience as they cope with large quantities of new material in the course of a semester or year of classroom language learning. It is this classroom context that poses the more immediate problem for the language teacher. Ausubel's solution to that problem would lie in the initial learning process: systematic, meaningful subsumption of material at the outset will enhance the retention process.

Ausubel's theory of learning has important implications for second language learning and teaching. The importance of meaning in language and of meaningful contexts for linguistic communication has been discussed in the first three chapters. Too much rote activity, at the expense of meaningful communication in language classes, could stifle the learning process.

Subsumption theory provides a strong theoretical basis for the rejection of conditioning models of practice and repetition in language teaching. In a meaningful process like second language learning, mindless repetition, imitation, and other rote practices in the language classroom have no place. The audiolingual method, which has emerged as a widely used and accepted method of foreign language teaching, is based almost exclusively on a behavioristic theory of conditioning that relies heavily on rote learning. The mechanical "stamping in" of the language through saturation with little reference to meaning is seriously challenged by subsumption theory. Rote learning can be effective on a short-term basis, but for any long-term retention it fails because of the tremendous buildup of interference. In those cases in which efficient long-term retention *is* attained in rote-learning situations like those often found in the audiolingual method, it would appear that by sheer dogged determination, the learner has somehow subsumed the material meaningfully *in spite of* the method!

The notion that forgetting is systematic also has important implications for language learning and teaching. In the early stages of language learning, certain devices (definitions, paradigms, illustrations, or rules) are often used to facilitate subsumption. These devices can be made initially meaningful by assigning or "manufacturing" meaningfulness. But in the process of making language automatic, the devices serve only as interim entities, meaningful at a low level of subsumption, and then they are systematically pruned out at later stages of language learning. We might thus better achieve the goal of communicative competence by removing unnecessary barriers to automaticity. A definition or a paraphrase, for example, might be initially facilitative, but as its need is minimized by larger and more global conceptualizations, it is pruned.

While we are all fully aware of the decreasing dependence upon such devices in language learning, Ausubel's theory of learning may help to give explanatory adequacy to the notion. Language teachers might consider urging students to "forget" these interim, mechanical items as they make progress in a language and instead to focus only on the communicative use (comprehension or production) of language.

Ausubel's conception of meaningful learning provides valuable insights, but it also presents a number of problems. We do not know, especially in early "nucleation" stages, exactly how subsumption occurs in human learning in general, much less in second language acquisition in particular. Also, while meaningful learning of all kinds is certainly facilitated linguistically, it is not clear whether language acquisition should be explained in terms of the acquisition of added subsumers, the reshaping of existing subsumers, or perhaps some other cognitive change. And the "meaningfulness" of hypothetical grammatical rules is yet to be determined; we can only assume that semantic processes that grammatical rules attempt to explain are of prime importance in that they clearly relate to cognitive functioning. Despite these questions and problems, there is a good deal of promise in cognitively oriented models for understanding second language learning, a promise earlier psychological theories were not able to offer.

# Rogers's Humanistic Psychology

Carl Rogers is not traditionally thought of as a "learning" psychologist, yet he and his colleagues and followers have had a significant impact on our present understanding of learning, particularly learning in an educational or pedagogical context. Rogers's humanistic psychology has more of an affective focus than a cognitive one, and so the impact of his thought may be more fully appreciated in the context of discussion on personality and sociocultural variables (Chapters Six and Seven). For the present, however, we take a brief look here at the contribution of Rogers's viewpoint to our understanding of learning, for his perspective gives us a fuller picture of the depth and breadth of human learning.

Rogers has devoted most of his professional life to clinical work in an attempt to be of therapeutic help to individuals. In his classic work *Client-Centered Therapy* (1951), Rogers carefully analyzed human behavior in general, including the learning process, by means of the presentation of 19 formal principles of human behavior. All 19 principles are concerned with learning to some degree, from a "phenomenological" perspective, a perspective that is in sharp contrast to that of Skinner. Rogers studied the "whole person" as a physical and cognitive, but primarily emotional, being. His formal principles focused on the development of an individual's self-concept and of his or her personal sense of reality, those internal forces which cause a person to act. Rogers felt that inherent in principles of behavior is the ability of human beings to adapt and to grow in the direction that enhances their existence. Given a nonthreatening environment, a person will form a picture of reality that is indeed congruent with reality and will grow and learn.

The "fully functioning person," according to Rogers, lives at peace with all of his feelings and reactions; he is able to be what he potentially is; he exists as a process of being and becoming himself. This fully functioning person, in his self-knowledge, is fully open to his experience, is without defensiveness, and creates himself anew at each moment in every action taken and in every decision made.

Rogers's position has important implications for education (see Rogers 1983, Curran 1972). The focus is away from "teaching" and toward "learning." The goal of education is the facilitation of change and learning. Learning how to learn is more important than being "taught" something from the "superior" vantage point of a teacher who unilaterally decides what shall be taught. Our present system of education, in prescribing curricular goals and dictating what shall be learned, denies persons both freedom and dignity. What is needed, according to Rogers, is real facilitators of learning, and one can only facilitate by establishing an interpersonal relationship with the learner. Teachers, to be facilitators, must first of all be real and genuine, discarding masks of superiority and omniscience. Second, teachers need to have genuine trust, acceptance, and a prizing of the other person—the student—as a worthy, valuable individual. And third, teachers need to communicate openly and empathically with their students and vice versa. Teachers with these characteristics will not only understand themselves better but will also be effective teachers, who, having set the optimal stage and context for learning, will succeed in the goals of education.

We can see in the Rogers's humanism quite a departure from the scientific analysis of Skinnerian psychology and even from Ausubel's rationalistic theory. Rogers is not as concerned about the actual cognitive process of learning since, he feels, if the *context* for learning is properly created, then human beings will, in fact, learn everything they need to.

Rogers's theory is not without its flaws. The educator may be tempted to take the nondirective approach too far, to the point that valuable time is lost in the process of allowing students to "discover" facts and principles for themselves. Also, a nonthreatening environment might become so nonthreatening that the facilitative tension needed for learning is removed. There is ample research documenting the positive effects of competitiveness in a classroom, as long as that competitiveness does not damage self-esteem and hinder motivation to learn (see Bailey 1983).

One much talked-about educational theorist in the Rogers tradition is the well-known Brazilian educator Paolo Freire, whose seminal work, *Pedagogy of the Oppressed* (1970), has inspired many a teacher to consider the importance of the *empowerment* of students in classrooms. Freire vigorously objected to traditional "banking" concepts of education in which teachers think of their task as one of "filling" students "by making deposits of information which [they] consider to constitute true knowledge—deposits which are detached from reality." (1970:62) Instead, Freire has continued to argue, students should be allowed to negotiate learning outcomes, to cooperate with teacher and other learners in a process of discovery, to engage in critical thinking, and to relate everything they do in school to their reality outside the classroom. Thus empowered to achieve solutions to real problems in the real world, learners are "liberated."

The work of Rogers (1983), Freire (1970) and other educators of a similar frame of mind have contributed significantly in recent years to a redefinition of the educational process. In adapting Rogers's ideas to language teaching and learning, we need to see to it that learners understand themselves and communicate this self to others freely and nondefensively. Teachers as facilitators must therefore provide the nurturing context for learning and not see their mission as one of rather programmatically feeding students quantities of knowledge which they subsequently devour. The latter practice fosters a climate of *defensive* learning in which learners try to protect themselves from failure, from criticism, from competition with fellow students, and possibly from punishment. Classroom activities and materials in language learning should therefore utilize meaningful contexts of genuine communication with persons together engaged in the process of becoming persons.

## Types of Learning

Theories of learning of course do not capture all of the possible elements of general principles of human learning. Beyond the four learning theories just considered are various taxonomies of types of human learning and other mental processes universal to all. The educational psychologist, Robert Gagné (1965), for example, ably demonstrated the importance of identifying a number of *types* of learning which all human beings use. Types of learning vary according to the context and subject matter to be learned, but a complex task such as language learning involves every one of Gagné's types of learning—from simple signal learning to problem solving. Gagné (1965:58–59) identified eight types of learning:

1. *Signal learning.* The individual learns to make a general diffuse response to a signal. This is the classical conditioned response of Pavlov.

2. *Stimulus-response learning.* The learner acquires a precise response to a discriminated stimulus. What is learned is a connection or, in Skinnerian terms, a discriminated operant, sometimes called an instrumental response.

3. *Chaining.* What is acquired is a chain of two or more stimulus-response connections. The conditions for such learning have also been described by Skinner.

4. *Verbal association.* Verbal association is the learning of chains that are verbal. Basically, the conditions resemble those for other (motor) chains. However, the presence of language in the human being

makes this a special type because internal links may be selected from the individual's previously learned repertoire of language.

5.   Multiple discrimination. The individual learns to make a number of different identifying responses to many different stimuli, which may resemble each other in physical appearance to a greater or lesser degree. Although the learning of each stimulus-response connection is a simple occurrence, the connections tend to interfere with one another.

6.   Concept learning. The learner acquires the ability to make a common response to a class of stimuli even though the individual members of that class may differ widely from each other. The learner is able to make a response that identifies an entire class of objects or events.

7.   Principle learning. In simplest terms, a principle is a chain of two or more concepts. It functions to organize behavior and experience. In Ausubel's terminology, a principle is a "subsumer"—a cluster of related concepts.

8.   Problem solving. Problem solving is a kind of learning that requires the internal events usually referred to as "thinking." Previously acquired concepts and principles are combined in a conscious focus on an unresolved or ambiguous set of events.

It is apparent from just a cursory definition of these eight types of learning that some types are better explained by certain theories than others. For example, the first five types seem to fit easily into a behavioristic framework, while the last three are better explained by Ausubel's or Rogers's theories of learning. Since all eight types of learning are relevant to second language learning, the implication is that certain "lower"-level aspects of second language learning may be more adequately treated by behavioristic approaches and methods, while certain "higher"-order types of learning are more effectively taught by methods derived from a cognitive approach to learning.

The second language learning process can be rather efficiently categorized and sequenced in cognitive terms by means of the eight types of learning. (1) Signal learning generally occurs in the total language process: human beings make a general response of some kind (emotional, cognitive, verbal, or nonverbal) to language. (2) Stimulus-response learning is quite evident in the acquisition of the sound system of a foreign language in which, through a process of conditioning and trial and error, the learner makes closer and closer approximations to nativelike pronunciation. Simple lexical items are, in one sense, acquired by stimulus-response connections; in another sense they are related to higher-order types of learning. (3) Chaining is evident in the acquisition of phonological sequences and syntactic patterns—the stringing together of several responses—though we should not be misled into believing that verbal chains are necessarily linear; generative linguists (like McNeill, as we saw in Chapter Two) have wisely shown that sentence structure is hierarchical. (4) The fourth type of learning involves Gagné's distinction between verbal and nonverbal chains, and is not really therefore a separate type of language learning. (5) Multiple discriminations are necessary particularly in second language learning where, for example, a word has to take on several meanings, or a rule in the native language is reshaped to fit a second language context. (6) Concept learning includes the notion that language and cognition are inextricably interrelated, also that rules themselves—rules of syntax, rules of conversation—are linguistic concepts that have to be acquired. (7) Principle learning is the extension of concept learning to the formation of a linguistic system, in which rules are not isolated in rote memory but conjoined and subsumed in a total system. (8) Finally, problem solving is clearly evident in second language learning as the learner is continually faced with sets of events that are truly problems to be solved—problems every bit as difficult as algebra problems or other "intellectual" problems. Solutions to the problems involve the creative interaction of all eight types of learning as the learner sifts and weighs previous information and knowledge in order to correctly determine the meaning of a word, the interpretation of an utterance, the rule that governs a common class of linguistic items, or a conversationally appropriate response.

It is not difficult, upon some reflection, to discern the importance of varied types of learning in the second language acquisition process (see Larsen-Freeman 1991). Teachers and researchers have all too often dismissed certain theories of learning as irrelevant or useless because of the misperception that language learning consists of only one type of learning. "Language is concept learning" say some; "Language is a conditioning process" say others. Both are correct in that part of language learning consists of each of the above. But both are incorrect to assume that all of language learning can be so simply classified. Methods of teaching, in recognizing different levels of learning, need to be consonant with whichever aspect of language is being taught at a particular time while also recognizing the interrelatedness of all levels of language learning.

# Transfer, Interference, and Overgeneralization

Human beings approach any new problem with an existing set of cognitive structures and, through insight, logical thinking, and various forms of hypothesis testing, call upon whatever prior experiences they have had and whatever cognitive structures they possess to attempt a solution. In the literature on language learning processes, three terms have commonly been singled out for explication: transfer, interference, and overgeneralization. The three terms are sometimes mistakenly considered to be separate processes; they are more correctly understood as several manifestations of one principle of learning—the interaction of previously learned material with a present learning event. From the beginning of life the human organism, or any organism for that matter, builds a structure of knowledge by the accumulation of experiences and by the storage of aspects of those experiences in memory. Let us consider these common terms in two associated pairs.

Transfer is a general term describing the carryover of previous performance or knowledge to subsequent learning. Positive transfer occurs when the prior knowledge benefits the learning task—that is, when a previous item is correctly applied to present subject matter. Negative transfer occurs when the previous performance disrupts the performance on a second task. The latter can be referred to as interference, in that previously learned material interferes with subsequent material—a previous item is incorrectly transferred or incorrectly associated with an item to be learned.

It has been common in second language teaching to stress the role of interference—that is, the interfering effects of the native language on the target (the second) language. It is of course not surprising that this process has been so singled out, for native-language interference is surely the most immediately noticeable source of error among second language learners. The saliency of interference has been so strong that some have viewed second language learning as exclusively involving the overcoming of the effects of the native language. It is clear from learning theory that a person will use whatever previous experience he or she has had with language in order to facilitate the second language learning process. The native language is an obvious set of prior experiences. Sometimes the native language is negatively transferred, and we say then that interference has occurred. For example, a French native speaker might say in English "I am in New York since January," a perfectly logical transfer of the comparable French sentence "Je suis à New York depuis janvier." Because of the negative transfer of the French verb form to English, the French system has, in this case, interfered with the person's production of a correct English form.

It is exceedingly important to remember, however, that the native language of a second language learner is often positively transferred, in which case the learner benefits from the facilitating effects of the first language. In the above sentence, for example, the correct one-to-one word order correspondence, the personal pronoun, and the preposition have been positively transferred from French to English. We often mistakenly overlook the facilitating effects of the native language in our penchant for analyzing errors in the second language and for overstressing the interfering effects of the first language. A more detailed discussion of the syndrome is provided in Chapter Eight.

In the literature on second language acquisition, interference is almost as frequent a term as overgeneralization, which is, of course, a particular subset of generalization. Generalization is a crucially important and pervading strategy in human learning. To generalize means to infer or derive a law, rule, or conclusion, usually from the observation of particular instances. The principle of generalization can be explained by Ausubel's concept of meaningful learning. Meaningful learning is, in fact, generalization: items are subsumed (generalized) under high-order categories for meaningful retention. Much of human learning involves generalization. The learning of concepts in early childhood is a process of generalizing. A child who has been exposed to various kinds of animals gradually acquires a generalized concept of "animal." That same child, however, at an early stage of generalization, might in his or her familiarity with dogs see a horse for the first time and overgeneralize the concept of "dog" and call the horse a dog. Similarly, a number of animals might be placed into a category of "dog" until the general attributes of a larger category, "animal," have been learned.

In second language acquisition it has been common to refer to overgeneralization as a process that occurs as the second language learner acts within the target language, generalizing a particular rule or item in the second language—irrespective of the native language—beyond legitimate bounds. We have already observed that children, at a particular stage of learning English as a native language, overgeneralize regular past-tense endings (walked, opened) as applicable to all past-tense forms (goed, flied) until they recognize a subset of verbs that belong in an "irregular" category. After gaining some exposure and familiarity with the second language, second language learners similarly will overgeneralize within the target language. Typical examples in learning English as a second language are past-tense regularization and utterances like "John doesn't can study" (negativization requires insertion of the do auxiliary before verbs) or "He told me when should I get off the train" (indirect discourse requires normal word order, not question word order, after the wh-word). Unaware that these rules have special constraints, the learner overgeneralizes. Such overgeneralization is committed by learners of English from almost any native language background. (Chapter Eight gives a more detailed discussion of linguistic overgeneralization.)

Many have been led to believe that there are only two processes of second language acquisition: interference and overgeneralization. This is obviously a misconception. First, interference and overgeneralization are the negative counterparts of the facilitating processes of transfer and generalization. Second, while they are indeed aspects of somewhat different processes, they represent fundamental and interrelated components of all human learning, and when applied to second language acquisition, are simply extensions of general psychological principles. Interference of the first language in the second is simply a form of generalizing that takes prior first language experiences and applies them incorrectly. Overgeneralization is the incorrect application—negative transfer—of previously learned second language material to a present second language context. All generalizing involves transfer, and all transfer involves generalizing.

# Inductive and Deductive Reasoning

Inductive and deductive reasoning are two polar aspects of the generalization process. In the case of inductive reasoning, one stores a number of specific instances and induces a general law or rule or conclusion that governs or subsumes the specific instances. Deductive reasoning is a movement from a generalization to specific instances: specific subsumed facts are inferred or deduced from a general principle. Second language learning in the "field" (natural, untutored language learning), as well as first language learning, involves a largely inductive process, in which learners must infer certain rules and meanings from all the data around them.

Classroom learning tends to rely more than it should on deductive reasoning. Traditional—especially Grammar Translation—methods have overemphasized the use of deductive reasoning in language teaching. While it may be appropriate at times to articulate a rule and then proceed to its instances, most of the evidence in communicative second language learning points to the superiority of an inductive approach to rules and generalizations. However, both inductively and deductively oriented teaching methods can be effective, depending on the goals and contexts of a particular language teaching situation.

An interesting extension of the inductive/deductive dichotomy was reported in Peters's (1981) case study of a child learning a first language. Peters pointed out that we are inclined, too often, to assume that a child's linguistic development proceeds from the parts to the whole, that is, children first learn sounds, then words, then sentences, and so forth. However, Peters's subject manifested a number of "Gestalt" characteristics, perceiving the whole before the parts. The subject demonstrated the perception of these wholes in the form of intonation patterns that appeared in his speech well before the particular words that would make up sentences. Peters cited other evidence of Gestalt learning in children and concluded that such "sentence learners" (versus "word learners") may be more common than researchers had previously assumed.

The implications of Peters's study for second language teaching are rather tantalizing. We should perhaps pay close attention to learners' production of overall, meaning-bearing intonation patterns. Wong (1986) capitalizes on just such a concept in a discussion of teaching communicative oral production.

# Intelligence and Second Language Learning

The learning theories, types of learning, and other processes that have so far been explained in this chapter deal with mental perception, storage, and recall. Little has been said, however, about one of the more controversial issues in learning psychology: intelligence. What is intelligence? How is intelligence defined in terms of the learning process? In terms of memory storage and recall? These questions are not easily answered, even by experts in the field.

Traditionally, intelligence is defined and measured in terms of linguistic and logical-mathematical abilities. Our notion of "IQ" (intelligence quotient) is based on several generations of testing of these two domains, stemming from the research of Alfred Binet in the early years of the century. Success in educational institutions and in life in general seems to be a correlate of high IQ. In terms of Ausubel's meaningful learning model, high intelligence would no doubt imply a very efficient process of storing items that are particularly useful in building conceptual hierarchies and systematically pruning those that are not useful. Other cognitive psychologists have dealt in a much more sophisticated way with memory processing and recall systems.

In relating intelligence to second language learning, can we say simply that a "smart" person will be capable of learning a second language more successfully because of greater intelligence? After all, the greatest barrier to second language learning seems to boil down to a matter of memory, in the sense that if you could just remember everything you were ever taught, or you ever heard, you would be a very successful language learner. Or would you? It appears that our language-learning "IQs" are much more complicated than that.

Howard Gardner (1983) advanced a controversial theory of intelligence that blows apart our traditional thoughts about IQ. Gardner describes seven different forms of knowing which, in his view, give us a much more comprehensive picture of intelligence. Beyond the usual two forms of (1) linguistic and (2) logical-mathematical abilities, his list consists of: (3) spatial intelligence (the ability to find your way around an environment, to form mental images of reality, and to transform them readily); (4) musical intelligence (the ability to perceive and create pitch and rhythmic patterns); (5) bodily-kinesthetic intelligence (fine motor movement, athletic prowess); (6) interpersonal intelligence (the ability to understand others, how they feel, what motivates them, how they interact with one another); and (7) intrapersonal intelligence (the ability to see oneself, to develop a sense of self-identity). Gardner maintains that by looking only at the first two categories we rule out a great number of the human being's mental abilities; we only see a portion of the total capacity of the human mind. Moreover, he shows that our traditional definitions of intelligence are culture-bound. The "sixth sense" of a hunter in New Guinea or the navigational abilities of a sailor in Micronesia are not accounted for in our Westernized definitions of IQ.

In a likewise revolutionary style, Robert Sternberg (1985, 1988) has also been shaking up the world of traditional intelligence measurement. In his "triarchic" view of intelligence, Sternberg says there are three types of "smartness:" (a) componential ability for analytical thinking; (b) experiential ability to engage in creative thinking, combining disparate experiences in insightful ways; and (c) contextual ability, "street smartness" that enables people to "play the game" of manipulating their environment (others, situations, institutions, contexts). Sternberg contends that too much of psychometric theory is obsessed with mental speed and has therefore dedicated his research to tests that measure insight, real-life problem solving, "common sense," getting a wider picture of things, and other practical tasks that are closely related to success in the real world.

By broadly defining intelligence as Gardner and Sternberg have done, we can more easily discern a relationship between intelligence and second language learning. In its traditional definition, intelligence may have little to do with one's success as a second language learner: people with both high and low IQs have proven to be successful in acquiring a second language. But Gardner attaches other important attributes to the notion of intelligence, attributes that could be crucial to second language success. Musical intelligence could explain the relative ease that some learners have in perceiving and producing the intonation patterns of a language. Bodily-kinesthetic modes have already been discussed in connection with the learning of the phonology of a language. Interpersonal intelligence is of obvious importance in the communicative process. Intrapersonal factors will be discussed in detail in Chapter Six of this book. One might even be able to speculate on the extent to which spatial intelligence, especially a "sense of direction," may assist the second culture learner in growing comfortable in new surroundings. Sternberg's experiential and contextual abilities further enhance our understanding of the relationship of intelligence to second language learning.

Oller (1981a) suggested, in an eloquent essay, that intelligence may after all be language based. "Language may not be merely a vital link in the social side of intellectual development, it may be the very foundation of intelligence itself" (1981a:466). While we must not equate speech with language, nevertheless, according to Oller, arguments from genetics and neurology suggest "a deep relationship, perhaps even an identity, between intelligence and language ability" (p. 487). The implications of Oller's hypothesis for second language learning are interesting. Both first and second languages must be closely tied to meaning in its deepest sense. Effective second language learning thus links surface forms of a language with meaningful experiences, as we have already noted in Ausubel's learning theory. The strength of that link may indeed be a factor of intelligence.

We have much to gain from the understanding of learning principles that have been presented here, and of the various ways of understanding what intelligence is. There are aspects of language learning that may call upon a conditioning process; other aspects require a meaningful cognitive process; others depend upon the security of supportive fellow learners interacting freely and willingly with one another; still others are related to one's total intellectual structure. Each aspect is important, but there is no consistent combination of theories that works for every context of second language learning. Each teacher has to adopt a somewhat intuitive process of discerning the best synthesis of theory for the most enlightening analysis of the particular context at hand. That intuition will be nurtured by an integrated understanding of the appropriateness and of the strengths and weaknesses of each theory of learning.

## In the Classroom: The "Designer" Methods of the Seventies

The age of audiolingualism, with its emphasis on surface forms and on the rote practice of scientifically produced patterns, began to wane when the Chomskyan revolution in linguistics turned linguists and language teachers toward the "deep structure" of language and when psychologists began to recognize the fundamentally affective and interpersonal nature of all learning. The decade of the 1970s was a chaotic but exceedingly fruitful era during which second language research not only came into its own but also began to inspire innovative methods for language teaching. As we increasingly recognized the importance of both cognitive and affective factors in second language learning, certain teaching methods came into vogue. These methods attempted to capitalize on the perceived importance of psychological factors in language learners' success. At the same time they were touted as "innovative" and "revolutionary," especially when compared to Audiolingual or Grammar Translation methodology. Claims for their success, originating from their proprietary founders and proponents, were often overstated in the interest of attracting teachers to weekend workshops and seminars, to new books and tapes and videos, and, of course, to getting their learners to reach the zenith of their potential. These claims, often overstated and overgeneralized, led David Nunan (1989:97) to refer to the methods of the day as "designer" methods, prescriptive, and ostensibly appropriate for all learners in all contexts.

Despite the overly strong claims that were made for such methods, nevertheless, (a) they were an important part of our language teaching history, and (b) they gave us some insights about language learning that still enlighten our teaching practices. What follows here is a brief summary of five of the most popular of the "designer" methods.

### *Community Language Learning*

In his "Counseling-Learning" model of education Charles Curran (1972) was inspired by Carl Rogers's view of education in which students and teacher join together to facilitate learning in a context of valuing and prizing each individual in the group. In such a surrounding each person lowers the defenses that prevent open interpersonal communication. The anxiety caused by the educational context is lessened by means of the supportive community. The teacher's presence is not perceived as a threat, nor is it the teacher's purpose to impose limits and boundaries, but rather, as a "counselor," to center his or her attention on the clients (the students) and their needs.

Curran's model of education was extended to language learning contexts in the form of Community Language Learning (CLL) (La Forge, 1973). While particular adaptations of CLL are numerous, the basic methodology is explicit. The group of clients (learners), having first established in their native language an interpersonal relationship and trust, are seated in a circle with the counselor (teacher) on the outside of the circle. The students may be complete beginners in the foreign language. When one of them wishes to say something to the group or to an individual, he or she says it in the native language (say, English) and the counselor translates the utterance back to the learner in the second language (say, Japanese). The learner then repeats that Japanese sentence as accurately as possible. Another client responds, in English; the utterance is translated by the counselor; the client repeats it; and the conversation continues. If possible the conversation is taped for later listening, and at the end of each session the learners inductively attempt together to glean information about the new language. If desirable, the counselor may take a more directive role and provide some explanation of certain linguistic rules or items.

As the learners gain more and more familiarity with the foreign language, more and more direct communication can take place with the counselor providing less and less direct translation and information, until after many sessions, perhaps many months or years later, the learner achieves fluency in the spoken language. The learner has at that point become independent.

There are advantages and disadvantages to a method like CLL. CLL is an attempt to put Carl Rogers's philosophy into action and to overcome some of the threatening affective factors in second language learning. But there are some practical and theoretical problems with CLL. The counselor-teacher can become too nondirective. While some intense inductive struggle is a necessary component of second language learning, the initial grueling days and weeks of floundering in ignorance in CLL could be alleviated by more directed, deductive, learning "by being told." Perhaps only later, when the learner has moved to more independence, is an inductive strategy really successful. And, of course, the success of CLL depends largely on the translation expertise of the counselor. Translation is an intricate and complex process that is often "easier said than done"; if subtle aspects of language are mistranslated, there could be a less than effective understanding of the target language.

Despite its weaknesses, CLL offers certain insights to teachers. We are reminded to lower learners' anxiety, to create as much of a supportive group in our classrooms as possible, to allow students to initiate language, and to point learners toward autonomous learning in preparation for the day when they no longer have the teacher around to guide them.

## *Suggestopedia*

Suggestopedia was another educational movement that promised great results if we would simply use the human brain power within us. According to Lozanov (1979), people are capable of learning much more than they give themselves credit for. Drawing on insights from Soviet psychological research on extrasensory perception and from yoga, Lozanov created a method for learning that capitalized on relaxed states of mind for maximum retention of material. Music was central to his method. Baroque music, with its 60 beats per minute and its specific rhythm, created the kind of "relaxed concentration" that led to "superlearning" (Ostrander and Schroeder 1979:65). According to Lozanov, during the soft playing of Baroque music, one can take in tremendous quantities of material, due to an increase in alpha brain waves and a decrease in blood pressure and pulse rate.

In applications of Suggestopedia to foreign language learning, Lozanov and his followers experimented with the presentation of vocabulary, readings, dialogs, role-plays, drama, and a variety of other typical classroom activities. Some of the classroom methodology did not have any particular uniqueness. The difference was that a significant proportion of activity was carried on with classical music in the background, and with students sitting in soft, comfortable seats in relaxed states of consciousness. Students were encouraged to be as "childlike" as possible, yielding all authority to the teacher and sometimes assuming the roles (and names) of native speakers of the foreign language. Students thus became "suggestible."

Suggestopedia was criticized on a number of fronts. Scovel (1979) showed quite eloquently that Lozanov's experimental data, in which he reported astounding results with Suggestopedia, were highly questionable. Moreover, the practicality of using Suggestopedia was an issue that teachers faced where music and comfortable chairs were not available. More serious was the issue of the place of memorization in language learning. On a more positive note, we can adapt certain aspects of Suggestopedia in our communicative classrooms without "buying into" the whole method. A relaxed and unanxious mind, achieved through music and/or any other means, will often help a learner to build confidence. Role playing, drama, and other "games" may be very helpful techniques to stimulate meaningful interaction in the classroom. And perhaps we should never underestimate the "superlearning" powers of the human brain.

## *The Silent Way*

Like Suggestopedia, the Silent Way rested on more cognitive than affective arguments for its theoretical sustenance. While Caleb Gattegno, its founder, was said to be interested in a "humanistic" approach (Chamot and McKeon 1984:2) to education, much of the Silent Way was characterized by a problem-solving approach to learning. Richards and Rodgers (1986:99) summarize the theory of learning behind the Silent Way:

1. Learning is facilitated if the learner discovers or creates rather than remembers and repeats what is to be learned.

2.   Learning is facilitated by accompanying (mediating) physical objects.

3.   Learning is facilitated by problem solving involving the material to be learned.

The Silent Way capitalizes on discovery-learning procedures. Gattegno (1972) believed that learners should develop independence, autonomy, and responsibility. At the same time, learners in a classroom must cooperate with each other in the process of solving language problems. The teacher—a stimulator but not a hand-holder—is silent much of the time, thus the name of the method. Teachers must resist their instinct to spell everything out in black and white—to come to the aid of students at the slightest downfall—and must "get out of the way" while students work out solutions.

In a language classroom the Silent Way typically utilized as materials a set of Cuisinere rods—small colored rods of varying lengths—and a series of colorful wall charts. The rods are used to introduce vocabulary (colors, numbers, adjectives [long, short, and so on], verbs [give, take, pick up, drop]) and syntax (tense, comparatives, pluralization, word order, and the like). The teacher provides single-word stimuli, or short phrases and sentences once or twice, and then the students must refine their understanding and pronunciation among themselves, with minimal corrective feedback from the teacher. The charts introduce pronunciation models, grammatical paradigms, and the like.

Like Suggestopedia, the Silent Way had its share of criticism. In one sense, the Silent Way was too harsh a method, and the teacher too distant, to encourage a communicative atmosphere. There are a number of aspects of language that can indeed be "told" to students to their benefit; they need not, as in CLL as well, struggle for hours or days with a concept that could be easily clarified by the teacher's direct guidance. The rods and charts wear thin after a few lessons, and other materials must be introduced, at which point the Silent Way can look like any other language classroom. There are, of course, insights to be derived. All too often we are tempted as teachers to provide everything for our students, served up on a silver platter. We could benefit from injecting healthy doses of discovery learning into our classroom activities and from providing less teacher talk than we usually do to let the students work things out on their own. These are some of the contributions of innovation. They expose us to new thoughts that we can—through our developing theoretical rationale for language teaching—sift through, weigh, and adapt to multiple contexts.

## Total Physical Response

The founder of the Total Physical Response (TPR), James Asher (1977) noted that children, in learning their first language, appear to do a lot of listening before they speak, and that their listening is accompanied by physical responses (reaching, grabbing, moving, looking, and so forth). He also gave some attention to right-brain learning. According to Asher, motor activity is a right-brain function that should precede left-brain language processing. Asher was also convinced that language classes were often the locus of too much anxiety and wished to devise a method that was as stress-free as possible, where learners would not feel overly self-conscious and defensive. The TPR classroom, then, is one in which students do a great deal of listening and acting. The teacher is very directive in orchestrating a performance: "The instructor is the director of a stage play in which the students are the actors" (Asher 1977:43).

Typically, TPR heavily utilizes the imperative mood, even into more advanced proficiency levels. Commands are an easy way to get learners to move about and to loosen up: Open the window, Close the door, Stand up, Sit down, Pick up the book, Give it to John, and so on. No verbal response is necessary. More complex syntax can be incorporated into the imperative: Draw a rectangle on the chalkboard. Walk quickly to the door and hit it. Humor is easy to introduce: Walk slowly to the window and jump. Put your toothbrush in your book (Asher 1977:55). Interrogatives are also easily dealt with: Where is the book? Who is John? (students point to the book or to John). Eventually students, one by one, will feel comfortable enough to venture verbal responses to questions, then to ask questions themselves, and the process continues.

Like other methods discussed here, TPR—as a method—had its limitations. It was especially effective in the beginning levels of language proficiency, but then lost its distinctiveness as learners advanced in their competence. But today TPR is used more as a technique, which is a more useful way to view it. Many successful communicative, interactive classrooms utilize TPR activities to provide both auditory input and physical activity.

## *The Natural Approach*

Stephen Krashen's (1982) theories of second language acquisition have been widely discussed and hotly debated in the last decade or so of research in the field. (Chapter Eleven will offer further details on Krashen's influence on second language acquisition theory—you may wish to look ahead at that section.) The major methodological offshoot of Krashen's work was manifested in the Natural Approach, developed by one of Krashen's colleagues, Tracy Terrell (Krashen and Terrell 1983). Acting on many of the claims that Asher made for TPR, Krashen and Terrell felt that learners would benefit from delaying production until speech "emerges," that learners should be as relaxed as possible in the classroom, and that a great deal of communication and "acquisition" should take place, as opposed to analysis. In fact, the Natural Approach advocated the use of TPR activities at the beginning level of language learning, when "comprehensible input" is essential for triggering the acquisition of language.

The Natural Approach was aimed at the goal of basic interpersonal communication skills, that is, everyday language situations—conversations, shopping, listening to the radio, and the like. The initial task of the teacher was to provide comprehensible input, that is, spoken language that is understandable to the learner, or just a little beyond the learner's level. Learners did not need to say anything during this "silent period" until they felt ready to do so. The teacher was the source of the learners' input and the creator of an interesting and stimulating variety of classroom activities—commands, games, skits, and small-group work.

The most controversial aspects of the Natural Approach were its "silent period" and its reliance on the notion of "comprehensible input." One could argue, with Gibbons (1985), that the delay of oral production can be pushed too far and that at an early stage it is important for the teacher to step in and encourage students to talk. And determining just what we mean by "comprehensible" is exceedingly difficult (see Chapter Eleven for further comments). Language learning is an interactive process, and therefore an over-reliance on the role of input at the expense of the stimulation of output coulds thwart the second language acquisition process.

But, of course, we also can look at the Natural Approach and be reminded that sometimes we insist that students speak much too soon, thereby raising anxiety and lessening the possibility of further risk-taking as the learner tries to progress. And so, once again your responsibility as a teacher is to choose the best of what others have experimented with, and adapt those insights to your own situation. There is a good deal of insight to be gained, and intuition to be developed, from examining the merits of all of these five "designer" methods. Those insights and intuitions can become a part of your own cautious, enlightened eclecticism.

## Suggested Readings

Most introductory psychology textbooks will provide useful summaries of behavioristic and cognitive theories of psychology. Such summaries can help to flesh out your understanding beyond what has been gained in this and preceding chapters.

Millhollan and Forisha (1972) provide an excellent summary of both Skinner's and Rogers's theories of learning and their implications for education.

Weltens's (1987) article on the loss of language skills is an informative summary of research on the topic. While some studies are a bit technical, others can be understood by a beginner in the field.

Rogers's (1951) classic is serious and difficult reading at times but contains valuable insights. Rogers provides a "counterpoint" in learning theory.

Another very frequently cited reference is Freire's (1970) seminal book on the need for worldwide educational reform so that students are "empowered" through the act of learning.

Howard Gardner's (1983) and Robert Sternberg's (1985, 1988) books on intelligence are fascinating reading for the lay psychologist. The implications of new definitions of intelligence for language learning are worth exploring seriously.

## Topics and Questions for Study and Discussion

1.  At the beginning of the chapter a sketch was made of considerations that must be given to training a mouse to walk backward in a circle. Go through the same procedure (that is, specify entry behavior,

explicit goals, methods of training, and an evaluation procedure) for the following three general tasks:

    a.   Train an aardvark (anteater) to find hidden anthills in an apartment.

    b.   Train a 10-month-old baby to clap hands together in rhythm to nursery rhymes.

    c.   Train an adult to put together a do-it-yourself radio kit (that the person has never seen before) without an instruction sheet.

2.   Think of some of the language teaching methods you have been exposed to (or perhaps have used in your own teaching). Evaluate those teaching methods in reference to the different types of learning theories presented in this chapter. How might you justify certain practices? or reject certain other practices?

3.   Summarize the distinction between elicited and emitted behavior and between respondent and operant conditioning. Can you specify some operants that are emitted by the learner in a foreign language class? and some responses that are elicited? Specify some of the reinforcers that are present in language classes. How effective are certain reinforcers?

4.   Can you think of ways that foreign language teachers might administer a form of punishment? A teacher's correction of student errors in the classroom could be viewed by the student as punishment. How can a teacher avoid such a perception? (We will discuss this issue again in Chapter Eight.)

5.   In foreign language classes you have taken (or are teaching), identify some practices you could consider rote and others that are meaningful. Evaluate the effectiveness of those practices. Is Ausubel's distinction between rote and meaningful learning clear? Think of some examples of learning that fall into a rather fuzzy gray area between the two.

6.   Explain the notion of "cognitive pruning." What is the difference between systematic forgetting and simply the interference of previous experience? Can you think of examples of necessary systematic forgetting in the foreign language classroom?

7.   Some researchers (notably Schumann et al. 1978) have suggested that hypnosis might help people to remember forgotten languages. What do we mean when we use the word "forget"? Do we ever (neurophysiologically) really "forget" anything in the sense that no remnants of memory are left? How can we teachers maximize memory?

8.   In one sense Skinner, Ausubel, and Rogers represent quite different points of view—at least they focus on different facets of human

learning. Do you think it is possible to synthesize the three points of view? In what way are all three psychologists expressing the "truth"? In what way do they differ substantially? Try to formulate an integrated understanding of human learning by taking the best of all three points of view. Does your integrated theory tell you something about how people learn a second language? or how you should teach a second language?

9.  Some linguistic examples were given of Gagné's eight types of learning. Give further examples of the use of these types of learning in the foreign language classroom. Identify certain aspects of the learning process that are more readily explained by "lower" levels of learning and certain others that relate to "higher" levels. Does such categorizing help to resolve certain apparent contradictions between Skinner's and Ausubel's theories of learning?

10. What are some advantages and disadvantages of inductive and deductive learning in the classroom? Consider the variables of situation, goals, age of the learner, and language skill (speaking, reading, and so forth). How could each type be pushed too far? How can a teacher avoid pushing each type of learning too far?

11. Review the implications of Gardner's and Sternberg's definitions of intelligence for language learning and teaching.

# Chapter 5

# STYLES AND STRATEGIES

Theories of learning, Gagné's "types" of learning, transfer processes, and intelligence models are all attempts to describe universal human traits in learning. They seek to explain globally how people perceive, filter, store, and recall information. Such *processes,* the unifying theme of the previous chapter, do not account for the plethora of differences across individuals in the way they learn items, or differences within any one individual. While we all exhibit inherently human traits of learning, every individual approaches a problem or learns a set of facts or organizes a combination of feelings from a unique perspective. This chapter deals with cognitive variations in learning a second language: variations in learning *styles* that differ across individuals, and in *strategies* employed by individuals to attack particular problems in particular contexts.

## Process, Style, and Strategy

Before we look specifically at some styles and strategies of second language learning, a few words are in order to explain the differences among *process, style,* and *strategy* as the terms are used in the literature on second language acquisition. There has been a good deal of confusion in the use of these three terms. We can find instances of "transfer" and "interference" being referred to as "strategies" (Taylor 1975, for example). Sometimes "process" and "strategy" are synonymous (Tarone et al. 1976, for example). And "styles" and "strategies" are often similarly interchanged. It is important to define more carefully the use of such terms.

*Process* is the most general of the three concepts. All human beings engage in certain universal processes. Just as we all need air, water, and food for our survival, so do all humans of normal intelligence engage in certain levels or types of learning such as those defined by Gagné (1965) in the previous chapter. We universally use principles of *transfer* in the process of learning and retention. Process is characteristic of every human being.

*Style* is a term that refers to consistent and rather enduring tendencies or preferences *within* an individual. Styles are those general characteristics of intellectual functioning (and personality type, as well) that especially pertain to you as an individual, that differentiate you from someone else. For example, you might be more visually oriented, more tolerant of ambiguity, or more reflective than someone else—these would be styles that characterize a general pattern in your thinking or feeling.

*Strategies* are specific methods of approaching a problem or task, modes of operation for achieving a particular end, planned designs for controlling and manipulating certain information. They are contextualized "battle plans" that might vary from moment to moment, or day to day, or year to year. Strategies vary *intra*individually; each of us has a whole host of possible ways to solve a particular problem and we choose one—or several of those in sequence—for a given problem.

As we turn to a study of styles and strategies in second language learning, we can benefit by understanding these "layers of an onion," or points on a continuum ranging from universal properties of learning to specific intraindividual variations in learning.

# Learning Styles

Suppose you are visiting a foreign country whose language you don't speak or read. You have landed in the airport and your contact person, whose name you don't know, is not there to meet you. To top it off, your luggage is missing. It's 3:00 A.M. and no one in the sparsely staffed airport speaks English. What will you do? There is obviously no single solution to this multifaceted problem. Your solution will be based to a great extent on the *styles* you happen to bring to bear. For example, if you are *tolerant of ambiguity,* you will not get easily flustered by your unfortunate circumstances. If you are *reflective,* you will exercise patience, and not jump quickly to a conclusion about how to approach the situation; if you are *field-independent* you will focus on the necessary and relevant details and not be distracted by surrounding but irrelevant details.

The way we learn things in general and the particular attack we make on a problem seem to hinge on a rather amorphous link between personality and cognition; this link is referred to as *cognitive style.* When cognitive styles are specifically related to an educational context, where affective and physiological factors are intermingled, they are usually more generally referred to as *learning styles.*

Learning styles might be thought of as "cognitive, affective, and physiological traits that are relatively stable indicators of how learners perceive, interact with, and respond to the learning environment." (Keefe 1979:4) Or, more simply, perhaps, as "a general predisposition, voluntary or not, toward processing information in a particular way." (Skehan 1991:288) In the enormous task of learning a second language, one that so deeply involves affective factors, a study of learning style brings very important variables to the forefront. Such styles can contribute significantly to the construction of a unified theory of second language acquisition.

Learning styles mediate between emotion and cognition, as you will soon discover. For example, a reflective style invariably grows out of a reflective personality or a reflective mood. An impulsive style, on the other hand, usually arises out of an impulsive emotional state. People's styles are determined by the way they internalize their total environment, and since that internalization process is not strictly cognitive, we find that physical, affective, and cognitive domains merge in learning styles. Some would claim that styles are stable traits in adults. This is a questionable view. It would appear that individuals show general tendencies toward one style or another, but that differing contexts will evoke differing styles in one individual. Perhaps an "intelligent" and "successful" person is one who is "bicognitive"—one who can manipulate both ends of a style continuum.

If I were to try to enumerate all the learning styles that educators and psychologists have identified, a very long list would emerge. Ausubel (1968:171) identified at least 18 different styles. Joseph Hill (1972) defined some 29 different factors that make up the cognitive-style "map" of a learner; these include just about every imaginable sensory, communicative, cultural, affective, cognitive, and intellectual factor. Dunn *et al.* (1989), Trayer (1991), Hartnett (1985), and H.D. Brown (1973) reviewed a number of styles relating to the teaching-learning process in general and specifically to second language learning. However, only a few of the possible number of styles have received the attention of second language researchers in recent years. These will be discussed in the following sections.

# Field Independence

Do you remember, in those coloring books you pored over as a child, a picture of a forest scene with exotic trees and flowers, and a caption under the picture saying "Find the hidden monkeys in the trees"? If you looked carefully, you soon began to spot them, some upside-down, some sideways, some high and some low, a dozen or so monkeys camouflaged by the lines of what at first sight looked like just leaves and trees. The ability to find those hidden monkeys hinged upon your *field-independent* style: your ability to perceive a particular, relevant item or factor in a "field" of distracting items. In general psychological terms, that "field" may be perceptual or it may be more abstract in referring to a set of thoughts, ideas, or feelings from which your task is to perceive specific relevant subsets. *Field dependence* is, conversely, the tendency to be "dependent" on the total field so that the parts embedded within the field are not easily perceived, though that total field is perceived more clearly as a unified whole.

There are positive and negative characteristics to both field independence and field dependence. A field-independent style enables you to distinguish parts from a whole, to concentrate on something (like reading a book in a noisy train station), to analyze separate variables without the contamination of neighboring variables. On the other hand, *too much* field independence can backfire: cognitive "tunnel vision" forces you to see only the parts and fail to see their relationship to a whole. "You can't see the forest for the trees," as the saying goes. Seen in this light, development of a field-dependent style has positive effects: you perceive the whole picture, the larger view, the general configuration of a problem or idea or event. It is clear, then, that some degree of *both* field independence and field dependence is necessary for most of the cognitive and affective problems we face.

The literature on field independence-dependence has shown that persons tend to be dominant in one mode of field independence-dependence or the other, that field independence-dependence is a relatively stable trait, and that field independence increases as a child matures to adulthood. It has been found in Western culture that males tend to be more field-independent, and that field independence is related to one of the three main factors used to define intelligence (the analytical factor), but not to the other two factors (verbal-comprehension and attention-concentration). Cross-culturally, the extent of the development of a field-independent style as children mature is a factor of the type of society and home in which the child is reared. Authoritarian or agrarian societies, which are usually highly socialized and utilize strict rearing practices, tend to produce more field dependence. A democratic, industrialized, competitive society with freer rearing norms tends to produce more field-independent persons.

Affectively, persons who are more predominantly field independent tend to be generally more independent, competitive, and self-confident. Field-dependent persons tend to be more socialized, tend to derive their self-identity from persons around them, and are usually more empathic and perceptive of the feelings and thoughts of others.

How does all this relate to second language learning? Two conflicting hypotheses can be proposed. First, we could conclude that field independence is closely related to classroom learning that involves analysis, attention to details, and mastering of exercises, drills, and other focused activities. Indeed recent research is supportive of such a hypothesis. Naiman et al. (1978) found in a study of English-speaking eighth, tenth, and twelfth graders who were learning French in Toronto that field independence correlated positively and significantly with language success in the classroom. Other more recent studies (Hansen and Stansfield 1981, Stansfield and Hansen 1983, L. Hansen 1984) found relatively strong evidence in groups of adult second language learners of a relationship between field independence and cloze testing (see Chapter Eleven for a discussion of cloze tests), which in some respects requires analytical abilities. Chapelle and Roberts (1986) found support for the correlation of a field-independent style with language success as measured both by traditional, analytic, paper-and-pencil tests and by an oral interview. (The latter finding—the correlation with the oral interview—was a bit surprising in light of the second of our two hypotheses, to be taken up below.) Abraham (1985) found that second language learners who were field independent performed better in deductive lessons while those with field-dependent styles were more successful with inductive lesson designs. Other more recent studies (Alptekin and Atakan 1990, Chapelle and Abraham 1990, Chapelle and Green 1992) provide further evidence of superiority of a field independent style for second language success.

The second of the conflicting hypotheses leads us to conclude that primarily field-dependent persons will, by virtue of their empathy, social outreach, and perception of other people, be successful in learning the communicative aspects of a second language. While no one seems to deny the plausibility of this second hypothesis, little evidence has been gathered to support it. The principal reason for the dearth of such evidence is the absence of a true test of field dependence. The standard test of field independence requires subjects to discern small geometric shapes embedded in larger geometric designs. A high score on such embedded-figures tests indicates field independence, but a low score does *not* necessarily imply relatively high field dependence. (This latter fact has unfortunately not been recognized by all who have interpreted results of embedded-figures tests.) So we are left with no standardized means of measuring field dependence, and thus the second hypothesis remains largely untestable.

The two hypotheses could be seen as paradoxical: how could field dependence be most important on the one hand and field independence equally important? The answer to the paradox would appear to be that clearly *both* styles are important. The two hypotheses deal with two different kinds of language learning. One kind of learning implies natural, face-to-face communication, the kind of communication that occurs too rarely in the average language classroom. The second kind of learning involves the familiar classroom activities: drills, exercises, tests, and so forth. It could well be that "natural" language learning in the "field," beyond the constraints of the classroom, requires a field-dependent style and the classroom type of learning requires, conversely, a field-independent style.

There is some research to support such a conclusion. Guiora et al. (1972b) showed that empathy is related to language acquisition, and though one could argue with some of his experimental design factors (see H.D. Brown 1973), the conclusion seems highly reasonable and also supportable by observational evidence and intuition. Some pilot studies of field independence-dependence (Brown 1977a) indicated that field independence correlated *negatively* with informal oral interviews of adult English learners in the United States. And so it would appear that field independence-dependence might provide one construct which differentiates "classroom" (tutored) second language learning from "natural" (untutored) second language learning.

Field independence-dependence may also prove to be a valuable tool for differentiating child and adult language acquisition. The child, more predominantly field-dependent, may have a cognitive style advantage over the more field-independent adult. Stephen Krashen (1977) has suggested that adults use more "monitoring," or "learning," strategies (conscious attention to forms) for language acquisition while children utilize strategies of "acquisition" (subconscious attention to functions). This distinction between acquisition and learning could well be explicated by the field independence-dependence dichotomy. (See Chapter Nine for further discussion of Krashen's Monitor model.)

Field independence-dependence has been conceived by psychological researchers as a construct in which a person is relatively stable. Unfortunately, there seems to be little room in such research for considering the possibility that field independence-dependence is contextualized and variable. Logically and observationally, field independence-dependence is quite variable within one person. Depending upon the context of learning, individual learners can vary their utilization of field independence or field dependence. If a task requires field independence, individuals may invoke their field-independent style; if it requires field dependence, they may invoke a field-dependent style. Such ambiguities fueled Griffiths and Sheen's (1992) passionate attempt to discredit the whole field independence construct, where they concluded that this "theoretically flawed" notion "does not have, and has never had, any relevance for second language learning" whatever. (p. 133)

Carol Chapelle (1992; see also Chapelle and Green 1992), in a more balanced and optimistic viewpoint on the relevance of field independence to communicative language ability, exposes flaws in Griffiths and Sheen's remarks and suggests avenues of future research. I surmise from her comments that her optimism springs from—among other things—our acceptance of the view that field independence and dependence are *not* in complementary distribution within an individual. Some persons might be both highly field-dependent and highly field-independent as contexts vary. Such variability is not without its parallels in almost every other psychological construct. A generally extroverted person might, for example, be relatively introverted at certain times. In second language learning, then, it may be incorrect to assume that learners should be *either* field-independent *or* field-dependent; it is more likely that persons have general inclinations, but, given certain contexts, can exercise a sufficient degree of an appropriate style. The burden on the learner is to invoke the appropriate style for the context. The burden on the teacher is to understand the preferred styles of each learner and to sow the seeds for flexibility.

# Left- and Right-Brain Functioning

We have already observed in Chapter Three that left- and right-brain dominance is an important issue in developing a theory of second language acquisition. As the child's brain matures, various functions become *lateralized* to the left or right hemisphere. The left hemisphere is associated with logical, analytical thought, with mathematical and linear processing of information. The right hemisphere perceives and remembers visual, tactile, and auditory images; it is more efficient in processing holistic, integrative, and emotional information. Torrance (1980) lists the following characteristics of left- and right-brain dominance. (See Table 5-1.)

While we can cite many differences between left- and right-brain characteristics, it is important to remember that the left and right hemispheres operate together as a "team." Through the *corpus collosum,* messages are sent back and forth such that both hemispheres are involved in most of the neurological activity of the human brain. Most problem solving involves the capacities of both hemispheres, and often the best solutions to problems are those in which each hemisphere has participated optimally (see Danesi 1988). We must also remember Scovel's (1982) warning that left- and right-brain differences tend to draw more attention than the research warrants at the present time.

Nevertheless, the left-/right-brain construct helps to define another useful learning style continuum, with implications for second language learning and teaching. Danesi (1988), for example, uses "neurological bimodality" to analyze the way in which various language teaching methods have failed: by appealing too strongly to left-brain processes, past methods were inadequately stimulating important right-brain processes in the language classroom. Krashen, Seliger, and Hartnett (1974) found support for the hypothesis that left-brain-dominant second language learners preferred a deductive style of teaching, while right-brain-dominant learners appeared to be more successful in an inductive classroom environment. Stevick (1982) concluded that left-brain-dominant second language learners are better at producing separate words, gathering the specifics of language, carrying out sequences of

## TABLE 5–1.    Left- and Right-Brain Characteristics

| LEFT-BRAIN DOMINANCE | RIGHT-BRAIN DOMINANCE |
| --- | --- |
| Intellectual | Intuitive |
| Remembers names | Remembers faces |
| Responds to verbal instructions and explanations | Responds to demonstrated, illustrated or symbolic instructions |
| Experiments systematically and with control | Experiments randomly and with less restraint |
| Makes objective judgments | Makes subjective judgments |
| Planned and structured | Fluid and spontaneous |
| Prefers established, certain information | Prefers elusive, uncertain information |
| Analytic reader | Synthesizing reader |
| Reliance on language in thinking and remembering | Reliance on images in thinking and remembering |
| Prefers talking and writing | Prefers drawing and manipulating objects |
| Prefers multiple choice tests | Prefers open-ended questions |
| Control feelings | More free with feelings |
| Not good at interpreting body language | Good at interpreting body language |
| Rarely uses metaphors | Frequently uses metaphors |
| Favors logical problem solving | Favors intuitive problem solving |

operations, and dealing with abstraction, classification, labeling, and reorganization. Right-brain-dominant learners, on the other hand, appear to deal better with whole images (not with reshuffling parts), with generalizations, with metaphors, and with emotional reactions and artistic expressions. In Chapter Three I noted the role of the right hemisphere in second language learning. This may suggest a greater need to perceive whole meanings in those early stages, and to analyze and monitor oneself more in the later stages.

You may be asking yourself how left- and right-brain functioning differs from field independence and dependence. While few studies have set out explicitly to correlate the two factors, intuitive observation of learners and conclusions from studies of both hemispheric preference and field independence show a strong relationship. Thus, in dealing with either type of cognitive style, we are dealing with two styles that are highly parallel. Conclusions that were drawn above for field independence and dependence seem to apply well for left- and right-brain functioning as well.

# Ambiguity Tolerance

A third style concerns the degree to which you are cognitively willing to tolerate ideas and propositions that run counter to your own belief system or structure of knowledge. Some people are, for example, relatively "open-minded" in accepting ideologies and events and facts that contradict their own views; they are more content than others to entertain and even internalize contradictory propositions. Others, more "closed-minded," more dogmatic, tend to reject items that are contradictory or slightly incongruent with their existing system; they wish to see every proposition fit into an acceptable place in their cognitive organization, and if it does not fit, it is rejected.

Again, advantages and disadvantages are present in each style. The person who is tolerant of ambiguity is free to entertain a number of innovative and creative possibilities and not be congnitively or affectively disturbed by ambiguity and uncertainty. In second language learning a great amount of apparently contradictory information is encountered: words that differ from the native language, rules that not only differ but that are internally inconsistent because of certain "exceptions," and sometimes a whole cultural system that is distant from that of the native culture. Successful language learning necessitates tolerance of such ambiguities, at least for interim periods or stages, during which time ambiguous items are given a chance to become resolved. On the other hand, too much tolerance of ambiguity can have a detrimental effect. People can become "wishy-washy," accepting virtually every proposition before them, not efficiently subsuming necessary facts into their cognitive organizational structure. Such excess tolerance has the effect of hampering or preventing meaningful subsumption of ideas. Linguistic rules, for example, might not be effectively integrated into a whole system; rather, they may be gulped down in meaningless chunks learned by rote.

Intolerance of ambiguity also has its advantages and disadvantages. A certain intolerance at an optimal level enables one to guard against the wishy-washiness referred to above, to close off avenues of hopeless possibilities, to reject entirely contradictory material, and to deal with the reality of the system that one has built. But clearly intolerance can close the mind too soon, especially if ambiguity is perceived as a threat; the result is a rigid, dogmatic, brittle mind that is too narrow to be creative. This may be particularly harmful in second language learning.

A few research findings are available on this style in second language learning. Naiman et al. (1978) found that ambiguity tolerance was one of only two significant factors in predicting the success of their high school learners of

French in Toronto. Chapelle and Roberts (1986) measured tolerance of ambiguity in learners of English as a second language in Illinois. They found that learners with a high tolerance for ambiguity were slightly more successful in certain language tasks. These findings suggest—though not strongly so—that ambiguity tolerance may be an important factor in second language learning. The findings have intuitive appeal. It is hard to imagine a compartmentalizer—a person who sees everything in black and white with no shades of gray—ever being successful in the overwhelmingly ambiguous process of learning a second language.

# Reflectivity and Impulsivity

It is common for us to show in our personalities certain tendencies toward *reflectivity* sometimes and at other times *impulsivity*. Psychological studies have been conducted to determine the degree to which, in the cognitive domain, a person tends to make either a quick or gambling (impulsive) guess at an answer to a problem or a slower, more calculated (reflective) decision. David Ewing (1977) refers to two styles that are closely related to the reflectivity-impulsivity dimension: systematic and intuitive styles. An intuitive style implies an approach in which a person makes a number of different gambles on the basis of "hunches," with possibly several successive gambles before a solution is achieved. Systematic thinkers tend to weigh all the considerations in a problem, work out all the loopholes, then, after extensive reflection, carefully venture a solution.

The implications for language acquisition are numerous. It has been found that children who are conceptually reflective tend to make fewer errors in reading than impulsive children (Kagan 1965); however, impulsive persons are usually faster readers, and eventually master the "psycholinguistic guessing game" (Goodman 1970) of reading so that their impulsive style of reading may not necessarily deter comprehension. In another study inductive reasoning was found to be more effective with reflective persons (Kagan, Pearson, and Welch 1966), suggesting that generally reflective persons could benefit more from inductive learning situations. Virtually all research on reflective/impulsivity has used the Matching Familiar Figures Test (Kagan 1964; revised by Cairns & Cammock 1989) in which subjects are required to find, among numerous minimally different drawings of figures (people, ships, buildings, etc.), the drawing that matches the criterion figure. And most of the research to date on this cognitive style has looked at American, monolingual English-speaking children.

Only a few studies have been conducted relating reflectivity/impulsivity to second language learning. Doron (1973) found that among her sample of adult learners of ESL in the USA, reflective students were slower but more accurate than impulsive students in reading. In another study of adult ESL students, Abraham (1981) concluded that reflection was weakly related to performance on a proofreading task. More recently, Jamieson (1992) reported on yet another study of adult ESL learners. She found that "fast-accurate" learners, or, good guessers, were better language learners as measured by the standardized Test of English as a Foreign Language, but warned against assuming that impulsivity always implies accuracy. Some of her subjects were fast and *inaccurate.*

Reflectivity-impulsivity has some important considerations for classroom second language learning and teaching. Teachers tend to judge mistakes too harshly, especially in the case of a learner with an impulsive style who may be more willing than a reflective person to gamble at a correct answer. On the other hand, a reflective person may require patience from the teacher, who must allow more time for the student to struggle with responses. It is also quite conceivable that those with impulsive styles may go through a number of rapid transitions of semigrammatical stages of interlanguage, with reflective persons tending to remain longer at a particular stage with "larger" leaps from stage to stage.

# Visual and Auditory Styles

Yet another dimension of learning style—one that is very salient in a formal classroom setting—is the preference that learners show toward either visual or auditory input. Visual learners tend to prefer reading and studying charts, drawings, and other graphic information, while an auditory style is characterized by a preference for listening to lectures and audiotapes. Of course, most successful learners utilize both visual and auditory input, but slight preferences one way or the other may distinguish one learner from another, an important factor for classroom instruction.

In one study of adult learners of ESL, Joy Reid (1987) found some significant cross-cultural differences in visual and auditory styles. By means of a self-reporting questionnaire, the subjects rated their own preferences. The students rated statements like "When I read instructions, I learn them better," and "I learn more when I make drawings as I study," on a five-point scale ranging from "strongly agree" to "strongly disagree." Among Reid's results: Korean students were significantly more visually oriented than native English-speaking Americans; Japanese students were the least auditory students, significantly less auditorily inclined than Chinese and Arabic students. Reid also found that some of the preferences of her subjects were a factor of gender, length of time in the US, academic field of study, and level of education. Such findings underscore the importance of recognizing learners' varying style preferences, but also of not assuming that they are easily predicted by cultural/linguistic backgrounds alone.

# Strategies

We now turn to the second of our principal categories in this chapter, the level at which activity varies considerably *within* individuals as well as across individuals. Styles are general characteristics that differentiate one individual from another; strategies are those specific "attacks" that we make on a given problem. They are the moment by moment techniques that we employ to solve "problems" posed by second language input and output. The field of second language acquisition has distinguished between two types of strategy: *learning* strategies and *communication* strategies. The former relates to input—to processing, storage, and retrieval, that is, to taking in messages from others. The latter pertain to output, how we productively express meaning, how we deliver messages to others. We will examine both types of strategy here.

First, a brief historical note on the study of second language learners' strategies. As our knowledge of second language acquisition increased markedly during the 1970s, teachers and researchers came to realize that no single research finding and no single method of language teaching would usher in an era of utopia of absolute, predictable success in teaching a second language. We saw that certain learners seemed to be successful in spite of methods or techniques of teaching. We began to see the importance of individual *variation* in language learning. Certain people appeared to be endowed with abilities to succeed, others lacked those abilities. This observation led Rubin (1975) and Stern (1975) to describe "good" language learners in terms of personal characteristics, styles, and strategies. Rubin (Rubin and Thompson 1982) later summarized fourteen such characteristics. Good language learners

1. find their own way, taking charge of their learning.

2. organize information about language.

3. are creative, developing a "feel" for the language by experimenting with its grammar and words.

4. make their own opportunities for practice in using the language inside and outside the classroom.

5. learn to live with uncertainty by not getting flustered and by continuing to talk or listen without understanding every word.

6. use mnemonics and other memory strategies to recall what has been learned.

7. make errors work for them and not against them.

8. use linguistic knowledge, including knowledge of their first language, in learning a second language.

9. use contextual cues to help them in comprehension.

10. learn to make intelligent guesses.

11. learn chunks of language as wholes and formalized routines to help them perform "beyond their competence."

12. learn certain tricks that help to keep conversations going.

13. learn certain production strategies to fill in gaps in their own competence.

14. learn different styles of speech and writing and learn to vary their language according to the formality of the situation.

Such lists, speculative as they were in the mid 70s, inspired a group of collaborators in Toronto to undertake a study of good language learning traits (Naiman et al. 1978). While the empirical results of the Toronto study were somewhat disappointing, they nevertheless spurred many other researchers in the years since then to try to identify characteristics of "successful" language learners (see Stevick 1989 for example). Such research has led some (Rubin and Thompson 1982; Brown 1989, 1991; Marshall 1989) to offer advice to would-be students of foreign language on how to become better learners.

## Learning Strategies

The research of the mid-1970s has now led to some very careful defining of specific *learning* strategies. In some of the most impressive research of this kind, Michael O'Malley and Anna Chamot and colleagues (O'Malley et al. 1983, 1985a, 1985b, 1987, 1989; O'Malley and Chamot 1990; Chamot and O'Malley 1986, 1987) have studied the use of strategies by learners of English as a second language (ESL) in the United States. Typically, strategies are divided into three main categories, as noted in Table 5-2. "Metacognitive" is a term used in information-processing theory to indicate an "executive" function, strategies that involve planning for learning, thinking about the learning process as it is taking place, monitoring of one's production or comprehension, and evaluating learning after an activity is completed. "Cognitive" strategies are more limited to specific learning tasks and involve more direct manipulation of the learning material itself. "Socioaffective" strategies have to do with social-mediating activity and transacting with others. You will note that the latter category, along with some of the other strategies listed in Table 5-2, are actually *communication* strategies.

In recent years numerous studies have been carried out on the effectiveness of learners' using a variety of strategies in their quest for language competence. O'Malley, Chamot, and Kupper (1989) found that second language learners developed effective listening skills through the use of monitoring, elaboration, and inferencing. Forty-seven different reading strategies were identified by Anderson (1991). Men and women appear to use listening comprehension strategies differentially (Bacon 1992). And even studies of

### TABLE 5–2.   Learning Strategies (O'Malley et al. 1985b:582–584)

| LEARNING STRATEGY | DESCRIPTION |
| --- | --- |
| **METACOGNITIVE STRATEGIES** | |
| Advance Organizers | Making a general but comprehensive preview of the organizing concept or principle in an anticipated learning activity |
| Directed Attention | Deciding in advance to attend in general to a learning task and to ignore irrelevant distractors |
| Selective Attention | Deciding in advance to attend to specific aspects of language input or situational details that will cue the retention of language input |
| Self-Management | Understanding the conditions that help one learn and arranging for the presence of those conditions |
| Functional Planning | Planning for and rehearsing linguistic components necessary to carry out an upcoming language task |
| Self-Monitoring | Correcting one's speech for accuracy in pronunciation, grammar, vocabulary, or for appropriateness related to the setting or to the people who are present |
| Delayed Production | Consciously deciding to postpone speaking in order to learn initially through listening comprehension |
| Self-Evaluation | Checking the outcomes of one's own language learning against an internal measure of completeness and accuracy |
| **COGNITIVE STRATEGIES** | |
| Repetition | Imitating a language model, including overt practice and silent rehearsal |
| Resourcing | Using target language reference materials |
| Translation | Using the first language as a base for understanding and/or producing the second language |
| Grouping | Reordering or reclassifying, and perhaps labeling, the material to be learned based on common attributes |
| Note Taking | Writing down the main idea, important points, outline, or summary of information presented orally or in writing |

## TABLE 5–2.    (Continued)

| LEARNING STRATEGY | DESCRIPTION |
| --- | --- |

### COGNITIVE STRATEGIES

| | |
| --- | --- |
| Deduction | Consciously applying rules to produce or understand the second language |
| Recombination | Constructing a meaningful sentence or larger language sequence by combining known elements in a new way |
| Imagery | Relating new information to visual concepts in memory via familiar, easily retrievable visualizations, phrases, or locations |
| Auditory Representation | Retention of the sound or a similar sound for a word, phrase, or longer language sequence |
| Keyword | Remembering a new word in the second language by (1) identifying a familiar word in the first language that sounds like or otherwise resembles the new word and (2) generating easily recalled images of some relationship between the new word and the familiar word |
| Contextualization | Placing a word or phrase in a meaningful language sequence |
| Elaboration | Relating new information to other concepts in memory |
| Transfer | Using previously acquired linguistic and/or conceptual knowledge to facilitate a new language learning task |
| Inferencing | Using available information to guess meanings of new items, predict outcomes, or fill in missing information |

### SOCIOAFFECTIVE STRATEGIES

| | |
| --- | --- |
| Cooperation | Working with one or more peers to obtain feedback, pool information, or model a language activity |
| Question for Clarification | Asking a teacher or other native speaker for repetition, paraphrasing, explanation, and/or examples |

unsuccessful learners (Vann and Abraham 1990, for example) are yielding important information.

# Communication Strategies

While learning strategies deal with the receptive domain of intake, memory, storage, and recall, *communication strategies* pertain to the employment of verbal or nonverbal mechanisms for the productive communication of information. In the arena of linguistic interaction, it is sometimes difficult, of course, to distinguish between the two, as Tarone (1983) aptly noted, since comprehension and production can occur almost simultaneously. Nevertheless, as long as you can appreciate the slipperiness of such a dichotomy, it remains a useful distinction in understanding the nature of strategies.

The speculative early research of the 1970s (Varadi 1973 and others) has now led to great deal of recent attention to communication strategies (see, for example, Rost and Ross 1991, Bialystok 1990a, Bongaerts and Poulisse 1989, Oxford and Crookall 1989). Some time ago, Faerch and Kasper (1983a:36) defined communication strategies as "potentially conscious plans for solving what to an individual presents itself as a problem in reaching a particular communicative goal." While the research of the last decade does indeed focus largely on the *compensatory* nature of communication strategies, more recent studies seem to take a more "positive" view of communication strategies as elements of an overall *strategic* competence (see Chapter Nine) in which learners bring to bear all the possible facets of their growing competence in order to send clear messages in the second language. Moreover, such strategies may or may not be "potentially conscious;" support for such a conclusion comes from observations of first language acquisition strategies that are similar to those used by adults in second language learning contexts (Bongaerts and Poulisse 1989).

Perhaps the best way to understand what is meant by communication strategy is to look at a typical list of such strategies. Elaine Tarone (1981:286) provided a taxonomy that has now withstood the test of time (see Table 5-3).

Tarone's categories are a good basis for some further comments on communication strategies. We will look at four broad strategies.

## *Avoidance*

Avoidance is a common communication strategy that can be broken down into several subcategories and thus distinguished from other types of strategies. The most common type of avoidance strategy is *syntactic* or *lexical* avoidance within a semantic category. Consider the following conversation:

### TABLE 5–3.    Classification of Communication Strategies
### (Tarone 1981:286)

**PARAPHRASE**

| | |
|---|---|
| Approximation | use of a single target language vocabulary item or structure, which the learner knows is not correct, but which shares enough semantic features in common with the desired item to satisfy the speaker (e.g., *pipe* for *waterpipe*) |
| Word Coinage | the learner makes up a new word in order to communicate a desired concept (e.g., *airball* for *balloon*) |
| Circumlocution | the learner describes the characteristics or elements of the object or action instead of using the appropriate target language (TL) item or structure ("She is, uh, smoking something. I don't know what's its name. That's, uh, Persian, and we use in Turkey, a lot of.") |

**BORROWING**

| | |
|---|---|
| Literal Translation | the learner translates word for word from the native language ("He invites him to drink," for "They toast one another.") |
| Language Switch | the learner uses the native language (NL) term without bothering to translate (e.g., *balon* for *balloon, tirtil* for *caterpillar*) |

**APPEAL FOR ASSISTANCE**

| | |
|---|---|
| | the learner asks for the correct term ("What is this? What called?") |

**MIME**

| | |
|---|---|
| | the learner uses nonverbal strategies in place of a lexical item or action (e.g., clapping one's hands to illustrate applause) |

**AVOIDANCE**

| | |
|---|---|
| Topic Avoidance | the learner simply tries not to talk about concepts for which the TL item or structure is not known |
| Message Abandonment | the learner begins to talk about a concept but is unable to continue and stops in mid-utterance |

> L:   I lost my road.
>
> NS:  You lost your *road?*
>
> L:   Uh, . . . I lost. I lost. I got lost.

The learner avoided the lexical item *road* entirely, not being able to come up with the word *way* at that point. A French learner who wishes to avoid the use of the subjunctive in the sentence "Il faut que nous partions" may for example commonly use instead the sentence "Il nous faut partir," or, not being sure of the use of *en* in the sentence "J'en ai trois," the learner might simply say "J'ai trois pommes." *Phonological* avoidance is also common, as in the case of a Japanese tennis partner of mine who avoids using the word "rally" (because of its phonological difficulty) and instead opts to say, simply, "hit the ball."

A more direct type of avoidance is *topic* avoidance, in which a whole topic of conversation (say, talking about what happened yesterday if the past tense is unfamiliar) might be avoided entirely. Learners manage to devise ingenious methods of topic avoidance: changing the subject, pretending not to understand (a classical means for avoiding answering a question), simply not responding at all, or noticeably abandoning a message when a thought becomes too difficult to continue expressing.

### Prefabricated Patterns

Another common communication device is to memorize certain stock phrases or sentences without internalized knowledge of the components of the phrase. "Tourist survival" language is full of prefabricated patterns, most of which can be found in pocket bilingual "phrase" books which list hundreds of stock sentences for various occasions. "How much does this cost?" "Where is the toilet?" "I don't speak English" "I don't understand you" are the sorts of prefabricated patterns that one sometimes learns at the beginning of a language learning experience when the structure of the language is not known. Such phrases are memorized by rote to fit their appropriate context. Prefabricated patterns are sometimes the source of some merriment. In the first few days of Kikongo learning in Africa I tried to say, in Kikongo, "I don't know Kikongo" to those who attempted to converse with me beyond my limits; I was later embarrassed to discover that, in the first few attempts at producing this prefabricated avoidance device, instead of saying "Kizeyi Kikongo ko," I said "Kizolele Kikongo ko" (I don't *like* Kikongo), which brought on reactions ranging from amusement to hostility from Kikongo listeners.

Kenji Hakuta (1974, 1976) reported on prefabricated patterns in the second language development of a Japanese child learning English. He noted that children learning a first language develop certain prefabricated patterns (/ǰu/—"did you"; *gonna*—"going to"; *I dunno*—"I don't know"; /aõwana/—"I don't want to"), and both adults and children do the same in second language learning. Patterns like *can you, where's, what's, let's,* and many other useful phrases are sometimes mastered early in the acquisition process, before the structures are really known. Hakuta (1976:333) notes that prefabricated patterns "enable learners to express functions which they are yet unable to construct from their linguistic system, simply storing them in a sense like large lexical items."

But in the process of storing such items errors are often made, as in the Kikongo example. The errors are due largely to the rote nature of the items, but their roteness is a factor of a lack of knowledge of the structural rules for forming the particular utterance. Errors will also occur in connecting a prefabricated pattern to adjacent forms, such as the English sentence often produced by learners: "I don't know how do you do that," in which possibly even two prefabricated patterns were juxtaposed without the necessary deletion.

### Appeal to Authority

A common strategy of communication is a direct appeal to authority. Learners may, if "stuck" for a particular word or phrase, directly ask a native speaker (the authority) for the form ("How do you say____?"). Or they might venture a possible guess and then ask for verification from the native speaker of the correctness of the attempt. They might also choose to look a word or structure up in a bilingual dictionary. The latter case can also produce some rather amusing situations. Once a foreign student of English as a second language, when asked to introduce himself to the class and the teacher, said, "Allow me to introduce myself and tell you some of the . . ." At this point he quickly got out his pocket dictionary and, finding the word he wanted, continued, ". . . some of the *headlights* of my past."

### Language Switch

Finally, when all else fails—when appeal, avoidance, transfer, and other strategies are all incapable of producing a meaningful utterance—learners may resort to language switch. That is, they may simply use their native language whether the hearer knows that native language or not. Sometimes the learner slips in just a word or two, in the hope that the hearer will get the gist of what is being communicated. But at other times relatively long stretches of native language discourse emerge from learners. Surprisingly, the context of communication coupled with some of the universals of nonverbal expression sometimes enable learners to communicate an idea in their own language to someone unfamiliar with that language. Such marvels of communication are a tribute to the universality of human experience and a balm for those who feel the utter despair of attempting to communicate in a foreign tongue.

A classroom related view of communication strategies was offered by Chesterfield and Chesterfield (1985:49–50). Table 5-4 summarizes 12 strategies that they found being used by Mexican-American preschool and first-grade children learning English as a second language.

### TABLE 5–4.   Second Language Communication Strategies (Chesterfield and Chesterfield 1985:49–50)

| STRATEGY | EXAMPLE |
|---|---|
| *Repetition:* Echo/imitation of a word modeled by another, or incorporation of a word or structure used previously into an utterance | When the aide corrects someone else, saying "only" in a correcting tone, Ivette repeats "only." |
| *Memorization:* recall by rote of songs, rhymes, or sequences of numbers or related concepts | When the teacher asks the children, "What are the days we go to school?" Ramón rattles off automatically, "Monday, Tuesday, Wednesday, Thursday, Friday, Saturday." The teacher corrects, "No not Saturday. Who said Saturday?" |
| *Formulaic expression:* words or phrases which function as unanalysed automatic speech units for the speaker, often serving the function of initiating or continuing a conversation and giving the impression of command of the target language. | When Lupe, placing the last piece in her puzzle, exclaims, "Yo gané" (I won), Miguel protests, "No, no dije 'ready let's go'" (No, I didn't say "ready let's go"). |
| *Verbal attention getter:* any means by which the speaker attracts the attention of another to him/herself so as to initiate interaction | The teacher is discussing with the class the subject of bee stings, and reminding them of a bee sting incident of the previous year. Marcela pipes up, "It was me" to focus the teacher's attention on her, and the teacher asks "You?" Marcela, having succeeded, continues, "It got real red." |
| *Answer in unison:* response by providing the answer aloud together with others | During the large group session, the teacher asks: "Bottle starts with what letter?" and Dominga responds aloud with others: "b." When the teacher asks, "What's that next picture?" Dominga says loudly in unison, "hen." |

## TABLE 5–4.    (Continued)

| STRATEGY | EXAMPLE |
| --- | --- |
| *Talk to self:* practice in target language by engaging in verbal behavior directed to him/herself | Enrique, solving his math problems, counts on his fingers, saying to himself, "Five take away two," then "One, two, three, four," as he counts the remaining four problems. |
| *Elaboration:* providing information beyond that which is necessary to carry on the interaction | After the teacher explains that they must sign their names on a postcard, Enrique continues on the topic: "Miss, we sended a mail. At Christmas I had colored—we write it, my mother and dad and I colored back of it. It didn't have a picture." |
| *Anticipatory answer:* guessing from context to provide a response for an anticipated question, or prematurely fill in a word or phrase in another's statement. | The teacher, holding flashcards, begins, "When you put 'st' in front—." Maria interjects, "stop," interrupting the teacher before she finishes. The teacher continues her sentence, "—of it—stop" and writes the word on the board. |
| *Monitoring:* recognition and verbal correction of one's own error in vocabulary, style, grammar, etc. | When the teacher goes to her desk to check papers, Marcela says, "Miss, I need some pencil—a pencil." |
| *Appeal for assistance:* spontaneously asking another for the correct term or structure, or for help in solving a problem | Adriana, trying to complete her spelling assignment, asks the teacher, "Miss, how do you spell star?" The teacher responds, "s-t and then look at car" (referring to the word "car" on the board). |
| *Request for clarification:* attempt to broaden understanding or knowledge of the target language by asking the speaker to explain or repeat a previous statement | Cesar and two girls are cutting out masks for Halloween. One of the girls tells him, "We have to decorate them." He responds, "Decorate? What does decorate mean?" The other girl tells him, "That means you draw pictures on it." |

**TABLE 5–4.    (Continued)**

| STRATEGY | EXAMPLE |
| --- | --- |
| *Role-play:* spontaneous practice of the target language in interaction with another by taking on the role of another and fantasy play | Roberto announces, "I'm gonna be the teacher." Cesar joins in, "Me too." He gets up in the chair at the head of the table and asks: "What are you gonna do?" Then, turning to Eduardo, he asks: "Where are you gonna go, Eduardo? The art area?" |

The list of potentially useful communication strategies identified by researchers has grown steadily. Cohen and Aphek (1981) found that successful learners in their study made use of word association and generating their own rules. Rost and Ross (1991) discovered that learners benefitted from using continuation signals, asking for repetition, and seeking various forms of clarification. Huang and Van Naerssen (1987) attributed the oral production success of Chinese learners of English to functional practice (using language for communication) and, interestingly enough, reading practice. And the research continues.

# Learner Strategy Training

Much of the work of researchers and teachers on the application of both learning and communication strategies to classroom learning has come to be known generically as *learner strategy training.* As we seek to make the language classroom an effective milieu for learning, it has become increasingly apparent that "teaching learners how to learn" is crucial. Wenden (1985) was among the first to assert that learner strategies are the key to learner autonomy, and that one of the most important goals of language training should be the facilitating of that autonomy. Teachers, therefore, can benefit from an understanding of what makes learners successful and unsuccessful, and establish in the classroom a milieu for the realization of successful strategies. Teachers cannot always expect instant success in that effort since students often bring with them certain preconceived notions of what "ought" to go on in the classroom (Bialystok 1985). Nevertheless, our efforts to teach students some "technical know-how about how to tackle a language" are well advised.

Several different models of learner strategy training are now being practiced in language classes around the world. (1) As part of a standard communicative methodology, teachers help students to become aware of their own style preferences and the strategies that are derived from those styles (see the

"In the Classroom" vignette at the end of this chapter for some details). Through checklists (see, for example, Oxford 1990a), tests, and interviews, teachers can become aware of students tendencies and then offer advice on beneficial in-class and extra-class strategies. (2) Teachers can embed actual strategy practice into their techniques and materials. As they utilize such techniques as communicative games, rapid reading, fluency exercises, error analysis, they can help students either consciously or subconsciously to practice successful strategies. (3) Certain compensatory techniques are sometimes practiced to help students overcome certain weaknesses. Well over a decade ago, Omaggio (1981) provided diagnostic instruments and procedures for determining students' preferences, then outlined exercises which help students to overcome certain blocks or to develop successful strategies where they are weak. (4) Finally, recent textbooks (Chamot, O'Malley and Küpper 1992; Ellis and Sinclair 1989) are now including strategy training as part of a content-centered approach.

One of the most useful manuals of learner strategy training currently available is Rebecca Oxford's (1990a) practical guide for teachers. She outlined a host of learning and communication strategies that have been successful among learners. Her taxonomy (see Figure 5-1), which distinguishes between *direct* and *indirect* (similar to O'Malley et al.'s [1985] "cognitive" and "metacognitive" strategies, respectively) strategies, is both comprehensive and practical.

We have much to learn in the creation of practical techniques for training learners in strategy use, but this remains a very exciting and promising area of pedagogical research at the present time.

In this chapter we have looked at a number of both relevant and salient cognitive variables in the learning of a foreign language. It should by now be apparent that cognitive variables alone represent a quagmire of factors that must be channeled into an understanding of the total second language acquisition process. An awareness of these factors will help you, the teacher, to perceive in the learners you encounter some wide-ranging individual differences. Not all learners are alike. No one can be neatly pigeon-holed into a cognitive type. With many styles and strategies operating within a person, hundreds of cognitive "profiles" might be identified! If we could discover some overriding and all-pervading variable that classifies learners neatly into categories of "successful" and "unsuccessful," then of course we could make a case for typing language learners. But, as Earl Stevick (1989) showed in his profile of seven successful language learners, such is not the case. Instead, teachers need to recognize and understand a multiplicity of cognitive variables active in the second language learning process and to make appropriate judgments about individual learners, meeting them where they are and providing them with the best possible opportunities for learning.

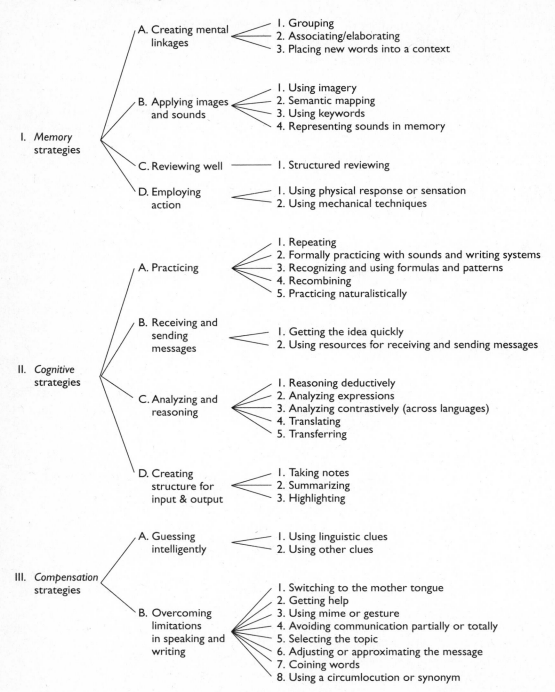

FIGURE 5–1.   Oxford's Strategy Classification System
Direct Strategies: Memory, Cognitive, and Compensation Strategies

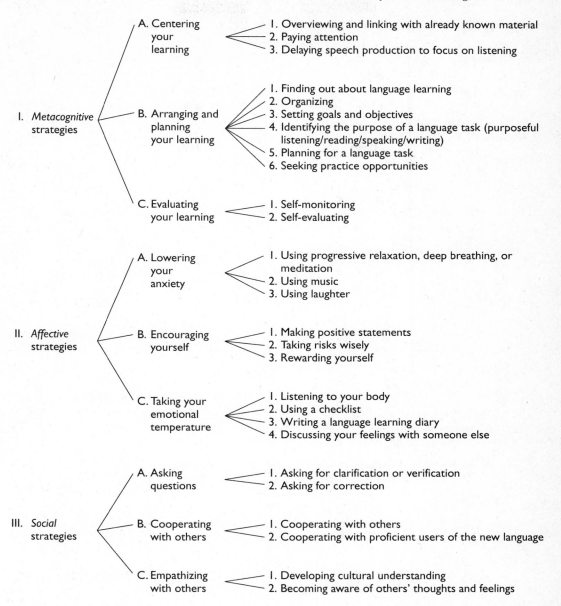

A. Centering
your
learning
  1. Overviewing and linking with already known material
  2. Paying attention
  3. Delaying speech production to focus on listening

I. *Metacognitive*
strategies

B. Arranging and
planning
your learning
  1. Finding out about language learning
  2. Organizing
  3. Setting goals and objectives
  4. Identifying the purpose of a language task (purposeful listening/reading/speaking/writing)
  5. Planning for a language task
  6. Seeking practice opportunities

C. Evaluating
your learning
  1. Self-monitoring
  2. Self-evaluating

A. Lowering
your
anxiety
  1. Using progressive relaxation, deep breathing, or meditation
  2. Using music
  3. Using laughter

II. *Affective*
strategies

B. Encouraging
yourself
  1. Making positive statements
  2. Taking risks wisely
  3. Rewarding yourself

C. Taking your
emotional
temperature
  1. Listening to your body
  2. Using a checklist
  3. Writing a language learning diary
  4. Discussing your feelings with someone else

A. Asking
questions
  1. Asking for clarification or verification
  2. Asking for correction

III. *Social*
strategies

B. Cooperating
with others
  1. Cooperating with others
  2. Cooperating with proficient users of the new language

C. Empathizing
with others
  1. Developing cultural understanding
  2. Becoming aware of others' thoughts and feelings

Indirect Strategies: Metacognitive, Affective, and Social Strategies

# In the Classroom: Styles and Strategies in Practice

Learner strategy training, discussed above, has a number of possible manifestations in the classroom. Sometimes textbooks themselves include exercises in style awareness and strategy development. Or teachers might consult a manual of techniques (e.g., Oxford 1990a) which offers guidelines on constructing their own strategy-building activities. Or students might fill out inventories to determine which of a host of possible strategies they use or fail to use. Or, teachers might simply provide impromptu advice to learners as the occasions arise. To give you an idea here of just a few examples of how learner strategy training works, three suggestions are offered.

1. **Students fill out a check list.** More often than not, language students enter a classroom with little or no conception of what good language learning strategies are. They dutifully sit at their desks waiting for the teacher to tell them to "open your books" or to "repeat after me." One thing that teachers can do to begin to open up students' minds to the possibility that they may *not* be engaging in strategies that could make them successful is to administer a very simple little check list on which students rate themselves. Figure 5-2 is an example of just such a check list. Once students have had a chance, with no advance "coaching," to fill out such a check list, you can then engage them in any or all of the following: (a) a discussion of why they responded as they did, (b) small group sharing of feelings underlying their responses, (c) an informal tabulation of how many people responded to each lettered box for each item, (d) some advice, from your own experience, on why certain practices may be either successful or not, or (e) reaching the general consensus that responses in the A and B categories are usually indicative of successful approaches to language learning.

2. **Engage in frequent spontaneous hints about successful learning and communications strategies.** In spite of the fact that a good deal of what we know about second language acquisition is not unequivocally proven, we nevertheless know quite a lot about what generally applies to most learners most of the time. Most learners, for example, come to language classes with raised inhibitions and fears that prevent them taking the necessary risks that learners must take in order to try out language and receive constructive feedback. Such principles may be stated for learners in the form of ten "commandments" (or, you might want to simply call them "suggestions") for learners. A teacher's version (in somewhat more technical jargon) and a learner's version of these ten rules for successful classroom learning are given in Table 5-5. These rules might simply take on the form of little reminders sprinkled into your classroom routines. You will note that each rule corresponds to the numbered items in the check list above. Caution should be taken in both cases, of course, in assuming that *all* learners will benefit from the directionality of the advice in these suggestions; a few learners, for example, may be too confident or too right-brain oriented.

3. **Build strategic techniques.** Perhaps a more subtle but no less effective way to manifest learner strategy training in a classroom is to make sure that

Check one box in each item that best describes you. Boxes A and E would indicate that the sentence is very much like you. Boxes B and D would indicate that the sentence is somewhat descriptive of you. Box C would indicate that you have no inclination one way or another.

A    B    C    D    E

1. I don't mind if people laugh at me when I speak.
☐ ☐ ☐ ☐ ☐
I get embarrassed if people laugh at me when I speak.

2. I like to try out new words and structures that I'm not completely sure of.
☐ ☐ ☐ ☐ ☐
I like to use only language that I am certain is correct.

3. I feel very confident in my ability to succeed in learning this language.
☐ ☐ ☐ ☐ ☐
I feel quite uncertain about my ability to succeed in learning this language.

4. I want to learn this language because of what I can personally gain from it.
☐ ☐ ☐ ☐ ☐
I am learning this language only because someone else is requiring it.

5. I really enjoy working with other people in groups.
☐ ☐ ☐ ☐ ☐
I would much rather work alone than with other people.

6. I like to "absorb" language and get the general "gist" of what is said or written.
☐ ☐ ☐ ☐ ☐
I like to analyze the many details of language and understand exactly what is said or written.

7. If there is an abundance of language to master, I just try to take things one step at a time.
☐ ☐ ☐ ☐ ☐
I am very annoyed by an abundance language material presented all at once.

8. I am not overly conscious of myself when I speak.
☐ ☐ ☐ ☐ ☐
I "monitor" myself very closely and consciously when I speak.

9. When I make mistakes, I try to use them to learn something about the language.
☐ ☐ ☐ ☐ ☐
When I make a mistake, it annoys me because that's a symbol of how poor my performance is.

10. I find ways to continue learning the language outside of the classroom.
☐ ☐ ☐ ☐ ☐
I look to the teacher and the classroom activities for everything I need to be successful.

FIGURE 5-2.    Learning Styles Check List

### TABLE 5–5. "Ten Commandments" for Good Language Learning

| TEACHER'S VERSION | LEARNER'S VERSION |
| --- | --- |
| 1. Lower inhibitions | Fear not! |
| 2. Encourage risk-taking | Dive in |
| 3. Build self-confidence | Believe in yourself |
| 4. Develop intrinsic motivation | Seize the day |
| 5. Engage in cooperative learning | Love thy neighbor |
| 6. Use right-brain processes | Get the BIG picture |
| 7. Promote ambiguity tolerance | Cope with the chaos |
| 8. Practice intuition | Go with your hunches |
| 9. Process error feedback | Make mistakes work FOR you |
| 10. Set personal goals | Set your own goals |

techniques are directed as much as possible toward good language learning behaviors. Overt admonition or calling students' conscious attention to principles need not be the major approach; instead, teachers can encourage successful subconscious strategy employment through their choice, among several options, of classroom techniques that enhance strategy building. Extending the "ten commandments" into classroom activities, suggestions for building strategic competence emerge, as shown in Table 5-6.

These three suggestions for bring learner strategy training into the classroom of course only begin to provide an idea of what can be done to sensitize learners to the importance of taking charge of their own learning—of taking some responsibility for their eventual success and not just leaving it all up to the teacher to "deliver" everything to them. If teachers everywhere would, however, just follow the above suggestions alone, significant steps would be made toward encouraging students to make a *strategic investment* in their language learning.

### TABLE 5–6. Building Strategic Techniques

1. **to lower inhibitions:** play guessing games and communication games; do role plays and skits; sing songs; use plenty of group work; laugh **with** your students; have them share their fears in small groups.

2. **to encourage risk taking:** praise students for making sincere efforts to try out language; use fluency exercises where errors are not corrected at that time; give outside-of-class assignments to speak or write or otherwise try out the language.

3. **to build students' self-confidence:** tell students explicitly (verbally and nonverbally) that you do indeed believe in them; have them make lists of their strengths, of what they know or have accomplished so far in the course.

4. **to help them to develop intrinsic motivation:** remind them explicitly about the rewards for learning English; describe (or have students look up) jobs that require English; play down the final examination in favor of helping students to see rewards for themselves beyond the final exam.

5. **to promote cooperative learning:** direct students to share their knowledge; play down competition among students; get your class to think of themselves as a team; do a considerable amount of small group work.

6. **to encourage them to use right-brain processing:** use movies and tapes in class; have them read passages rapidly; do skimming exercises; do rapid "free writes;" do oral fluency exercises where the object is to get students to talk (or write) a lot without being corrected.

7. **to promote ambiguity tolerance:** encourage students to ask you, and each other, questions when they don't understand something; keep your theoretical explanations very simple and brief; deal with just a few rules at a time; occasionally you can resort to translation into a native language to clarify a word or meaning.

8. **to help them use their intuition:** praise students for good guesses; do not always give explanations of errors—let a correction suffice; correct only selected errors, preferably just those that interfere with learning.

9. **to get students to make their mistakes work FOR them:** tape record students' oral production and get them to identify errors; let students catch and correct each other's errors; do not always give them the correct form; encourage students to make lists of their common errors and to work on them on their own.

10. **to get students to set their own goals:** explicitly encourage or direct students to go beyond the classroom goals; have them make lists of what they will accomplish on their own in a particular week; get students to make specific time commitments at home to study the language; give "extra credit" work.

## Suggested Readings

Two readily available articles on the relationship of cognitive and learning styles to second language acquisition can be found in *Snow and Shapira* (1985) and *Hartnett* (1985).

For a lively little debate, read *Griffiths and Sheen's* (1992) spirited attempt to discredit the whole field-independence construct; then read *Chapelle's* (1992) reasoned response. For an update on field-independence, look at *Chapelle and Green* (1992).

An interesting, readable study of visual and auditory learning styles is found in *Reid's* (1987) account ESL learners in the United States.

For an interesting popularized book on left- and right-brain differences and implications for an entirely different field—drawing—look through *Edwards* (1979).

An excellent survey of research and issues on styles and strategies is found in *Crookall and Oxford's* (1989) very readable article.

*Bialystok* (1990) has written a whole book on research on communication strategies.

The most comprehensive book available on teaching learning strategies in the classroom is *Oxford's* (1990) very useful guide for teachers.

Take a look at *Brown's* (1989) practical guide for language learners themselves, a book that is now available in Japanese, Thai, and Spanish.

## Topics and Questions for Study and Discussion

1.  Make sure you understand the continuum of process, style, and strategy in order to sort out differences between those things that all people do and those that vary tremendously even within an individual.

2.  In a class or conversation group of second language learners, observe the varying cognitive and learning styles. Do you see evidence of degrees of field independence, reflectivity, or tolerance of ambiguity? What is that evidence? Is it linguistic or behavioral evidence? Is there a connection between such styles and the apparent success of the learner?

3.  Review the argument that the field-independence/dependence dichotomy helps give explanatory power to the differentiation between natural (untutored) language learning and classroom (tutored) learning. How does this pose a dilemma for the foreign language teacher? Can you compromise between the two styles in the classroom?

4.  Someone once claimed (source unknown) that field dependence is related to farsightedness. That is, farsighted people tend to be more field-dependent, and vice versa. If that is true, how would you theoretically justify such a finding?

5.  If you were asked to make *your* list of characteristics of "good language learners," what would that list look like? Can you justify each of the ideas on your list?

6.  The distinction is made here between metacognitive (or indirect) strategies and cognitive (or direct) strategies. What is that distinction? Why is it an important one to make?

7.  Review both Tarone's and the Chesterfields' lists of communication strategies. How might you teach such strategies in the classroom?

8. List some possible prefabricated patterns in English and/or any other language. What are the limitations of their use?

9. How far can a teacher be expected to take the advice that students be taught certain strategies and "technical know-how about how to tackle a language"? When you were learning a foreign language, what advice would you like to have had that you did not have at the time?

10. Look again at the "ten commandments" for successful language learning in the "in the classroom" vignette at the end of the chapter. Are there any you would like to add or subtract or reword?

# Chapter 6

# PERSONALITY FACTORS

The previous two chapters dealt with two facets of the cognitive domain of language learning: human learning processes in general, and cognitive variations in learning—styles and strategies. Similarly, this chapter and Chapter Seven deal with two facets of the affective domain of second language acquisition. The first of these is the intrinsic side of affectivity: personality factors within a person that contribute in some way to the success of language learning. The second facet, treated in Chapter Seven, encompasses extrinsic factors—sociocultural variables that emerge as the second language learner brings not just two languages into contact but two cultures, and in some sense must learn a second culture along with a second language.

If we were to devise theories of second language acquisition or teaching methods that were based only on cognitive considerations, we would be omitting the most fundamental side of human behavior. Ernest Hilgard, well known for his study of human learning and cognition, once noted that "purely cognitive theories of learning will be rejected unless a role is assigned to affectivity" (1963:267). In recent years there has been an increasing awareness of the necessity in second language research and teaching to examine human personality in order to find solutions to perplexing problems.

The affective domain is difficult to describe within definable limits. A large number of variables are implied in considering the emotional side of human behavior in the second language learning process. One problem in striving for affective explanations of language success is presented by the task of subdividing and categorizing the factors of the affective domain. We are often tempted to use rather sweeping terms as if they were carefully defined.

For example, it is easy enough to say that "culture conflict" accounts for most language learning problems, or that "motivation" is the key to success in a foreign language; but it is quite another matter to define such terms with precision. Psychologists also experience a difficulty in defining terms. Abstract concepts such as empathy, aggression, extroversion, and other common terms are difficult to define operationally. Standardized psychological tests often form an empirical definition of such concepts, but constant revisions are evidence of an ongoing struggle for validity. Nevertheless, the elusive nature of affective and cognitive concepts need not deter us from seeking answers to questions. Careful, systematic study of the role of personality in second language acquisition has already led to a greater understanding of the language learning process and to improved language teaching methods.

# The Affective Domain

What is the affective domain? How is it to be delimited and understood? *Affect* refers to emotion or feeling. The affective domain is the emotional side of human behavior, and it may be juxtaposed to the cognitive side. The development of affective states or feelings involves a variety of personality factors, feelings both about ourselves and about others with whom we come into contact.

Three decades ago, Benjamin Bloom and his colleagues (Krathwohl, Bloom, and Masia 1964) provided a useful extended definition of the affective domain that is still widely used today:

1.  At the first and fundamental level, the development of affectivity begins with *receiving.* Persons must be aware of the environment surrounding them, be conscious of situations, phenomena, people, objects; be willing to receive, willing to tolerate a stimulus, not avoid it, and give a stimulus their controlled or selected attention.

2.  Next, persons must go beyond receiving to *responding,* committing themselves in at least some small measure to a phenomenon or a person. Such responding in one dimension may be in acquiescence, but in another, higher, dimension the person is willing to respond voluntarily without coercion, and then to receive satisfaction from that response.

3.  The third level of affectivity involves *valuing,* placing worth on a thing, a behavior, or a person. Valuing takes on the characteristics of beliefs or attitudes as values are internalized. Individuals do not merely accept a value to the point of being willing to be identified with it, but commit themselves to the value to pursue it, seek it out, and to want it, finally to the point of conviction.

4.  The fourth level of the affective domain is the *organization* of values into a system of beliefs, determining interrelationships among them, and establishing a hierarchy of values within the system.

5.  Finally, individuals become characterized by and understand themselves in terms of their *value system.* Individuals act consistently in accordance with the values they have internalized and integrate beliefs, ideas, and attitudes into a total philosophy or world view. It is at this level that problem solving, for example, is approached on the basis of a total, self- consistent system.

Bloom's taxonomy was devised for educational purposes, but it has been used for a general understanding of the affective domain in human behavior. The fundamental notions of receiving, responding, and valuing are universal. In second language acquisition learners need to be receptive both to those with whom they are communicating and to the language itself, responsive to persons and to the context of communication, and to place a certain value on the communicative act of interpersonal exchange.

Lest you feel at this point that the affective domain as described by Bloom is just a bit too far removed from the essence of language, it is appropriate to recall that language is inextricably bound up in virtually every aspect of human behavior. Language is so pervasive a phenomenon in our humanity that it cannot be separated from the larger whole—from the whole persons that live and breathe and think and feel. Kenneth Pike (1967:26) said that

> language is behavior, that is, a phase of human activity which must not be treated in essence as structurally divorced from the structure of nonverbal human activity. The activity of man constitutes a structural whole in such a way that it cannot be subdivided into neat "parts" or "levels" or "compartments" with language in a behavioral compartment insulated in character, content, and organization from other behavior.

Understanding how human beings feel and respond and believe and value is an exceedingly important aspect of a theory of second language acquisition.

We turn now to a consideration of specific personality factors in human behavior and how they relate to second language acquisition.

# Self-Esteem

Self-esteem is probably the most pervasive aspect of any human behavior. It could easily be claimed that no successful cognitive or affective activity can be carried out without some degree of self-esteem, self-confidence, knowledge of yourself, and belief in your own capabilities for that activity. Malinowski (1923) noted that all human beings have a need for *phatic communion*—defining oneself and finding acceptance in expressing that self in relation to valued others. Personality development universally involves the growth of a person's concept of self, acceptance of self, and reflection of self as seen in the interaction between self and others.

The following is a well-accepted definition of *self-esteem* (Coopersmith 1967:4–5):

> By self-esteem, we refer to the evaluation which the individual makes and customarily maintains with regard to himself; it expresses an attitude of approval or disapproval, and indicates the extent to which an individual believes himself to be capable, significant, successful and worthy. In short, self-esteem is a personal judgement of worthiness that is expressed in the attitudes that the individual holds towards himself. It is a subjective experience which the individual conveys to others by verbal reports and other overt expressive behavior.

People derive their sense of self-esteem from the accumulation of experiences with themselves and with others and from assessments of the external world around them. General, or *global,* self-esteem is thought to be relatively stable in a mature adult, and is resistant to change except by active and extended therapy. But since no personality or cognitive trait is predictably stable for all situations and at all times, self-esteem has been categorized into three levels, only the first of which is global self-esteem. *Situational* or *specific* self-esteem is a second level of self-esteem, referring to one's appraisals of oneself in certain life situations, such as social interaction, work, education, home, or on certain relatively discretely defined traits—intelligence, communicative ability, athletic ability, or personality traits like gregariousness, empathy, and flexibility. The degree of specific self-esteem a person has may vary depending upon the situation or the trait in question. The third level, *task* self-esteem, relates to particular tasks within specific situations. For example, within the educational domain task self-esteem might refer to particular subject-matter areas. In an athletic context, skill in a particular sport—or even a facet of a sport such as net play in tennis or pitching in baseball—would be evaluated on the level of task self-esteem. Specific self-esteem might refer to second language acquisition in general, and task self-esteem might appropriately refer to one's self-evaluation of a particular aspect of the process: speaking, writing, a particular class in a second language, or even a special kind of classroom exercise.

Adelaide Heyde (1979) studied the effects of the three levels of self-esteem on performance of an oral production task by American college students learning French as a foreign language. She found that all three levels of self-esteem correlated positively with performance on the oral production measure, with the highest correlation occurring between task self-esteem and performance on oral production measures. Watkins *et al.* (1991), Brodkey and Shore (1976), and Gardner and Lambert (1972) all included measures of self-esteem in their studies of success in language learning. The results revealed that self-esteem appears to be an important variable in second language acquisition, particularly in view of cross-cultural factors of second language learning that will be discussed in the next chapter.

What we do not know at this time is the answer to the classic chicken-or-egg question: does high self-esteem cause language success or does language success cause high self-esteem? Clearly, both are interacting factors. It is difficult to say whether teachers should try to "improve" global self-esteem or simply improve a learner's proficiency and let self-esteem take care of itself. Heyde (1979) found that certain sections of a beginning college French course had better oral production and self-esteem scores than other sections after only 8 weeks of instruction. This finding suggests that teachers really can have a positive and influential effect on both the linguistic performance and the emotional well-being of the student. Perhaps those "good" teachers succeeded because they gave optimal attention to linguistic goals and to the personhood of their students.

# Inhibition

Closely related to and in some cases subsumed under the notion of self-esteem is the concept of inhibition. All human beings, in their understanding of themselves, build sets of defenses to protect the ego. The newborn baby has no concept of its own self; gradually it learns to identify a self that is distinct from others. Then in childhood, the growing degrees of awareness, responding, and valuing begin to create a system of affective traits that individuals identify with themselves. In adolescence, the physical, emotional, and cognitive changes of the preteenager and teenager bring on mounting defensive inhibitions to protect a fragile ego, to ward off ideas, experiences, and feelings that threaten to dismantle the organization of values and beliefs on which appraisals of self-esteem have been founded. The process of building defenses continues on into adulthood. Some persons—those with higher self-esteem and ego strength—are more able to withstand threats to their existence and thus their defenses are lower. Those with weaker self-esteem maintain walls of inhibition to protect what is self-perceived to be a weak or fragile ego, or a lack of self-confidence in a situation or task.

The human ego encompasses what Guiora called the *language ego* to refer to the very personal, egoistic nature of second language acquisition. Meaningful language acquisition involves some degree of identity conflict as language learners take on a new identity with their newly acquired competence. An adaptive language ego enables learners to lower the inhibitions that may impede success. Guiora et al. (1972a) produced one of the few studies on inhibition in relation to second language learning. Claiming that the notion of ego boundaries is relevant to language learning, Guiora designed an experiment using small quantities of alcohol to induce temporary states of less than normal inhibition in an experimental group of subjects. The performance on a pronunciation test in Thai of subjects given the alcohol was significantly better than the performance of a control group. Guiora concluded that a direct relationship existed between inhibition (a component of language ego) and pronunciation ability in a second language. But there were some serious problems in his conclusion. Alcohol may lower inhibitions, but alcohol also tends to affect muscular tension, and while "mind" and "body" in this instance may not be clearly separable, the physical effect of the alcohol may have been a more important factor than the mental effect in accounting for the superior pronunciation performance of the subjects given alcohol. Furthermore, pronunciation may be a rather poor indicator of overall language competence. Nevertheless, Guiora provided an important hypothesis that has tremendous intuitive—if not experimental—support.

In another experiment (Guiora et al. 1980), Guiora and his associates studied the effect of valium on pronunciation of a second language. Inspired by a study (Schumann et al. 1978) that showed that hypnotized subjects performed well on pronunciation tests, Guiora and colleagues hypothesized that various dosages of a chemical relaxant would have a similar effect on subjects' pronunciation performance. Unfortunately, the results were nonsignificant, but interestingly enough the test*er* made a significant difference. In other words, the person doing the testing made a bigger difference on scores than did the dosage of valium. I wonder if this result says something about the importance of teachers!

Some have facetiously suggested that the moral to Guiora's experiments is that we should provide cocktails—or prescribe tranquilizers—for foreign language classes! While students might take delight in such a proposal, the experiments have highlighted a most interesting possibility: that the inhibitions, the defenses, which we place between ourselves and others are important factors contributing to second language success. Recently, Ehrman (1993) provided further support for the importance of language ego in a study of learners with "thin" (permeable) and "thick" (not as permeable) ego boundaries. While neither extreme was found to have necessarily beneficial or deleterious effects on success, Ehrman suggested that the openness, vulnerability, and ambiguity tolerance of those with thin ego boundaries found different pathways to success from those with hard-driving, systematic, perfectionistic, thick ego boundaries.

Such findings, coupled with Guiora's earlier work, have given rise to a number of steps that have been taken in foreign language teaching practices to create techniques that reduce inhibition in the classroom. Language teaching approaches in the last quarter of the twentieth century have been characterized by the creation of contexts for meaningful classroom communication such that the interpersonal ego barriers are lowered to pave the way for free, unfettered communication.

Anyone who has learned a foreign language is acutely aware that second language learning actually necessitates the making of mistakes. We test out hypotheses about language by trial and many errors; children learning their first language and adults learning a second can really only make progress by learning from making mistakes. If we never ventured to speak a sentence until we were absolutely certain of its total correctness, we would likely never communicate productively at all. But mistakes can be viewed as threats to one's ego. They pose both internal and external threats. Internally, one's critical self and one's performing self can be in conflict: the learner performs something "wrong" and becomes critical of his or her own mistake. Externally, the learner perceives others exercising their critical selves, even judging his very person when he or she blunders in a second language. Earl Stevick (1976b) spoke of language learning as involving a number of forms of *alienation*, alienation between the critical me and the performing me, between my native culture and my target culture, between me and my teacher, and between me and my fellow students. This alienation arises from the defenses that we build around ourselves. These defenses do not facilitate learning; rather they inhibit learning, and their removal therefore can promote language learning, which involves self-exposure to a degree manifested in few other endeavors.

# Risk-Taking

In the last chapter we saw that one of the prominent characteristics of good language learners, according to Rubin and Thompson (1982), was the ability to make intelligent guesses. Impulsivity was also described as a style that could have positive effects on language success. And we have just seen that inhibitions, or building defenses around our egos, can be a detriment. These factors suggest that risk-taking is an important characteristic of successful learning of a second language. Learners have to be able to "gamble" a bit, to be willing to try out hunches about the language and take the risk of being wrong.

Beebe (1983:40) says risk-taking is important in both classroom and natural settings:

> In the classroom, these ramifications might include a bad grade in the course, a fail on the exam, a reproach from the teacher, a smirk from a classmate, punishment or embarrassment imposed by oneself. Outside the classroom, individuals learning a second language face other negative consequences if they make mistakes. They fear looking ridiculous; they fear the frustration coming from a listener's blank look, showing that they have failed to communicate; they fear the danger of not being able to take care of themselves; they fear the alienation of not being able to communicate and thereby get close to other human beings. Perhaps worst of all, they fear a loss of identity.

On a continuum ranging from high to low risk-taking, we may be tempted to assume with Ely (1986) that high risk-taking will yield positive results in second language learning; however, such is not usually the case. Beebe (1983:41) cited a study which claimed that "persons with a high motivation to achieve are . . . moderate, not high, risk-takers. These individuals like to be in control and like to depend on skill. They do not take wild, frivolous risks or enter into no-win situations." Successful second language learners appear to fit the same paradigm. A learner might be too bold in blurting out meaningless verbal garbage that no one can quite understand, while success lies in an optimum point where calculated guesses are ventured. As Rubin (1975) noted, the good language learner makes willing and *accurate* guesses.

Risk-taking variation seems to be a factor in a number of issues in second language acquisition and pedagogy. The silent student in the classroom is one who is unwilling to appear foolish when mistakes are made. Self-esteem seems to be closely connected to a risk-taking factor: when those foolish mistakes are made, a person with high global self-esteem is not daunted by the possible consequences of being laughed at. Beebe (1983) noted that fossilization, or the relatively permanent incorporation of certain patterns of error, may be due to a lack of willingness to take risks. It is "safe" to stay within patterns that accomplish the desired function even though there may be some errors in those patterns. (See Chapter Eight for further discussion of fossilization.) The implications for teaching are important. In a few uncommon cases, overly high risk-takers, as they dominate the classroom with wild gambles, may need to be "tamed" a bit by the teacher. But most of the time our problem as teachers will be to encourage students to guess somewhat more willingly than the usual student is prone to do, and to value them as persons for those risks that they take.

# Anxiety

Intricately intertwined with self-esteem and inhibition and risk-taking, the construct of anxiety, as it has been studied in the psychological domain, plays an important affective role in second language acquisition. Anxiety is almost impossible to define in a simple sentence. It is associated with feelings of uneasiness, frustration, self-doubt, apprehension, or worry. Scovel (1978:134) defined anxiety as "a state of apprehension, a vague fear. . . ." We all know what anxiety is and we all have experienced feelings of anxiousness. How does this construct relate to second language learning? Any complex task we undertake can have elements of anxiety in it, aspects in which we doubt our own abilities and wonder if we will indeed succeed. Second language learning is no exception to a long list of complex tasks that are susceptible to our human anxieties.

The research on anxiety suggests that, like self-esteem, anxiety can be experienced at various levels (e.g., MacIntyre and Gardner 1991c). At the deepest, or global, level, *trait* anxiety is a more permanent predisposition to be anxious. Some people are predictably and generally anxious about many things.

At a more momentary, or situational level, *state* anxiety is experienced in relation to some particular event or act. As we learned in the case of self-esteem, then, it is important in a classroom for a teacher to try to determine whether a student's anxiety stems from a more global trait or whether it comes from a particular situation at the moment.

Trait anxiety, because of its global and somewhat ambiguously defined nature, has not proved to be useful in predicting second language achievement (MacIntyre and Gardner 1991c). However, recent research on *foreign language anxiety,* as it has come to be known, focuses more specifically on the situational nature of state anxiety. Three components of foreign language anxiety have been identified (Horwitz et al. 1986, MacIntyre and Gardner 1989, 1991c) in order to break down the construct into researchable issues: (1) communication apprehension, arising from learners' inability to adequately express mature thoughts and ideas; (2) fear of negative social evaluation, arising from a learner's need to make a positive social impression on others; and (3) test anxiety, or apprehension over academic evaluation. Inspired by MacIntyre and Gardner's (1988, 1989, 1991a, 1991b, 1991c) studies of foreign language anxiety, other researchers (e.g., Young 1991, Phillips 1992), have recently collaborated to give us useful information on foreign language anxiety. All of these studies conclude that "foreign language anxiety can be distinguished from other types of anxiety and that it can have a negative effect on the language learning process." (MacIntyre and Gardner 1991c:112).

Yet another important insight to be applied to our understanding of anxiety lies in the distinction between *debilitative* and *facilitative* anxiety (Alpert and Haber 1960, cited by Scovel 1978). We may be inclined to view anxiety as a negative factor, something to be avoided at all costs. For example, we are all familiar with the feeling of "test anxiety" before a big examination (see Madsen 1982, Phillips 1992). But the notion of facilitative anxiety is that some concern—some apprehension—over a task to be accomplished is a positive factor. Otherwise, a learner might be inclined to be "wishy-washy," lacking that facilitative tension that keeps one poised, alert, and just slightly unbalanced to the point that one cannot relax entirely. The feeling of nervousness before giving a public speech is, in experienced speakers, often a sign of facilitative anxiety, a symptom of just enough tension to get the job done.

In Bailey's (1983) study of competitiveness and anxiety in second language learning, facilitative anxiety was one of the keys to success, and closely related to competitiveness. I noted in Chapter Four that Rogers's humanistic theory of learning promotes low anxiety among learners and a nondefensive posture where learners do not feel they are in competition with one another. Bailey found in her self-analysis, however, that while competitiveness sometimes hindered her progress (for example, the pressure to outdo her peers sometimes caused her to retreat even to the point of skipping class), at other times it motivated her to study harder (as in the case of carrying out an intensive review of material in order to feel more at ease in oral work in the class-room). She explained the positive effects of competitiveness by means of the construct of facilitative anxiety.

So the next time your language students are "anxious," you do well to ask yourself if that anxiety is truly debilitative. It could well be that a little nervous tension in the process is a good thing. Once again, we find that a construct has an optimal point along its continuum: Both too much and too little anxiety may hinder the process of successful second language learning.

# Empathy

The human being is a social animal, and the chief mechanism for main-taining the bonds of society is language. Some highly sophisticated methods of language teaching have failed to accomplish the goal of communicativity in the learner by overlooking the social nature of language. While we tend to rec-ognize the importance of the social aspect of language, we also tend to over-simplify that aspect by not recognizing the complexity of the relation between language and society, or by considering socially oriented problems in language learning as a simple matter of "acculturation." Chapter Seven demonstrates that acculturation is no simple process, and it will become clear in this chapter that the social *transactions* that the second language learner is called upon to make constitute complex endeavors.

Transaction is the process of reaching out beyond the self to others. The tools of language help to accomplish these feats. A variety of transactional variables comes to bear on second language learning: imitation, modeling, identification, empathy, extroversion, aggression, styles of communication, and others. Two of these variables, chosen for their relevance to a global under-standing of second language acquisition, will be treated here: empathy and extroversion.

*Empathy,* like so many personality variables, defies adequate definition. In common terminology, empathy is the process of "putting yourself into someone else's shoes," of reaching beyond the self and understanding and feel-ing what another person is understanding or feeling. It is probably the major factor in the harmonious coexistence of individuals in society. Language is one of the primary means of empathizing, but nonverbal communication facilitates the process of empathizing and must not be overlooked.

In more sophisticated terms, empathy is usually described as the projec-tion of one's own personality into the personality of another in order to under-stand him or her better. Empathy is not synonymous with *sympathy.* Empathy implies more possibility of detachment; sympathy connotes an agreement or harmony between individuals. Guiora (1972b:142) defined empathy as "a pro-cess of comprehending in which a temporary fusion of self-object boundaries permits an immediate emotional apprehension of the affective experience of another." The affective side of that definition could apply to the cognitive as well. Psychologists have found it difficult to define empathy. Hogan (1969:309), one of the leading researchers in empathy, at one point defined empathy as "a relatively discrete social phenomenon recognizable in the experience of laymen and psychologists alike." The circularity of this definition is reminiscent of the zoologist's definition of a *dog* as a four-legged animal recognizable as a dog by other dogs! Despite the difficulty of defining the concept, there is general consensus on what empathy is. Psychologists generally agree with Guiora's definition above and add that there are two necessary aspects to the development and exercising of empathy: first, an awareness and knowledge of one's own feelings, and second, identification with another person (Hogan 1969). In other words, you cannot fully empathize—or know someone else—until you adequately know yourself.

Communication requires a sophisticated degree of empathy. In order to communicate effectively you need to be able to understand the other person's affective and cognitive states; communication breaks down when false presuppositions or assumptions are made about the other person's state. From the very mechanical, syntactic level of language to the most abstract, meaningful level, we assume certain structures of knowledge and certain emotional states in any communicative act. In order to make those assumptions correctly we need to transcend our own ego boundaries, or using Guiora's term, to "permeate" our ego boundaries so that we can send and receive messages clearly.

Oral communication is a case in which, cognitively at least, it is easier to achieve empathic communication since there is immediate feedback from the hearer. A misunderstood word, phrase, or idea can be questioned by the hearer, and then rephrased by the speaker until a clear message is interpreted. Written communication requires a special kind of empathy—a "cognitive" empathy in which the writer, without the benefit of immediate feedback from the reader, must communicate ideas by means of a very clear empathic intuition and judgment of the reader's state of mind and structure of knowledge.

So in a second language learning situation the problem of empathy becomes acute. Not only must learner-speakers correctly identify cognitive and affective sets in the hearer, but they must do so in a language in which they are insecure. Then, learner-hearers, attempting to comprehend a second language, often discover that their own states of thought are misinterpreted by a native speaker, and the result is that linguistic, cognitive, and affective information easily passes "in one ear and out the other."

Guiora and his colleagues (1972a, 1972b) found that a modified version of the Micro-Momentary Expression (MME) test, a test claiming to measure degrees of empathy, successfully predicted authenticity of pronunciation of a foreign language. Naiman, Fröhlich, and Stern (1975) included an empathy measure (Hogan's Empathy Scale—see Hogan 1969) in their battery of tests used to try to discover characteristics of the "good language learner," but found no significant correlation between empathy and language success as measured by an imitation test and a listening test. However, their finding was not unexpected since they found field independence to be positively correlated with language success; the presumed antithesis of field independence—field dependence—has been shown to correlate highly with empathy (Witkin et al. 1971). But a great deal of the problem of the study of most personality variables lies in the accuracy of the tests used to measure traits. Serious methodological problems surround such measurement; the MME and Hogan's Empathy Scale are cases in point. It has been shown that such tests accurately identify personality *extremes* (schizophrenic, paranoid, or psychotic behavior, for example) but fail to differentiate among the vast "normal" population.

If indeed a high degree of empathy is predictive of success in language learning, it would be invaluable to discover how one could capitalize on that possibility in language teaching. It is one thing to claim to be able to predict success and quite another matter to cause success by fostering empathy in the language classroom. One would need to determine if empathy is something one can "learn" in the adult years, especially cross-culturally. If so, then it would not be unreasonable to incorporate empathy in language teaching methods. What kinds of drills and exercises could be devised that require a person to predict or guess another person's response? How worthwhile would it be to attempt to organize foreign language classes that operate on a high-empathy basis, as in Community Language Learning, in which principles of T-group therapy are used to aid the language learning process? These and other questions give rise to some creative issues in language teaching methodology.

Probably the most interesting implication of the study of empathy is the need to define empathy cross-culturally—to understand how different cultures express empathy. Most of the empathy tests devised in the United States are culture-bound to Western North American middle-class society. Chapter Seven will deal more specifically with empathy in cross-cultural settings, particularly with the role of empathy in defining the concept of acculturation.

# Extroversion

Extroversion, and its counterpart, introversion, are also potentially important factors in the acquisition of a second language. The terms are often misunderstood because of a tendency to stereotype extroversion. We are prone to think of an extroverted person as a gregarious, "life of the party" person. Introverted people, conversely, are thought of as quiet and reserved, with tendencies toward reclusiveness. Western society values the stereotypical extrovert. Nowhere is this more evident than in the classroom where teachers admire the talkative, outgoing student who participates freely in class discussions. On the other hand, introverts are sometimes thought of as not being as bright as extroverts.

Such a view of extroversion is misleading. Extroversion is the extent to which a person has a deep-seated need to receive ego enhancement, self-esteem, and a sense of wholeness *from other people* as opposed to receiving that affirmation within oneself. Extroverts actually need other people in order to feel "good." However, extroverts are not necessarily loudmouthed and talkative. They may be relatively shy but still need the affirmation of others. Introversion, on the other hand, is the extent to which a person derives a sense of wholeness and fulfillment apart from a reflection of this self from other people. Contrary to our stereotypes, introverts can have an inner strength of character that extroverts do not have.

Unfortunately, these stereotypes have influenced teachers' perceptions of students. Ausubel (1968:413) noted that introversion and extroversion are a "grossly misleading index of social adjustment," and other educators have warned against prejudging students on the basis of perceived extroversion. In language classes, where oral participation is highly valued, it is easy to view active participants with favor, and to assume that their visibility in the classroom is due to an extroversion factor (which may not be so). Culturally, American society differs considerably from a number of other societies where it is improper to speak out extensively in the classroom. Teachers need to consider cultural norms in their assessment of a student's presumed "passivity" in the classroom.

Extroversion is commonly thought to be related to empathy, but such may not be the case. The extroverted person may actually behave in an extroverted manner in order to protect his or her own ego, with extroverted behavior being symptomatic of defensive barriers and high ego boundaries. At the same time the introverted, quieter, more reserved person may show high empathy—an intuitive understanding and apprehension of others—and simply be more reserved in the outward and overt expression of empathy.

It is not clear then, that extroversion or introversion helps or hinders the process of second language acquisition. The Toronto study (Naiman et al. 1978) found no significant effect for extroversion in characterizing the good language learner. Busch (1982), in the most comprehensive study to date on extroversion, explored the relationship of introversion and extroversion to English proficiency in adult Japanese learners of English in Japan. She hypothesized that extroverted students (as measured by a standard personality inventory) would be more proficient than introverts. Her hypothesis was not supported. In fact, introverts were significantly *better* than extroverts in their pronunciation (one of four factors which were measured in an oral interview)! This latter result tends to blow apart our stereotype of the extroverted language learner who is presumably a frequent and willing participant in class activities. Busch's study, however, is just one study, and it was done in one culture with one group of learners. Much more research is needed before we can draw conclusions, as Skehan (1989a:100–106) ably pointed out.

Even in the light of an appropriate definition of extroversion, it is never-theless conceivable that extroversion may be a factor in the development of general oral communicative competence, which requires face to face interac-tion, but not in listening, reading, and writing. It is also readily apparent that cross-cultural norms of nonverbal and verbal interaction vary widely, and what in one culture (say, the United States) may appear as introversion is in another culture (say, Japan), respect and politeness. Nevertheless, on a practi-cal level, the facilitating or interfering effects of certain methods that invoke extroversion need to be carefully considered. How effective are methods that incorporate drama, pantomime, humor, role plays, and overt personality expo-sure? A teacher needs to beware of trying to "create" in a student more so-called extroversion than is really necessary. We need to be sensitive to cultural norms, to a student's willingness to speak out in class, and to optimal points between extreme extroversion and introversion that may vary from student to student.

# Myers-Briggs Character Types

In the last decade or so there has been a tremendous wave of interest, in Western society, in the relationship between personality "type" and one's suc-cess in a job, in management of time, in academic pursuits, in marriage, in childrearing, and perhaps a host of other contexts. We have become hypersen-sitized to the "different strokes for different folks" syndrome, that alerts us all to how unique every individual is and how each person can act on that uniqueness to succeed in business, school, sex life, and interpersonal relation-ships. The champions of this syndrome are Isabel Myers and Katheryn Briggs, whose research in the 1950s and 1960s has come to fruition in the form of the widespread use, today, of the Myers-Briggs Type Indicator (Myers 1962), com-monly referred to as the "Myers-Briggs test."

The Myers-Briggs test revived the work of Carl Jung of a half-century ear-lier. Jung (1923) said that people are different in fundamental ways, and that an individual has preferences for "functioning" in ways that are characteristic, or "typical," of that particular individual. Jung's work was all but forgotten with the boom of behavioristic psychology in the middle part of the century, but we have now returned to a recognition of the acute importance of individ-ual variation, especially in the realm of education. Borrowing from some of Jung's "types," the Myers-Briggs team tested four dichotomous styles of func-tioning in the Myers-Briggs test: (1) introversion versus extroversion, (2) sens-ing versus intuition, (3) thinking versus feeling, and (4) judging versus perceiving. Table 6-1 defines the four categories (Keirsey and Bates 1984:25–26) in simple words and phrases.

The Extroversion-Introversion (E/I) category relates to an aspect of per-sonality already discussed in this chapter, the way we either "turn inward" or

## TABLE 6–1. Myers-Briggs Character Types

| EXTROVERSION (B) | INTROVERSION (I) |
| --- | --- |
| Sociability | Territoriality |
| Interaction | Concentration |
| External | Internal |
| Breadth | Depth |
| Extensive | Intensive |
| Multiplicity of relationships | Limited relationships |
| Expenditure of energies | Conservation of energies |
| Interest in external events | Interest in internal reaction |

| SENSING (S) | INTUITION (N) |
| --- | --- |
| Experience | Hunches |
| Past | Future |
| Realistic | Speculative |
| Perspiration | Inspiration |
| Actual | Possible |
| Down-to-earth | Head-in-clouds |
| Utility | Fantasy |
| Fact | Fiction |
| Practicality | Ingenuity |
| Sensible | Imaginative |

| THINKING (T) | FEELING (F) |
| --- | --- |
| Objective | Subjective |
| Principles | Values |
| Policy | Social values |
| Laws | Extenuating circumstances |
| Criterion | Intimacy |
| Firmness | Persuasion |
| Impersonal | Personal |
| Justice | Humane |
| Categories | Harmony |
| Standards | Good or bad |
| Critique | Appreciative |
| Analysis | Sympathy |
| Allocation | Devotion |

| JUDGING (J) | PERCEIVING (P) |
|---|---|
| Settled | Pending |
| Decided | Gather more data |
| Fixed | Flexible |
| Plan ahead | Adapt as you go |
| Run one's life | Let life happen |
| Closure | Open options |
| Decision-making | Treasure hunting |
| Planned | Open ended |
| Completed | Emergent |
| Decisive | Tentative |
| Wrap it up | Something will turn up |
| Urgency | There's plenty of time |
| Deadline! | What deadline? |
| Get show on the road | Let's wait and see . . . |

"turn outward" for our sense of wholeness and self-esteem. The Sensing-Intuition (S/N) category has to do with the way we perceive and "take in" the world around us. Sensing types are data-oriented and empirically inclined to stick to observable, measurable facts, while intuitive types are more willing to rely on hunches, inspiration, and imagination for perceiving reality. The Thinking-Feeling (T/F) category describes ways of arriving at conclusions and of storing reality in memory. Thinking types are generally cognitive, objective, impartial, and logical. Feeling involves more affectivity, a desire for harmony, a capacity for warmth, empathy, and compassion. Myers and Briggs extended beyond Jung's types in adding the Judging-Perceiving (J/P) dichotomy, which has to do with one's attitude toward the "outer world." "Js" want closure, planning, organization, while "Ps" are spontaneous, flexible, and comfortable with open-ended contexts.

With four two-dimensional categories, 16 personality profiles, or combinations, are possible. Disciples of the Myers-Briggs research (Keirsey and Bates 1984, for example) describe the implications of being an "ENFJ" or an "ISTP," and all the 14 other combinations of types. Managers are aided in their understanding of employees by understanding their character type. ISTJs, for example, make better behind-the-scenes workers on jobs that require meticulous precision, while ENFPs might be better at dealing with the public. Young people seeking a career can understand better how certain occupations might be more or less suited to them by knowing their own character type. Lawrence (1984) stresses the importance of a teacher's understanding of the individual differences of learners in a classroom: Es will excel in group work; Is will prefer individual work; SJs are "linear learners with a strong need for structure" (Lawrence 1984:52); NTs are good at paper-and-pencil tests. The generalizations are many.

What might all this have to do with second language learner? So far, except for the research on extroversion referred to earlier in this chapter, only a few studies (Ehrman 1989, 1990; Ehrman and Oxford 1989, 1990; Moody 1988; Oxford and Ehrman 1988) have sought to discover a link between Myers-Briggs types and second language learning. Notable among these, however, is Ehrman and Oxford's (1990) study of 79 foreign language learners at the Foreign Service Institute. They found that their subjects exhibited some differences in *strategy* use, depending on their Myers-Briggs type. For example, extroverts (E) used social strategies consistently and easily while introverts (I) rejected them. Sensing (S) students displayed a strong liking for memory strategies; intuitives (N) were better at compensation strategies. The T/F distinction yielded the most dramatic contrast: thinkers (T) commonly used metacognitive strategies and analysis while feelers (F) rejected such strategies, and feelers used social strategies while thinkers did not. And judgers (J) rarely used the affective strategies that the perceivers (P) found so useful.

These findings notwithstanding, we should not be too quick to conclude that psychological type can predict successful and unsuccessful learning, as the authors readily admit. In another study, Ehrman (1989) outlines both the assets *and* the liabilities of each side of the Myers-Briggs continuum (see Table 6-2).

It would appear that success in a second language depends on the "mobilization [a] of the strategies associated with one's native learning-style preferences (indicated by the four MBTI letters) and [b] of the strategies associated with the less preferred functions that are the opposites of the four letters of a person's type." (Ehrman and Oxford 1990:323) In other words, successful learners know their preferences, their strengths, and their weaknesses, and effectively utilize strengths and compensate for weaknesses regardless of their "natural" preferences.

# Measuring Affective Factors

The measurement of affective factors has for many decades posed a perplexing problem. Most tests of personality are paper-and-pencil tests that ask for a self-rating of some kind. In typical tests, for example, "My friends have no confidence in me" and "I am generally very patient with people" are items on which a subject agrees or disagrees in order to measure self-esteem and empathy, respectively. Such tests present two problems. On the one hand they can be quite culturally ethnocentric, using concepts and references that are difficult to interpret cross-culturally. For instance, one item testing empathy

## TABLE 6–2.    Assets and Liabilities of Myers-Briggs Types (Ehrman 1989)

### MAJOR ASSETS ASSOCIATED WITH EACH PREFERENCE

| | |
|---|---|
| Extraversion | Willing to take conversational risks |
| Introversion | Concentration, self-sufficiency |
| Sensing | Hard, systematic work; attention to detail, close observation |
| Intuition | Inferencing and guessing from context, structuring own training, conceptualizing and model-building |
| Thinking | Analysis, self-discipline; instrumental motivation |
| Feeling | Integrative motivation, bonding with teachers, good relations lead to good self-esteem |
| Judging | Systematic work, get the job (whatever it is) done |
| Perceiving | Open, flexible, adaptable to change and new experiences |

### MAJOR LIABILITIES ASSOCIATED WITH EACH PREFERENCE
(Note: Not all students showed these liabilities.)

| | |
|---|---|
| Extraversion | Dependent on outside stimulation and interaction |
| Introversion | Need to process ideas before speaking sometimes led to avoidance of linguistic risks in conversation |
| Sensing | Hindered by lack of clear sequence, goals, syllabus, structure in language or course |
| Intuition | Inaccuracy and missing important details, sought excessive complexity of discourse |
| Thinking | Performance anxiety because self-esteem was attached to achievement, excessive need for control (language, process) |
| Feeling | Discouraged if not appreciated, disrupted by lack of interpersonal harmony |
| Judging | Rigidity, intolerance of ambiguous stimuli |
| Perceiving | Laziness, inconsistent pacing over the long haul |

requires the subject to agree or disagree with the following statement: "Disobedience to the government is sometimes justified." Such a concept could have wide variance in interpretation. A second and equally profound problem in the measurement of affective variables lies in the "self-flattery" syndrome (Oller 1981b, 1982). Generally, testees will try to discern "right" answers to such questions (that is, answers that make them look "good" or that do not "damage" them), even though directions to these tests say there are no "right" or "wrong" answers. In so doing, perceptions of self are likely to be considerably biased toward what the testee perceives as a highly desirable personality type. A word of caution is in order, then, as we interpret the results of affective tests. "No matter how many of us agree with the plausible claims of the theories, and in general I am pressed by intuition to go with the popular vote, the conclusions of the theorists [that achievement in a second language is related to affective variables] are no more nor less empirically secure than the measures of affect are valid" (Oller 1981b:24).

# Motivation

Motivation is probably the most frequently used catch-all term for explaining the success or failure of virtually any complex task. It is easy to figure that success in a task is due simply to the fact that someone is "motivated." It is easy in second language learning to claim that a learner will be successful with the proper motivation. Such claims are of course not erroneous, for countless studies and experiments in human learning have shown that motivation is a key to learning (see Crookes and Schmidt 1991). But these claims gloss over a detailed understanding of exactly what motivation is and what the subcomponents of motivation are. What does it mean to say that someone is motivated? How do you create, foster, and maintain motivation?

Motivation is commonly thought of as an inner drive, impulse, emotion, or desire that moves one to a particular action. Or, in more technical terms, motivation refers to "the choices people make as to what experiences or goals they will approach or avoid, and the degree of effort they will exert in that respect." (Keller 1983:389) Some psychologists define motivation in terms of certain *needs* or drives. Ausubel (1968:368–379), for example, identified six needs undergirding the construct of motivation: (1) the need for *exploration,* for seeing "the other side of the mountain," for probing the unknown; (2) the need for *manipulation,* for operating—to use Skinner's term—on the environment and causing change; (3) the need for *activity,* for movement and exercise, both physical and mental; (4) the need for *stimulation,* the need to be stimulated by the environment, by other people, or by ideas, thoughts, and feelings; (5) the need for *knowledge,* the need to process and internalize the results of exploration, manipulation, activity, and stimulation, to resolve contradictions, to quest for solutions to problems and for self-consistent systems of knowledge; (6) finally, the need for *ego enhancement,* for the self to be known and to be accepted and approved of by others.

There are other possible factors that could be listed in accounting for motivation. Maslow (1970) listed hierarchical human needs, from fundamental physical necessities (air, water, food) to higher needs of security, identity, and self-esteem, the fulfillment of which leads to *self-actualization.* Other psychologists have noted further basic needs: achievement, autonomy, affiliation, order, change, endurance, aggression, and other needs.

Examples abound to illustrate the "needs" concept of motivation. Consider children who are motivated to learn to read. They are motivated because certain needs are important to them, particularly exploration, stimulation, knowledge, self-esteem and autonomy. Children who are not motivated to read fail to see how reading meets the needs they have. The adult who learns to ski and learns to do so well no doubt is motivated by a need for exploration and stimulation and activity and maybe even ego enhancement. The foreign language learner who is either intrinsically or extrinsically meeting needs in learning the language will be positively motivated to learn.

Motivation is something that can, like self-esteem, be global, situational, or task-oriented. Learning a foreign language clearly requires some of all three levels of motivation. For example, a learner may possess high "global" motivation but low "task" motivation to perform well on, say, the written mode of the language. Motivation is also typically examined in terms of the *intrinsic* and *extrinsic* orientation of the learner. Those who learn for their own self-perceived needs and goals are intrinsically oriented and those who pursue a goal only to receive an external reward from someone else are extrinsically motivated. We will return to this extremely important concept below. Finally, studies of motivation in second language acquisition often refer to the distinction between *integrative* and *instrumental* orientations of the learner, which we now consider in the next section.

# Instrumental, Integrative, and Assimilative Motivation

One of the best-known and historically significant studies of motivation in second language learning was carried out by Robert Gardner and Wallace Lambert (1972). Over a period of 12 years they extensively studied foreign language learners in Canada, several parts of the United States, and the Philippines in an effort to determine how attitudinal and motivational factors affect language learning success. Motivation was examined as a factor of a number of different kinds of attitudes. Two different clusters of attitudes divided two basic types of motivation: instrumental and integrative motivation. *Instrumental* motivation refers to motivation to acquire a language as means for attaining instrumental goals: furthering a career, reading technical material, translation, and so forth. An *integrative* motive is employed when learners wish to integrate themselves within the culture of the second language group, to identify themselves with and become a part of that society. Many of Lambert's studies (see Lambert 1972) and one study by Spolsky (1969) found that integrative motivation generally accompanied higher scores on proficiency tests in a foreign language. The conclusion from these studies was that integrative motivation may indeed be an important requirement for successful language learning. And some teachers and researchers have even gone so far as to claim that integrative motivation is absolutely essential for successful second language learning.

Soon evidence began to accumulate that challenged such a claim. Yasmeen Lukmani (1972) demonstrated that among Marathi-speaking Indian students learning English in India, those with higher *instrumental* motivation scored higher in tests of English proficiency. Braj Kachru (1977, 1992) has noted that Indian English is but one example of a variety of Englis*es,* which, especially in Third World countries where English has become an international language, can be acquired very successfully for instrumental reasons alone.

In the face of claims and counter claims about integrative and instrumental motivation, Au (1988) reviewed twenty-seven different studies of the integrative-instrumental construct and concluded that both its theoretical underpinnings and the instruments used to measure motivation were suspect. Because the dichotomy is based on notions about cultural beliefs, numerous ambiguities have crept into the construct, making it difficult to attribute foreign language success to certain presumably integrative or instrumental causes. To further muddy the waters, even Gardner himself, with his associates, have recently found that certain contexts point toward instrumental orientation as an effective motive for language success (Gardner and MacIntyre 1991), and that others favor integrative motivation (Gardner, Day, and MacIntyre 1992).

Such variable findings in empirical investigations do not necessarily invalidate the integrative-instrumental construct. They point out once again that there is no single means of learning a second language: some learners in some contexts are more successful in learning a language if they are integratively oriented, and others in different contexts benefit from an instrumental orientation. The findings also suggest that the two types of motivation are not necessarily mutually exclusive. Second language learning is rarely motivated by attitudes that are exclusively instrumental or exclusively integrative. Most situations involve a mixture of each type of motivation. For example, Chinese speakers learning English in the United States for academic purposes may be relatively balanced in their desire to learn English both for academic (instrumental) purposes and to understand and become somewhat integrated with the culture and people of the United States.

The instrumental/integrative construct does, however, help to put some of the recent interest in affective variables into some perspective. It is easy to conclude that second language learning is an emotional activity involving countless affective variables, or to assert that learning a second language involves taking on a new identity (see Chapter Seven). But the findings of studies like those of Lukmani and Kachru warn us that while perhaps some contexts of foreign language learning involve an identity crisis, there are a good many legitimate language learning contexts in which that identity crisis may be minimized, or at least seen as less of a personal affective crisis and more of a cognitive crisis. Do children in French-speaking Africa, who must learn French in order to succeed in educational settings, and who are quite instrumentally motivated to do so, meet with an identity crisis? Must they take on a "French" identity? It is possible that they do not, just as children learning English in India tend to learn *Indian* English as an integral part of their own culture. In some cases, then, the foreign language does not carry with it the heavy cultural loading that some have assumed to be characteristic of all language learning contexts.

In an expansion of the construct of integrative motivation, Graham (1984) claimed that integrative motivation had been too broadly defined in previous research. He made a distinction between integrative and *assimilative* motivation. Integrative motivation is the desire on the part of a language learner to learn the second language in order to communicate with, or find out about, members of the second language culture, and does not necessarily imply direct contact with the second language group. Assimilative motivation is the drive to become an indistinguishable member of a speech community, and it usually requires prolonged contact with the second language culture. Assimilative motivation is characteristic of persons who, perhaps at a very young age, learn a second language and second culture in order to identify almost exclusively with that second culture. Seen in this light, integrative motivation takes on less of a pervading affective character and becomes more of a simple contrast to instrumental motivation. One can be integratively oriented without desiring to "lose oneself" in the target culture.

# Intrinsic and Extrinsic Motivation

Yet another but perhaps the most powerful dimension of the whole motivation construct in general is the degree to which learners are *intrinsically* or *extrinsically* motivated to succeed in a task. Edward Deci (1975:23) defined intrinsic motivation:

> Intrinsically motivated activities are ones for which there is no apparent reward except the activity itself. People seem to engage in the activities for their own sake and not because they lead to an extrinsic reward. . . . Intrinsically motivated

behaviors are aimed at bringing about certain internally rewarding consequences, namely, feelings of *competence* and *self-determination.*

Extrinsically motivated behaviors, on the other hand, are carried out in anticipation of a reward from outside and beyond the self. Typical extrinsic rewards are money, prizes, grades, and even certain types of positive feedback. Behaviors initiated solely to avoid punishment are also extrinsically motivated, even though numerous intrinsic benefits can ultimately accrue to those who, instead, view punishment avoidance as a challenge that can build their sense of competence and self-determination.

Which form of motivation is more powerful? Our growing stockpile of research on motivation (see Crookes and Schmidt 1991; Brown 1990) strongly favors intrinsic orientations, especially for long-term retention. Jean Piaget and others would point out that human beings universally view incongruity, uncertainty, and "disequilibrium" as motivating. In other words, we seek out a reasonable challenge. Then we initiate behaviors intended to conquer the challenging situation. Incongruity is not itself motivating, but optimal incongruity—or what Krashen (1985) called "i+1" (see Chapter Eleven)—presents enough of a possibility of being resolved that we will go after that resolution.

Maslow (1970) claimed that intrinsic motivation is clearly superior to extrinsic. According to his hierarchy of needs discussed above, we are ultimately motivated to achieve "self-actualization" once the basic physical, safety, and community needs are met. No matter what extrinsic rewards are present or absent, we will strive for self-esteem and fulfillment.

## TABLE 6–2.   Motivational Dichotomies

|  | INTRINSIC | EXTRINSIC |
|---|---|---|
| *Integrative* | L2 learner wishes to integrate with the L2 culture (e.g., for immigration or marriage) | Someone else wishes the L2 learner to know the L2 for integrative reasons (e.g., Japanese parents send kids to Japanese-language school) |
| *Instrumental* | L2 learner wishes to achieve goals utilizing L2 (e.g., for a career) | External power wants L2 learner to learn L2 (e.g., corporation sends Japanese businessman to U.S. for language training) |

Jerome Bruner (1962), praising the "autonomy of self-reward," claimed that one of the most effective ways to help both children and adults to think and learn is to free them from the control of rewards and punishments. One the principal weaknesses of extrinsically driven behavior is its addictive nature. Once captivated, as it were, by the lure of an immediate prize or praise, our dependency on those tangible rewards increases, even to the point that their withdrawal can then extinguish the desire to learn. Ramage (1990), for example, found that foreign language high school students who were interested in continuing their study beyond the college entrance requirement were positively and intrinsically motivated to succeed. In contrast, those who were only in the classes to fulfill entrance requirements exhibited low motivation and weaker performance.

It is important to distinguish the intrinsic-extrinsic construct from Gardner's integrative-instrumental motivation. While many instances of intrinsic motivation may indeed turn out to be integrative, some may not. For example, one could, for highly developed intrinsic purposes, wish to learn a second language in order to advance in a career or to succeed in an academic program. Likewise, one could develop a positive affect toward the speakers of a second language for extrinsic reasons: parental reinforcement, teacher's encouragement, etc. Kathleen Bailey (1986) illustrated the relationship between the two dichotomies with the following diagram (Table 6-2):

The intrinsic-extrinsic continuum in motivation is applicable to foreign language classrooms around the world. Regardless of the cultural beliefs and attitudes of learners and teachers, intrinsic and extrinsic factors can be quite easily identified—much more universally so than the integrative-instrumental continuum that relies exclusively on a social-psychological approach. One's attitude toward target language culture is but one of many aspects of this complex phenomenon that we call motivation. By looking at motivation "in terms of choice, engagement, and persistence, as determined by interest, relevance, expectancy, and outcomes, . . . the concept of motivation [will have] a more satisfactory connection to language-learning processes and language pedagogy." (Crookes and Schmidt 1991:502) And our fervent quest in this language teaching business is, of course, to see to it that our pedagogical tools can harness the power of intrinsically motivated learners who are striving for excellence, autonomy, and self-actualization.

## In the Classroom: Putting Methods into Perspective

In the century spanning the mid 1880s to the mid 1980s, the language teaching profession was involved in a search. That search was for what has popularly been called "methods," or ideally, a single method, generalizable across widely varying audiences, that would successfully teach students a foreign language in the classroom. Historical accounts of the profession tend therefore to describe a succession of methods each of which are more or less discarded in due course of time as a new method takes its place.

The first four of these end-of-chapter vignettes on classroom practice gave you a brief sketch of that hundred year "method-ical" history. From the revolutionary turn-of-the-century methods espoused by François Gouin and Charles Berlitz, through yet another revolution—the Audiolingual Method—in the middle of the twentieth century, and through the spirited "designer" methods of the seventies, we come now to the threshold of a new century. But this time around, *methods,* as distinct, theoretically unified clusters of teaching practices presumably appropriate for a wide variety of audiences, are no longer the object of our search. Instead, the last few years of the twentieth century have been characterized by an enlightened, dynamic *approach* to language teaching in which teachers and curriculum developers are searching for valid communicative, interactive techniques suitable for specified learners pursuing specific goals in specific contexts.

In order to understand this new paradigm shift in language teaching, it will be useful to examine what is meant by some commonly used terms—words like method, approach, technique, procedure, etc.

What is a method? Three decades ago Edward Anthony (1963) gave us a definition that has quite admirably withstood the test of time. His concept of method was the second of three hierarchical elements, namely, approach, method, and technique. An *approach,* according to Anthony, is a set of assumptions dealing with the nature of language, learning, and teaching. *Method* is an overall plan for systematic presentation of language based upon a selected approach. *Techniques* are the specific activities manifested in the classroom, which are consistent with a method and therefore in harmony with an approach as well.

To this day, Anthony's terms are still in common use among language teachers. A teacher may, for example, at the approach level, affirm the ultimate importance of learning in a relaxed state of mental awareness just above the threshold of consciousness. The method that follows might resemble, say, Suggestopedia. Techniques could include playing Baroque music while reading a passage in the foreign language, getting students to sit in the yoga position while listening to a list of words, learners adopting a new name in the classroom, or role-playing that new person.

A couple of decades later, Jack Richards and Theodore Rodgers (1982, 1986) proposed a reformulation of the concept of method. Anthony's approach, method, and technique were renamed, respectively, *approach, design,* and *procedure,* with a superordinate term to describe this three-step process now called *method.* A method, according to Richards and Rodgers, "is an umbrella term for the specification and interrelation of theory and practice." (1982:1564) An approach defines assumptions, beliefs, and theories about the nature of language and language learning. Designs specify the relationship of those theories to classroom materials and activities. Procedures are the techniques and practices that are derived from one's approach and design.

Through their reformulation, Richards and Rodgers made two principal contributions to our understanding of the concept of method:

1. First, they specified the necessary elements of language teaching "designs" that had heretofore been left somewhat vague. They named six important features of "designs:" objectives, syllabus (criteria for selection and organization of linguistic and subject/matter content), activities, learner roles, teacher roles, and the role of instructional materials.

2. Second, Richards and Rodgers nudged us into at last relinquishing the notion that separate, definable, discrete method*s* are the essential building blocks of *methodology.* By helping us to think in terms of an approach that undergirds our language designs (or, we could say, curricula), which are realized by various procedures (or, techniques), we could see that methods, as we still use and understand the term, are too restrictive, too pre-programmed, and too "pre-packaged." Virtually all language teaching methods make the oversimplified assumption that what teachers "do" in the classroom can be conventionalized into a set of procedures that fits all contexts. We are now all too aware that such is clearly not the case.

Richards and Rodgers' reformulation of the concept of method was soundly conceived; however, their attempt to give new meaning to an old term has not caught on in the pedagogical literature. What they would like us to call "method" is more comfortably referred to, I think, as "methodology," in order to avoid confusion with what we will no doubt always think of as those separate entities (like Audiolingual or Suggestopedia) that are no longer at the center of our teaching philosophy.

Another terminological problem lies in the use of the term "designs;" instead, we more comfortably refer to curricula or syllabuses when we refer to design features of a language program.

What are we left with in this lexicographic confusion? Interestingly, the terminology of the pedagogical literature in the field appears to be more in line with Anthony's original terms, but with some important additions and refinements. Following is a set of definitions that reflect the current usage.

**Methodology:** The study of pedagogical practices in general (including theoretical underpinnings and related research). Whatever considerations are involved in "how to teach" are methodological.

**Approach:** Theoretical positions and beliefs about the nature of language, the nature of language learning, and the applicability of both to pedagogical settings.

**Method:** A generalized, prescribed set of classroom specifications for accomplishing linguistic objectives. Methods tend to be primarily concerned with teacher and student roles and behaviors, and secondarily with such features as linguistic and subject-matter objectives, sequencing, and materials. They are almost always thought of as being broadly applicable to a variety of audiences in a variety of contexts.

**Curriculum/syllabus:** Designs for carrying out a particular language program. Features include a primary concern with the specification of linguistic and subject-matter objectives, sequencing, and materials to meet the needs of a designated group of learners in a defined context. (The term "syllabus" is used more customarily in the United Kingdom to refer to what is referred to as a "curriculum" in the United States.)

**Technique** (also commonly referred to by other terms[1]): Any of a wide variety of exercises, activities, or devices used in the language classroom for realizing lesson objectives.

And so, ironically, the **methods** that were such strong signposts of our century-old language teaching journey are no longer of great consequence in marking our progress. How did that happen?

In the seventies and early eighties, there was a good deal of hoopla about the "designer" methods described in the earlier vignettes. Even though they weren't widely adopted as standard methods, they were nevertheless symbolic of a profession at least partially caught up in a mad scramble to invent a new method when the very concept of method was eroding under our feet. We didn't need a new method. We needed, instead, to get on with the business of unifying our **approach** to language teaching and of designing effective tasks and techniques that are informed by that approach.

Today, those clearly identifiable and enterprising methods are an interesting if not insightful contribution to our professional repertoire, but few practitioners look to any one of them, or their predecessors, for a final answer on how to teach a foreign language. Method, as a unified, cohesive, finite set of design features is now given only minor attention.[2] The profession has at last reached the point of maturity where we recognize that the complexity of language learners in multiple worldwide contexts demands an eclectic blend of tasks each tailored for a particular group of learners in a particular place, studying for particular purposes in a given amount of time. David Nunan (1991b:228) sums it up nicely: ". . . It has been realised that there never was and probably never will be a method for all, and the focus in recent years has been on the development of classroom tasks and activities which are consonant with what we know about second language acquisition, and which are also in keeping with the dynamics of the classroom itself."

## Suggested Readings

*Bloom's* (Krathwohl, Bloom, and Masia 1964) classic taxonomy of the affective domain has been widely used in educational circles for a number of

---

[1]There is currently quite an intermingling of such terms as technique, task, procedure, activity, and exercise, often used in somewhat careless free variation across the profession. Of these terms, task has received the most concerted attention recently, viewed by such scholars as David Nunan (1991a) as incorporating specific communicative and pedagogical principles. Tasks, according to Nunan and others, should be thought of as a special kind of technique, and in fact, may actually include more than one technique.

[2]While we may have outgrown our need to search for such definable methods, nevertheless the term "methodology" continues to be used, as it would in any other behavioral science, to refer to the systematic application of validated principles to practical contexts. You need not therefore subscribe to a particular Method (with a capital M) in order to engage in a "methodology."

years. You will find that reading portions of it, especially pages 95–185, will provide a more technical understanding of levels of affectivity.

Because it is one of the earliest experiments on affective variables in second language acquisition, *Guiora's* (1972a) study of the effect of alcohol-induced inhibition on second language pronunciation is recommended reading. *Guiora's* (1972b) article on empathy in second language learning is also informative.

*Stevick's* (1976b) highly readable article on the alienation felt by language learners is an excellent resource for understanding the affective nature of language learning.

For an excellent set of summaries of research on risk-taking and anxiety, respectively, look at *Beebe's* (1983) and *MacIntyre and Gardner's* (1991) reviews of the research on the topics.

*Keirsey and Bates* (1984) is written for the lay psychologist. It has a wealth of information on the Myers-Briggs test. *Lawrence's* (1984) little volume, also directed toward a nontechnical audience, is an interesting application of Myers-Briggs categories to educational contexts.

A comprehensive summary of research and issues on motivation, especially integrative and instrumental motivation, can be found in *Gardner's* (1985) book.

Various theories of motivation, especially alternatives to Gardner's dichotomy, are offered in an excellent review article by *Crookes and Schmidt* (1991).

Intrinsic and extrinsic motivation are defined and applied to classroom practice by *Brown* (1990).

More information on Community Language Learning is available in *LaForge* (1971) and *Curran* (1976). The latter is a comprehensive treatment of the theory behind Community Language Learning. *Brown's* (1977b) critique of Community Language Learning put the method into some perspective.

## Topics and Questions for Study and Discussion

1. How would you relate Bloom's levels of affectivity to the second language learning process? Do you see the levels manifested in the classroom or in a conversation group?

2. Restate the chicken-or-egg question in relating self-esteem to second language learning. Can you *teach* self-esteem? What can a teacher do with a student who apparently has very low self-esteem?

3. Give some examples of the manifestation of inhibition in children. How about adults? And yourself? How might these inhibitions hamper language acquisition? In your own experience in language

learning, have you ever been troubled by your own inhibitions? How can a person overcome those inhibitions?

4.  Distinguish between empathy and sympathy. Give an example of a language learner empathizing with a native speaker but not sympathizing.

5.  What is meant by "cognitive empathy" (p. 144)? Why does written communication require a different kind of empathy than oral communication? Which mode of communication might therefore more readily reveal a person's degree of empathy?

6.  How is empathy expressed in cultures other than your own? Can empathy be defined cross-culturally? How might different manifestations of empathy be misunderstood in second language learning contexts?

7.  Virtually no research has been done so far to see if the Myers-Briggs categories bear any relationship to second language learning. What might some possible hypotheses be? How would you go about finding support for your hypotheses?

8.  Explain the connection between motivation and reinforcement.

9.  Distinguish between integrative and instrumental motivation to learn a language. In the case of your second language, do you feel you were more instrumentally or more integratively motivated? Why? Why does it appear that instrumental and integrative orientations are not mutually exclusive?

10. Review the definitions of intrinsic and extrinsic motivation. Is it idealistic to expect students to be totally intrinsically motivated? How can small doses of extrinsic motivation help to instill intrinsic? Illustrate, if possible, with classroom examples.

# Chapter 7

# SOCIOCULTURAL FACTORS

The previous chapter examined one aspect of the affective domain of second language acquisition: how those very personal variables within oneself and the reflection of that self to other people affect our communicative interaction. This chapter touches on a major and very crucial aspect of the communicative process, an aspect that is still very much a part of the egocentric self in a trans-actional process but a specialized subset of that process: the learning of another culture, the overcoming of the personal and transactional barriers presented by two cultures in contact, and the relationship of culture learning to second language learning.

Culture is a way of life. Culture is the context within which we exist, think, feel, and relate to others. It is the "glue" that binds a group of people together. Several centuries ago, John Donne (1624) had this to say about culture in his *Devotions upon Emergent Occasions* (number 17):

> No man is an island, entire of itself; every man is a piece of the continent, a part of the main; . . . any man's death diminishes me, because I am involved in mankind; and therefore never send to know for whom the bell tolls; it tolls for thee.

Culture is our continent, our collective identity. Larson and Smalley (1972:39) described culture as a "blueprint" that

> guides the behavior of people in a community and is incubated in family life. It governs our behavior in groups, makes us sensitive to matters of status, and helps

us know what others expect of us and what will happen if we do not live up to their expectations. Culture helps us to know how far we can go as individuals and what our responsibility is to the group. Different cultures are the underlying structures which make Round community round and Square community square.

Culture might be defined as the ideas, customs, skills, arts, and tools that characterize a given group of people in a given period of time. But culture is more than the sum of its parts. "It is a system of integrated patterns, most of which remain below the threshold of consciousness, yet all of which govern human behavior just as surely as the manipulated strings of a puppet control its motions" (Condon 1973:4). The fact that no society exists without a culture reflects the need for culture to fulfill certain biological and psychological needs in human beings. Consider the bewildering host of confusing and contradictory facts and propositions and ideas that present themselves every day to any human being; some organization of these facts is necessary to provide some order to potential chaos, and therefore conceptual networks of reality evolve within a group of people for such organization. The mental constructs that enable us thus to survive are a way of life that we call "culture."

These constructs are infinitely diverse, and therefore cultures have widely differing characteristics. Nevertheless, such patterns for living have, in the view of some anthropologists, universal characteristics. George Peter Murdock (1961:45–54) cites seven "universals" of cultural patterns of behavior: (1) they originate in the human mind; (2) they facilitate human and environmental interactions; (3) they satisfy basic human needs; (4) they are cumulative and adjust to changes in external and internal conditions; (5) they tend to form a consistent structure; (6) they are learned and shared by all the members of a society; and (7) they are transmitted to new generations.

Culture thus establishes for each person a context of cognitive and affective behavior, a blueprint for personal and social existence. But we tend to perceive reality strictly within the context of our own culture; this is a reality that we have "created," not necessarily "objective" reality, if indeed there is any such thing as objectivity in its ultimate sense. "The meaningful universe in which each human being exists is not a universal reality, but 'a category of reality' consisting of selectively organized features considered significant by the society in which he lives" (Condon 1973:17). Although the opportunities for world travel in the last quarter of this century are increasing, there is still a tendency for us to believe that our own reality is the "correct" perception. Perception, though, is always quite subjective. Perception involves the filtering of information even before it is stored in memory, resulting in a selective form of consciousness. What appears to you to be an accurate and objective perception of a person, a custom, an idea, is sometimes "jaded" or "stilted" in the view of someone from another culture. Misunderstandings are therefore likely to occur between members of different cultures. We will probably never be able to answer the question of how perception came to be shaped in different ways by different cultural groups; it is another chicken-or-egg question. But differences are real, and we must learn to deal with them in any situation in which two cultures come into contact.

It is apparent that culture, as an ingrained set of behaviors and modes of perception, becomes highly important in the learning of a second language. A language is a part of a culture and a culture is a part of a language; the two are intricately interwoven so that one cannot separate the two without losing the significance of either language or culture. The acquisition of a second language, except for specialized, instrumental acquisition (as may be the case, say, in "Indian" English), is also the acquisition of a second culture. Both linguists (see Lado 1957) and anthropologists (see Burling 1970) bear ample testimony to this observation.

The sections of this chapter attempt to capture some of the important aspects of the relationship between learning a second language and learning the cultural context of the second language. An examination of the notion of cultural stereotypes and attitudes will precede a discussion of what it means to "learn" another culture, followed by a section on the relationship among language, thought, and culture.

# Cultural Stereotypes

Mark Twain gave us a delightfully biased view of other cultures and other languages in *The Innocents Abroad.* In reference to the French language, Twain comments that the French "always tangle up everything to that degree that when you start into a sentence you never know whether you are going to come out alive or not." In *A Trump Abroad,* Twain notes that German is a most difficult language: "A gifted person ought to learn English (barring spelling and pronouncing) in 30 hours, French in 30 days, and German in 30 years." So he proposed to reform the German language, for "if it is to remain as it is, it ought to be gently and reverently set aside among the dead languages, for only the dead have time to learn it."

Twain, like all of us at times, has expressed caricatures of certain languages. Such caricatures are not unlike linguistic and cultural stereotypes. In the bias of our own culture-bound world view, we picture other cultures in an oversimplified manner, lumping cultural differences into exaggerated categories, and then we view every person in a culture as possessing corresponding stereotypical traits. Thus Americans are all rich, informal, materialistic, and overly friendly. Italians are passionate and demonstrative. The British are reserved, polite, thrifty, and drink tea. Germans are stubborn, industrious, methodical, and drink beer. Orientals are reserved, wise, cunning, and "inscrutable." François Lierres, writing in the Paris newsmagazine *Le Point,* gave some tongue-in-cheek advice to French people on how to get along with Americans: "They are the Vikings of the world economy, descending upon it in their jets as the Vikings once did in their *drakars.* They have money, technology, and nerve. . . . We would be wise to get acquainted with them." Upon which he offered some *do's* and *don't's.* Among the *do's:* Greet them, but after you have been introduced once, don't shake hands, merely emit a brief cluck of joy—"hi." Speak without emotion, with self-assurance, giving the impression you have a command of the subject even if you haven't. Check the collar of your jacket—nothing is uglier in the eyes of an American than dandruff. Radiate congeniality and show a good disposition—a big smile and a warm expression are essential. Learn how to play golf. Then, among the *don't's:* Don't tamper with your accent—Maurice Chevalier is well-liked in America. And don't allow the slightest smell of perspiration to reach the offended nostrils of your American friends.

How do stereotypes form? Our cultural milieu shapes our world view— our *Weltanschauung*—in such a way that reality is thought to be objectively perceived through our own cultural pattern, and a differing perception is seen as either false or "strange" and is thus oversimplified. If people recognize and understand differing world views, they will usually adopt a positive and open-minded attitude toward cross-cultural differences. A closed-minded view of such differences often results in the maintenance of a *stereotype*—an oversimplification and blanket assumption. A stereotype is a category that singles out an individual as sharing assumed characteristics on the basis of his or her group membership. The stereotype may be accurate in depicting the "typical" member of a culture, but it is inaccurate for describing a particular person, simply because every person is a unique individual and all of a person's behavioral characteristics cannot be accurately predicted on the basis of cultural norms.

Cross-cultural research has shown that there are indeed characteristics of culture that make one culture different from another. Condon (1973) concluded from cross-cultural research that American, French, and Hispanic world views are quite different in their concept of time and space. Americans tend to be dominated by a "psychomotor" view of time and space that is dynamic, diffuse, and nominalistic. French orientation is more "cognitive" with a static, centralized, and universalistic view. The Hispanic orientation is more "affectively" centered with a passive, relational, and intuitive world view. It is from these general but reasonably accurate descriptions that stereotypes emerge.

Are cultural stereotypes "bad"? Not necessarily, if a person recognizes positive effects of stereotyping. It was noted in Chapter Four that all human beings organize the environment by means of systematic and meaningful storage. Having developed one particular world view—one set of tools for storing experiences and for reacting to others in our culture—we place incongruous or different world views into categories for meaningful understanding. Since one person is not an integral part of another world view, that other world view is simplified. Sometimes these perceptions are accurate. To say that Americans think of distances in relatively broad categories (60 miles is an easy jaunt) and that the French view distances in narrower categories (60 miles, or 100 kilometers, is a considerable travel distance) is reasonably accurate. So the cautious accumulation of stereotyped images can help a person to understand another culture in general and the differences between that culture and his or her own.

But there are obvious negative connotations of stereotyping. One is the idea that all persons in a culture fit neatly into a group of rigid categories. Clearly not all Americans are rich, friendly, and materialistic even though that may be a fairly accurate stereotype of an American in general. And to judge a single member of a culture by overall traits of the culture is both to prejudge and to misjudge that person. The most destructive aspect of stereotyping is that which is derogatory or falls short of valuing and prizing people from different cultures. Mark Twain's comments about the French and German languages, while written in a humorous vein and without any malice, could be interpreted by some to be insulting.

False stereotyping is another negative aspect of cultural stereotyping. Sometimes our oversimplified concepts of members of another culture are downright false. Americans sometimes think of Japanese as being unfriendly because of their cultural norms of respect and politeness. The false view that members of another culture are "dirty" or "smelly"—with verbal and nonverbal messages conveying that view—in fact usually stems merely from different customs of so-called cleanliness. Muriel Saville-Troike (1976:51) notes that "Middle-class whites may objectively note that the lower socioeconomic classes frequently lack proper bathing facilities or changes of clothing, but may be surprised to discover that a common stereotype blacks hold of whites is that they 'smell like dogs coming in out of the rain.' Asians have a similar stereotype of Caucasians."

Both learners and teachers of a second language need to understand cultural differences, to recognize openly that everyone in the world is not "just like me," that people are *not* all the same beneath the skin. There are real differences between groups and cultures. We can learn to perceive those differences, appreciate them, and above all to respect, value, and prize the personhood of every human being.

# Attitudes

Stereotyping usually implies some type of *attitude* toward the culture or language in question. I recently happened upon an incredible example of a negative attitude stemming from a stereotype; the following passage is an excerpt from an item on "Chinese literature" in the *New Standard Encyclopedia* published in 1940:

> The Chinese Language is monosyllabic and uninflectional. . . . With a language so incapable of variation, a literature cannot be produced which possesses the qualities we look for and admire in literary works. Elegance, variety, beauty of imagery—these must all be lacking. A monotonous and wearisome language must give rise to a forced and formal literature lacking in originality and interesting in its subject matter only. Moreover, a conservative people . . . , profoundly reverencing all that is old and formal, and hating innovation, must leave the impress of its own character upon its literature. (Volume VI)

Fortunately, one would probably not find such views expressed in encyclopedias today. Such biased attitudes are based on insufficient knowledge, misinformed stereotyping, and extreme ethnocentric thinking.

Attitudes, like all aspects of the development of cognition and affect in human beings, develop early in childhood and are the result of parents' and peers' attitudes, contact with people who are "different" in any number of ways, and interacting affective factors in the human experience. These attitudes form a part of one's perception of self, of others, and of the culture in which one is living.

Gardner and Lambert's (1972) extensive studies were systematic attempts to examine the effect of attitudes on language learning. After studying the interrelationships of a number of different types of attitudes, they defined motivation as a construct made up of certain attitudes. The most important of these is group-specific, the attitude learners have toward the members of the cultural group whose language they are learning. Thus, in Gardner and Lambert's model, an English-speaking Canadian's positive attitude toward French-Canadians—a desire to understand them, and to empathize with them—will lead to high integrative motivation to learn French. That attitude is a factor of learners' attitudes toward their own native culture, their degree of ethnocentrism, and the extent to which they prefer their own language over the one they are learning as a second language. Among the Canadian subjects Gardner and Lambert distinguished between attitudes toward French-Canadians and attitudes toward people from France.

John Oller and his colleagues (see Oller, Hudson, and Liu 1977; Chihara and Oller 1978; Oller, Baca, and Vigil 1978) conducted several large-scale studies of the relationship between attitudes and language success. They looked at the relationship of Chinese, Japanese, and Mexican students' achievement in English to their attitudes toward self, the native language group, the target language group, their reasons for learning English, and their reasons for traveling to the United States. The researchers were able to identify a few meaningful clusters of attitudinal variables that correlated positively with attained proficiency. Each of the three studies yielded slightly different conclusions, but for the most part, positive attitudes toward self, the native language group, and the target language group enhanced proficiency. There were mixed results on the relative advantages and disadvantages of integrative and instrumental motivation. For example, in one study they found that better proficiency was attained by students who did not want to stay in the United States permanently. All of the above attitude studies, however, now need to be viewed in the light of Oller's (1981b, 1982) more recent remarks, referred to in the previous chapter, that cast some shadows of doubt on the validity of any study that relies on self-report measures of affective variables.

It seems intuitively clear, nevertheless, that second language learners benefit from positive attitudes and that negative attitudes may lead to decreased motivation and in all likelihood, because of decreased input and interaction, to unsuccessful attainment of proficiency. Yet the teacher needs to be aware that everyone has both positive and negative attitudes. The negative attitudes *can* be changed, often by exposure to reality—for example, by encounters with actual persons from other cultures. Negative attitudes usually emerge either from false stereotyping or from undue ethnocentrism. The quotation from the encyclopedia above might lead one to stereotype Chinese incorrectly and therefore to develop a negative attitude toward learning a language that reportedly lacks "elegance, variety, beauty of imagery." Teachers can aid in dispelling what are often myths about other cultures, and replace those myths with a realistic understanding of the other culture as one that is different from one's own, yet to be respected and valued. Learners can thus move through the hierarchy of affectivity as described by Bloom in the preceding chapter, through awareness and responding, to valuing, and finally to an organized and systematic understanding and appreciation of the foreign culture.

# Acculturation

In Chapter Six we saw that second language learning in some respects involves the acquisition of a second identity. Guiora introduced the concept of language ego to capture the deeply seated affective nature of second language learning, stressing the necessity for permeable ego boundaries in order to successfully overcome the barriers to second language learning. Others have placed strong emphasis on affective characteristics of second language learning because of the highly *social* context of language. Second language learning is often second culture learning. In order to understand just what second culture learning is, one needs to understand the nature of acculturation, culture shock, and social distance.

If a French person is primarily cognitive-oriented and an American is psychomotor-oriented and a Spanish speaker is affective-oriented, as claimed by Condon (1973:22), it is not difficult on this plane alone to understand the complexity of *acculturation,* the process of becoming adapted to a new culture. A reorientation of thinking and feeling, not to mention communication, is necessary.

For instance, to a European or a South American, the overall impression created by American culture is that of a frantic, perpetual round of actions which leave practically no time for personal feeling and reflection. But, to an American, the reasonable and orderly tempo of French life conveys a sense of hopeless backwardness and ineffectuality; and the leisurely timelessness of Spanish activities represents an appalling waste of time and human potential. And, to a Spanish speaker, the methodical essence of planned change in France may seem cold-blooded, just as much as his own proclivity toward spur-of-the-moment decisions may strike his French counterpart as recklessly irresponsible. (Condon 1973:25)

The process of acculturation runs even deeper when language is brought into the picture. To be sure, culture is a deeply ingrained part of the very fiber of our being, but language—the means for communication among members of a culture—is the most visible and available expression of that culture. And so a person's world view, self-identity, and systems of thinking, acting, feeling, and communicating can be disrupted by a change from one culture to another.

*Culture shock* is a common experience for a person learning a second language in a second culture. Culture shock refers to phenomena ranging from mild irritability to deep psychological panic and crisis. Culture shock is associated with feelings in the learner of estrangement, anger, hostility, indecision, frustration, unhappiness, sadness, loneliness, homesickness, and even physical illness. Persons undergoing culture shock view their new world out of resentment and alternate between being angry at others for not understanding them and being filled with self-pity. Edward Hall (1959:59) describes a hypothetical example of an American living abroad for the first time:

At first, things in the cities look pretty much alike. There are taxis, hotels with hot and cold running water, theatres, neon lights, even tall buildings with elevators and a few people who can speak English. But pretty soon the American discovers that underneath the familiar exterior there are vast differences. When someone says "yes" it often doesn't mean yes at all, and when people smile it doesn't always mean they are pleased. When the American visitor makes a helpful gesture he may be rebuffed; when he tries to be friendly nothing happens. People tell him that they will do things and don't. The longer he stays, the more enigmatic the new country looks. . . .

This case of an American in Japan illustrates the point that initially persons in a foreign culture are comfortable and delighted with the "exotic" surroundings. As long as they can perceptually filter their surroundings and internalize the environment in their *own* world view, they feel at ease. As soon as this newness wears off, and the cognitive and affective contradictions of the foreign culture mount up, they become disoriented.

Peter Adler (1972:8) described culture shock in more technical psychological terms:

Culture shock, then, is thought to be a form of anxiety that results from the loss of commonly perceived and understood signs and symbols of social intercourse. The individual undergoing culture shock reflects his anxiety and nervousness with cultural differences through any number of defense mechanisms: repression, regression, isolation and rejection. These defensive attitudes speak, in behavioral terms, of a basic underlying insecurity which may encompass loneliness, anger, frustration and self-questioning of competence. With the familiar props, cues, and clues of cultural understanding removed, the individual becomes disoriented, afraid of, and alienated from the things that he knows and understands.

The anthropologist George M. Foster (1962:87) thought of culture shock in extreme terms: "Culture shock is a mental illness, and as is true of much mental illness, the victim usually does not know he is afflicted. He finds that he is irritable, depressed, and probably annoyed by the lack of attention shown him."

It is feasible to think of culture shock as one of four successive stages of acculturation. The first stage is the period of excitement and euphoria over the newness of the surroundings. The second stage—culture shock—emerges as individuals feel the intrusion of more and more cultural differences into their own images of self and security. In this stage individuals rely on and seek out the support of their fellow countrymen in the second culture, taking solace in complaining about local customs and conditions, seeking escape from their predicament. The third stage is one of gradual, and at first tentative and vacillating, recovery. This stage is typified by what Larson and Smalley (1972) called *culture stress*: some problems of acculturation are solved while other problems continue for some time. But general progress is made, slowly but surely, as individuals begin to accept the differences in thinking and feeling that surround them, slowly becoming more empathic with other persons in the second culture. The fourth stage represents near or full recovery, either assimilation or adaptation, acceptance of the new culture and self-confidence in the "new" person that has developed in this culture.

Wallace Lambert's (1967) work on attitudes in second language learning referred often to Durkheim's (1897) concept of *anomie*—feelings of social uncertainty or dissatisfaction—as a significant aspect of the relationship between language learning and attitude toward the foreign culture. As individuals begin to lose some of the ties of their native culture and adapt to the second culture, they experience feelings of chagrin or regret, mixed with the fearful anticipation of entering a new group. Anomie might be described as the first symptom of the third stage of acculturation, a feeling of homelessness, where one feels neither bound firmly to one's native culture nor fully adapted to the second culture. Lambert's research has supported the view that the strongest dose of anomie is experienced when linguistically a person begins to "master" the foreign language. In Lambert's (1967) study, for example, when English-speaking Canadians became so skilled in French that they began to "think" in French, and even dream in French, feelings of anomie were markedly high. For Lambert's subjects the interaction of anomie and increased skill in the language sometimes led persons to revert or to "regress" back to English—to seek out situations in which they could speak English. Such an urge corresponds to the tentativeness of the third stage of acculturation—periodic reversion to the escape mechanisms acquired in the stage of culture shock. Only until a person is well into the third stage do feelings of anomie decrease as the learner is "over the hump" in the transition from one culture to another.

In keeping with these bleak descriptions of culture shock, Mark Clarke (1976:380) likened second language learning and second culture learning to *schizophrenia,* where "social encounters become inherently threatening, and defense mechanisms are employed to reduce the trauma." Clarke cited Gregory Bateson's (1972:208) description of the "double bind" that foreigners experience in a new culture:

1.  . . . the individual is involved in an intense relationship; that is, a relationship in which he feels it is vitally important that he discriminate accurately what sort of message is being communicated so that he may respond appropriately.

2.  . . . the individual is caught in a situation in which the other person in the relationship is expressing two orders of message and one of these denies the other.

3.  . . . the individual is unable to comment on the messages being expressed to correct his discrimination of what order of message to respond to, i.e., he cannot make a metacommunicative statement.

Clarke then goes on to note that virtually every encounter with people in a foreign culture is an "intense relationship" in which tremendous effort is expended to keep communication from breaking down. For example, "Getting a taxi driver to understand where you want to go; attempting to discover if he has indeed understood you, given that he says he has, but continues to drive in the wrong direction; and searching frantically all the while for the proper phrases to express yourself so that you don't appear stupid or patronizing; all of this combines to give a simple ride across town Kafkaesque proportions which cannot be easily put in perspective by the person who has suffered through them" (p. 380). That such behavior can be compared with schizophrenia is clear from Bateson's (1972:211) description of alternatives commonly adopted by a schizophrenic to defend himself:

1.  He might . . . assume that behind every statement there is a concealed meaning which is detrimental to his welfare. . . . If he chooses this alternative, he will be continually searching for meanings

behind what people say and behind chance occurrences in the environment, and he will be characteristically suspicious and defiant.

2.  He might . . . tend to accept literally everything people say to him; when their tone or gesture or context contradicted what they said he might establish a pattern of laughing off these metacommunicative signals.

3.  If he didn't become suspicious of metacommunicative messages or attempt to laugh them off, he might choose to ignore them. Then he would find it necessary to see and hear less and less of what went on around him, and do his utmost to avoid provoking a response in his environment.

The schizophrenic period of culture shock and of language learning is therefore indeed a crucial period during which time the learner will either "sink or swim."

The description I have given of culture shock paints a rather severe picture of an unwitting and helpless victim of an illness, and an illness for which there is no clearcut cure. Peter Adler (1972:14) points out that culture shock, while surely possessing manifestations of crisis, can also be viewed more positively as a profound cross-cultural learning experience:

> a set of situations or circumstances involving intercultural communication in which the individual, as a result of the experiences, becomes aware of his own growth, learning and change. As a result of the culture shock process, the individual has gained a new perspective on himself, and has come to understand his own identity in terms significant to himself. The cross-cultural learning experience, additionally, takes place when the individual encounters a different culture and as a result (a) examines the degree to which he is influenced by his own culture, and (b) understands the culturally derived values, attitudes and outlooks of other people.

# Culture in the Classroom

While most learners can indeed find positive benefits in cross-cultural living or learning experiences, nevertheless a number of people experience certain psychological blocks and other inhibiting effects of the second culture. Teachers can help students to turn such an experience into one of increased cultural and self-awareness.

Stevick (1976b) cautioned that learners can feel alienation in the process of learning a second language, alienation from people in their home culture, the target culture, and from themselves. In teaching an "alien" language we need to be sensitive to the fragility of students by using techniques that promote cultural understanding. Donahue and Parsons (1982) examined the use of role-play in ESL classrooms as a means of helping students to overcome cultural "fatigue"; role-play promotes the process of cross-cultural dialog while at the same time it provides opportunities for oral communication. Numerous other materials and techniques—readings, films, simulation games, culture assimilators, "culture capsules," and "culturgrams"—are now available to language teachers to assist them in the process of acculturation in the classroom (McGroarty and Galvan 1985, Levine *et al.* 1987, Kohls 1984).

While these techniques and materials are valuable to us, no one would say that culture shock can be prevented with "affective vaccinations." But teachers can play a therapeutic role in helping learners to move through stages of acculturation. If learners are aided in this process by sensitive and perceptive teachers, they can perhaps more smoothly pass through the second stage and into the third stage of culture learning and thereby increase their chances for succeeding in both second language learning and second culture learning.

It is important that teachers allow learners to proceed into and through that second stage, through the anomie, and not to force a quick bypass of the second stage. We should not expect learners to deny the anger, the frustration, the helplessness and homelessness they feel. Those are real feelings and they need to be openly expressed. To smother those feelings may delay and actually prevent eventual movement into the third stage. A teacher can enable learners to understand the source of their anger and frustration, to express those feelings, and then gradually to emerge from those depths to a very powerful and personal form of learning.

Another way of looking at cross-cultural differences in classrooms focuses on students' *expectations* and behavior in educational institutions. In most developed countries, for example, thousands of foreign students are enrolled in institutions of higher education and must study the language of the country in order to pursue their academic objectives. Or, one might simply consider the multitude of immigrants who enter the educational stream of their new country after having received their early schooling in their previous country. They bring with them the cultural mores and patterns of "good" behavior learned in their home culture, and tend to apply those expectations to their new situation.

Consider, for a moment, Kenji, a university student from Japan who is studying at a pre-university language institute in the United States. This student has some very specific roles that for 12 years of schooling he has been taught to play. He must give the utmost "respect" to his teacher, which means a number of things: never contradict the teacher; never speak in class unless spoken to—always let the teacher initiate communication; let the teacher's wisdom be "poured into" him; never call a teacher by a first name; respect older teachers even more than younger teachers. But, in his new language school, his teachers are very friendly and encourage a first-name basis, they ask students to participate in group work, they try to get students to come up with answers to problems rather than just giving the answer, and so on. Kenji is confused. Why?

Some means of conceptualizing such mismatches in expectations were outlined in a very thought-provoking article by Geert Hofstede (1986). Four different conceptual categories were used to study the cultural norms of 50 different countries. Hofstede (1986:307–308) described each category:

1. *Individualism* as a characteristic of a culture opposes *Collectivism* (the word is used here in an anthropological, not a political sense). Individualist cultures assume that any person looks primarily after his/her own interest and the interest of his/her immediate family (husband, wife and children). Collectivist cultures assume that any person through birth and possible later events belongs to one or more tight "in-groups," from which he/she cannot detach him/herself. The "in-group" (whether extended family, clan, or organization) protects the interest of its members, but in turn expects their permanent loyalty. A collectivist society is tightly integrated; an individualist society is loosely integrated.

2. *Power Distance* as a characteristic of a culture defines the extent to which the less powerful persons in a society accept inequality in power and consider it as normal. Inequality exists within any culture, but the degree of it that is tolerated varies between one culture and another ("All societies are unequal, but some are more unequal than others"—Hofstede, 1980:136).

3. *Uncertainty Avoidance* as a characteristic of a culture defines the extent to which people within a culture are made nervous by situations which they perceive as unstructured, unclear, or unpredictable, situations which they therefore try to avoid by maintaining strict codes of behaviour and a belief in absolute truths. Cultures with a strong uncertainty avoidance are active, aggressive, emotional, compulsive, security-seeking, and intolerant; cultures with a weak uncertainty avoidance are contemplative, less aggressive, unemotional, relaxed, accepting personal risks, and relatively tolerant.

4. *Masculinity* as a characteristic of a culture opposes *Femininity*. The two differ in the social roles associated with the biological fact of the existence of two sexes, and in particular in the social roles attributed to *men*. The cultures which I labelled as *masculine* strive for maximal distinction between what men are expected to do and what women are expected to do. They expect men to be assertive, ambitious and competitive, to strive for material success, and to respect whatever is big, strong, and fast. They expect women to serve and to care for the non-material quality of life, for children and for

the weak. *Feminine* cultures, on the other hand, define relatively overlapping social roles for the sexes, in which, in particular, men need not be ambitious or competitive but may go for a different quality of life than material success; men may respect whatever is small, weak, and slow. So, in masculine cultures these political/organizational values stress material success and assertiveness; in feminine cultures they stress other types of quality of life, interpersonal relationships, and concern for the weak.

Table 7–1 shows Hofstede's conception of the manifestation of the first of the above four categories, individualism/collectivism.

Teachers who are charged with educating students (like Kenji, referred to on p. 174) whose cultural backgrounds differ from their own must of course attend to such factors as those that Hofstede has brought to our attention. The climate for effective classroom language acquisition may be considerably clouded by what students see as contradictory expectations for their participation, and as a result, certain unnecessary blocks stand in the way of their success.

# Social Distance

The concept of *social distance* has emerged as an affective construct to give explanatory power to the place of culture learning in second language learning. Social distance refers to the cognitive and affective proximity of two cultures that come into contact within an individual. "Distance" is obviously used in an abstract sense, to denote dissimilarity between two cultures. On a very superficial level one might observe, for example, that Americans (people from the United States) are culturally similar to Canadians, while Americans and Chinese are, by comparison, relatively dissimilar. We could say that the social distance of the latter case exceeds the former.

John Schumann (1976c:136) described social distance as consisting of the following parameters:

> In relation to the TL [target language] group, is the 2LL [second language learning] group politically, culturally, technically or economically dominant, non-dominant, or subordinate? Is the integration pattern of the 2LL group assimilation, acculturation, or preservation? What is the 2LL group's degree of enclosure? Is the 2LL group cohesive? What is the size of the 2LL group? Are the cultures of the two groups congruent? What are the attitudes of the two groups toward each other? What is the 2LL group's intended length of residence in the target language area?

Schumann used the above factors (dominance, integration pattern, cohesiveness, congruence, attitude, and length of residence) to describe hypothetically "good" and "bad" language learning situations, and illustrated each situation

**TABLE 7–1. Differences in Teacher/Student and Student/Student Interaction Related to the Individualism versus Collectivism Dimension (Hofstede 1986:312)**

| COLLECTIVIST SOCIETIES | INDIVIDUALIST SOCIETIES |
| --- | --- |
| • positive association in society with whatever is rooted in tradition | • positive association in society with whatever is "new" |
| • the young should learn; adults cannot accept student role | • one is never too old to learn; "permanent education" |
| • students expect to learn how to do | • students expect to learn how to learn |
| • individual students will only speak up in class when called upon personally by the teacher | • individual students will speak up in class in response to a general invitation by the teacher |
| • individuals will only speak up in small groups | • individuals will speak up in large groups |
| • large classes split socially into smaller, cohesive subgroups based on particularist criteria (e.g., ethnic affiliation) | • subgroupings in class vary from one situation to the next based on universalist criteria (e.g., the task "at hand") |
| • formal harmony in learning situations should be maintained at all times | • confrontation in learning situations can be salutary; conflicts can be brought into the open |
| • neither the teacher nor any student should ever be made to lose face | • face-consciousness is weak |
| • education is a way of gaining prestige in one's social environment and of joining a higher status group | • education is a way of improving one's economic worth and self-respect based on ability and competence |
| • diploma certificates are important and displayed on walls | • diploma certificates have little symbolic value |
| • acquiring certificates even through [dubious] means is more important than acquiring competence | • acquiring competence is more important than acquiring certificates |
| • teachers are expected to give preferential treatment to some students (e.g., based on ethnic affiliation or on recommendation by an influential person) | • teachers are expected to be strictly impartial |

with two actual cross-cultural contexts. Two hypothetical "bad" language learning situations were described (p. 139):

1. One of the bad situations would be where the TL group views the 2LL group as dominant and the 2LL group views itself in the same way, where both groups desire preservation and high enclosure for the 2LL group, where the 2LL group is both cohesive and large, where the two cultures are not congruent, where the two groups hold negative attitudes toward each other, and where the 2LL group intends to remain in the TL area only for a short time.

2. The second bad situation has all the characteristics of the first except that in this case, the 2LL group would consider itself subordinate and would also be considered subordinate by the TL group.

The first situation is typical, according to Schumann, of Americans living in Riyadh, Saudi Arabia. The second situation is descriptive of Navajo Indians living in the southwestern part of the United States.

A "good" language learning situation, according to Schumann's model (p. 141),

> would be one where the 2LL group is non-dominant in relation to the TL group, where both groups desire assimilation (or at least acculturation) for the 2LL group, where low enclosure is the goal of both groups, where the two cultures are congruent, where the 2LL group is small and non-cohesive, where both groups have positive attitudes towards each other, and where the 2LL group intends to remain in the target language area for a long time. Under such conditions social distance would be minimal and acquisition of the target language would be enhanced.

Schumann cites as a specific example of a "good" language learning situation the case of American Jewish immigrants living in Israel.

Schumann's hypothesis is that the greater the social distance between two cultures, the greater the difficulty the learner will have in learning the second language, and conversely, the smaller the social distance (the greater the social solidarity between two cultures), the better will be the language learning situation.

# Pidginization

Schumann's research on social distance has also been extended to the concept of *pidginization*. A pidgin is a mixed language or jargon that arises from two (or sometimes more) languages in contact, and it is used for communication in commercial, political, or social contexts. Pidgins are marked by simplified and reduced forms of the languages in contact; for example, they tend to lack inflectional morphology ("He give me money.") and to eliminate certain grammatical transformations ("You go beach now?"). Schumann

(1976a) hypothesized that pidginization is, in part, a result of varying degrees of social distance. People develop their own pidgin as a symbol of their unique identity, separate from either of the cultures of the two languages in contact.

Some researchers (Schumann 1976a, 1978, 1982b, 1990; Bickerton 1981; Andersen 1979) also contend that the interlanguage (see Chapter Eight) of many second language learners is akin to pidginized forms of language. The implication is that what happens over perhaps several hundred years in pidginization is reproduced to some degree in the short duration of one learner's acquisition of a second language. One would conclude that the learner instinctively attempts to bring two languages—the target and the native—together to form a unique language, an interlanguage, possessing aspects of both languages. It is perhaps only with great persistence that learners overcome this apparently universal pidginization tendency, weed out interlanguage forms, and adopt the second language exclusively.

# Perceived and Optimal Social Distance

One of the difficulties in Schumann's hypothesis of social distance is the measurement of actual social distance. How can one determine *degrees* of social distance? By what means? And how would those means be quantifiable for comparison of relative distances? So far the construct has remained a rather subjectively defined phenomenon that, like empathy, self-esteem, and so many other psychological constructs, defies definition even though one can intuitively grasp the sense of what is meant.

William Acton (1979) proposed a solution to the dilemma. Instead of trying to measure *actual* social distance, he devised a measure of *perceived* social distance. His contention was that it is not particularly relevant what the actual distance is between cultures since it is what learners perceive that forms their own reality. We have already noted that human beings perceive the cultural environment through the filters and screens of their own world view and then act upon that perception, however "biased" it may be. According to Acton, when learners encounter a new culture, their acculturation process will be a factor of how they perceive their own culture in relation to the culture of the target language and vice versa. For example, objectively there may be a relatively large distance between Americans and Saudi Arabians, but an American learning Arabic in Saudi Arabia might for a number of reasons perceive little distance and in turn act on that perception.

By asking learners to respond to three dimensions of distance, Acton devised a measure of perceived social distance—the Professed Difference in Attitude Questionnaire (PDAQ)—which characterized the "good" or successful language learner (as measured by standard proficiency tests) with remarkable accuracy. Basically the PDAQ asked learners to quantify what they perceived to be the differences in attitude toward various concepts ("the automobile," "divorce," "socialism," "policemen," for example) on three dimensions: (1) distance (or difference) between themselves and their countrymen in general; (2) distance between themselves and members of the target culture in general; and (3) distance between their countrymen and members of the target culture. By using a semantic differential technique, three distance scores were computed for each dimension. Acton found that in the case of learners of English who had been in the United States for 4 months, there is an *optimal* perceived social distance ratio (among the three scores) that typifies the "good" language learner. If learners perceived themselves as either too *close* to or too *distant* from either the target culture or the native culture they fell into the category of "bad" language learners as measured by standard proficiency tests. The implication is that successful language learners see themselves as maintaining some distance between themselves and *both* cultures. Unfortunately, Acton's PDAQ did not *predict* success in language. However, this is no great surprise since we know of no adequate instrument to predict language success or to assess language aptitude. But what the PDAQ did was to describe empirically, in quantifiable terms, a relationship between social distance and second language acquisition.

Acton's theory of optimal perceived social distance supported Lambert's (1967) contention that mastery of the foreign language takes place hand in hand with feelings of anomie or homelessness, where learners have moved away from their native culture but are still not completely assimilated or adjusted in the target culture. More importantly, Acton's model led us closer to an understanding of culture shock and the relationship of acculturation to language learning by supplying an important piece to a puzzle. If you combine Acton's research with Lambert's a rather interesting hypothesis emerges— namely, that mastery or skillful fluency in a second language (within the second culture) occurs somewhere at the beginning of the third—recovery—stage of acculturation. The implication of such a hypothesis is that mastery might not effectively occur before that stage or, even more likely, that learners might never be successful in their mastery of the language if they have proceeded beyond early Stage 3 without accomplishing that linguistic mastery. Stage 3 may provide not only the optimal *distance,* but the optimal cognitive and affective *tension* to produce the necessary *pressure* to acquire the language, yet pressure that is neither too overwhelming (such as that which may be typical of Stage 2 [culture shock]) nor too weak (which would be found in Stage 4, adaptation/assimilation). Language mastery at Stage 3, in turn, would appear to be an instrument for progressing psychologically through Stage 3 and finally into Stage 4.

According to this *optimal distance model* (Brown 1980) of second language acquisition, an adult who fails to master a second language in a second culture may for a host of reasons have failed to synchronize linguistic and cultural development. Adults who have achieved nonlinguistic means of coping in the foreign culture will pass through Stage 3 and into Stage 4 with an undue number of *fossilized* forms of language (see Chapter Eight for a discussion of fossilization), never achieving mastery. They have no reason to achieve mastery since they have learned to cope without sophisticated knowledge of the language. They may have acquired a sufficient number of functions of a second language without acquiring the correct forms. What I have suggested in this optimal distance model might well be seen as a culturally based critical-period hypothesis, that is, a critical period that is independent of the age of the learner. While the optimal distance model applies more appropriately to adult learners, it could pertain to children, although less critically so. Because they have not built up years and years of a culture-bound world view (or view of themselves), children have fewer perceptive filters to readjust and therefore move through the stages of acculturation more quickly. They nevertheless move through the same four stages, and it is plausible to hypothesize that their recovery stages are also crucial periods of acquisition.

Some research evidence has been gathered in support of the optimal distance concept. In a study of returning Peace Corps volunteers who had remained in their assigned countries for two or more years, Day (1982) garnered some observational evidence of the coinciding of critical leaps in language fluency and cultural anomie. And Svanes (1987, 1988) found that university foreign students studying in Norway appeared to achieve higher language proficiency if they had "a balanced and critical attitude to the host people" (Svanes 1988:368) as opposed to uncritical admiration for all aspects of the target culture. The informal testimony of many teachers of ESL in the United States also confirms the plausibility of a motivational tension created by the need to "move along" in the sometimes long and frustrating process of adaptation to a new homeland. Teachers in similar contexts could benefit from a careful assessment of the current cultural stages of learners with due attention to possible optimal periods for language mastery.

# Sociopolitical Considerations

The relationship between language and society cannot be discussed for long without touching on the political ramifications of language and language policy. Virtually every country has some form of explicit, "official" or implicit, "unofficial" policy affecting the status of its native language(s) and one or more foreign languages. English, now as the major worldwide *lingua franca,* attracts widespread attention as a native, second, foreign, and international language.

Different *contexts* of learning a second language give us some categories for consideration. (1) One context is technically referred to as the learning of a *second* language, or learning another language either (a) within the culture of that second language (for example, an Arabic speaker learning English in the

United States) or (b) within one's own native culture where the second language is an accepted lingua franca used for education, government, or business within the country (for example, learning English in the Philippines or India). (2) Another context for learning another language is technically called *foreign* language learning—that is, learning a nonnative language in one's own culture with few immediate and widespread opportunities to use the language within the environment of one's own culture (for example, learning French or German in the United States). It should be pointed out that in this book no such restricted or technical connotations have been implied in the use of the term "second language learning." "Second" language learning and "foreign" language learning have been used interchangeably.

Each type of second language situation involves different degrees of acculturation. Second language learning in a foreign culture (Type 1a) potentially involves the deepest form of acculturation. Learners must survive in a strange culture as well as learn a language on which they are totally dependent for communication. Second language learning in the native culture (Type 1b) varies in the severity of acculturation experienced by the learner, depending upon the country, the cultural and sociopolitical status of the language, and the motivations or aspirations of the learner.

This latter category of second language learning has, in recent years, stimulated some interesting but often controversial discussion about the status of English as an International Language (EIL) in its varieties of what Kachru (1976, 1992) calls "World Englishes." Learning English in India, for example, really does not involve taking on a new culture since one is acquiring *Indian* English in India. According to Kachru, the "Indianization" of English in India has led to a situation where English has few if any British cultural attributes. This process of "nativization" or "indigenization" (Richards 1979) of English has spread to an "outer circle" (Kachru 1985) of countries that includes India, Singapore, the Philippines, Nigeria, Ghana, and others. In such cases the learning of English does not necessarily pose a serious *cultural* conflict; for school children the second language coupled with the new cognitive contexts of the educational setting may pose difficulties, but these are not correctly described as cultural difficulties.

The spread and stratification of EIL has led Kachru and others who have joined in the debate (Quirk 1988, Davies 1989, for example) to a "fresh conceptualisation" of contexts of English language use. "The traditional dichotomy between native and non-native is functionally uninsightful and linguistically questionable, particularly when discussing the functions of English in multilingual societies. The earlier distinction of English as a native language (ENL), second (ESL) and foreign (EFL) has come under attack for reasons other than sociolinguistic." (Kachru 1992:3) Instead, we are advised to view English in terms of a broad range of its functions and the degree of its penetration into a country's society.

These caveats notwithstanding, we still find ample and appropriate use of the terms *second* and *foreign* language learning, especially in languages other than English, which leads us finally to consider just what we mean by the latter category. The *foreign* language context (Type 2) produces diverse degrees of acculturation since people are attempting to learn a foreign language for a variety of possible reasons. Some people learn other languages simply out of an interest in languages, ranging from passing curiosity to a technical linguistic fascination. Others may learn a language in order to communicate someday with people in another country. Still others learn for specific purposes: say, a foreign language requirement or a need to gain a reading knowledge in a field of specialization. It is possible in such settings to function without the foreign language although that foreign language provides advantages in educational advancement, work, or social status (Olshtain 1985). In many foreign language (Type 2) situations, cultural topics provide added motivation for understanding the people of the second culture. Foreign language curricula therefore commonly attempt to deal with the cultural connotations of the foreign language itself.

# Language, Thought, and Culture

No discussion about cultural variables in second language acquisition is complete without some treatment of the relationship between language and thought. We saw in the case of first language acquisition that cognitive development and linguistic development go hand in hand, each interacting with and shaping the other. It is commonly observed that the manner in which an idea or "fact" is stated affects the way we conceptualize the idea. Words shape our lives. The advertising world is a prime example of the use of language to shape, persuade, and dissuade. "Weasel words" tend to glorify very ordinary products into those that are "unsurpassed," "ultimate," "supercharged," and "the right choice." In the case of food that has been sapped of most of its nutrients by the manufacturing process, we are told that these products are now "enriched" and "fortified." A foreigner in the United States once remarked that in the United States there are no "small" eggs, only "medium," "large," "extra-large," and "jumbo." Euphemisms—or "telling it like it isn't"—abound in American culture where certain thoughts are taboo or certain words connote something less than desirable. We are persuaded by industry, for example, that "receiving waters" are the lakes or rivers into which industrial wastes are dumped and that "assimilative capacity" refers to how much of the waste you can dump into the river before it starts to show. Garbage men are "sanitary engineers"; toilets are "rest rooms"; slums are "substandard dwellings." Even a common word like "family" has for some social scientists been replaced by "a microcluster of structured role expectations."

Verbal labels can shape the way we store events for later recall. In a classic study, Carmichael, Hogan, and Walter (1932) found that when subjects were briefly exposed to figures like those in Figure 7–1 and later asked to reproduce them, the reproductions were influenced by the labels assigned to the figures.

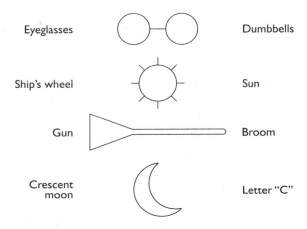

FIGURE 7-1.   Sample stimulus figures used by Carmichael, Hogan, and Walter (1932).

For example, the first drawing tended to be reproduced as something like this:

if subjects had seen the "eyeglasses" label, and on the other hand like this:

if they had seen the "dumbbells" label.

Words are not the only linguistic category affecting thought. The way a sentence is structured will affect nuances of meaning. Elizabeth Loftus (1976) discovered that subtle differences in the structure of questions can affect the answer a person gives. For example, upon viewing a film of an automobile accident subjects were asked questions like "Did you see *the* broken headlight?" in some cases, and in other cases "Did you see *a* broken headlight?" Questions using *the* tended to produce more false recognition of events. That is, the presence of the definite article led subjects to believe that there *was* a broken headlight whether they saw it or not. Similar results were found for questions like "Did you see some people watching the accident?" versus "Did you see any people watching the accident?" or even for questions containing a presupposition: "How fast was the car going when it hit the stop sign?" (presupposing both the existence of a stop sign and that the car hit a stop sign whether the subject actually saw it or not).

On the discourse level of language we are familiar with the persuasiveness of an emotional speech or a well-written novel. How often has a gifted orator swayed opinion and thought? or a powerful editorial moved one to action or change? These are common examples of the influence of language on our cognitive and affective organizations.

Culture is really an integral part of the interaction between language and thought. Cultural patterns, customs, and ways of life are expressed in language; culture-specific world views are reflected in language. Cultures have different ways of dividing the color spectrum, for example, illustrating differing world views on what color is and how to identify color. Gleason (1961:4) noted that the Shona of Rhodesia and the Bassa of Liberia have fewer color categories than speakers of European languages and they break up the spectrum at different points. Of course, the Shona or Bassa are able to perceive and describe other colors, in the same way that an English speaker might describe a "dark bluish green," but the labels that the language provides tend to shape the person's overall cognitive organization of color and to cause varying degrees of color discrimination. Eskimo tribes commonly have as many as seven different words for *snow* to distinguish among different types of snow (falling snow, snow on the ground, fluffy snow, wet snow, and so forth), while certain African cultures in the equatorial forests of Zaire have no word at all for snow.

But even more to the point than such geographically conditioned aspects of language are examples from the Hopi language (see Whorf 1956). Hopi does not use verbs in the same way that English does. For example, in English we might say "he is running," but in Hopi we would have to choose from a number of much more precise verbal ideas, depending upon the knowledge of the speaker and the validity of the statement. A different form of the verb expresses: "I know that he is running at this very moment," "I know that he is running at this moment even though I cannot see him," "I remember that I saw him running and I presume he is still running," or "I am told that he is running." Also, *duration* and *time* are expressed differently in Hopi. Time, for example, is not measured or wasted or saved in Hopi. Time is expressed in terms of events, sequences, and development. Plant a seed and it will grow; the span of time for growth is not important. It is the development of events—planting, germination, growth, blossoming, bearing fruit—that are important.

A tantalizing question emerges from such observations. Does language *reflect* a cultural world view or does language actually *shape* the world view? Drawing on the ideas of Wilhelm von Humboldt (1767–1835), who claimed that language shaped a person's *Weltanschauung,* Edward Sapir and Benjamin Whorf proposed a hypothesis that has now been given several alternative labels: the *Sapir-Whorf hypothesis,* the *Whorfian hypothesis, linguistic relativity,* or *linguistic determinism.* Whorf (1956:212–214) sums up the hypothesis:

> The background linguistic system (in other words, the grammar) of each language is not merely a reproducing instrument for voicing ideas but rather is itself the shaper of ideas, the program and guide for the individual's mental activity, for his analysis of impressions, for his synthesis of his mental stock in trade. Formulation of ideas is not an independent process, strictly rational in the old sense, but is part of a particular grammar and differs, from slightly to greatly, as between different grammars. We dissect nature along lines laid down by our native languages. The categories and types that we isolate from the world of phenomena we do not find there because they stare every observer in the face; on the contrary, the world is presented in a kaleidoscopic flux of impressions which has to be organized by our minds—and this means largely by the linguistic systems in our minds. We cut nature up, organize it into concepts, and ascribe significance as we do, largely because we are parties to an agreement to organize it in this way—an agreement that holds through our speech community and is codified in the patterns of our language. The agreement is, of course, an implicit and unstated one, but its terms are absolutely obligatory; we cannot talk at all except by subscribing to the organization and classification of data which the agreement decrees.

Ronald Wardhaugh (1976:74) expresses the antithesis of the Whorfian hypothesis:

> The most valid conclusion to all such studies is that it appears possible to talk about anything in any language provided the speaker is willing to use some degree of circumlocution. Some concepts are more "codable," that is, easier to express, in some languages than in others. The speaker, of course, will not be aware of the circumlocution in the absence of familiarity with another language that uses a more succinct means of expression. Every natural language provides both a language for talking about every other language, that is, a metalanguage, and an entirely adequate apparatus for making any kinds of observations that need to be made about the world. If such is the case, every natural language must be an extremely rich system which readily allows its speakers to overcome any predispositions that exist.

The Whorfian hypothesis has unfortunately been misinterpreted by a number of linguists and other scholars. In one case, Guiora (1981:177) criticized Whorf's claim that the influence of language on behavior was "undifferentiated, all pervasive, permanent and absolute"; Guiora called these claims "extravagant." It would appear that it was Guiora's interpretation that was extravagant, for he put ideas into Whorf's writings that were never there. Clarke et al. (1984:57), in a careful review of Whorf's writings, eloquently demonstrated that the Whorfian hypothesis was not nearly as monolithic or causal as some would interpret it to be. "The 'extravagant claims' made in the name of linguistic relativity were not made by Whorf, and attributing to him simplistic views of linguistic determination serves only to obscure the usefulness of his insights."

The language teaching profession today has actually attended to a more moderate view of the Whorfian hypothesis, if only because of the intuitive evidence of the *interaction* of language and culture. Aspects of language do indeed seem to provide us with cognitive mind sets. In English, the passive voice, our verb system, and numerous lexical items already referred to in this section all contribute to influencing our thinking. But we can also recognize that through both language and culture, some universal properties bind us all together in one world. The act of learning to *think* in another language may require a considerable degree of mastery of that language, but a second language learner does not have to learn to think, in general, all over again. As in every other human learning experience, the second language learner can make positive use of prior experiences to facilitate the process of learning by retaining that which is valid and valuable for second culture learning and second language learning.

## In the Classroom: Toward a Principled Approach to Language Pedagogy

It should be clear from the vignette of the previous chapter that as an "enlightened, eclectic" teacher, you can think in terms of a number of possible methodological options at your disposal for tailoring classes to particular contexts. Your **approach**—or theory of language and language learning—therefore takes on great importance. Your approach to language teaching methodology is your theoretical rationale that underlies everything that you do in the classroom.

Your approach actually draws on most of what is presented in this book—issues and findings and conclusions and *principles* of language learning and teaching, principles such as:

- Intrinsic motivation is a powerful incentive for learning.
- A moderate to high level of risk-taking behavior is important.
- Language and culture are inextricably intertwined.
- Successful learners make a strategic investment in their learning.
- Self-confidence is an important precursor to success.

Your understanding of these principles forms a set of foundations stones upon which you build curricular plans, lesson designs, and moment by moment techniques and activities. (For more on principled approaches to language teaching, see Brown 1994.)

Your approach to language pedagogy is not just a set of static principles, "set in stone." It is, in fact, a dynamic composite of energies within you that changes (or should change, if you are a growing teacher) with your experiences in your own learning and teaching. The way you understand the language learning process—what makes for successful and unsuccessful learning—may be relatively stable across months or years, but it doesn't pay to be too smug. There is far too much that we do not know collectively about this process, and there are far too many new research findings pouring in, to assume that you can confidently assert that you know everything you already need know about language and language learning.

The interaction between your approach and your classroom practice is the key to dynamic teaching. The best teachers always take a few calculated risks in the classroom, trying new activities here and there. The inspiration for such innovation comes from the approach level, but the feedback that they gather from actual implementation then informs their overall understanding of what learning and teaching is. Which, in turn, may give rise to a new insight and more innovative possibilities, and the cycle continues.

Consider an example of this cycle. Intrinsic motivation, as explained in Chapter 6, is indeed a powerful factor in the learning of a second language. It is therefore a "keystone" in one's approach to language teaching. How does that keystone interact with classroom techniques? In a number of ways, the principle of intrinsic motivation points toward certain techniques and away from others. The following check list will illustrate how techniques get generated, shaped, and revised according to just this one principle.

## Intrinsically Motivating Techniques: A Check List

1. Does the technique appeal to the genuine interests of your students? Is it relevant to their lives?

2. Do you present the technique in a positive, enthusiastic manner?

3. Are students clearly aware of the purpose of the technique?

4. Do students have some choice in:
   (a) choosing some aspect of the technique?
   (b) determining how they go about fulfilling the goals of the technique?

5. Does the technique encourage students to discover for themselves certain principles or rules (rather than simply being "told")?

6. Does it encourage students in some way to develop or use effective strategies of learning and communication?

7. Does it contribute—at least to some extent—to students' ultimate autonomy and independence (from you)?

8. Does it foster cooperative negotiation with other students in the class? Is it a truly interactive technique?

9. Does the technique present a "reasonable challenge?"

10.  Do students receive sufficient feedback on their performance (from each other or from you)?

The ten criteria in the check list represent various facets of the principle of intrinsic motivation. As each item gets applied to a technique that is either being planned or has already been taught, evaluation takes place, and the technique thereby becomes a manifestation of a principled approach. All of the principles in your approach could easily lead to similar check lists for the validation of techniques.

In the process of actual teaching in the classroom, it is quite possible that you will be led to modify certain aspects of your approach. For example, item number 3 above stresses the importance, following intrinsic motivation theory, of students' awareness of the purpose of what they are doing in the classroom. But you might find, as you teach, that your understanding of the principle is too strong and that there are times when students really should not know the ultimate purpose of an activity. Classroom experience then moves you to revise your approach slightly.

As you continue to read this book, you may do well to pay increasing attention now to your growing stockpile of language learning/teaching principles that are together forming a composite approach to language learning and teaching. Consider the pedagogical implications and classroom applications of every finding, every issue, every conclusion, and every generalization that is made. In so doing your overall approach will not only be more enlightened but more readily applicable to classroom practice.

## Suggested Readings

*McGroarty and Galvan* (1985) offer a concise summary of culture and second language learning, including a summary of teaching techniques.

You can get some valuable insights from reading one or all of *Oller*'s studies on attitudes (Oller, Hudson, and Liu 1977; Oller, Baca, and Vigil 1978; Chihara and Oller 1978). Those articles provide a picture of the type of instrumentation that is used to measure attitudes and also give more technical information supporting their conclusions on the relationship between attitudes and language learning. *Gardner and Lambert* (1972) is also a good background resource for this chapter and Chapter Six.

For a fascinating look at cultural factors at play in the classroom, read *Hofstede*'s (1986) study of cultural norms in some fifty different countries.

*Kohls*'s (1984) survival kit for overseas living is a very practical resource for understanding other cultures.

The relatively recent interest in "World Englishes" and the sociopolitical dimensions of the spread of English are the subject of a comprehensive review article by *Kachru* (1992). Related to this issue is that of "linguistic imperialism," the subject of *Phillipson*'s (1992) recent book.

For a bit of history, why not take a look at *Whorf*'s (1956) classic on linguistic determinism?

*Ostrander and Schroeder*'s (1979) fascinating book on "superlearning" is written for the lay public. If read with a grain of salt, it can provide some stimulating ideas for language teaching.

## Topics and Questions for Study and Discussion

1.  Think of everyday examples of the subjectivity of perceiving people and behavior through the eyes of your own cultural viewpoint. Refer to eating customs, daily work patterns, family life, marriage customs, politeness patterns, and the like. Does your own pattern somehow seem more reasonable or sensible than that of some other culture with which you are familiar?

2.  Consider some of the cultures with which you are familiar and list various stereotypes of those cultures. Share your stereotypes with those of a classmate or friend and compare your perceptions. How might those stereotypes *help* you to understand someone from another culture? How might they *hinder* your understanding?

3.  Discuss sensitive cross-cultural differences (religious, political, social, or personal issues) with someone from another culture. Can you empathize (not necessarily sympathize) with those differences? In your discussion, what attitudes were reflected toward your culture? What attitudes do you think you expressed toward the other culture?

4.  Try to think of some area of your affective or cognitive self in which you feel some prejudice toward members of another culture or even a subculture (such as people from different parts of your own country). What are the deeply seated causes of that prejudice? Should you overcome that prejudice? How might a person go about eradicating such negative attitudes?

5.  If you have ever lived in another country, can you now identify some of the stages of acculturation in your own experience? Describe your feelings. Did you move through all four stages? Did you reach assimilation? Or adaptation? Did you experience *anomie*?

6.  Is Clarke pushing matters a little too far in likening culture shock to schizophrenia?

7.  Summarize the notion of the "optimal distance" model. In your own experiences or the experiences of those you have known, would you say there is support for the notion of a culturally defined critical period? Have you known people who progressed well into Stage 3

without linguistic mastery? What happened eventually to their language proficiency?

8. Have you known people who mastered a language too *soon,* before going through stages of acculturation? What effect, if any, did that have on eventual cultural adaptation or assimilation?

9. Why is language learning and teaching a political issue? In countries with which you are familiar, discuss the extent to which government dictates language policy.

10. In considering so-called "world Englishes," where do you draw the line in recognizing the "legitimacy" of a variety of English? If Indian English, for example, is a legitimate variety of English, is Japanese English ("Japlish") in the same category? Think of other examples and try to arrive at a conclusion.

11. Review the distinction between *second* language learning and *foreign* language learning. How might your teaching materials and techniques vary depending upon whether you were teaching a second or a foreign language?

12. In your second language, find examples that support the contention that language (specific vocabulary items, perhaps) seems to shape the way the speaker of a language views the world. In what way does the Whorfian hypothesis present yet another chicken-or-egg issue?

# Chapter 8

# CONTRASTIVE ANALYSIS, INTERLANGUAGE, AND ERROR ANALYSIS

Up to this point in the treatment of principles of second language acquisition I have focused essentially on psychological variables, making references to linguistic factors within a psychological framework. The reason for such a focus is that the psychological principles of second language acquisition form the foundation stones for building a comprehensive understanding of the acquisition of the linguistic system—the units and structures of language. Linguistic systems cannot be examined fruitfully without recognition and understanding of the relationship of language to the total human being. The *forms* of language—the sounds, sound systems, grammatical structures, words, and discourse features—are utilized to accomplish certain intended *functions* of communication. We have encountered a good many of those functions of language in our examination of first and second language acquisition, human learning, cognitive processes, styles, and strategies, personality variables, and sociocultural dimensions of second language acquisition. We have considered some of the physical, cognitive, and affective factors that come to bear on this most complex process. In this chapter we will begin to examine the most salient aspect of second language acquisition—the learning of the linguistic system itself.

# The Contrastive Analysis Hypothesis

In the middle part of the twentieth century, one of the most popular pursuits for applied linguists was the study of two languages in contrast. Eventually the stockpile of comparative and contrastive data on a multitude of pairs of languages yielded what commonly came to be known as the *Contrastive Analysis Hypothesis* (CAH). Deeply rooted in the behavioristic and structuralist approaches of the day, the CAH claimed that the principal barrier to second language acquisition is the interference of the first language system with the second language system, and that a scientific, structural analysis of the two languages in question would yield a taxonomy of linguistic contrasts between them which in turn would enable the linguist to predict the difficulties a learner would encounter. It was at that time considered feasible that the tools of structural linguistics, such as Fries's (1952) slot-filler grammar, would enable a linguist to describe accurately the two languages in question, and to match those two descriptions against each other to determine valid contrasts, or differences, between them. Behaviorism contributed to the notion that human behavior is the sum of its smallest parts and components, and therefore that language learning could be described as the acquisition of all of these discrete units. Moreover, human learning theories highlighted *interfering* elements of learning, concluding that where no interference could be predicted, no difficulty would be experienced since one could *transfer* positively all other items in a language. The logical conclusion from these various psychological and linguistic assumptions was that second language learning basically involved the overcoming of the *differences* between the two linguistic systems—the native and target languages.

Intuitively the CAH has appeal in that we commonly observe in second language learners a plethora of errors attributable to the negative transfer of the native language to the target language. It is quite common, for example, to detect certain foreign accents and to be able to infer, from the speech of the learner alone, where the learner comes from. English learners from such native language backgrounds as German, French, Spanish, and Japanese, for example, usually can readily be detected by native English speakers by easily identifiable—stereotypical, if you will—accents that we have grown accustomed to hearing. Such accents can even be represented in the written word. Consider again Mark Twain's *The Innocents Abroad* (1869:111), in which the French-speaking guide introduces himself: "If ze zhentlemans will to me make ze grande honneur to me rattain in hees serveece, I shall show to him everysing zat is magnifique to look upon in ze beautiful Paree. I speaky ze Angleesh parfaitmaw." Or William E. Callahan's Juan Castaniegos, a young Mexican in *Afraid of the Dark,* who says: "Help me to leave from thees place. But, Señor Capitán, me, I 'ave do notheeng. Notheeng, Señor Capitán." These excerpts also capture the transfer of vocabulary and grammatical rules from the native language.

Some rather strong claims were made of the CAH among language teaching experts and linguists. One of the strongest was made by Robert Lado (1957:vii) in the preface to *Linguistics Across Cultures:* "The plan of the book rests on the assumption that we can predict and describe the patterns that will cause difficulty in learning, and those that will not cause difficulty, by comparing systematically the language and the culture to be learned with the native language and culture of the student." Then, in the first chapter of the book, Lado continues: ". . . in the comparison between native and foreign language lies the key to ease or difficulty in foreign language learning. . . . Those elements that are similar to [the learner's] native language will be simple for him and those elements that are different will be difficult" (pp. 1–2). An equally strong claim was made by Banathy, Trager, and Waddle (1966:37): "The change that has to take place in the language behavior of a foreign language student can be equated with the differences between the structure of the student's native language and culture and that of the target language and culture."

For a number of years materials in foreign languages were prepared on these "fundamental assumptions" about the relationship between two linguistic systems in learning a foreign language. Randal Whitman (1970) noted that contrastive analysis involved four different procedures. The first of these is *description:* the linguist or language teacher, using the tools of formal grammar, explicitly describes the two languages in question. Second, a *selection* is made of certain forms—linguistic items, rules, structures—for contrast, since it is virtually impossible to contrast every possible facet of two languages. Whitman admits that the selection process "reflects the conscious and unconscious assumptions of the investigator" (p. 193), which in turn affect exactly what forms are selected. The third procedure is the *contrast* itself, the mapping of one linguistic system onto the other, and a specification of the relationship of one system to the other which, like selection, "rests on the validity of one's reference points" (p. 196). Finally, one formulates a *prediction* of error or of difficulty on the basis of the first three procedures. That prediction can be arrived at through the formulation of a hierarchy of difficulty or through more subjective applications of psychological and linguistic theory.

It is not difficult to discern from Whitman's outline of procedures the subjectivity of contrastive analysis, something that falls short of a "scientific description" (Fries 1945:9) in the rigorous tradition of behavioristic psychology.

# Hierarchy of Difficulty

In the heyday of the CAH, attempts were made to formalize the prediction stage of contrastive analysis and to remove some of the subjectivity involved.

The best-known attempt was made by Stockwell, Bowen, and Martin (1965), who proposed what they called a *hierarchy of difficulty* by which a teacher or linguist could make a *prediction* of the relative difficulty of a given aspect of the second language. Though the authors devised their hierarchy for English and Spanish, they claimed a universal application of the hierarchy. For phonological systems in contrast, Stockwell and his associates suggested eight possible degrees of difficulty. These degrees were based upon the notions of transfer (positive, negative, and zero) and of optional and obligatory choices of certain phonemes in the two languages in contrast. Through a very careful, systematic analysis of the properties of the two languages in reference to the hierarchy of difficulty, applied linguists were able to derive a reasonably accurate inventory of phonological difficulties that a second language learner would encounter. That inventory included a prediction of the difficulty—relative to other items in the inventory—of a particular unit of contrast. Stockwell and his associates also constructed a hierarchy of difficulty for grammatical structures of two languages in contrast. Their grammatical hierarchy included 16 levels of difficulty, based on the same notions used to construct phonological criteria with the added dimensions of "structural correspondence" and "functional/semantic correspondence."

Clifford Prator (1967) captured the essence of this grammatical hierarchy in six categories of difficulty. Prator's hierarchy is applicable to both grammatical and phonological features of language. The six categories, in ascending order of difficulty, are discussed below. Most of the examples are taken from English and Spanish (a native English speaker learning Spanish as a second language); a few examples illustrate other pairs of contrasting languages.

### Level 0—Transfer

No difference or contrast is present between the two languages. The learner can simply transfer (positively) a sound, structure, or lexical item from the native language to the target language. Such transfer is posited to be of no difficulty, hence the label of "level zero." Examples can be found in certain phonemes and their distribution in English and Spanish (cardinal vowels, /s/, /z/, /m/, /n/, structures (say, general word order), or words (*mortal, inteligente, arte, americanos*).

### Level 1—Coalescence

Two items in the native language become coalesced into essentially one item in the target language. This requires that learners overlook a distinction they have grown accustomed to. For example, English third-person possessives require gender distinction (*his/her*), and in Spanish they do not (*su*). It is difficult to provide phonological instances of coalescence because of the theoretical difficulty of claiming that two sounds actually "merge." One might, for example, claim that the English-speaking learner of Japanese can overlook the distinction between /r/ and /l/, and simply produce an /r/ in Japanese. But such a contrast can also be argued merely as a case of a phoneme (/l/) that is *absent* (see Level 2) in the target language. A good lexical example of coalescence is found in the case of an English speaker learning French who must overlook the distinction between *teach* and *learn,* and use just the one word *apprendre* in French.

## Level 2—Underdifferentiation

An item in the native language is absent in the target language. The learner must avoid that item. English learners of Spanish must "forget," as it were, such items as English *do* as a tense carrier, indefinite determiners (*other, certain*), possessive forms of *wh-* words (*whose*), or the use of *some* with mass nouns. A number of phonemes that are present in English are absent in Spanish: several vowels (/I/, /æ/, among others), and consonants like the interdental fricatives (/th/) and velar nasal (/ng/).

## Level 3—Reinterpretation

An item that exists in the native language is given a new shape or distribution. Though it is difficult to argue that Level 3 is distinct from *any* of the other levels, Prator (1967) claimed that in some cases items in the target language are perceived as reinterpreted native language items. The English speaker who learns French, for example, must learn a new distribution for nasalized vowels. Or, when in English we use a determiner (He's *a* philosopher), in Spanish the determiner is optional (El es (*un*) filósofo); learners of Spanish must reinterpret their English system of determiners.

## Level 4—Overdifferentiation

A new item entirely, bearing little if any similarity to the native language item, must be learned. For example, in learning Spanish the native English speaker must learn to include determiners in generalized nominals (Man is mortal/*El* hombre es mortal), to use *se* with intransitive verbs for an indefinite subject (*Se* come bien aquí), or, most commonly, to learn Spanish grammatical gender inherent in nouns.

## Level 5—Split

One item in the native language becomes two or more in the target language, requiring the learner to make a new distinction. The split is the counterpart of coalescence. Typical of such items in learning Spanish are the learning of the distinction between *ser* and *estar* (to be) and between *tú* and *usted* (you), or even learning the distinction between Spanish indicative and subjunctive moods where in English the indicative alone is appropriate.

Prator's reinterpretation, and Stockwell and his associates' original hierarchy of difficulty, are based on principles of human learning. The first, or "zero," degree of difficulty represents complete one-to-one correspondence and transfer while the fifth degree of difficulty is the height of interference. Prator and Stockwell both claimed that their hierarchy could be applied to virtually any two languages and would thus yield some form of objectivity to the prediction stage of contrastive analysis procedures.

Using the hierarchy of difficulty and the procedures for contrastive analysis described by Whitman, one can make simple predictions about difficulties learners will encounter. Let us look, for example, at the learning of English consonants by a native speaker of Turkish. The *description* and *selection* stages of contrastive analysis are fulfilled in the chart of Turkish and English consonants (Subuktekin 1975:33) in Table 8–1. (Bowen's [1975] phonemic symbols are used here for simplified reading.)

By "mapping" one language onto the other, you can engage in the process of *contrasting* the systems—the third of Whitman's procedures. The following six statements will suffice for a superficial contrast:

1. English /t/, /d/, and /n/ are alveolar; the corresponding consonants in Turkish are dental.

2. English has interdental fricatives /th/ and /dh/; Turkish does not.

3. English has a velar nasal /ng/; Turkish does not.

4. English has a velar glide /w/; Turkish does not.

5. Turkish has palatal /K/, /G/, and /L/ which do not occur in English.

6. From a phonetic viewpoint, English /r/ and Turkish /r/ are of very different natures.

Next, the *prediction* procedure can be accomplished by subjecting the above contrastive description to a hierarchy of difficulty:

0. Of no difficulty will be all those consonants that do not appear in the six contrastive statements above. We will assume such consonants bear one-to-one correspondence.

1. No apparent instance of coalescence, unless items in Level 2 below might be so analyzed.

2. Palatal stops /K/ and /G/ and palatal /L/ are absent in English.

3. English alveolar consonants /t/, /d/, and /n/ will have to be reshaped by the Turkish speaker from Turkish dental counterparts.

4. English consonants /th/, /dh/, /ng/, and /w/ are new to the Turkish speaker. Also American English /r/ is phonetically virtually new.

5. No apparent instance of a split.

The contrastive analysis procedure has identified and contrasted selected features of the two languages and predicted basically three levels of difficulty.

**TABLE 8-1.**   Turkish and English consonants (English consonants are underlined)

| | | BILABIAL | LABIO-DENTAL | INTER-DENTAL | DENTAL | ALVEOLAR | PALATAL | VELAR | GLOTTAL |
|---|---|---|---|---|---|---|---|---|---|
| Stops | vl | p p̲ | | | t | t̲ | K | k k̲ | |
| | vd | b b̲ | | | d | d̲ | G | g g̲ | |
| Fricatives | vl | | f f̲ | th̲ | | s s̲ | sh sh̲ | | h h̲ |
| | vd | | v v̲ | dh̲ | | z z̲ | zh zh̲ | | |
| Affricates | vl | | | | | ch ch̲ | | | |
| | vd | | | | | j j̲ | | | |
| Nasals | | m m̲ | | | n | n̲ | | ng̲ | |
| Laterals | | | | | | l l̲ | L | | |
| Glides | | | | | | r r̲ | y y̲ | w̲ | |

The procedure is not without glaring shortcomings. For one thing, the process illustrated above is oversimplified. Subtle phonetic distinctions between phonemes have been ignored. Phonological environments and allophonic variants of phonemes have been overlooked. For example, Sebuktekin (1975) noted that Turkish /v/ has an allophone /w/ which occurs between some vowels in Turkish. Therefore, English /w/ would probably not present a fourth level of difficulty to a Turkish learner of English. With attention to such details you might, on the one hand, find it most difficult to use the hierarchy as prescribed and yet on the other hand find that more than three levels of difficulty can be defined. Surely, for example, the Turkish speaker will find varying degrees of difficulty within Level 4.

Other problems with the model are apparent. It is very difficult, even with six categories, to determine exactly which category a particular contrast fits into. For example, is learning the English /r/ really a case of learning an entirely new item? Phonetically that is the case. But in the underlying structures of the two languages the American English /r/ and the Turkish /r/ have very similar distributions and phonemic value. Moreover, the English learner can indeed substitute the Turkish /r/ in English and be understood. The latter is an argument for placing the /r/ contrast into Level 3 rather than 4. Yet intuitively we know that learning the English /r/ may be the most difficult item phonetically for learners from many backgrounds to master. Should not the /r/, therefore, be assigned the fifth degree of difficulty? In such a question lies a hint of some of the subjectivity of "scientific" hierarchies of difficulty.

# Moderating the Contrastive Analysis Hypothesis

The problems touched on above only begin to hint at the tentativeness of the Contrastive Analysis Hypothesis. The attempt to *predict* difficulty by means of contrastive analysis is what Ronald Wardhaugh (1970) called the *strong version* of the CAH, a version that he believed was quite unrealistic and impracticable. Wardhaugh noted (p. 125) that "at the very least, this version demands of linguists that they have available a set of linguistic universals formulated within a comprehensive linguistic theory which deals adequately with syntax, semantics, and phonology." He went on to point out the difficulty (p. 126), already noted, of an adequate procedure, built on sound theory, for actually contrasting the forms of languages: "Does the linguist have available to him an over-all contrastive system within which he can relate the two languages in terms of mergers, splits, zeroes, over-differentiations, under-differentiations, reinterpretations, and so on . . . ?" And so, while many linguists claimed to be using a scientific, empirical, and theoretically justified tool in contrastive analysis, in actuality they were operating more out of mentalistic subjectivity.

Wardhaugh noted, however (p. 126), that contrastive analysis has intuitive appeal, and that teachers and linguists have successfully used "the best linguistic knowledge available . . . in order to account for observed difficulties in second language learning." He termed such observational use of contrastive analysis the *weak version* of the CAH. The weak version does not imply the *a priori* prediction of certain fine degrees of difficulty. It recognizes the significance of interference across languages, the fact that such interference does exist and can explain difficulties, but it also recognizes that linguistic difficulties can be more profitably explained *a posteriori*—after the fact. As learners are learning the language and errors appear, the teacher can utilize their knowledge of the target and native languages to understand sources of error. Clearly, gross predictions can be made by observation and intuition and experience, but a language is made up of hundreds of thousands of items, and it is impossible to predict difficulty beyond some very glaring phonological differences between two languages. In fact, it is really *only* in the phonological component of language that contrastive analysis is mildly successful. In early stages of second language acquisition, learners produce the sounds of a foreign language in fairly consistent patterns, largely because pronunciation is a *psychomotor* skill and, with its reliance on muscular coordination, is a factor of more predictable interference. Syntactic, semantic, or lexical interference is far less predictable, since "cognitive coordination" (thinking, processing, storing, recalling, and the like), in all its tremendous variability, becomes more of a factor than muscular coordination. While one might *expect* a French speaker who is beginning to learn English to say "I am in New York since January," the *prediction* that a learner will make that error is a gamble. But if a learner then makes that error, a contrastive analysis of present-perfect usage in English with its French counterpart will reveal the source of the error.

The most convincing criticism of the strong version of the CAH was offered by Whitman himself, who with Kenneth Jackson (Whitman and Jackson 1972) undertook to test empirically the practicability of the Contrastive Analysis hypothesis. The predictions of four separate contrastive analyses (including that of Stockwell, Bowen, and Martin 1965) were applied to a 40-item test of English grammar to determine, *a priori,* the relative difficulty of the test items for speakers of Japanese. The test was administered to 2500 Japanese learners of English who did not know, of course, the predictions of the contrastive analyses. The results of the test were compared with the predictions. Whitman and Jackson found no support for the predictions of the contrastive analyses so carefully worked out by linguists! They concluded (p. 40) that "contrastive analysis, as represented by the four analyses tested in this project, is inadequate, theoretially and practically, to predict the interference problems of a language learner." While it is of interest to note that the Whitman and Jackson study was performed on *grammar,* which I have already pointed out to be less predictable than phonology, nevertheless the Contrastive

Analysis hypothesis—which purported to apply to any aspect of two languages—was found to be inadequate.

While Wardhaugh (1970) called for a "period of quiescence" for the CAH, Oller and Ziahosseiny (1970) hinted at a compromise between the strong and weak versions of the hypothesis. They proposed a *moderate* form of the CAH on the basis of a rather intriguing study of spelling errors. They found that for learners of English as a second language, English spelling proved to be more difficult for people whose native language used a Roman script (for example, French, Spanish) than for those whose native language used a non-Roman script (Arabic, Japanese). The strong form of the CAH would have predicted that the learning of an entirely new writing system (Level 4 in the hierarchy of difficulty) would be more difficult than reinterpreting (Level 3) spelling rules. Oller and Ziahosseiny found the opposite to be true and reasoned that knowledge of one Romanized system made it more difficult, not less, to acquire another Roman spelling system. They concluded that the strong form was too strong and the weak form too weak, but that a moderate version that centers on the nature of human learning, and not just on the contrast between two languages, has more explanatory power.

That moderate version of the CAH was technically defined as follows (p. 186): "The categorization of abstract and concrete patterns according to their perceived similarities and differences is the basis for learning; therefore, wherever patterns are minimally distinct in form or meaning in one or more systems, confusion may result." In other words, the learning of sounds, sequences, and meanings will be the most difficult where the most subtle distinctions are required either between the target language and native language or within the target language itself. In the case of their research on spelling English, there were more *differences* between non-Roman writing and Roman writing, but learners from a non-Roman writing system had to make fewer *subtle* distinctions than did those from the Roman writing system. We have all experienced learning an entirely new game or skill perhaps more easily than one that is somewhat similar to a skill already learned previously. The principle at work is common in human learning: interference can actually be greater when items to be learned are more similar to existing items than when items are entirely new and unrelated to existing items.

Oller and Ziahosseiny's moderate version put the CAH into some perspective. They rightly emphasized the generalizing nature of human learning. It is common to overgeneralize to the extent that minimal differences are overlooked; at the same time gross differences—because of their saliency—are often more easily perceived and stored in memory. Greater differences do not always result in greater learning difficulty. Such a perspective underscores the significance of *intra*lingual errors, which are as much a factor in second language learning as *inter*lingual errors. The forms within one language are often perceived to be minimally distinct in comparison to the vast distinctions between the native and target language, yet those intralingual factors can lead to some of the greatest difficulties.

The CAH in its strong form was, as Wardhaugh predicted, quietly laid to rest—if even with the cautious hope that someday, when the tools of linguistic and cultural analysis are perfected, we would then revive this methodology that did not deliver to language teachers the last word in applied linguistics. Meanwhile, teachers of foreign languages and researchers in second language acquisition were rightfully dissatisfied with too weak a version of contrastive analysis that only lent an explanation to certain errors after the fact. This state of professional anomie was somewhat soothed by moderate forms of the CAH that enabled us to get a larger picture of the nature of human learning and to understand a number of factors contributing to learning and forgetting.

# Markedness and Universal Grammar

Fred Eckman (1977) proposed a useful method for determining directionality of difficulty. His Markedness Differential Hypothesis (otherwise known as *markedness* theory) accounted for relative degrees of difficulty by means of principles of universal grammar. Celce-Murcia and Hawkins (1985:66) sum up markedness theory:

> It distinguishes members of a pair of related forms or structures by assuming that the marked member of a pair contains at least one more feature than the unmarked one. In addition, the unmarked (or neutral) member of the pair is the one with a wider range of distribution than the marked one. For example, in the case of the English indefinite articles (*a* and *an*), *an* is the more complex or marked form (it has an additional sound) and *a* is the unmarked form with the wider distribution.

Eckman (1981) showed that marked items in a language will be more difficult to acquire than unmarked, and that degrees of markedness will correspond to degrees of difficulty. Rutherford (1982) used markedness theory to explain why there seems to be a certain order of acquisition of morphemes in English: marked structures are acquired later than unmarked structures.

More recently, the attention of some second language researchers has expanded beyond markedness hypotheses alone to the broader framework of linguistic universals in general (see Eckman 1991, Carroll and Meisel 1990, Comrie 1990, Gass 1989). Some of these arguments focus on the applicability of notions of *universal grammar* (UG) to second language acquisition (White 1990, Schachter 1988, among others). "Rules" that are shared by all languages comprise this UG. Such rules are a set of limitations or *parameters* (Flynn 1987) of language. Different languages set their parameters differently, thereby creating the characteristic grammar for that language. The hope is that by discovering innate linguistic principles that govern what is possible in human languages, we may be better able to understand and describe contrasts between native and target languages and the difficulties encountered by adult second language learners. Research on UG has only just barely begun to identify such universal properties and principles, but it is nevertheless an avenue of some promise.

Markedness theory and UG perspectives provide a more sophisticated understanding of difficulty in learning a second language than we had previously from the early formulations of the CAH. But describing and predicting difficulty amidst all the variables of human learning is still an elusive process. As is the case with virtually every problem in linguistic analysis, our scientific methodological capacities are currently inadequate to give a complete account.

# Interlanguage

The CAH stressed the interfering effects of the first language on second language learning and claimed, in its strong form, that second language learning is primarily, if not exclusively, a process of acquiring whatever items are different from the first language. Such a narrow view of interference ignored the *intralingual* effects of learning, among other factors. In recent years researchers and teachers have come more and more to understand that second language learning is a creative process of constructing a system in which learners are consciously testing hypotheses about the target language from a number of possible sources of knowledge: limited knowledge of the target language itself, knowledge about the native language, knowledge about the communicative function of language, knowledge about language in general, and knowledge about life, human beings, and the universe. The learners, in acting upon their environment, construct what to them is a legitimate system of language in its own right—a structured set of rules that for the time being provide order to the linguistic chaos that confronts them.

By the late 1960s, second language learning began to be examined in much the same way that first language learning had been studied for some time: learners were looked on not as producers of malformed, imperfect language replete with mistakes but as intelligent and creative beings proceeding through logical, systematic stages of acquisition, creatively acting upon their linguistic environment as they encounter its forms and functions in meaningful contexts. By a gradual process of trial and error and hypothesis testing, learners slowly and tediously succeed in establishing closer and closer approximations to the system used by native speakers of the language. A number of terms have been coined to describe the perspective which stresses the legitimacy of learners' second language systems. The best known of these terms is *interlanguage,* a term that Selinker (1972) adapted from Weinreich's (1953) term "interlingual." Interlanguage refers to the separateness of a second language learner's system, a system that has a structurally intermediate status between the native and target languages. Nemser (1971) referred to the same general phenomenon in second language learning but stressed the successive approximation to the target language in his term *approximative system*. Corder (1971:151) used the term *idiosyncratic dialect* to connote the idea that the learner's language is unique to a particular individual, that the rules of the learner's language are peculiar to the language of that individual alone. While each of these designations emphasizes a particular notion, they share the concept that second language learners are forming their own self-contained linguistic systems. This is neither the system of the native language nor the system of the target language, but instead falls between the two; it is a system based upon the best attempt of learners to provide order and structure to the linguistic stimuli surrounding them. The interlanguage hypothesis led to a whole new era of second language research and teaching and presented a significant breakthrough from the shackles of the contrastive analysis hypothesis.

The most obvious approach to analyzing interlanguage is to study the speech and writing of learners, or, what has come to be called *learner language* (James 1990). Production data is publicly observable and is presumably reflective of a learner's underlying competence—production competence, that is. Comprehension of a second language is more difficult to study since it is not directly observable and must be inferred by overt verbal and nonverbal responses, by artificial instruments, or by the intuition of the teacher or researcher. It follows that the study of the speech and writing of learners is largely the study of the errors of learners. "Correct" production yields little information about the actual interlanguage system of learners, only information about the target language system that learners have already acquired. Therefore, our focus in the rest of this chapter will be on the significance of errors in learners' interlanguage systems, otherwise known as *error analysis.*

## Error Analysis

Human learning is fundamentally a process that involves the making of mistakes. Mistakes, misjudgments, miscalculations, and erroneous assumptions form an important aspect of learning virtually any skill or acquiring information. You learn to swim by first jumping into the water and flailing arms and legs until you discover that there is a combination of movements—a structured pattern—that succeeds in keeping you afloat and propelling you through the water. The first mistakes of learning to swim are giant ones, gradually diminishing as you learn from making those mistakes. Learning to swim, to play tennis, to type, or to read all involve a process in which success comes by profiting from mistakes, by using mistakes to obtain feedback from the environment and with that feedback to make new attempts which successively more closely approximate desired goals.

Language learning, in this sense, is like any other human learning. We have already seen in the second chapter that children learning their first language make countless "mistakes" from the point of view of adult grammatical language. Many of these mistakes are logical in the limited linguistic system within which children operate, but by carefully processing feedback from others such children slowly but surely learn to produce what is acceptable speech in their native language. Second language learning is a process that is clearly not unlike first language learning in its trial-and-error nature. Inevitably learners will make mistakes in the process of acquisition, and indeed will even impede that process if they do not commit errors and then benefit in turn from various forms of feedback on those errors.

Researchers and teachers of second languages soon came to realize that the mistakes a person made in this process of constructing a new system of language needed to be analyzed carefully, for they possibly held in them some of the keys to the understanding of the process of second language acquisition. As Corder (1967:167) noted: "A learner's errors . . . are significant in [that] they provide to the researcher evidence of how language is learned or acquired, what strategies or procedures the learner is employing in the discovery of the language."

## Mistakes and Errors

In order to analyze learner language in a proper perspective, it is crucial to make a distinction between *mistakes* and *errors,* technically two very different phenomena. A mistake refers to a performance error that is either a random guess or a "slip," in that it is a failure to utilize a known system correctly. All people make mistakes, in both native and second language situations. Native speakers are normally capable of recognizing and correcting such "lapses" or mistakes, which are not the result of a deficiency in competence but the result of some sort of breakdown or imperfection in the process of producing speech. These hesitations, slips of the tongue, random ungrammaticalities, and other performance lapses in native-speaker production also occur in second language speech.

Such mistakes must be carefully distinguished from *errors* of a second language learner, idiosyncrasies in the interlanguage of the learner that are direct manifestations of a system within which a learner is operating at the time. Dulay and Burt (1972) referred to errors as "goofs," defined in an earlier work—*The Gooficon* (Burt and Kiparsky 1972:1)—as "an error . . . for which no blame is implied." Put in another way, an error is a noticeable deviation from the adult grammar of a native speaker, reflecting the interlanguage competence of the learner. If a learner of English asks, "Does John can sing?" he is probably reflecting a competence level in which all verbs require a pre-posed *do* auxiliary for question formation. He has committed an error, most likely not a mistake, and an error which reveals a portion of his competence in the target language.

Can you tell the difference between an error and a mistake? Not always. If, on one or two occasions, for example, an English learner says "John cans sing," but on other occasions says "John can sing," it is difficult to determine whether "cans" is a mistake or an error. If, however, further examination of the learner's speech reveals such utterances as "John wills go," "John mays come," and so forth, with very few instances of correct third-person singular usage of modal auxiliaries, you might then conclude that "cans," "mays," and other such forms are errors indicating that the learner has not distinguished modals from other verbs, though perhaps—because of the few correct instances—she is on the verge of making the necessary differentiation between the two types of verbs in her systematic conception of the second language. You can thus appreciate the subjectivity of determining the difference between a mistake and an error in learner speech. That undertaking always bears with it the chance of a faulty assumption on the part of a teacher or researcher.

The fact that learners do make errors and that these errors can be observed, analyzed, and classified to reveal something of the system operating within the learner, led to a surge of study of learners' errors, called *error analysis*. Error analysis became distinguished from contrastive analysis by its examination of errors attributable to *all* possible sources, not just those which result from negative transfer of the native language. Error analysis easily superseded contrastive analysis, as we discovered that only *some* of the errors a learner makes are attributable to the mother tongue, that learners do not actually make all the errors that contrastive analysis predicted they should, and that learners from disparate language backgrounds tend to make similar errors in learning one target language. Errors—overt manifestations of learners' systems—arise from several possible general sources: interlingual errors of interference from the native language, intralingual errors within the target language, the sociolinguistic context of communication, psycholinguistic or cognitive strategies, and no doubt countless affective variables.

### Errors in Error Analysis

There is a danger in too much attention to learners' errors. While errors are indeed revealing of a system at work, the classroom foreign language teacher can become so preoccupied with noticing errors that the correct utterances in the second language go unnoticed. In our observation and analysis of errors—for all that they do reveal about the learner—we must beware of placing too much attention on errors and not lose sight of the value of positive reinforcement of clear, free communication. While the diminishing of errors is an important criterion for increasing language proficiency, the ultimate goal of second language learning is the attainment of communicative fluency in a language.

Another shortcoming in error analysis is an overstressing of production data. Language is speaking *and* listening, writing *and* reading. The comprehension of language is as important as production. It so happens that production lends itself to analysis and thus becomes the prey of researchers; but comprehension data is equally important in developing an understanding of the process of second language acquisition.

Jacqueline Schachter (1974) and others (see Kleinmann 1977) have shown in research that error analysis fails to account for the strategy of *avoidance.* A learner who for one reason or another avoids a particular sound, word, structure, or discourse category may be assumed incorrectly to have no difficulty therewith. Schachter found, for example, that it was misleading to draw conclusions about relative-clause errors among certain English learners; native Japanese speakers were largely avoiding that structure and thus not manifesting nearly as many errors as some native Persian speakers. The absence of error therefore does not necessarily reflect nativelike competence since learners may be avoiding the very structures that pose difficulty for them.

Finally, error analysis can keep us too closely focused on specific languages rather than viewing *universal* aspects of language. Gass (1984) recommended that researchers pay more attention to linguistic elements that are common to all languages. The interlanguage systems of learners may have elements that reflect neither the target language nor the native language but rather a universal feature of some kind. Such assertions are in keeping with the bio-programming theories referred to in Chapter Two. But there are problems, of course, with the search for universal properties of learner's errors. "It is not at all clear in any precise way when the influence of the universal will appear in the interlanguage of learners rather than a violation of it based on influence from either the source or target language" (Celce-Murcia and Hawkins 1985:66).

We do well, therefore, in the analysis of learners' interlanguage errors, to engage in "performance analysis"—or perhaps more simply, "interlanguage analysis" (Celce-Murcia and Hawkins 1985:64), a less restrictive concept that places a healthy investigation of errors within the larger perspective of the learner's total interlanguage performance. While a significant portion of this chapter deals with error analysis, let us nevertheless remember that production errors are only a subset of the overall performance of the learner.

# Identifying and Describing Errors

One of the common difficulties in understanding the linguistic systems of both first and second language learners is the fact that such systems cannot be directly observed. They must be inferred by means of analyzing production and comprehension data. What makes the task even thornier, however, is the *instability* of learners' systems. Systems are in a constant state of flux as new information flows in and, through the process of subsumption, causes existing structures to be revised. Repeated observations of a learner will often reveal apparently unpredictable or even contradictory data. In undertaking the task of performance analysis, the teacher and researcher are called upon to infer order and logic in this unstable and variable system.

The first step in the process of analysis is the identification and description of errors. Corder (1971) provided a model for identifying erroneous or idiosyncratic utterances in a second language. That model is schematized in Figure 8–1. According to Corder's model, any sentence uttered by the learner and subsequently transcribed can be analyzed for idiosyncrasies. A major distinction is made at the outset between "overt" and "covert" errors. Overtly erroneous utterances are unquestionably ungrammatical at the sentence level. Covertly erroneous utterances are grammatically well-formed at the sentence level but are not interpretable within the context of communication. Covert errors, in other words, are not really covert at all if you attend to surrounding discourse (before or after the utterance). "I'm fine, thank you" is grammatically correct at the sentence level, but as a response to "Who are you?" it is very obviously an error. A simpler and more straightforward set of terms, then, would be "sentence level" and "discourse level" errors.

Corder's model in Figure 8–1 indicates that, in the case of both overt and covert errors, if a plausible interpretation can be made of the sentence then one should form a reconstruction of the sentence in the target language, compare the reconstruction with the original idiosyncratic sentence, and then describe the differences. If the native language of the learner is known, the model indicates using translation as a possible indicator of native language interference as the source of error. In some cases, of course, no plausible interpretation is possible at all, and the researcher is left with no analysis of the error ($OUT_3$).

Consider the following examples of idiosyncratic utterances of learners, and let us allow them to be fed through Corder's procedure for error analysis:

1.  Does John can sing?

    A.  NO

    C.  YES

    D.  Can John sing?

    E.  Original sentence contained pre-posed *do* auxiliary applicable to most verbs, but not to verbs with modal auxiliaries, $OUT_2$

2.  I saw their department.

    A.  YES

    B.  NO (context was in a conversation about living quarters in Mexico)

    C.  NO

    F.  YES, Spanish.

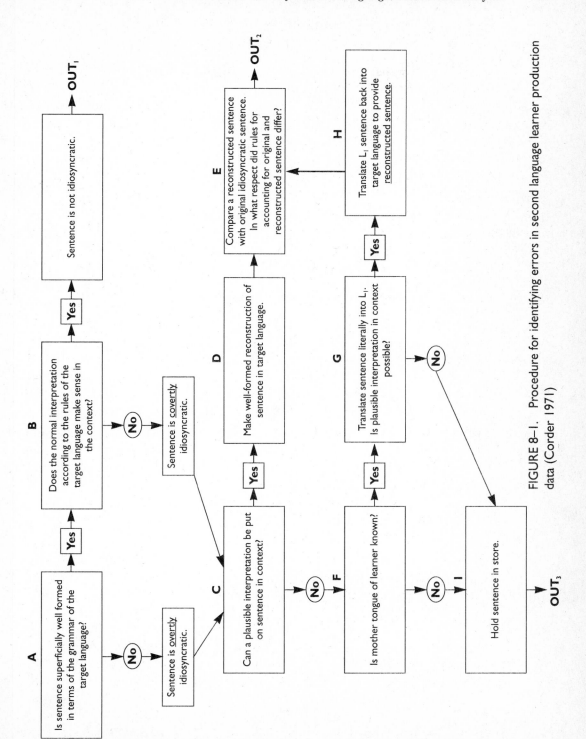

FIGURE 8–1.  Procedure for identifying errors in second language learner production data (Corder 1971)

G.    Yo vi su departamento. YES

H.    I saw their apartment.

E.    *Departamento* was translated to false cognate *department*. OUT₂

3.  The different city is another one in the another two.

A.    NO

C.    NO

F.    YES, Spanish.

G.    No plausible translation or interpretation.

I.    No analysis. OUT₃

It can be seen that the model is not complicated and represents a procedure that teachers and researchers might intuitively follow. However, once an error is identified, the next step is to describe it adequately, something the above procedure has only begun to accomplish.

A number of different categories for description of errors have been identified in research on learner language (for an overview, see Lennon 1991):

1.   The most generalized breakdown can be made by identifying errors of addition, omission, substitution, and ordering, following standard mathematical categories. In English a *do* auxiliary might be added (Does can he sing?), a definite article omitted (I went to movie), an item substituted (I lost my road), or a word order confused (I to the store went). But such categories are clearly very generalized.

2.   Within each category, *levels* of language can be considered: phonology or orthography, lexicon, grammar, and discourse. Often, of course, it is difficult to distinguish different levels of errors. A word with a faulty pronunciation, for example, might hide a syntactic or lexical error. A French learner who says "[zhey] suis allé à l'école" might be mispronouncing the grammatically correct "je," or correctly pronouncing a grammatically incorrect "j'ai."

3.   Errors may also be viewed as either *global* or *local* (Burt and Kiparsky 1974). Global errors hinder communication; they prevent the hearer from comprehending some aspect of the message. For example, "Well, it's a great hurry around," in whatever context, may be difficult or impossible to interpret. Local errors do not prevent the message from being heard, usually because there is only a minor violation of one segment of a sentence, allowing the hearer/reader to make an accurate guess about the intended meaning. "A scissors," for example, is a local error. The global-local distinction is discussed in the vignette at the end of this chapter.

4.  Finally, Lennon (1991) suggests that two related dimensions of error, *domain* and *extent* should be considered in any error analysis. Domain is the rank of linguistic unit (from phoneme to discourse) that must be taken as context in order for the error to become apparent, and extent is the rank of linguistic unit that would have to be deleted, replaced, supplied, or reordered in order to repair the sentence. Lennon's categories help to operationalize Corder's overt-covert distinction discussed above. So, in the example just cited above, "a scissors," the domain is the phrase, and the extent is the indefinite article.

# Stages of Interlanguage Development

There are many different ways to describe the progression of linguistic development that learners manifest as their attempts at production successively approximate the target language system. Indeed, learners are so variable in their acquisition of a second language that stages of development defy description. Borrowing some insights from an earlier model proposed by Corder (1973), I have found it useful to think in terms of four stages, based on observations of what the learner does in terms of errors alone.

The first is a stage of *random errors,* a stage that Corder called "presystematic," in which the learner is only vaguely aware that there is some systematic order to a particular class of items. The example in the previous section, "The different city is another one in the another two," surely comes out of a random error stage in which the learner is making rather wild guesses at what to write. Inconsistencies like "John cans sing," "John can to sing," and "John can singing," said by the same learner within a short period of time, might indicate a stage of experimentation and inaccurate guessing.

The second, or *emergent,* stage of interlanguage finds the learner growing in consistency in linguistic production. The learner has begun to discern a system and to internalize certain rules. These rules may not be "correct" by target language standards, but they are nevertheless legitimate in the mind of the learner. This stage is characterized by some "backsliding," in which the learner seems to have grasped a rule or principle and then regresses to some previous stage. Generally the learner is still, at this stage, unable to correct errors when they are pointed out by someone else. Avoidance of structures and topics is typical. Consider the following conversation between a learner (L) and a native speaker (NS) of English:

L:   I go New York.
NS:   You're going to New York?
L:   [doesn't understand] What?

NS:    You will go to New York?

L:     Yes.

NS:    When?

L:     1972.

NS:    Oh, you went to New York in 1972.

L:     Yes, I go 1972.

Such a conversation is reminiscent of those mentioned in Chapter Two where children in first language situations could not discern any error in their speech.

A third stage is a truly *systematic* stage in which the learner is now able to manifest more consistency in producing the second language. While those rules inside the head of the learner are still not all "well-formed," they are more internally self-consistent and, of course, they are more closely approximating the target language system. The most salient difference between the second and third stage is the ability of learners to correct their errors when they are pointed out—even very subtly—to them. Consider the English learner who described a popular fishing-resort area.

L:     Many fish are in the lake. These fish are serving in the restaurants near the lake.

NS:    [laughing] The fish are serving?

L:     [laughing] Oh, no, the fish are served in the restaurants!

A final stage, which I will call the *stabilization* stage in the development of interlanguage systems, is akin to what Corder (1973) called a "postsystematic" stage. Here the learner has relatively few errors and has mastered the system to the point that fluency and intended meanings are not problematic. This fourth stage is characterized by the learner's ability to self-correct. The system is complete enough that attention can be paid to those few errors that occur and corrections made without waiting for feedback from someone else. It is at this point that learners can stabilize too fast, allowing minor errors to slip by undetected, and thus manifest *fossilization* of their language, a concept that will be defined and discussed later in this chapter (see Selinker and Lamendella 1979).

Lest you be tempted to assume that all learner language is orderly and systematic, a caveat is in order. A great deal of attention has been recently given to the *variability* of interlanguage development (Littlewood 1981, Tarone 1988, James 1990, Ellis 1987). Just as native speakers of a language vacillate between expressions like "It has to be you," and "It must be you," learners also exhibit variation, sometimes within the parameters of acceptable norms, sometimes not. Some variability in learner language can be explained by what Gatbonton (1983) described as the "gradual diffusion" of incorrect forms of language in emergent and systematic stages of development: first, incorrect forms coexist with correct, then, the incorrect are expunged. Context has also been identified as a source of variation. In classrooms, the type of task can affect variation (Tarone and Parrish 1988). And variability can be affected, in both tutored and untutored learning, by the exposure that a learner gets to norms. In short, one simply must expect a good proportion of interlanguage data to fall beyond our capacity for systematic categorization.

It should also be made clear that the four stages of systematicity outlined above do not describe a learner's total second language system. We would find it hard to assert, for example, that a learner is an emergent stage, globally, for all of the linguistic subsystems of language. One might be in a second stage with respect to, say, the perfect-tense system, and in the third or fourth stage when it comes to simple present and past tenses. Nor do these stages, which are based on error analysis, adequately account for sociolinguistic, functional, or nonverbal strategies, all of which are important in assessing the total competence of the second language learner. Finally, we need to remember that production errors alone are inadequate measures of overall competence. They happen to be salient features of second language learners' interlanguage and present us with grist for error-analysis mills, but *correct* utterances deserve our attention, and especially in the teaching-learning process, deserve positive reinforcement.

# Sources of Error

Having examined procedures of error analysis used to identify errors in second language learner production data, our final step in the analysis of learner speech is that of determining the *source* of error. Why are certain errors made? What cognitive strategies and styles or even personality variables underlie certain errors? While the answers to these questions are somewhat speculative in that sources must be inferred from available data, in such questions lies the ultimate value of interlanguage analysis in general. By trying to identify sources we can begin to arrive at an understanding of how the learner's cognitive and affective self relates to the linguistic system and to formulate an integrated understanding of the process of second language acquisition.

## *Interlingual Transfer*

The beginning stages of learning a second language are characterized by a good deal of interlingual transfer from the native language, or, interference. In these early stages, before the system of the second language is familiar, the native language is the only linguistic system in previous experience upon which the learner can draw. We have all heard English learners say "sheep" for "ship," or "the book of Jack" instead of "Jack's book"; French learners may say,

"Je sais Jean," for "Je connais Jean," and so forth. All these errors are attributable to negative interlingual transfer. While it is not always clear that an error is the result of transfer from the native language, many such errors are detectable in learner speech. Fluent knowledge of a learner's native language of course aids the teacher in detecting and analyzing such errors; however, even familiarity with the language can be of help in pinpointing this common source.

The learning of a *third language* (and subsequent languages) provides an interesting context for research. Depending upon a number of factors including the linguistic and cultural relatedness of the languages and the context of learning, there are varying degrees of interlingual interference from both the first and second language to the third language, especially if the second and third languages are closely related or the learner is attempting a third language shortly after beginning a second language.

## *Intralingual Transfer*

One of the major contributions of error analysis was its recognition of sources of error that extend beyond just interlingual errors in learning a second language. It is now clear that intralingual transfer (within the target language itself) is a major factor in second language learning. In Chapter Four we discussed overgeneralization, which is the negative counterpart of intralingual transfer. Researchers (see especially Taylor 1975) have found that the early stages of language learning are characterized by a predominance of interference (interlingual transfer), but once learners have begun to acquire parts of the new system, more and more intralingual transfer—generalization within the target language—is manifested. This of course follows logically from the tenets of learning theory. As learners progress in the second language, their previous experience and their existing subsumers begin to include structures within the target language itself.

Negative intralingual transfer, or overgeneralization, has already been illustrated in such utterances as "Does John can sing?" Other examples abound—utterances like "He goed," "I don't know what time is it," and "Il a tombé." Once again, the teacher or researcher cannot always be certain of the source of an apparent intralingual error, but repeated systematic observations of a learner's speech data will often remove the ambiguity of a single observation of an error.

The analysis of intralingual errors in a corpus of production data can become quite complex. For example, in Barry Taylor's (1975:95) analysis of English sentences produced by ESL learners, just the class of errors in producing the main verb following an auxiliary yielded nine different types of error:

1.  Past tense form of verb following a modal
2.  Present tense -*s* on a verb following a modal

3.  *-ing* on a verb following a modal

4.  *are* (for *be*) following *will*

5.  Past tense form of verb following *do*

6.  Present tense *-s* on a verb following *do*

7.  *-ing* on a verb following *do*

8.  Past tense form of a verb following *be* (inserted to replace a modal or *do*)

9.  Present tense *-s* on a verb following *be* (inserted to replace a modal or *do*)

And of course these are limited to the particular data that Taylor was analyzing and are therefore not exhaustive within a grammatical category. Moreover, they pertain only to errors of overgeneralization, excluding another long list of categories of errors that he found attributable to interlingual transfer. Similarly, Jack C. Richards (1971:185–187) provided a list of typical English intralingual errors in the use of articles (see Table 9–1). These are not exhaustive either but only exemplary of some of the errors one commonly encounters in English learners from disparate native language backgrounds. Both Taylor's and Richards's lists are restricted to English, but clearly their counterparts exist in other languages.

### *Context of Learning*

A third major source of error, though it overlaps both types of transfer, is the context of learning. "Context" refers, for example, to the classroom with its teacher and its materials in the case of school learning or the social situation in the case of untutored second language learning. In a classroom context the teacher or the textbook can lead the learner to make faulty hypotheses about the language, what Richards (1971) called "false concepts" and what Stenson (1974) termed "induced errors." Students often make errors because of a misleading explanation from the teacher, faulty presentation of a structure or word in a textbook, or even because of a pattern that was rotely memorized in a drill but not properly contextualized. Two vocabulary items presented contiguously—for example, *point at* and *point out*—might in later recall be confused simply because of the contiguity of presentation. Or a teacher may out of some ignorance provide incorrect information—not an uncommon occurrence—by way of a misleading definition, word, or grammatical generalization. Another manifestation of language learned in classroom contexts is the occasional tendency on the part of learners to give uncontracted and inappropriately formal forms of language. We have all experienced foreign learners whose "bookish" language gives them away as classroom language learners.

The social context of language acquisition will produce other types of errors. The sociolinguistic context of natural, untutored language acquisition

## TABLE 8–2.    Typical English Intralingual Errors in the Use of Articles
### (From Richards 1971:187)

---

1.  **OMISSION OF** *THE*

    (a)  before unique nouns        Sun is very hot
                                                  Himalayas are . . .

    (b)  before nouns of nationality     Spaniards and Arabs . . .

    (c)  before nouns made particular   At the conclusion of article
            in context                                 She goes to bazaar every day
                                                    She is mother of that boy

    (d)  before a noun modified by a participle    Solution given in this article
    (e)  before superlatives            Richest person
    (f)  before a noun modified by an *of-phrase*   Institute of Nuclear Physics

---

2.  *THE* **USED INSTEAD OF** ∅

    (a)  before proper names         The Shakespeare, the Sunday
    (b)  before abstract nouns       The friendship, the nature,
                                                  the science

    (c)  before nouns behaving like     After the school, after the
            abstract nouns                      breakfast

    (d)  before plural nouns          The complex structures are
                                                  still developing

    (e)  before *some*                  The some knowledge

---

3.  *A* **USED INSTEAD OF** *THE*

    (a)  before superlatives          a worst, a best boy in the
                                                  class

    (b)  before unique nouns         a sun becomes red

---

4.  *A* **INSTEAD OF** ∅

    (a)  before a plural noun qualified by   a holy place, a human beings,
            an adjective                       a bad news
    (b)  before uncountables        a gold, a work
    (c)  before an adjective          . . . taken as a definite

---

5.  **OMISSION OF** *A*

    before class nouns defined by adjectives    he was good boy
                                                              he was brave man

---

can give rise to certain dialect acquisition that may itself be a source of error. Corder's term *idiosyncratic dialect* applies especially well here. For example, a Japanese immigrant lived in a predominantly Mexican-American area of a city in the United States, and his interlanguage was a rather interesting blend of Mexican-American English and the standard English to which he was exposed in the university.

### Communication Strategies

In Chapter Five, communication strategies were defined and related to learning styles. Learners obviously use production strategies in order to enhance getting their messages across, but at times these techniques can themselves become a source of error. Once an ESL learner said, "Let us work for the well done of our country." While it exhibited a nice little twist of humor, the sentence had an incorrect approximation of the word "welfare." Likewise, word coinage, circumlocution, false cognates (from Tarone 1981), and prefabricated patterns can all be sources of error.

# Fossilization

It is a common experience to witness in a learner's language various erroneous features that persist despite what is otherwise a fluent command of the language. This phenomenon is ordinarily manifested phonologically in "foreign accents" in the speech of many of those who have learned a second language after adolescence. We also commonly observe syntactic and lexical errors persisting in the speech of those who have otherwise learned the language quite well. The relatively permanent incorporation of incorrect linguistic forms into a person's second language competence has been referred to as *fossilization.* Interestingly enough, the internalization of incorrect forms takes place by means of the same learning processes as the internalization of correct forms, but we refer to the latter, of course, as "learning." So, fossilization should not be viewed as some sort of terminal illness, in spite of the forbidding metaphor that depicts an unchangeable situation, etched in the stone of time. A better metaphor might be something like "cryogenation"—the process of freezing matter at very low temperatures; we would then have a picture of a situation that could be reversed, given some warmth, of course!

How do items become fossilized? Until recently there was little attempt to grapple with the cognitive or affective dimensions of fossilization. But now fossilization can be seen as consistent with the laws of human learning. Vigil and Oller (1976) provided a formal account of fossilization as a factor of positive and negative affective and cognitive feedback. They noted that there are two kinds of information transmitted between sources (learners) and audiences (in this case, native speakers): information about the *affective* relationship between source and audience, and *cognitive* information—facts, suppositions, beliefs. Affective information is primarily encoded in terms of kinesic mechanisms—gestures, tone of voice, facial expressions—while cognitive information is usually conveyed by means of linguistic devices—sounds, phrases, structures, discourse. The feedback learners get from their audience can be either positive, negative, or neutral. Illustrations of different types of feedback were given by Vigil and Oller (p. 286):

### AFFECTIVE FEEDBACK

POSITIVE:  "I like it" (more of the same)
NEUTRAL:  "Waiting . . ." (reaction undecided)
NEGATIVE:  "I don't like it" (try something else)

### COGNITIVE FEEDBACK

POSITIVE:  "I understand" (message and direction are clear)
NEUTRAL:  "Still processing . . ." (undecided)
NEGATIVE:  "I don't understand" (message and/or direction are not clear)

Various combinations of the two major types of feedback are possible. For example, an audience can indicate positive affective feedback ("I affirm you and value what you are trying to communicate") but give neutral or even negative cognitive feedback to indicate that the message itself is unclear. Vigil and Oller astutely observe that negative affective feedback, regardless of the degree of cognitive feedback, will likely result in the abortion of future attempts to communicate. This is, of course, consistent with the overriding affective nature of human interaction: if people are not at least affirmed and their communication valued, there is little reason for communication. So, one of the first requirements for meaningful communication, as has been pointed out in earlier chapters, is an affective affirmation of the other person.

Vigil and Oller's model thus holds that a positive affective response is imperative to the learner's desire to continue attempts to communicate. Cognitive feedback then determines the degree of internalization. Negative or neutral feedback in the cognitive dimension will, with the prerequisite positive affective feedback, encourage learners to "try again," to restate, to reformulate, or to draw a different hypothesis about a rule. Positive feedback in the cognitive dimension will result in reinforcement of the forms used and a conclusion on the part of learners that their speech is well-formed. Fossilized items, then, are those *un*grammatical or *in*correct items in the speech of a learner that gain first positive affective feedback ("I like it") then positive cognitive feedback ("I understand"), reinforcing an incorrect form of language. Learners with fossilized items have acquired them through the same positive feedback and reinforcement with which they acquired correct items.

We need to be careful in interpreting Vigil and Oller's model. While it is most helpful, for example, in understanding models of error correction as we shall see in the vignette to follow at the end of this chapter, there are flaws in attributing such importance to feedback alone. Selinker and Lamendella (1979) noted that Vigil and Oller's model relies on the notion of *extrinsic* feedback, and that there are other factors internal to the learner which affect fossilization. We are not merely a product of our environment. Internal motivating factors, the need for interaction with other people, and innate and universal factors could all account for various instances of fossilization. As teachers, we may, and rightly so, attach great importance to the feedback we give to students, but we must recognize that there are other forces at work in the process of internalizing a second language.

## In the Classroom: Error Correction

As the focus of classroom instruction has shifted over the past few decades from an emphasis on language forms to attention to functional language within communicative contexts, the question of the place of error correction has become more and more important. The research on this issue (Long 1988, Lightbown and Spada 1990) suggests that form-focused instruction can indeed increase learner's levels of attainment, but that the "neanderthal" (Long 1988:136) practices (grammatical explanations, discussion of rules, rote practice) of bygone years is clearly not justified. Error treatment and focus on language forms appears to be most effective when incorporated into a communicative, learner-centered curriculum, and least effective when error correction is a dominant pedagogical feature, occupying the focal attention of students in the classroom.

How, then, might one judiciously approach error treatment in the communicative classroom? One of the keys, but not the only key, of course, to successful learning lies in the *feedback* that a learner receives from others, as we have just seen in the Vigil and Oller model above. Figure 8–2 metaphorically depicts what happens in that model.

The "green light" of the affective feedback mode allows the sender to continue attempting to get a message across; a "red light" causes the sender to abort such attempts. (The metaphorical nature of such a chart is evident in the fact that affective feedback does not precede cognitive feedback, as this chart may lead you to believe; both modes can take place simultaneously.) The traffic signal of cognitive feedback is the point at which error correction enters in. A green light here symbolizes noncorrective feedback that says "I understand your message." A red light symbolizes corrective feedback that takes on a myriad of possible forms (outlined below) and causes the learner to make some kind of alteration in production. To push the metaphor further, a yellow light could represent those various shades of color that are interpreted by the learner as falling somewhere in between a complete green light and a red light, causing the learner to adjust, to alter, to recycle back, to try again in some way. Note that fossilization may be the result of too many green lights when there should have been some yellow or red lights.

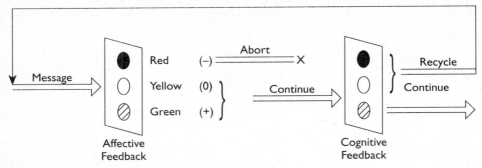

FIGURE 8–2.   Affective and cognitive feedback

The most useful implication of Vigil and Oller's model for a theory of error correction is that cognitive feedback must be *optimal* in order to be effective. Too much negative cognitive feedback—a barrage of interruptions, corrections, and overt attention to malformations—often leads learners to shut off their attempts at communication. They perceive that so much is wrong with their production that there is little hope to get anything right. On the other hand, too much positive cognitive feedback—willingness of the teacher-hearer to let errors go uncorrected, to indicate understanding when understanding may not have occurred—serves to reinforce the errors of the speaker-learner. The result is the persistence, and perhaps the eventual fossilization, of such errors. The task of the teacher is to discern the optimal tension between positive and negative cognitive feedback: providing enough green lights to encourage continued communication, but not so many that crucial errors go unnoticed, and providing enough red lights to call attention to those crucial errors, but not so many that the learner is discouraged from attempting to speak at all.

We do well to recall at this point the application of Skinner's operant conditioning model of learning discussed in Chapter Four. The affective and cognitive modes of feedback are *reinforcers* to speakers' *responses*. As speakers perceive "positive" reinforcement, or the "green lights" of Figure 8–3, they will be led to internalize certain speech patterns. Corrective feedback can still be "positive" in the Skinnerian sense, as we shall see below. However, ignoring erroneous behavior has the effect of a positive reinforcer; therefore teachers must be very careful to discern the possible reinforcing consequences of neutral feedback. What we must avoid at all costs is the administration of *punitive* reinforcement, or, correction that is viewed by learners as an affective red light—devaluing, dehumanizing, or insulting their personhood.

Against this theoretical backdrop we can evaluate some possibilities of when and how to treat errors in the language classroom. Long (1977:288) suggested that the question of *when* to treat an error (that is, which errors to provide some sort of feedback on) has no simple answer.

Having noticed an error, the first (and, I would argue, crucial) decision the teacher makes is whether or not to treat it at all. In order to make the decision the teacher may have recourse to factors with immediate, temporary bearing, such as the importance of the error to the current pedagogical focus on the lesson, the teacher's perception of the chance of eliciting correct performance from the student if negative feedback is given, and so on. Consideration of these ephemeral factors may be preempted, however, by the teacher's beliefs (conscious or unconscious) as to what a language is and how a new one is learned. These beliefs may have been formed years before the lesson in question.

In a most practical and clearly written article on error correction, Hendrickson (1980) advised teachers to try to discern the difference between *global* and *local* errors, already described earlier in this chapter. Once a learner of English was describing a quaint old hotel in Europe and said, "There is a French widow in every bedroom." The local error is clearly, and humorously, recognized. Hendrickson recommended that local errors usually need not be corrected since the message is clear and correction might interrupt a learner in the flow of productive communication. Global errors need to be corrected in some way since the message may otherwise remain garbled. "I saw their department" is a sentence that would most likely need correcting if the hearer is confused about the final word in that sentence. Many utterances are not clearly global or local, and it is difficult to discern the necessity for corrective feedback. A learner once wrote, "The grammar is the basement of every language." While this witty little proclamation may indeed sound more like Chomsky than Chomsky does, it behooves the teacher to ascertain just what the learner meant here (no doubt "basis" rather than "basement"), and to provide some feedback to clarify the difference between the two. The bottom line is that we simply must not stifle our students' attempts at production by smothering them with corrective feedback.

The matter of *how* to correct errors gets exceedingly complex. Research on error correction methods is not at all conclusive on the most effective method or technique for error correction. It seems quite clear that students in the classroom generally want and expect errors to be corrected (Cathcart and Olsen 1976). However, some methods recommend no direct treatment of error at all (Krashen and Terrell 1983). In "natural," untutored environments nonnative speakers generally get corrected by native speakers on only a small percentage of errors that they make (Chun et al. 1982); native speakers will attend basically only to global errors and then usually not in the form of interruptions but at transition points in conversations (Day et al. 1984). Balancing these various perspectives, I think we can safely conclude that a sensitive and perceptive language teacher should make the language classroom a happy optimum between some of the overpoliteness of the real world and the expectations that learners bring with them to the classroom.

Error treatment options can be classified in a number of possible ways (see Gaies 1983, Long 1977), but one useful taxonomy is recommended by Bailey (1985), who drew from the work of Allwright (1975). Seven "basic options" are complemented by eight "possible features" within each option (Bailey 1985:111).

## BASIC OPTIONS:

1. To treat or to ignore
2. To treat immediately or to delay

3. To transfer treatment [to, say, other learners] or not
4. To transfer to another individual, a subgroup, or the whole class
5. To return, or not, to original error maker after treatment
6. To permit other learners to initiate treatment
7. To test for the efficacy of the treatment

## POSSIBLE FEATURES:

1. Fact of error indicated
2. Location indicated
3. Opportunity for new attempt given
4. Model provided
5. Error type indicated
6. Remedy indicated
7. Improvement indicated
8. Praise indicated

All of the basic options and features within each option are conceivably viable modes of error correction in the classroom. The teacher needs to develop the intuition, through experience and solid eclectic theoretical foundations, for ascertaining which option or combination of options is appropriate at given moments. Principles of optimal affective and cognitive feedback, of reinforcement theory, and of communicative language teaching, all combine to form those theoretical foundations.

At least one general conclusion that can be drawn from the study of errors in the interlanguage systems of learners is that learners are indeed creatively operating on a second language—constructing, either consciously or subconsciously, a system for understanding and producing utterances in the language. That system should not necessarily be treated as an imperfect system; it is such only insofar as native speakers compare their own knowledge of the language to that of the learners. It should rather be looked upon as a variable, dynamic, approximative system, reasonable to a great degree in the mind of the learners, albeit idiosyncratic. Learners are processing language on the basis of knowledge of their own interlanguage, which, as a system lying between two languages, ought not to have the value judgments of either language placed upon it. The teacher's task is to value learners, prize their attempts to communicate, and then to provide optimal feedback for the system to evolve in successive stages until learners are communicating meaningfully and unambiguously in the second language.

## Suggested Readings

*Celce-Murcia and Hawkins* (1985) provide a readable summary of contrastive analysis, error analysis, and interlanguage.

For some of the earlier statements, pro and con, on the efficacy of the Constrastive Analysis Hypothesis, you might like to look at *Lado* (1957) and *Banathy, Trager, and Waddle* (1966), who are favorably inclined, and at *Wardhaugh* (1970), who offered a more balanced perspective.

The entire June, 1990 issue of the journal *Studies in Second Language Acquisition* (*White* 1990) was devoted to articles reflecting current research on Universal Grammar. *Birdsong* (1990) also reviewed issues in Universal Grammar.

A great deal of literature on error analysis appeared in the 1970s. Some anthologies are available which almost exclusively deal with topics in error analysis. The best of these are *Oller and Richards* (1973), *Richards* (1974), and *Hatch* (1978b). All three contain pivotal works in second language error analysis. *Corder* (1967), *Selinker* (1972), and *Nemser* (1971) wrote important articles which pioneered error and analysis efforts.

For a current overview of research on learner language, consult the review article by *James* (1990), a comprehensive look at where we have been and where we are in interlanguage research.

One of the themes in this chapter that underlies virtually every question about the role of error in the development of learner language is the effect of classroom instruction. An excellent overview of what we know about this effect is found in *Ellis's* (1990b) book. For a shorter, but nonetheless comprehensive review of the research, look at *Long* (1988).

For an excellent, practically oriented article on error correction in the classroom, consult *Hendrickson* (1980). *Bailey* (1985) summarized research on the effectiveness of error correction. *Lightbown and Spada* (1990) added some important empirical support for the positive effect of error correction on learners' interlanguage development.

## Topics and Questions for Study and Discussion

1. Why do you think the Contrastive Analysis Hypothesis received such widespread attention and acceptance in the 1950s? Refer to concurrent linguistic, psychological, and methodological trends to support your response.

2. Try to mimic "typical" accents of a French, German, Japanese, or Latin American person trying to speak English. What features do you adopt in your mimicry? Can you identify those features as a product of interference? In your contact with second language learners try to identify features of speech that are attributable to interference from the native language.

3. Using Whitman's four procedures of contrastive analysis, try to perform a contrastive analysis of a segment of your second language with the corresponding segments in English. The most practical seg-

ment might be the consonant systems of the two languages, or the vowel systems. Grammatical systems could be attempted if just one small slice of the total language pie is carefully defined. Use the six categories described by Prator in order to arrive at a hierarchy of difficulty.

4. Review the *strong* and *weak* versions of the Contrastive Analysis hypothesis. Do you agree with Oller that there should be a *moderate* version? Can you think of instances in learning other skills and subject matter in which this moderate principle holds true?

5. In Chapter Two (page 36), some grammatical universals were listed. Look again at that list and try to think of examples of each that apply both to English and any other language you know. Do the universals hold?

6. Why must the study of the speech of learners inevitably be the study of the *errors* of learners? How does "performance analysis"—in theory, at least—attempt to overcome negative connotations of error analysis? What are some of those negative connotations or dangers?

7. What is the difference between a mistake and an error? How can a foreign language teacher tell the difference between the two in the speech of learners? Why is it important to distinguish between mistakes and errors?

8. What did Corder mean by *overt* and *covert* errors? Why is the terminology misleading? Can you think of examples of common sentence-level and discourse-level errors in your foreign language?

9. If possible, record a few minutes of the conversation of a second language learner. Then select a few sentences that contain errors and transcribe those sentences. Perform an error analysis of those sentences using Corder's procedures for identifying errors in second language speech. If you wish to record and transcribe even more speech, some insights could be gained from the careful examination of another learner's oral production in a conversation. Certain interlanguage rules might be inferred from cross-referencing the data.

10. The learning of a third language is given passing reference on page 214. Cite a specific example of third language learning. What kinds of interlingual transfer might occur? What other factors are present in the context that would need to be considered?

11. Taylor's and Richards' lists of errors are restricted to subsystems of English. Attempt a listing of typical intralingual errors in a language other than English. Share this list with others and try to arrive at a consensus.

12. Fossilization and learning are actually the result of the same cognitive processes at work. Explain this. Then, try to think of factors other than "feedback" that could cause or contribute to fossilization. Once a language form is fossilized, can it ever be corrected?

13. Observe a language class or conversation group and take note of instances of teacher or peer correction of errors. Using Bailey's (1985) list of error correction options (pages 221–222), classify the corrections that were made. Were all corrections equally effective? Did corrections facilitate or impede the "flow" of communication? Justify your judgments.

# Chapter 9

# COMMUNICATIVE COMPETENCE

The subject matter of the previous chapter and this one represent a historical development of research on teaching second languages. The middle part of this century was characterized by a zeal for the scientific, linguistic analysis of the structures of languages and for the application of such analysis to behavioristic approaches to language teaching. This was followed by a period of intense research into the nature of the legitimate interlanguage systems of learners, with a focus on errors as important keys to understanding the makeup of those systems. Both of those strains of research continue to be important as we head toward the twenty-first century. But a new wave of interest has characterized the last two decades of the twentieth century, a focus on *communicative language teaching*—teaching second languages for the ultimate goal of communication with other speakers of the second language. Such a focus has centered on speaking and listening skills, on writing for specific communicative purposes, and on "authentic" reading texts. (We will come back to a more detailed discussion of communicative language teaching in a later section in this chapter.) Underlying the communicative language teaching movement are a number of important theoretical principles of language behavior. We turn now to a study of those principles, the first and foremost of which is a definition of what is now a "household word" in second language research and teaching, *communicative competence.*

# On Defining Communicative Competence

The term "communicative competence" was coined by Dell Hymes (1967, 1972), a sociolinguist who was convinced that Chomsky's (1965) notion of competence (see Chapter Two) was too limited. Chomsky's "rule-governed creativity" that so aptly describes a child's mushrooming grammar at the age of 3 or 4 did not, according to Hymes, account sufficiently for the social and functional rules of language. Communicative competence, then, is that aspect of our competence that enables us to convey and interpret messages and to negotiate meanings interpersonally within specific contexts. Savignon (1983:9) notes that "communicative competence is relative, not absolute, and depends on the cooperation of all the participants involved." It is not so much an intrapersonal construct as we saw in Chomsky's early writings but rather a dynamic, interpersonal construct that can only be examined by means of the overt performance of two or more individuals in the process of negotiating meaning.

In the 1970s, research on communicative competence distinguished between *linguistic* and *communicative* competence (Hymes 1967, Paulston 1974) to highlight the difference between knowledge "about" language forms and knowledge that enables a person to communicate functionally and interactively. In a similar vein, James Cummins (1979, 1980) proposed a distinction between *cognitive/academic language proficiency* (CALP) and *basic interpersonal communicative skills* (BICS). CALP is that dimension of proficiency in which the learner manipulates or reflects upon the surface features of language outside of the immediate interpersonal context. It is what learners often use in classroom exercises and tests that focus on form. BICS, on the other hand, is the communicative capacity that all children acquire in order to be able to function in daily interpersonal exchanges. Cummins (1981) later modified his notion of CALP and BICS in the form of *context-reduced* and *context-embedded* communication, where the former resembles CALP and the latter BICS, but with the added dimension of considering the context in which language is used. A good share of classroom, school-oriented language is context-reduced, while face-to-face communication with people is context-embedded. By referring to the *context* of our use of language, then, the distinction becomes more feasible to operationalize.

Seminal work on defining communicative competence was carried out by Michael Canale and Merrill Swain (1980), now the reference point for virtually all discussions of communicative competence vis-á-vis second language teaching. In Canale and Swain's (1980), and later in Canale's (1983) definition, four different components, or subcategories, make up the construct of communicative competence. The first two subcategories reflect the use of the linguistic system itself. (1) *Grammatical* competence is that aspect of communicative

competence that encompasses "knowledge of lexical items and of rules of morphology, syntax, sentence-grammar semantics, and phonology" (Canale and
Swain 1980:29). It is the competence that we associate with mastering the linguistic code of a language, the "linguistic" competence of Hymes and
Paulston, referred to above. (2) The second subcategory is *discourse* competence, the complement of grammatical competence in many ways. It is the ability we have to connect sentences in stretches of discourse and to form a
meaningful whole out of a series of utterances. Discourse means everything
from simple spoken conversation to lengthy written texts (articles, books, and
the like). While grammatical competence focuses on sentence-level grammar,
discourse competence is concerned with intersentential relationships.

The last two subcategories define the more functional aspects of communication. (3) *Sociolinguistic* competence is the knowledge of the sociocultural
rules of language and of discourse. This type of competence "requires an
understanding of the social context in which language is used: the roles of the
participants, the information they share, and the function of the interaction.
Only in a full context of this kind can judgments be made on the *appropriateness* of a particular utterance" (Savignon 1983:37). (4) The fourth subcategory
is *strategic* competence, a construct that is exceedingly complex. Canale and
Swain (1980:30) described strategic competence as "the verbal and nonverbal
communication strategies that may be called into action to compensate for
breakdowns in communication due to performance variables or due to insufficient competence." Savignon (1983:40) paraphrases this as "the strategies that
one uses to compensate for imperfect knowledge of rules—or limiting factors
in their application such as fatigue, distraction, and inattention." In short, it is
the competence underlying our ability to make repairs, to cope with imperfect
knowledge, and to sustain communication through "paraphrase, circumlocution, repetition, hesitation, avoidance, and guessing, as well as shifts in register and style" (Savignon 1983:40–41).

Strategic competence occupies a special place in an understanding of
communication. Actually, definitions of strategic competence that are limited
to the notion of "compensatory strategies" fall short of encompassing the full
spectrum of the construct. In a follow-up to the previous (Canale and Swain
1980) article, Swain (1984:189) amended the earlier notion of strategic competence to include "communication strategies that may be called into action
either *to enhance the effectiveness of communication* or to compensate for
breakdowns." (my italics) Similarly, Yule and Tarone (1990:181) refer to strategic competence as "an ability to select an effective means of performing a communicative act that enables the listener/reader to identify the intended
referent." So, all communication strategies—such as those discussed in Chapter Five—may be thought of as arising out of a person's strategic competence.
In fact, strategic competence is the way we *manipulate* language in order to
meet communicative goals. An eloquent speaker possesses and uses a sophisti-

cated strategic competence. A salesman utilizes certain strategies of communication to make a product seem irresistible. A friend persuades you to do something extraordinary because he or she has mustered communicative strategies for the occasion.

Canale and Swain's (1980) definition of communicative competence has undergone some other modifications over the years. These newer views are perhaps best captured in Lyle Bachman's (1990) schematization of what he simply calls Language Competence, as shown in Figure 9–1. Bachman places grammatical and discourse (renamed "textual") competence under one node which he appropriately calls *organizational* competence: all those rules and systems that dictate what we can do with the *forms* of language, whether they be sentence-level rules (grammar) or rules that govern how we "string" sentences together (discourse). Canale and Swain's sociolinguistic competence is now broken down into two separate *pragmatic* categories: functional aspects of language (illocutionary competence, or, pertaining to sending and receiving *intended* meanings) and sociolinguistic aspects (which deal with such considerations as politeness, formality, metaphor, register, and culturally related aspects of language). And, in keeping with current waves of thought, Bachman adds strategic competence as an entirely separate element of communicative language ability (see Figure 9–2). Here, strategic competence almost serves an "executive" function of making the final "decision," among many possible options, on wording, phrasing, and other productive and receptive means for negotiating meaning.

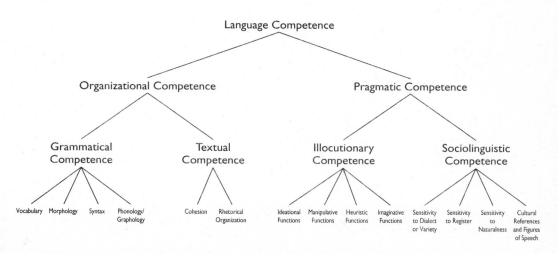

FIGURE 9–1. Components of language competence (Bachman 1990:87)

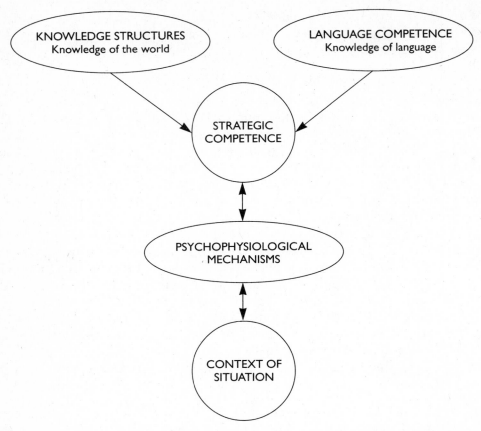

FIGURE 9–2.   Components of communicative language ability in communicative language use (Bachman 1990:85)

# Pragmatics

The importance of *pragmatics* in recent theories of communicative competence must not be underestimated, as Margie Berns (1990) and others have pointed out. Pragmatic constraints on language production and interpretation may be loosely thought of as the effect of *context* on strings of linguistic events. Consider the following conversation:

[Phone rings, a child picks up the phone]

STEFANIE:   Hello.

VOICE:   Hi, Stef, is your Mom there?

S:   Just a minute. [cups the phone, and yells] Mom! Phone!

MOM:   [from upstairs] I'm in the tub!

S:   [returning to the phone] She can't talk now. Wanna leave a message?

V:   Oh, [pause] I'll call back later. Bye.

Pragmatic considerations allowed all three participants to interpret what would otherwise be ambiguous sentences. "Is your Mom there?" is not, in a telephone context, a question that requires a yes or no answer. Stefanie's "Just a minute" confirmed to the caller that her mother was indeed home, and in so saying, let the caller know that she would either (a) check to see if she is home, and/or (b) get her to come to the phone. Then, Stefanie's "Mom! Phone!" was easily interpreted by her mother as "Someone is on the phone who wants to talk with you." Mom's response, otherwise a rather worthless bit of information, in fact informed Stefanie that she couldn't come to the phone, which was then conveyed to the caller. The caller, didn't explicitly respond "no" to Stefanie's offer to take a message, but implicitly did so with "I'll call back later."

Second language acquisition becomes an exceedingly difficult task when these *sociopragmatic* or *pragmalinguistic* constraints are brought to bear. Holmes and Brown (1987), Harlow (1990), and Kitao (1990) have demonstrated the difficulty of teaching such conventions because of subtle cross-cultural contrasts. Variations in politeness and formality are particularly touchy:

AMERICAN:   What an unusual necklace. It's beautiful!

SAMOAN RECIPIENT:   Please take it. (Holmes and Brown 1987:526)

AMERICAN TEACHER:   Would you like to read?

RUSSIAN STUDENT:   No, I would not. (Harlow 1990:328)

In both cases the non-native English speakers misunderstood the illocutionary force (intended meaning) of the utterance within the contexts. Learning the organizational rules of a second language are almost simple when compared to the complexity of catching on to a seemingly never-ending list of pragmatic constraints.

# Language Functions

Pragmatic conventions of language are sometimes difficult to learn because of the disparity between language *forms* and *functions*. The acquisition of vocabulary, grammar rules, discourse rules, and other organizational competencies results in nothing if the learner cannot use those forms for the functional purpose of transmitting and receiving thoughts, ideas, and feelings between speaker and hearer or writer and reader. While forms are the outward manifestation of language, functions are the realization of those forms.

Forms of language generally serve specific functions. "How much does that cost?" is usually a form functioning as a question, and "He bought a car" functions as a statement. But linguistic forms are not always unambiguous in their function. "I can't find my umbrella," uttered by a frustrated adult who is late for work on a rainy day may be a frantic request for all in the household to join in a search. A child who says "I want some ice cream" is rarely stating a simple fact or observation but requesting ice cream in her own intimate register. A sign on the street that says "one way" functions to guide traffic in only one direction. A sign in a church parking lot in a busy downtown area was subtle in form but direct in function: "We forgive those who trespass against us, but we also tow them;" that sign functioned effectively to prevent unauthorized cars from parking in the lot!

Communication may be regarded as a combination of *acts,* a series of elements with purpose and intent. Communication is not merely an event, something that happens; it is functional, purposive, and designed to bring about some effect—some change, however subtle or unobservable—on the environment of hearers and speakers. Communication is a series of communicative acts or *speech acts,* to use John Austin's (1962) term, which are used systematically to accomplish particular purposes. Austin stressed the importance of consequences, the *per*locutionary force, of linguistic communication. Researchers have since been led to examine communication in terms of the effect that utterances achieve. That effect has implications for both the production and comprehension of an utterance; both modes of performance serve to bring the communicative act to its ultimate purpose. Second language learners need to understand the purpose of communication, developing an awareness of what the purpose of a communicative act is and how to achieve that purpose through linguistic forms.

The *functional* approach to describing language is one that has its roots in the traditions of British linguist J.R. Firth who viewed language as interactive and interpersonal, "a way of behaving and making others behave" (quoted by Berns 1984a:5). Since then the term *function* has been variously interpreted. Michael Halliday (1973), who provided one of the best expositions of language functions, used the term to mean the purposive nature of communication, and outlined seven different functions of language:

1. The *instrumental* function serves to manipulate the environment, to cause certain events to happen. Sentences like "This court finds you guilty," "On your mark, get set, go!" or "Don't touch the stove" have an instrumental function; they are communicative acts that bring about a particular condition.

2. The *regulatory* function of language is the control of events. While such control is sometimes difficult to distinguish from the instrumental function, regulatory functions of language are not so much the "unleashing" of certain power as the maintenance of control. "I pronounce you guilty and sentence you to three years in prison"

serves an instrumental function, but the sentence "Upon good behavior, you will be eligible for parole in ten months" serves more of a regulatory function. The regulation of encounters among people—approval, disapproval, behavior control, setting laws and rules, are all regulatory features of language.

3.  The *representational* function is the use of language to make statements, convey facts and knowledge, explain, or report—that is, to "represent" reality as one sees it. "The sun is hot," "The president gave a speech last night," or even "The world is flat" all serve representational functions though the last representation may be highly disputed.

4.  The *interactional* function of language serves to ensure social maintenance. "Phatic communion," Malinowski's term referring to the communicative contact between and among human beings that simply allows them to establish social contact and to keep channels of communication open, is part of the interactional function of language. Successful interactional communication requires knowledge of slang, jargon, jokes, folklore, cultural mores, politeness and formality expectations, and other keys to social exchange.

5.  The *personal* function allows a speaker to express feelings, emotions, personality, "gut-level" reactions. A person's individuality is usually characterized by his or her use of the personal function of communication. In the personal nature of language, cognition, affect, and culture all interact in ways that have not yet been explored.

6.  The *heuristic* function involves language used to acquire knowledge, to learn about the environment. Heuristic functions are often conveyed in the form of questions that will lead to answers. Children typically make good use of the heuristic function in their incessant "why" questions about the world around them. Inquiry is a heuristic method of eliciting representations of reality from others.

7.  The *imaginative* function serves to create imaginary systems or ideas. Telling fairy tales, joking, or writing a novel are all uses of the imaginative function. Using language for the sheer pleasure of using language—as in poetry, tongue twisters, puns—are also instances of imaginative functions. Through the imaginative dimensions of language we are free to go beyond the real world to soar the heights of the beauty of language itself, and through that language to create impossible dreams if we so desire.

These seven different functions of language are neither discrete nor mutually exclusive. A single sentence or conversation might incorporate many different functions simultaneously. Yet it is the understanding of how to use linguistic forms to achieve these functions of language that comprises the crux of second language learning. A learner might acquire correct word order, syntax, and lexical items but not understand how to achieve a desired and intended function through careful selection of words, structure, intonation, nonverbal signals, and astute perception of the context of a particular stretch of discourse.

Halliday's seven functions of language tend to mask the almost infinite variety and complexity of functions that we accomplish through language. Van Ek and Alexander's (1975) taxonomy lists almost 70 different functions to be taught in English curricula. Some of these functions are listed below:

1. Greeting, parting, inviting, accepting
2. Complimenting, congratulating, flattering, seducing, charming, bragging
3. Interrupting
4. Requesting
5. Evading, lying, shifting blame, changing the subject
6. Criticizing, reprimanding, ridiculing, insulting, threatening, warning
7. Complaining
8. Accusing, denying
9. Agreeing, disagreeing, arguing
10. Persuading, insisting, suggesting, reminding, asserting, advising
11. Reporting, evaluating, commenting
12. Commanding, ordering, demanding
13. Questioning, probing
14. Sympathizing
15. Apologizing, making excuses

All of these fall into one or more of Halliday's seven functions, and all of them are common everyday acts whose performance requires a knowledge of language. Subtle differences between functions must be learned. The appropriate contexts of various speech acts must be discerned. The forms of language used to accomplish the functions must become part of the total linguistic repertoire of the second language learner.

If learners are attempting to acquire written as well as spoken competence in the language, they must also discern differences in forms and functions between spoken and written discourse. Such differences are both significant and salient. However, we are centering in this chapter, particularly in the next section, on spoken discourse for several reasons. First, it is the most common goal of foreign language classes. Second, the teaching of writing—beyond perfunctory levels of written discourse—is a highly technical task that varies greatly depending upon the goal of written discourse and upon the particular language that is in question. The study of written discourse, or *stylistics,* is best undertaken with a specific language in focus. Third, many of the general principles of discourse analysis apply, as we have already seen, to both spoken and written modes of performance.

# Discourse Analysis

The analysis of the functions of language can be referred to as *discourse analysis* to capture the notion that language is more than a sentence-level phenomenon. A single sentence can seldom be fully analyzed without considering its context. We use language in stretches of discourse. We string many sentences together in interrelated, cohesive units. In speaking a language our discourse is marked by exchanges with another person or several persons in which a few sentences spoken by one participant are followed and built upon by sentences spoken by another. Both the production and the comprehension of language are a factor of our ability to perceive and process stretches of discourse, to formulate representations of meaning from not just a single sentence but referents in both previous sentences and following sentences. In fact, a single sentence sometimes contains certain presuppositions or entailments that are not overtly manifested in surrounding surface structure but that are clear from the total context and the understanding of one's cognitive and linguistic environment. So, while linguistic science has traditionally centered on the sentence for the purposes of analysis, recent trends in linguistics have increasingly emphasized the importance of intersentential relations in discourse. In written language, the same intersentential discourse relations hold true as the writer builds a network of ideas or feelings and the reader interprets them.

Without the intersentential relationships of discourse, it would be difficult to communicate unambiguously with one another. Through discourse, we greet, request, agree, persuade, question, command, criticize, and much more. The sentence "I didn't like that casserole" could be agreement, disagreement, criticism, argument, complaint, apology, or simply comment if we only considered sentence-level surface structure. The surface structure of a sentence in the pragmatic context of total discourse, in conjunction with its prosodic features (stress, intonation, and other phonological nuances) and its nonverbal features (gestures, eye contact, body language), determine the actual interpretation of that single sentence. A second language learner not familiar with contextual discourse constraints of English might utter such a sentence or sentences like it with perfect pronunciation and perfect grammar, but fail to achieve the communicative purpose of, say, apologizing to a dinner host or hostess, and instead appear to be impolitely critical or complaining.

For several decades, as I have already noted, linguistic research focused on linguistic forms and on descriptions of the structure of language that were basically at the sentence level. In recent years the emphasis on communicative competence has shifted the focus to the discourse level. Second language research has followed the same trend. We now realize that formal approaches that emphasize the speech product of the learner overlook important functions of language. Wagner-Gough (1975), for example, noted that acquisition by a learner of the *-ing* morpheme of the present progressive tense does not necessarily mean acquisition of varying functions of the morpheme: to indicate present action, action about to occur immediately, future action, or repeated actions. Formal approaches have also tended to shape our conception of the whole process of second language learning. Evelyn Hatch (1978a:404) spoke of the dangers. "In second language learning the basic assumption has been . . . that one first learns how to manipulate structures, that one gradually builds up a repertoire of structures and then, somehow, learns how to put the structures to use in discourse. We would like to consider the possibility that just the reverse happens. One learns how to do conversation, one learns how to interact verbally, and out of this interaction syntactic structures are developed."

One of the most salient and significant modes of discourse is conversation. Conversations are excellent examples of the interactive and interpersonal nature of communication. "Conversations are cooperative ventures" (Hatch and Long 1980:4). What are the rules that govern our conversations? How do we get someone's attention? How do we initiate topics? terminate topics? avoid topics? How does a person interrupt, correct, or seek clarification? These questions form an area of linguistic competence that every adult native speaker of a language possesses, yet few foreign language curricula traditionally deal with these important aspects of communicative competence. Once again our consideration of conversation rules will be general, since specific languages differ.

Very early in life, children learn the first and essential rule of conversation: *attention getting.* If you wish linguistic production to be functional and to accomplish its intended purpose, you must of course have the attention of the hearer or audience. The attention-getting conventions within each language—both verbal and nonverbal—need to be carefully assimilated by learners. Without knowledge and use of such conventions second language learners may be reluctant to participate in a conversation because of their own inhibitions, or they may become obnoxious in securing attention in ways that "turn off" their hearer to the topic they wish to discuss.

Once speakers have secured the hearer's attention, their task becomes one of *topic nomination.* There are few explicit rules for accomplishing topic nomination in a language. Usually a person will simply embark on an issue by making a statement or a question that leads to a particular topic. H.P. Grice (1971) noted that certain conversational "maxims" enable the speaker to nominate and maintain a topic of conversation: (1) *quantity:* say only as much as is necessary for understanding the communication; (2) *quality:* say only what is true; (3) *relevance:* say only what is relevant; (4) *manner:* be clear. Robin Lakoff (1976) incorporated Grice's maxims into what she defined as rules of communicative competence.

Once a topic is nominated, participants in a conversation then embark on *topic development,* using conventions of *turn-taking* to accomplish various functions of language. Allwright (1980) showed how students of English as a second language failed to use appropriate turn-taking signals in their interactions with each other and with the teacher. Turn-taking is another of those culturally oriented sets of rules that require finely tuned perceptions in order to communicate effectively. Aside from turn-taking itself, topic development, or maintenance of a conversation, involves *clarification, shifting, avoidance,* and *interruption.* Topic clarification manifests itself in various forms of heuristic functions. In the case of conversations between second language learners and native speakers, topic clarification often involves seeking or giving *repair* (correction) of linguistic forms that contain errors. According to Schwartz (1980), repair is part of the process of negotiation that is so important in communication; her study provided many examples of both "self-initiated" and "other-initiated" repair. Topic shifting and avoidance may be affected through both verbal and nonverbal signals. Interruptions are a typical feature of all conversations. Language users learn how to interrupt politely—a form of attention getting. Children typically have to be "taught" how and when to interrupt.

*Topic termination* is an art that even native speakers of a language have difficulty in mastering at times. We commonly experience situations in which a conversation has ensued for some time and neither participant seems to know how to terminate it. Usually, in American English, conversations are terminated by various interactional functions—a glance at a watch, a nicety, or a "Well, I have to be going now." Each language has verbal and nonverbal signals for such termination. It is important for teachers to be acutely aware of the rules of conversation in the second language and to aid learners both to perceive those rules and follow them in their own conversations.

Conversation rules are one major category of discourse analysis (Hatch and Long 1980), but also of great interest in second language learning is the acquisition of the discoursal conventions for accomplishing certain functions. Second language researchers have studied such varied functions as apologizing (Olshtain and Cohen 1983), complimenting (Wolfson 1981), disapproving (D'Amico-Reisner 1983), inviting (Wolfson, D'Amico-Reisner, and Huber 1983), and even "how to tell when someone is saying 'no'" (Rubin 1976). There is no end to the possibility for research on such topics. The applications to teaching are equally numerous, apparent in a perusal of the many foreign language textbooks now aimed at focusing on functional aspects of language.

Of further interest to second language researchers is the process of reading and writing. The last few years have seen a mushrooming of work on second language reading strategies. Techniques in the teaching of reading skills have gone far beyond the traditional passage, comprehension questions, and vocabulary exercises. "Text attack skills" now include sophisticated techniques for recognizing and interpreting cohesive devices (for example, reference and ellipsis), discourse markers (*then, moreover, therefore*), rhetorical organization, and other textual discourse features (Nuttall 1982). "Cohesion" and "coherence" are common terms that need to be considered in teaching reading (Carrell 1982, 1986). Likewise the analysis of writing skills has progressed to a recognition of the full range of pragmatic and organizational competence that is necessary to write effectively in a second language.

Discourse analysis, then, is a multifaceted and exceedingly important consideration in the teaching of a second language. No longer can an adequate theory of second language acquisition be constructed without accounting for the stretches of language that characterize communicative acts.

# Styles and Registers

Another important issue in describing communicative competence is the way we use language in different *styles* depending on the context of a communicative act in terms of subject matter, audience, occasion, shared experience, and purpose of communication. A style is not a social or regional dialect, but a variety of language used for a specific purpose. Styles, vary considerably within a single language user's idiolect. When you converse informally with a friend, you use a different style than that used in an interview for a job with a prospective employer. Native speakers, as they mature into adulthood, learn to adopt appropriate styles for widely different contexts. An important difference between a child's and an adult's "fluency" in a native language is the degree to which an adult is able to vary styles for different occasions and persons. Adult second language learners must acquire stylistic adaptability in order to be able to encode and decode the discourse around them correctly.

Martin Joos (1967) provided one of the most common classifications of speech styles using the criterion of *formality,* which tends to subsume subject matter, audience, and occasion. Joos described five levels of formality: (1) oratorical, or "frozen"; (2) deliberative, or formal; (3) consultative; (4) casual; and (5) intimate. An *oratorical* style is used in public speaking before a large audience; wording is carefully planned in advance, intonation is somewhat exaggerated, and numerous rhetorical devices are appropriate. A *deliberative* style is also used in addressing audiences, usually audiences too large to permit effective interchange between speaker and hearers, though the forms are normally not as polished as those in an oratorical style. A typical university classroom lecture is often carried out in a deliberative style. A *consultative* style is typically a dialogue though formal enough that words are chosen with some care. Business transactions, doctor-patient conversations, and the like are usually consultative in nature. *Casual* conversations are between friends or colleagues or sometimes members of a family; in this context words need not be guarded and social barriers are moderately low. An *intimate* style is one characterized by complete absence of social inhibitions. Talk with family, loved ones, and very close friends, where you tend to reveal your inner self, is usually in an intimate style.

Categories of style can apply to written discourse as well. Most writing is addressed to readers who cannot respond immediately; that is, long stretches of discourse—books, essays, even letters—are read from beginning to end before the reader gives a response. Written style is therefore usually more deliberative with the exception of friendly letters, notes, or literature intended to capture a more personal style. Even the latter, however, often carry with them reasonably carefully chosen wording with relatively few performance variables.

Styles are manifested by both verbal and nonverbal features. Differences in register can be conveyed in body language, gestures, eye contact, and the like—all very difficult aspects of "language" for the learner to acquire. (Nonverbal communication is discussed below.) Verbal aspects of style are difficult enough to learn. Syntax in many languages is characterized by more contractions and other deletions in lower registers. Lexical items vary, too. Bolinger (1975) gave a somewhat tongue-in-cheek illustration of lexical items that have one semantic meaning but represent each of the five styles: *on the ball, smart, intelligent, perceptive,* and *astute*—from intimate to frozen, respectively. He of course recognized other meanings besides those of style that intervene to make the example somewhat overstated. Style distinctions in pronunciation are likely to be most noticeable in the form of hesitations and other misarticulations, phonological deletion rules in informal speech, and perhaps a more affected pronunciation in formal language.

Related to stylistic variation is another factor called *register*. Registers are commonly identified by certain phonological variants, vocabulary, idioms, and other expressions that are associated with different occupational or socioeconomic groups. Registers sometimes enable people to identify with a particular group and to maintain solidarity. Colleagues in the same occupation or profession will use certain jargon to communicate with each other, to the exclusion of eavesdroppers. Truckers, airline pilots, salespersons, and farmers, for example, use words and phrases unique to their own group. Register is also sometimes associated with social class distinctions, but here the line between register and dialect is difficult to define (see Wardhaugh 1992 and Chaika 1989 for further comments).

The acquisition of styles and registers poses no simple problem for second language learners. Cross-cultural variation is a primary barrier—that is, understanding cognitively and affectively what levels of formality are appropriate or inappropriate. North American culture tends generally to accept more informal styles for given occasions than some other cultures. Some English learners in the United States consequently experience difficulty in gauging appropriate formality distinctions and tend to be overly formal. Such students, are often surprised by the level of informality expressed by their American professors. The acquisition of both styles and registers thus combines a linguistic and culture-learning process.

# Language and Gender

Another major factor affecting the acquisition of sociopragmatic competence in virtually every language, and one that has received considerable attention recently, is the effect of one's sex on both production and reception of language. Differences between the way males and females speak have been noted for some time now (R. Lakoff 1975, Nilsen et al. 1977, Tannen 1990, Holmes 1989, 1991). Among American English speakers, girls have been found to produce more "standard" language than boys, a pattern that continues on through adulthood. Women appear to use language that expresses more uncertainty (hedges, tag questions, rising intonation on declaratives, etc.) than men, suggesting less confidence in what they say. Men have been reported to interrupt more than women, and to use stronger expletives, while the latter use more polite forms. Tannen (1990) and others have found that males place more value, in conversational interaction, on *status* and *report* talk, competing for the floor, while females value *connection* and *rapport,* fulfilling their role as more "cooperative and facilitative conversationalists, concerned for their partner's positive face needs" (Holmes 1991:210).

These studies of language and gender, which were conducted in English-speaking cultures, do not even begin to deal with some of the more overtly formal patterns for men's and women's talk in other languages. Among the Carib Indians in the Lesser Antilles, for example, male and female Caribs must use entirely different gender markings for abstract nouns. In several languages males and females use different phonological variants. In Japanese, women's and men's language is differentiated by formal (syntactic) variants, intonation patterns, and nonverbal expression. It is not uncommon for American men learning Japanese from a female native-speaking Japanese teacher to inadvertently "say things like a woman," much to their embarrassment when, say, conducting business with Japanese men.

In English, another twist on the language and gender issue has lately focused us on "sexist" language: language that either calls unnecessary attention to gender or is demeaning to one gender—almost always women in today's overly male dominated world. Writers are cautioned to refrain from using what we used to call the "generic" *he* and instead to pluralize or to use *he* or *she.* What used to be *stewardesses, chairmen,* and *policemen* are now more commonly called *flight attendants, chairs,* and *police officers.*

Words/phrases like *broads, skirtchasers, the wife,* etc., are now marked as demeaning perpetuations of negative stereotypes of women. The list of sexist terms, phrases, and metaphors goes on and on. Fortunately, the research of linguists like Robin Lakoff and Deborah Tannen has called the attention of the public to such sexism, and we are seeing signs of the decline of this sort of language. All these factors, however, are subtleties that a second language learner must contend with. They all form a significant, intricately interwoven tapestry in our sociopragmatic competence.

# Nonverbal Communication

We communicate so much information nonverbally in conversations that often the verbal aspect of the conversation is negligible. This is particularly true for interactive language functions in which social contact is of key importance and in which it is not *what* you say that counts but *how* you say it—what you convey with body language, gestures, eye contact, physical distance, and other nonverbal messages. Nonverbal communication, however, is so subtle and subconscious in a native speaker that verbal language seems, by comparison, quite mechanical and systematic. Language becomes distinctly human through its nonverbal dimension, or what Edward Hall (1959) called the "silent language." The expression of culture is so bound up in nonverbal communication that the barriers to culture learning are more nonverbal than verbal. Verbal language requires the use of only one of the five sensory modalities: hearing. But there remain in our communicative repertoire three other senses by which we communicate every day, if we for the moment rule out taste as falling within a communicative category (though messages are indeed sent and received through the taste modality). We will examine each of these.

### *Gesture and Body Language*

Every culture and language uses "body language" or kinesics, in unique but clearly interpretable ways. "There was speech in their dumbness, language in their very gesture," wrote Shakespeare in *The Winter's Tale.* All cultures throughout the history of humankind have relied on kinesics for conveying important messages. Books like Edward Hall's *The Silent Language* (1959), *The Hidden Dimension* (1966), and Julius Fast's *Body Language* (1970) were just the first of a long string of self-help manuals offering lighthearted but provocative insights on the use of kinesics in North American culture. Today, virtually every book on communication explains how you communicate—and miscommunicate—when you fold your arms, cross your legs, stand, walk, move your eyes and mouth, and so on.

But as universal as kinesic communication is, there is tremendous variation cross-culturally and cross-linguistically in the specific interpretations of gestures. Human beings all move their heads, blink their eyes, move their arms and hands, but the significance of these movements varies from society to society. Consider the following categories and how you would express them in American culture:

1. Agreement, "yes"
2. "No!"
3. "Come here"
4. Disinterest, "I don't know"
5. Flirting signals, sexual signals
6. Insults, obscene gestures

There are conventionalized gestural signals to convey these semantic categories. Are those signals the same in another language and culture? Sometimes they are not. And sometimes a gesture that is appropriate in one culture is obscene or insulting in another. Nodding the head, for example, means "yes" among most European language speakers. But in the Eskimo gestural system, head nodding means "no" and head shaking means "yes." Among the Ainu of Japan, "yes" is expressed by bringing the arms to the chest and waving them. The pygmy Negritos of interior Malaya indicate "yes" by thrusting the head sharply forward, but people from the Punjab of India throw their heads sharply backward. The Ceylonese curve their chins gracefully downward in an arc to the left shoulder, whereas Bengalis rock their heads rapidly from one shoulder to the other.

### Eye Contact

Is eye contact appropriate between two participants in a conversation? When is it permissible not to maintain eye contact? What does eye contact or the absence thereof signal? Cultures differ widely in this particular visual modality of nonverbal communication. In American culture it is permissible, for example, for two participants of unequal status to maintain prolonged eye contact. In fact, an American might interpret lack of eye contact as discourteous lack of attention, while in Japanese culture eye contact might be considered rude. Intercultural interference in this nonverbal category can lead to misunderstanding.

Not only is eye contact itself an important category, but the gestures, as it were, of the eyes are in some instances keys to communication. Eyes can signal interest, boredom, empathy, hostility, attraction, understanding, misunderstanding, and other messages. The nonverbal language of each culture has different ways of signaling such messages. An important aspect of unfettered and unambiguous conversation in a second language is the acquisition of conventions for conveying messages by means of eye signals.

## Proxemics

Physical proximity is also a meaningful communicative category. Cultures vary widely in acceptable distances for conversation. Edward Hall (1966) calculated acceptable distances for public, social-consultative, personal, and intimate discourse. He noted, for example, that Americans feel that a certain personal space "bubble" has been violated if a stranger stands closer than 20 to 24 inches away unless there is restricted space, such as in a subway or an elevator. However, a typical member of a Latin American culture would feel that such a physical distance would be too great.

> The interesting thing is that neither party is specifically aware of what is wrong when the distance is not right. They merely have vague feelings of discomfort or anxiety. As the Latin American approaches the North American backs away; both parties take offense without knowing why. When a North American, having had the problem pointed out to him, permits the Latin American to get close enough, he will immediately notice that the latter seems much more at ease. (Hall 1974:76–77)

Sometimes objects—desks, counters, other furniture—serve to maintain certain physical distances. Such objects tend to establish both the overall register and relationship of participants. Thus, a counter between two people maintains a consultative mood. Similarly, the presence of a desk or a typewriter will set the tone of a conversation. Again, however, different cultures interpret different messages in such objects. In some cultures, objects might enhance a communicative act, but in other cases they impede the communicative process.

## Artifacts

The nonverbal messages of clothing and ornamentation are also important aspects of communication. Clothes often signal a person's sense of self-esteem, socioeconomic class, and general character. Jewelry also conveys certain messages. In a multicultural conversation group such artifacts, along with other nonverbal signals, can be a significant factor in lifting barriers, identifying certain personality characteristics, and setting a general mood.

## Kinesthetic Dimensions

Touching, sometimes referred to as kinesthetics, is another culturally loaded aspect of nonverbal communication. How we touch others and where we touch them is sometimes the most misunderstood aspect of nonverbal communication. Touching in some cultures signals a very personal or intimate register, while for other cultures extensive touching is commonplace. Knowing the limits and conventions is important for clear and unambiguous communication.

### *Olfactory Dimensions*

Our noses also receive sensory nonverbal messages. The olfactory modality is of course an important one for the animal kingdom, but for the human race, too, different cultures have established different dimensions of olfactory communication. The twentieth century has created in most technological societies a penchant for perfumes, lotions, creams, and powders as acceptable and even necessary; natural human odors, especially perspiration, are thought to be undesirable. In some societies, of course, the smell of human perspiration is quite acceptable and even attractive. Second language and especially second culture learners need to be aware of the accepted mores of other cultures in the olfactory modality.

We cannot underestimate the importance of nonverbal communication in second language learning and in conversational analysis (see Kellerman 1992). Communicative competence includes nonverbal competence—knowledge of all the varying nonverbal semantics of the second culture, and an ability both to send and receive nonverbal signals unambiguously.

# Communicative Language Teaching

As the field of second language pedagogy has developed and matured over the past few decades, we have experienced a number of reactions and counter-reactions in methods and approaches to language teaching. We can look back over a century of foreign language teaching and observe the trends as they came and went. How will we look back 100 years from now and characterize the present era? Almost certainly the answer lies in our recent efforts to engage in *communicative language teaching* (CLT). The "push toward communication" (Higgs and Clifford 1982) has been relentless. Researchers have defined and redefined the construct of communicative competence. They have explored the myriad functions of language that learners must be able to accomplish. They have described spoken and written discourse. They have examined the nature of styles, registers, gender factors, and nonverbal communication. With this storehouse of knowledge we have pressed valiantly toward the goal of learning how best to teach communication.

One glance at current journals in second language teaching reveals quite an array of material on CLT. Numerous textbooks for teachers and teacher trainers expound on the nature of communicative approaches and offer techniques for varying ages and purposes. In short, wherever you look in the literature today, you will find reference to the communicative nature of language classes.

CLT is best understood as an *approach,* not a method. (For some comments on the difference between a method and an approach, refer to the vignettes at the end of chapters Six and Seven.) It is therefore a unified but broadly-based theoretical position about the nature of language and of language learning and teaching. It is nevertheless difficult to synthesize all of the various definitions that have been offered. From Widdowson's (1978b) earlier work to Breen and Candlin's (1980) seminal article to Savignon's (1983) practical applications of communicative competence, to a recent special issue of *Applied Linguistics* (Angelis and Henderson 1989), we have definitions enough to send us reeling. For the sake of simplicity and directness, I offer the following four interconnected characteristics as a definition of CLT:

1. Classroom goals are focused on *all* of the components of communicative competence and not restricted to grammatical or linguistic competence.

2. Language techniques are designed to engage learners in the pragmatic, authentic, functional use of language for meaningful purposes. Organizational language forms are not the central focus but rather aspects of language that *enable* the learner to accomplish those purposes.

3. Fluency and accuracy are seen as complementary principles underlying communicative techniques. At times fluency may have to take on more importance than accuracy in order to keep learners meaningfully engaged in language use.

4. In the communicative classroom, students ultimately have to *use* the language, productively and receptively, in *unrehearsed* contexts.

These four characteristics reveal some major departures from earlier approaches. In some ways those departures are a product of the growth of knowledge that you have already seen illustrated in numerous methods (such as CLL or the Natural Approach) that have been discussed in preceding chapters. In other ways those departures are radical. Structurally (grammatically) sequenced curricula were a mainstay of language teaching for centuries. CLT suggests that grammatical structure might better be subsumed under various functional categories. In CLT we pay considerably less attention to the overt presentation and discussion of grammatical rules than we traditionally did. A great deal of use of *authentic* language is implied in CLT, as we attempt to build fluency. It is important to note, however, that fluency should *never* be encouraged at the expense of clear, unambiguous, direct communication. And much more spontaneity is present in communicative classrooms. Students are encouraged to deal with unrehearsed situations under the guidance, but not control, of the teacher.

The latter characteristic of CLT often makes it difficult for a nonnative speaking teacher who is not very proficient in the second language to teach effectively. Dialogues, drills, rehearsed exercises, and discussions of grammatical rules are much simpler for the average nonnative speaking teacher to contend with. This drawback should not deter one, however, from pursuing communicative goals in the classroom. Technology (films, videos, television, audio tapes, computer software) can come to the aid of such teachers. Teacher training and certification programs may need to stiffen their language proficiency requirements for teachers. As educational and political institutions in various countries become more sensitive to the importance of teaching foreign languages for communicative purposes (not just for the purpose of fulfilling a "requirement" or of "passing a test"), we may be better able, worldwide, to accomplish the goals of communicative language teaching.

We have seen in this chapter alone that communicative competence is such an intricate web of psychological, sociocultural, physical, and linguistic features that it is easy to get entangled in but one part of that web. And it is probably impossible in the near future to describe the whole of human discourse in such a way that language teachers are provided with ready solutions to the teaching of a foreign language. But some of the features of human communication are becoming clearer, and I believe we are moving in positive and creative directions. The language teacher and researcher can be a part of that creative event by fashioning an integrated and cohesive understanding of how learners acquire the ability to communicate clearly and effectively in a second language.

## In the Classroom: Notional-Functional Syllabuses

An important forerunner of what we now call communicative language teaching was the *notional-functional syllabus.* ("Syllabus," in this case, is a term used mainly in the United Kingdom to refer to what is commonly known as a "curriculum" in the United States.) Beginning with the work of the Council of Europe (Van Ek and Alexander 1975) and later followed by numerous interpretations of "notional" syllabuses (Wilkins 1976), notional-functional syllabuses began to grow in popularity in the United Kingdom in the 1970s. The distinguishing characteristic of the notional-functional syllabus is its attention to functions as the organizing elements of a foreign language curriculum. Grammar is attended to only in that it explains the various forms used to accomplish certain functions.

"Notions," according to Van Ek and Alexander (1975) are both general and specific. General notions are abstract concepts such as existence, space, time, quantity, and quality. They are domains in which we use language to express thought and feeling. Within the general notion of space and time, for example, are the concepts of location, motion, dimension, speed, length of time, frequency, and so forth. "Specific" notions correspond more closely to what we have become accustomed to calling "contexts" or "situations." Personal identification, for example, is a specific notion, or topic, under which name, address, phone number, and other personal information is subsumed. Other specific notions include travel, health and welfare, education, shopping, services, and free time.

The "functional" part of the notional-functional syllabus corresponds to what we have already defined as language functions. Curricula are organized around such functions as identifying, reporting, denying, declining an invitation, asking permission, and apologizing. Van Ek and Alexander's (1975) list of language functions (discussed previously in this chapter) has become a basic reference for notional-functional syllabus development.

Notional-functional (often simply referred to as either "functional" or "notional") approaches to language have become popular underpinnings for the development of communicative textbooks and materials in foreign language courses. The table of contents of Coffey's (1983) *Fitting In* is an appropriate example:

1. Introduction
2. Greetings, Goodbyes
3. Invitations
4. Apologies, Condolences
5. Gratitude, Compliments, Congratulations
6. Requests, Commands, Warnings, Directions
7. Offers, Seeking Permission
8. Advice, Intentions
9. Pleasure, Displeasure
10. Expressing Your Opinion
    Asking People to Repeat Themselves
    Interrupting Someone
    Changing the Topic of Conversation

A typical unit in this textbook includes presentation of dialogues, conversation practice with a classmate, situations in which the student figures out "what would I say," role-plays, chart work, multiple-choice exercises on functional considerations, one-sided dialogs in which the student fills in responses, nonverbal considerations, discussion activities, and "community exercises" for extra class practice.

A weakness of the structural syllabus, in its focus on grammar, is its tendency to highlight a grammatical feature to the exclusion of practical application in real situations. While a "situational approach" to a structural syllabus is possible, sometimes the very fact that situations are devised to illustrate grammar, instead of grammar illustrating a function, keys the student artificially into grammatical categories that may later impede the communicative process. Notional syllabuses seek to overcome that weakness in their attention to the ultimate purpose of language: functional, pragmatic communication between and among human beings.

Both types of syllabus might claim to provide the necessary components of language in terms of learner needs. On the one hand, learners may need a basic knowledge of the lexical and grammatical forms of the language on the assumption that this knowledge will provide the essential basis for communication when they are faced with a need to communicate. On the other hand, those who favor the notional syllabus might argue that learners need to learn appropriate communicative behavior during the course of studies and that on such a foundation they will more meaningfully acquire the grammar of a language; in essence, learners cannot simply be left to their own devices in developing an ability to communicate.

Henry Widdowson (1978a) noted that while the notional syllabus claims to develop communicative competence within the actual design of the syllabus itself, such is not necessarily the case, since the notional syllabus still presents language as an inventory of units—functional rather than structural units, but still isolates. "Communicative competence is not a compilation of items in memory but a set of strategies or creative procedures for realizing the value of linguistic elements in contexts of use, an ability to make sense as a participant in discourse, whether spoken or written, by the skillful deployment of shared knowledge of code resources and rules of language use" (Widdowson 1978a:34). Similarly, Margie Berns (1984b:15) warned teachers that textbooks that claim to have a functional base may be "sorely inadequate and even misleading in their representation of language as interaction." She went on to show how *context* is the real key to giving meaning to both form and function and therefore materials, in and of themselves, will continue to fall short of developing a learner's communicative competence. The notional syllabus deals with the components of discourse but may not deal with discourse itself.

The notional syllabus, then, is not a panacea or "last word" for language teachers. Nor is it merely "structural lamb served up as notional-functional mutton" (Campbell 1978:18). What notional syllabuses do give us is, first of all, an organization of language content by functional categories. Second, they provide a means of developing structural categories within a general consideration of the functions of language. We have not arrived at a final solution with the notional-functional syllabus, but we have rather begun an avenue of exploration that we should continue with the full awareness that communication in a foreign language is something so complex that it will probably never be reduced to a simple formula or a neatly packaged syllabus. Communication is qualitative and infinite; a syllabus is quantitative and finite.

## Suggested Readings

A *sine qua non* for a complete understanding of communicative competence is the seminal article by *Canale and Swain* (1980), which still stands as a viable treatise on the construct. For a good sense of practical classroom applications of their definitions, look at *Savignon*'s (1983) book on communicative competence, followed by *Savignon and Berns* (1984).

Since 1980, of course, new research has appeared. For a good update, look at the whole June, 1989 issue of *Applied Linguistics* (*Angelis and Henderson* 1989), in which you will find nine major articles on communicative competence.

Excellent discussions of strategic competence are found in *Bachman* (1990) and in *Yule and Tarone* (1990).

*Berns* (1990) gives a good overview of social and cultural considerations in communicative competence.

*Joos*'s (1968) classic treatise on the "five clocks" or five styles used in human communication will give you a more technical understanding of the meaning and uses of the registers summarized in the chapter.

The language and gender issue presents some thorny but challenging issues. *Holmes* (1989) gave an excellent review of research and issues. Some very effective books have been written by *Tannen* (1986, 1990) directed at lay readers.

If you have never read either of *Hall*'s (1959, 1966) books, at least read the latter in the near future for your own pleasure. Also *Fast*'s (1970) humorous but informative paperback makes enjoyable armchair reading.

For more information on communicative language teaching, consult books like *Brown* (1994), *Nunan* (1991), and *Richards and Rodgers* (1986).

*Finocchiaro and Brumfit*'s (1983) book is a comprehensive summary of notional-functional principles, but you should look at *Berns*'s (1984b) highly critical review of their book for a balanced perspective.

## Topics and Questions For Study and Discussion

1.  How does Cummins's CALP/BICS distinction differ from the earlier distinction between linguistic and communicative competence? How does the addition of *context* help one to operationalize differences between CALP and BICS? why is context important?

2.  Look at Bachman's (1990) graphic depiction of language competence (Figures 9-1 and 9-2). Explain the relationship of strategic competence to language competence. What is the relationship between "compensatory" strategies and "executive" strategies?

3.  Review once again the distinction between the *form* and the *function* of language. Why is an analysis of second language acquisition incomplete if it includes only forms and not functions? In what way does Skinner's theory account for both form and function in language?

4.  Hatch contended that in second language learning "one learns how to do conversation" first, and then builds up a repertoire of structures. This suggests that learning may be in some sense a deductive process: one learns linguistic "wholes" and then learns "parts." Do you agree with Hatch? What are the classroom implications of her contention?

5.  In a conversation group or a conversation period in a class, take note of the use of the various *rules of conversation* described in this

chapter. If a tape recording of the conversation is available you might engage in a mini-discourse analysis of the conversation. Note personality dynamics, nonverbal features of the conversation, and the discourse itself. Can you learn something about the second language learning process through such an exercise? or about a particular learner?

6. In your routine language discourse over the next day or two, notice how people get attention, change topics, clarify topics, terminate topics, take turns, avoid topics, and interrupt. What are some major differences between English conversation and the discourse of another language you are familiar with?

7. Give examples of language in Joos's five styles. How many styles are appropriate to teach in a foreign language class? What are some surface linguistic manifestations of differences in style? nonverbal manifestations? How do styles vary cross-culturally?

8. Compare English with another language, if possible, in terms of gender issues. Are there differences in the way one addresses women and men? In the way women and men talk? in grammatical (or morphological) gender loading? In what ways might that other language reflect sexism?

9. Compare nonverbal expressions in English-speaking culture with those of a second culture. How might such expressions interfere with second language communication? How might they facilitate communication?

10. In what way are principles of communicative language teaching operating in methods that have been summarized in previous "in the classroom" vignettes?

11. What is wrong with "structural lamb served up as notional mutton?" How does the notional-functional syllabus help us to reach communicative competence in the classroom? What are the limitations of the notional-functional syllabus?

# Chapter 10

# LANGUAGE TESTING

The principal theme running through this book has been the importance of theory building in teaching foreign languages. The assumption is that the best teacher is the teacher who devises classroom methods and techniques that derive from a comprehensive knowledge of the total process of language learning, of what is happening within the learner and within the teacher and in the interaction between the two. All of this knowledge, however, remains somewhat abstract in the mind of the teacher unless it can be empirically tested in the real world. It is one thing to have a thorough grasp of the principles of foreign language learning and teaching and another to creatively formulate specific hypotheses about language learning in particular contexts and to garner empirical support for those hypotheses.

That support can be gathered by means of careful measurement of the language competence of learners in given situations. That is, your theory of second language acquisition can be put into practice every day in the classroom, but you will never know how valid your theory is unless you systematically measure the success of your learners and consequently, your theory-in-practice. It is to that end that this chapter takes up general considerations of what it is that you, the teacher, need to know about *language testing*.

## What is a Test?

Whether we realize it or not, we test every day in virtually every cognitive effort we make. When we read a book, listen to the news on TV, or prepare a meal, we are testing hypotheses and making judgments. Anytime we "try" something—a new recipe, a different tennis racquet, a new pair of shoes—we are testing. We are formulating a judgment about something on the basis of a sample of behavior. Language learners are testing their newly acquired forms of language almost every time they speak. They devise hypotheses about how the language forms are structured and how certain functions are expressed in forms. On the basis of the feedback they receive, they make judgments and decisions. Language teachers also test, informally and intuitively, in every contact with learners. As a learner speaks or writes or indicates either aural or reading comprehension, the teacher makes a judgment about the performance and from that judgment infers certain competence on the part of the learner. Classroom-oriented informal testing is an everyday and very common activity in which teachers engage almost intuitively.

A test, in plain, ordinary words, is a method of measuring a person's ability or knowledge in a given area. The definition captures the essential components of a test. A test is first *a method*. There is a set of techniques, procedures, test items, that constitute an instrument of some sort. And that method generally requires some performance or activity on the part of either the testee or the tester or both. The method may be quite intuitive and informal, as in the case of judging offhand someone's authenticity of pronunciation. Or it may be quite explicit and structured, as in a multiple-choice technique in which correct responses have already been specified by some "objective" means.

Next, a test has the purpose of *measuring*. Some measurements are rather broad and inexact while others are quantified in mathematically precise terms. The difference between formal and informal testing exists to a great degree in the nature of the quantification of data. Informal tests, the everyday intuitive judging that we do as laypersons or teachers, are difficult to quantify. Judgments are rendered in rather global terms. For example, it is common to speak of a "good" tennis player, "fair" performance by an actor in a play, or a "poor" reader. In formal testing, in which carefully planned techniques of assessment are used, quantification is important, especially for comparison either within an individual (say, at the beginning and the end of a course) or across individuals.

A test measures *a person's* ability or knowledge. Care must be taken in any test to understand who the *testees* are. What is their previous experience—their entry behavior? Is the test appropriate for them? How are scores to be interpreted for individuals?

Also being measured in a test is *ability or knowledge*—that is, competence. A test samples performance but infers certain competence. A driving test for a driver's license is a test requiring a sample of performance, but that performance is used by the tester to infer someone's general competence to drive a car. A language test samples language behavior and infers general ability in a language. A test of reading comprehension may consist of some questions following one or two paragraphs, a tiny sample of a second language learner's total reading behavior. From the results of that test the examiner infers a certain level of general reading ability.

Finally, a test measures *a given area*. In the case of a proficiency test, even though the actual performance on the test involves only a sampling of skills, that *area* is overall proficiency in a language—general competence in all skills of a language. Other tests may have more specific criteria. A test of pronunciation might well be a test only of a particular phonemic minimal pair in a language. One of the biggest obstacles to overcome in constructing adequate tests is to measure the *criterion* and not inadvertently something else.

# Practicality

The foregoing discussion implicitly dealt with the three requirements of a "good" test: practicality, reliability, and validity. If these three axiomatic criteria are carefully met, a test should then be administerable within given constraints, be dependable, and actually measure what it intends to measure.

A test ought to be *practical*—within the means of financial limitations, time constraints, ease of administration, and scoring and interpretation. A test that is prohibitively expensive is impractical. A test of language proficiency that takes a student 10 hours to complete is also impractical. A test that requires individual one-to-one proctoring is impractical for a group of 500 people and only a handful of examiners. A test that takes a few minutes for a student to take and several hours for the examiner to correct is impractical for a large number of testees and one examiner if results are expected within a short time. A test that can be scored only by computer is impractical if the test takes place a thousand miles away from the nearest computer. The value and quality of a test are dependent upon such nitty-gritty, practical considerations.

One important aspect of practicality that testing researchers have pointed out is that a test ought to have what Oller (1979:52) called *instructional value,* that is, "it ought to be possible to use the test to enhance the delivery of instruction in student populations." Testing and teaching are interrelated, as we shall see later in this chapter. Teachers need to be able to make clear and useful interpretations of test data in order to understand their students better. A test that is too complex or too sophisticated may not be of practical use to the teacher.

# Reliability

A *reliable* test is a test that is consistent and dependable. Sources of unreliability may lie in the test itself or in the scoring of the test, known respectively as test reliability and rater (or scorer) reliability. If you give the same test to the same subject or matched subjects on two different occasions, the test itself should yield similar results; it should have *test reliability*. A test of skating ability, for example, should be reasonably consistent from one day to the next. However, if one skating test is conducted on bumpy ice and another on smooth ice, the reliability of the test—of one aspect of the test, at least—is suspect. I once witnessed the administration of a test of aural comprehension in which a tape recorder played items for comprehension, but because of street noise outside the testing room, some students in the room were prevented from hearing the tape accurately. That was a clear case of unreliability. Sometimes a test yields unreliable results because of factors beyond the control of the test writer, such as illness, a "bad day," or no sleep the night before.

*Scorer reliability* is the consistency of scoring by two or more scorers. If very subjective techniques are employed in the scoring of a test, one would not expect to find high scorer reliability. A test of authenticity of pronunciation in which the scorer is to assign a number between one and five might be unreliable if the scoring directions are not clear. If scoring directions are clear and specific as to the exact details the judge should attend to, then such scoring can become reasonably consistent and dependable. In tests of writing skills scorer reliability is not easy to achieve since writing proficiency involves numerous traits that are difficult to define. But as Brown and Bailey (1984) pointed out, the careful specification of an analytical scoring instrument can increase scorer reliability.

## Validity

By far the most complex criterion of a good test is *validity,* the degree to which the test actually measures what it is intended to measure. A valid test of reading ability is one that actually measures reading ability and not 20/20 vision, previous knowledge in a subject, or some other variable of questionable relevance. To measure writing ability, one might conceivably ask students to write as many words as they can in 15 minutes, then simply *count* the words for the final score. Such a test would be practical and reliable; the test would be easy to administer, and the scoring quite dependable. But it would hardly constitute a valid test of writing ability unless some consideration were given to the communication and organization of ideas, among other factors. Some have felt that standard language proficiency tests, with their context-reduced, CALP-oriented language and limited stretches of discourse, are not valid measures of language "proficiency" since they do not appear to tap into the communicative competence of the learner. There is good reasoning behind such criticism (Duran 1985); nevertheless, what such proficiency tests lack in validity, they gain in practicality and reliability. We will return to the question of large-scale proficiency testing in a later section of this chapter.

How does one establish the validity of a test? Statistical correlation with other related measures is a standard method. But ultimately, validity can only be established by observation and theoretical justification. There is no final, absolute, and objective measure of validity. We have to ask questions that give us convincing evidence that a test accurately and sufficiently measures the testee for the particular purpose, or *objective,* or *criterion,* of the test.

Consider, for example, the common practice in the United States of testing a person's ability to drive an automobile. Intuitively, we would conclude that a valid test of driving ability should include an actual sample of a person's behind-the-wheel behavior. However, in many localities a paper-and-pencil test of road signs and traffic regulations is a sufficient criterion for renewal of a driver's license. Is such a test valid? Observational studies seem to bear out the contention that no subsequent driving test is needed, but it is doubtful that the written test actually predicts the quality of driving ability. It is more likely that simply previous experience in driving is the best predictor of good driving ability. The paper-and-pencil license-renewal test probably has little validity for predicting good driving; what it does measure is knowledge of various regulations, which is only a small part of total driving ability.

In tests of language, validity is supported most convincingly by subsequent personal observation of teachers and peers. The validity of a high score on the final exam of a foreign language course will be substantiated by "actual" proficiency in the language (if the claim is that a high score is indicative of high proficiency). A classroom test designed to assess mastery of a point of grammar in communicative use will have validity if test scores correlate either with observed subsequent behavior or with other communicative measures of the grammar point in question.

How can teachers be somewhat assured that a test, whether it is a standardized test or one which has been constructed for classroom use, is indeed valid? The technical procedures for validating tests are complex and require specialized knowledge. But two major types of validation are important for classroom teachers: content validity and construct validity.

### Content Validity

If a test actually samples the class of situations, that is, the universe of subject matter about which conclusions are to be drawn, it is said to have *content validity.* The test actually involves the testee in a sample of the behavior that is being measured. You can usually determine content validity, observationally, if you can clearly define the achievement that you are measuring. A test of tennis competency that asks someone to run a 100-yard dash lacks content validity. If you are trying to assess a person's ability to speak a second language in a conversational setting, a test that asks the learner to answer paper-and-pencil multiple-choice questions requiring grammatical judgments does not achieve content validity. A test that requires the learner actually to speak within some sort of authentic context does.

A concept that is very closely related to content validity is *face validity,* which asks the question: does the test, on the "face" of it, *appear* to test what it is designed to test? Face validity is very important from the learner's perspective. To achieve "peak" performance on a test, a learner needs to be convinced that the test is indeed testing what it claims to test. Once I administered a dictation test and a cloze test (see below, for a discussion of cloze tests) as a placement test for an experimental group of learners of English as a second language. Some learners were upset because such tests, on the face of it, did not appear to them to test their true abilities in English. Face validity is almost always perceived in terms of content: if the test samples the actual content of what the learner has achieved or expects to achieve, then face validity will be perceived.

In most human situations we are best tested in something when we are required to perform a sampling of the criterion behavior. But there are a few cases of highly specialized and sophisticated testing instruments which do not have high content validity yet are nevertheless valid. Projective personality tests are a prime example. The Thematic Apperception Test and the Rorschach "inkblot" tests have little content validity, yet they have been shown to be accurate in assessing certain types of deviant personality behavior. Other well-known psychological tests have little content validity. The Micro-Momentary Expression test (MME) is a test of empathy that requires subjects to detect facial changes in a participant in a conversation. The more facial changes a testee detects, the more empathic he or she is said to be. Such a test has little content validity, especially if the astute detection of facial changes might be argued to require field independence, which has been shown to correlate negatively with empathy! A test of field independence as a prediction of language success in the classroom is another example of a test with potentially good criterion validity but poor content validity in that the ability to detect an embedded geometric figure bears little direct resemblance to the ability to speak and hear a language.

## Construct Validity

A second category of validity that teachers must be aware of in considering language tests is *construct validity.* One way to look at construct validity is to ask the question: does this test actually tap into the theoretical construct as it has been defined? "Proficiency" is a construct. "Communicative competence" is a construct. "Self-esteem" is a construct. Virtually every theoretical category we have discussed in this book is a theoretical construct. Tests are, in a manner of speaking, *operational definitions* of such constructs, in that they operationalize the entity that is being measured (see Davidson, Hudson, and Lynch 1985). A teacher, then, needs to be satisfied that a particular test is an adequate definition of a construct. A general proficiency test that consists of, say, grammatical judgment items, reading comprehension items, and listening comprehension items is defining "proficiency" as either consisting of, or being correlated with, those three modes of performance.

In many cases such theoretical constructs are perceived as being adequately defined in the content of the test itself. But when there is low, or questionable, content validity in a test, it becomes very important for a teacher to be assured of its construct validity. In this instance, validation of the construct has to be empirically demonstrated by means of research that shows that the behavior required of the testee is *correlated* with the total construct of behaviors in question. For example, the empirical justification for using the MME as a test of empathy is found in research that shows the MME to be correlated with other tests of empathy. The Embedded Figures Test of field independence, in which the testee is to discern smaller geometric shapes within larger and more complex geometric designs, has likewise been related in research studies to other forms of assessing field independence. If you were to claim that such a test is valid for, say, predicting success in a second language, you would be forced to do (or find) research that would empirically demonstrate the correlation of scores on the Embedded Figures Test with scores on other measures of language aptitude. The construct underlying such a claim would theorize that the same cognitive strategies or styles required to perform well on the Embedded Figures Test are also required for successful learning of a second language.

Validity is a complex concept. However, it is indispensable to the teacher's understanding of what makes a "good" test. If in your language teaching you can attend to the practicality, reliability, and validity of tests of language, whether those tests are classroom tests related to a part of a lesson or final exams or proficiency tests, then you are well on the way to making accurate and viable judgments about the competence of the learners with whom you are working.

# Kinds of Tests

There are many kinds of tests, each with a specific purpose, a particular criterion to be measured. The purpose of this chapter is not to expound on the many varieties of tests, nor to instruct you on how exactly to devise even a few varieties. However, in examining the general underlying principles of language testing, it is appropriate and necessary to devote a few brief words to outlining some categories of language tests. Your training as a teacher of a particular language should then involve the more specific matters of test construction and interpretation for that language.

## *Proficiency Tests*

If your aim in a test is to tap global competence in a language, then you are, in conventional terminology, testing *proficiency*. A proficiency test is not intended to be limited to any one course, curriculum, or single skill in the language. Proficiency tests have traditionally consisted of standardized multiple-choice items on grammar, vocabulary, reading comprehension, aural comprehension, and sometimes of a sample of writing. Such tests often have validity weaknesses: they may confuse oral proficiency with literacy skills, or they may confuse knowledge *about* a language with ability to *use* a language; a number of other weaknesses may pertain (Dieterich, Freeman, and Crandall 1979). Proficiency tests need not be defined in such limited terms, however, as we shall see later in this chapter; some great strides have been made toward defining communicative proficiency tests that depart from tradition in radical ways.

A rather typical example of a standardized proficiency test is the Test of English as a Foreign Language (TOEFL) produced by the Educational Testing Service. It is used by nearly 1000 institutions of higher education in the United States as an indicator of a prospective student's ability to undertake academic work in an English medium. The TOEFL consists of the following three sections:

Section 1, Listening Comprehension, measures the ability to understand English as it is spoken in the United States. The oral aspects of the language are stressed. The problems tested include vocabulary that is more frequently used in spoken English, structures that are primarily peculiar to spoken English, and sound and intonation distinctions that have proven to be difficult for nonnative speakers. The stimulus material is recorded in standard American English; the response options are printed in the test books.

Section 2, Structure and Written Expression, measures mastery of important structural and grammatical points in standard written English. The language tested is formal, rather than conversational. The topics of the sentences are of a general academic nature so that individuals in specific fields of study or from specific national or linguistic groups have no particular advantage. When topics have a national context, they refer to United States history, culture, art, or literature.

Section 3, Vocabulary and Reading Comprehension, tests the ability to understand the meanings and uses of words in written English as well as the ability to understand a variety of reading materials. So that there is no advantage to individuals in any one field of study, the questions based on reading materials do not require outside knowledge of the subject matter.

Proficiency tests sometimes add sections that involve free writing (e.g., ETS's Test of Written English) and/or oral production (e.g., ETS's Test of Spoken English), but these responses diminish the practicality of scoring on a high-volume basis. The TOEFL and virtually every other large-scale proficiency test is machine scorable; when scorers must either read writing samples or judge audiotapes of spoken proficiency, a great deal of administrative cost and time are involved.

### *Diagnostic and Placement Tests*

A *diagnostic* test is designed to diagnose a particular aspect of a particular language. A diagnostic test in pronunciation might have the purpose of determining which particular phonological features of the language pose difficulty for a learner. Prator's (1972) Diagnostic Passage, for example, is a short written passage that a student of English as a second language reads orally; the teacher or tester then examines a tape recording of that reading against a very detailed checklist of pronunciation errors. The checklist serves to diagnose certain problems in pronunciation. Some proficiency tests can serve as diagnostic tests by isolating and analyzing certain sets of items within the test. An achievement test on a particular module in a curriculum might include a number of items on modal auxiliaries; these particular items could serve to diagnose difficulty on modals.

Certain proficiency tests and diagnostic tests can act in the role of *placement tests* whose purpose is to place a student in a particular level or section of a language curriculum or school. A placement test typically includes a sampling of material to be covered in the curriculum (that is, it has content validity), and it thereby provides an indication of the point at which the student will find a level or class to be neither too easy nor too difficult but to be appropriately challenging.

### *Achievement Tests*

An *achievement test* is related directly to classroom lessons, units, or even a total curriculum. Achievement tests are limited to particular material covered in a curriculum within a particular time frame.

### *Aptitude Tests*

Finally, we need to consider the type of test that is given to a person prior to *any* exposure to the second language, a test that predicts a person's future success. A foreign language *aptitude test* is designed to measure a person's capacity or general ability to learn a foreign language and to be successful in that undertaking. Aptitude tests are considered to be independent of a particular foreign language, predicting success in the acquisition of any foreign language. Two standardized aptitude tests have been used in the United States—the Modern Language Aptitude Test (Carroll and Sapon 1958) and the Pimsleur Language Aptitude Battery (Pimsleur 1966). Both of these are English language tests and require students to perform such tasks as learning numbers, listening, detecting spelling clues and grammatical patterns, and memorizing.

While these two aptitude tests were once rather popular in the foreign language profession, few attempts have been made since then to experiment with new measures of language aptitude (see Parry and Child 1990). Two major issues account for this decline. First, even though the MLAT and the PLAB *claimed* to measure "language" aptitude, it appears that they simply reflected the general intelligence or academic ability of the student (see Skehan 1989a). At best, they measured ability to perform focused, analytical, field-independent, context-reduced activities that occupy a student in a traditional language classroom. They hardly even began to tap into the kinds of learning strategies and styles that recent research (Oxford 1990b, Ehrman 1990, for example) has shown to be crucial in the acquisition of *communicative* competence in context-embedded situations. As we have already noted in previous chapters, especially in Chapter Five, learners can be successful for a multitude of reasons, many of which are much more related to motivation and determination than to "native" abilities (Lett and O'Mara 1990).

Second, how is one to interpret a language aptitude test? Rarely does an institution have the luxury or freedom to test people *before* they take a foreign language to counsel certain people out of their decision to do so. So, an aptitude test biases both student and teacher. They are each led to believe that they will be successful or unsuccessful, depending on the aptitude test score, and a self-fulfilling prophecy occurs. It is better for teachers to be optimistic for students, and in the early stages of a student's process of language learning, to monitor styles and strategies carefully, leading the student toward strategies that will aid in the process of learning and away from those blocking factors that will hinder the process.

The importance of these four different kinds of language tests lies in the fact that different tests serve different purposes. In order to select tests adequately and to interpret their results accurately, teachers need to be aware of the ultimate purpose of the testing context.

Within each category of test above there is a variety of different possible techniques and procedures. These range from objective to subjective techniques, open-ended to structured, multiple-choice to fill-in-the-blank, written to oral. Moreover, language has been viewed traditionally as consisting of four separate skills; therefore language tests have attempted to measure differential ability in speaking, listening, reading, and writing. It is not uncommon to be quite proficient in reading a foreign language but not in speaking, or of course for aural comprehension to outstrip speaking ability.

Beyond such considerations, tests of each of the modes of performance can be focused on a continuum of linguistic units, from smaller to larger: phonology and orthography, words, sentences, and discourse. In interpreting a test it is important to note which linguistic units are being tested. Oral production tests can be tests of overall conversational fluency or pronunciation of a particular subset of phonology, and can take the form of imitation, structured responses, or free responses. Similarly, listening-comprehension tests can concentrate on a particular feature of language or on overall listening for general meaning. Tests of reading can cover the range of language units and can aim to test comprehension of long or short passages, single sentences, or even phrases and words. Writing tests can take on an open-ended form with free composition, or be structured to elicit anything from correct spelling to discourse-level competence.

# Historical Perspectives

In order to examine two language testing issues that characterize the development of the field over the past half-century, we will first glance at some historical trends. For some further historical background, see Spolsky (1978b), Davies (1990), Skehan (1988, 1989b), and Alderson (1991).

The history of language testing seems to break itself into several chronological periods, according to Spolsky (1978b). The first of those periods, the "prescientific" period, prior to the early 1950s, had no language testing research as such to turn to. Since language teaching itself was not a distinct discipline, language testing followed whatever general principles of testing were available in the humanities or social sciences. By and large, teachers constructed their own classroom tests, which were an outgrowth of Grammar-Translation or reading-oriented methods that they were using.

The second period was identified as the "psychometric-structuralist" period, from the early 1950s through the late 1960s. You will recall from previous chapters that this was a time when contrastive analysis was a thriving discipline, and that structural linguistics and behavioral psychology combined to provide a "scientific" air to language teaching. Likewise, testing focused on specific language elements such as phonological, grammatical, and lexical contrasts between two languages (see Lado 1961). It was during this era that language testers adopted the practice of testing single, minute elements of language in a test, so that each item tested an element. This approach came to be known as the "discrete point" approach to language testing, to be carefully distinguished from "integrative" approaches (see Carroll 1961).

The third period, dating from the late 1960s to the present time, is labeled the "integrative-sociolinguistic" period. The growing dissatisfaction with structuralism and behaviorism led, as we have seen, to linguistic research on communicative competence and on the contexts of language. In short, testers were realizing that "the whole of the communicative event was considerably greater than the sum of its linguistic elements" (Clark 1983:432). Today, language testing specialists like Lyle Bachman (1991) are continuing to experiment with more accurate methods of assessing communicative language ability.

You can see that trends in testing followed the disciplinary trends in linguistics and psychology that we have already seen in earlier chapters of this book. As second language acquisition research grew and developed, paradigms and theories were reflected in the thinking of testing specialists. It is against that brief historical backdrop that we now look at two major issues in language testing.

# Discrete Point and Integrative Testing

The first of two major issues in language testing reflects the debate and research primarily of the decade of the 1970s, namely, the controversy between *discrete point* and *integrative* testing methods. Discrete point tests were constructed on the assumption that language can be broken down into its component parts and those parts adequately tested. Those components are basically the "four skills" (listening, speaking, reading, writing), the various hierarchical units of language (phonology/graphology, morphology, lexicon, syntax) within each skill, and subcategories within those units. So, for example, it was claimed that a typical proficiency test with its sets of multiple-choice questions divided into grammar, vocabulary, reading, and the like, with some items attending to smaller units and others to larger units, can measure these discrete points of language and, by adequate sampling of these units, can achieve validity. Such a rationale is not unreasonable if one considers types of testing theory in which certain constructs are measured by the breaking down of their componential parts.

The discrete point approach obviously met with some criticism as we emerged into the "integrative-sociolinguistic" era with its emphasis on communication, authenticity, and context. The criticism came largely from John Oller (1976, 1979), who argued that language competence is a unified set of interacting abilities that cannot be separated apart and tested adequately. The claim is, in short, that communicative competence is so global and requires such *integration* (hence the term "integrative" testing) that it cannot be captured in additive tests of grammar and reading and vocabulary and other discrete points of language. "If discrete items take language skill apart, integrative tests put it back together. Whereas discrete items attempt to test knowledge of language one bit at a time, integrative tests attempt to assess a learner's capacity to use many bits all at the same time" (Oller 1979:37). While some testing researchers (for example, Farhady 1979) argued the validity of discrete point tests, others (Cziko 1982, Savignon 1982) embraced the assumption that integrative tests are distinctive in their capacity to assess communicative abilities of second language learners.

Just what does an integrative test look like? Two types of test have been held up as prime examples of integrative tests: cloze tests and dictations. A *cloze test* is a reading passage (of, say, 150 to 300 words) that has been "mutilated" by the deletion of roughly every sixth or seventh word; the testee is required to supply words that fit into those blanks. Oller (1976, 1979) and others have claimed that cloze test results are good measures of overall proficiency. According to theoretical constructs underlying this claim, the ability to supply appropriate words in blanks requires a number of abilities that lie at the very heart of competence in a language: knowledge of vocabulary, grammatical structure, and discourse structure, reading skills and strategies, and an internalized "expectancy" grammar (that enables one to predict an item that will come next in a sequence). It is argued that successful completion of cloze items taps into all of those abilities, which are the essence of global language proficiency.

Cloze tests have a variety of formats. A *Fixed-ratio* deletion method establishes the deletion of every *n*th word (usually every sixth or seventh word), regardless of what that word may be, and of the predicted difficulty of the testee "guessing" it. *Rational* deletion provides an alternative to the fixed-ratio method by selecting words for deletion that meet certain discourse criteria. Current research on cloze testing yields divergent data on the relative merits of each test method. Some earlier studies (e.g., Bachman 1982, 1984) concluded that rational deletion enables the tester to be more specific in pinpointing grammatical and discourse criteria. More recent studies (Sciarone and Schoorl 1989, Jonz 1990, Fotos 1991) support the contention that fixed-ratio deletions are quite valid. Other studies (Chapelle and Abraham 1990) came up with somewhat equivocal results, suggesting that both methods may be appropriate, depending on the test's goals.

Another variation in cloze test administration lies in its scoring method. Scoring can vary from requiring the testee to supply the *exact word* that was deleted, to supplying an *acceptable word* (which "makes sense" in the context of the passage). The latter is often more psychologically reassuring for the testee, an especially important consideration in classroom uses of cloze tests. However, Sciarone and Schoorl (1989) found that as long as there are at least 100 blanks (deletions) in a test, exact-word scoring is as valid as acceptable-word scoring. Exact-word scoring is more efficient for large-scale testing and can be adapted to a multiple-choice format for easier scoring mechanics. In fact, recent research on the TOEFL (Duran 1985) suggested that cloze testing could provide an added functional dimension to the TOEFL and still maintain the administrative practicality that is so important for a test that is taken by over a half-million students every year.

The *dictation* test is familiar to virtually all classroom language learners. A relatively short passage (say, 100 to 200 words) is read by the teacher to the students. In the first of what are usually three readings, the passage is read through at "normal" speed while students listen. In the second reading, the passage is broken up into phrases or chunks of language long enough to challenge learners; the learners write what they hear during pauses. In the third reading, students hear the passage again at normal speed and can check their written renditions. Dictations also have a tremendous variety of administration and scoring procedures. The length of the chunks can vary considerably; the pace of the second reading obviously can vary; the length of pauses for writing can vary; dictations and cloze tests can combine to form "partial dictations" or "oral cloze" tests; and there are myriad scoring criteria that have been used in the many decades, if not centuries, of dictation testing.

Dictation, along with cloze, is said to be a potentially appropriate integrative test (Savignon 1982, Oller 1979, Oller and Streiff 1975). The argument is that it, too, taps into certain grammatical and discourse competencies and that dictation test results tend to correlate strongly with other tests of proficiency. Success on a dictation requires careful listening, reproduction in writing of what is heard, efficient short-term memory, and, to an extent, some expectancy rules to aid the short-term memory. Dictation testing remains more classroom centered since large-scale administration of dictations is quite impractical from a scoring standpoint. Reliability of scoring criteria is also a problem that is not presented in multiple-choice, exact-word cloze test scoring.

# Language Proficiency: Unitary or Divisible?

The debate over whether or not there is such a thing as an integrative test of language proficiency continued in various manifestations for some time. Initially, the discussion centered on the issue of whether or not language ability can be divided up into separately testable components. Proponents of the "indivisible" view proposed the *unitary trait hypothesis* (Oller 1979; see also Lowe 1988), which suggested that language proficiency is more unitary than the discrete point testers contended. That is, vocabulary, grammar, phonology, the "four skills," and other discrete points of language cannot, in fact, be distinguished from each other. The unitary trait hypothesis contended that there is a general factor of language proficiency such that all the discrete points do *not* add up to that whole.

Others argued strongly against the unitary trait position, noting, among other things, that "language proficiency is one of the most poorly defined concepts in the field of language testing" (Farhady 1982:44). As evidence against the unitary trait hypothesis, Farhady found significant and widely varying differences in performance on six different components of an ESL proficiency test depending on subjects' native country, major field of study, and graduate versus undergraduate status. So for example, Brazilians scored very low in listening comprehension and relatively high in reading comprehension. Filipinos, whose scores on five of the six components of the test were considerably higher than Brazilians' scores, were actually lower than Brazilians in reading comprehension scores. Farhady's contentions were supported in other research (Bachman and Palmer 1981, 1982; Upshur and Homburg 1983) that seriously questioned the unitary trait hypothesis. Finally, in the face of the evidence, Oller (1983:352) backed down, and admitted that "the unitary trait hypothesis was wrong."

Meanwhile, language testing research was gradually pointing to the viability of the hypothesis that language proficiency consists of several distinct abilities, but the research of the 1980s was not in any way a return to discrete point testing. Far from it. Instead, researchers were—and continue to be—

focused on the components of communicative competence in their efforts to specify the multiple language *traits* that must be measured in a valid test. Listening, speaking, reading, and writing are but one dimension of a multi-trait approach to testing. In fact, Bachman's (1990) model of communicative language proficiency discussed in the previous chapter has become a template for experimenting with a multiplicity of methods of language assessment. Along with the components of organizational (phonology, grammar, discourse) competence, language tests of the 90s are focusing on the pragmatic (sociolinguistic, functional) and strategic components of language ability (Skehan 1988, 1989b; Bachman 1991). While the integrative properties of cloze and dictation testing still appear to hold some promise, most testing specialists now agree that valid tests of communicative competence must tap into all of these communicative components.

# Assessing Communicative Language Ability

In the last decade or so, some important strides have been taken toward the objective of accurate assessment of communicative language ability. With the continued refinement of our definitions of communicative competence coupled with vigorous research on forms of communicative testing, particularly the testing of communicative production of language, we have begun to make some significant progress.

A communicative test has to meet some rather stringent criteria (see Wesche 1983, Swain 1984, Bachman 1991). It has to test for grammatical, discourse, sociolinguistic, and illocutionary competence as well as strategic competence. It has to be *pragmatic* in that it requires the learner to *use* language *naturally* for genuine communication and to relate to thoughts and feelings, in short, to put *authentic* language to use within a *context.* It should be *direct* (as opposed to indirect tests that may lose validity as they lose content validity). And it should test the learner in a variety of language functions.

How does such a test differ from its historical predecessors? Bachman (1991:678) offers four distinguishing characteristics:

> First, such tests create an "information gap," requiring test takers to process complementary information through the use of multiple sources of input. Test takers, for example, might be required to perform a writing task that is based on input from both a short recorded lecture and a reading passage on the same topic. A second characteristic is that of task dependency, with tasks in one section of the test building upon the content of earlier sections, including the test taker's answers to those sections. Third, communicative tests can be characterized by their integration of test tasks and content within a given domain of discourse. Finally, communicative tests attempt to measure a much broader range of language abilities—including knowledge of cohesion, functions, and sociolinguistic appropriateness—than did earlier tests, which tended to focus on the formal aspects of language—grammar, vocabulary, and pronunciation.

Along more practical, classroom-oriented lines, Merrill Swain (1984) recommended four criteria for the construction of communicative tests:

1. **Start from somewhere.** Tests should build on existing knowledge and principles. In other words, a theoretical framework, such as that which you have been developing in the study of this book, is an important foundation for creating communicative tests.

2. **Concentrate on content.** The "traditional" language test might have hundreds of unrelated topics that require the testee to jump from topic to topic in a matter of a few seconds, a far cry from natural communicative situations. Swain suggests that our tests need to have motivating, interesting, and substantive content. For example, students can be given a sample situation, such as "job opportunities in two locales," which form the setting for the test. The situation is motivating to the students and provides some new information to deal with. Tests that concentrate on content also need to be integrated and interactive. Integration provides *context,* that all-important element of communication. And by eliciting opinions and the expression of one's own ideas, an interactive element can occur.

3. **Bias for best.** Our tests need to do everything possible to elicit the very best performance from students. They can do their best if their anxieties are lowered, if they have adequate time to complete· the task, and if they are made to feel they can indeed succeed. In another article, not cited by Swain, Canale (1984) suggested that learners perform best if a test has four phases: (a) *warmup,* where the testee gets accustomed to the test format; (b) *level check,* where items confirm that testees are where they are assumed to be; (c) *probe,* where the limits of one's abilities are ascertained through challenging, difficult items; and (d) *wind down,* where the learner is allowed to relax with some easier questions that set the mind at ease. These appear to be appropriate principles for "biasing for best."

4. **Work for washback.** "Washback" is the effect a test has on teaching in the classroom. While we should not teach "toward" a test, we can use tests as teaching tools. Tests become feedback devices whereby a student perceives elements of communicative performance that need improvement. Our tests, then, should be designed to provide that feedback, as was noted at the beginning of this chapter.

To begin to enumerate all of the varieties of tests of communicative ability is not possible within this chapter. Tests in all four skills (speaking, listening, reading, and writing) have been developed, many of which of course involve more than one skill simultaneously. In some more recent research, Swain

(1990) offered an excellent example of a test that attempts to fulfill communicative criteria enumerated above as well as some criteria stemming from considerations of practicality. Swain's test battery includes a paper and pencil multiple-choice format as one component of a three-part test; the other two parts measure oral communication skills and written proficiency. Each of these parts is subdivided into grammatical, discourse, and sociolinguistic traits. Table 10–1 describes the 3 × 3 design of the test. Of course, for a classroom teacher, and even more so for large, institutional testing contexts, this format takes time to administer because of the individualization involved, but time well invested in order to test several traits of communicative competence through several methods.

# Oral Proficiency Testing

One of the toughest challenges of communicative testing has been the construction of practical, reliable, and valid tests of oral production ability. Production, unlike comprehension, takes time, money, and ingenuity to measure. The best tests of oral proficiency involve a one-on-one tester/testee relationship, "live" performance (as opposed to taped), a careful specification of tasks to be accomplished during the test, and a scoring rubric that is truly descriptive of ability.

For several decades now, what was formerly the Foreign Service Institute's (FSI) Oral Proficiency Interview (OPI) has been widely used across dozens of languages around the world. "FSI[1] levels" (zero through five) have become standard indicators within the profession of a person's speaking proficiency in a given foreign language (see Table 10–2). In a series of structured tasks, the OPI is carefully designed to elicit pronunciation, fluency/integrative ability, sociolinguistic and cultural knowledge, grammar, and vocabulary. Performance is judged by the interviewer, through a detailed checklist, to fall between level zero (the interviewee cannot perform at all in the language) and level five (speaking proficiency equivalent to that of an educated native speaker).

---

[1]It should be noted that FSI levels are no longer referred to as such among language testing researchers. Through a historical progression of collaboration with different agencies, what was known as the FSI test has now fallen under the administration of the American Council for the Teaching of Foreign Languages (ACTFL). However, ACTFL's interest in this Oral Proficiency Interview (OPI) has involved collaboration with the Educational Testing Service (ETS) and another group of researchers known as the Interagency Language Roundtable (ILR). This chaotic potpourri of acronyms has prompted most people simply to call the old FSI (now revised several times) the OPI. This nomenclature, thankfully, saves us from having to call it the FSIACTFLET-SILROPI!

**TABLE 10–1.  Operationalization of traits in second language proficiency test (Swain 1990:403)**

| Trait / Method | Grammar | Discourse | Sociolinguistic |
|---|---|---|---|
| | focus on grammatical accuracy within sentences | focus on textual cohesion and coherence | focus on social appropriateness of language use |
| **Oral** | structured interview scored for accuracy of verb morphology, prepositions, syntax | story retelling and argumentation/suasion detailed ratings for e.g., identification, logical sequence, time orientation, and global ratings for coherence | role-play of speech acts: requests, offers, complaints scored for ability to distinguish formal and informal register |
| **Multiple Choice** | sentence-level 'select the correct form' exercise (45 items) involving verb morphology, prepositions, and other items | paragraph-level 'select the coherent sentence' exercise (29 items) | speech-act-level 'select the appropriate utterance' exercise (28 items) |
| **Written Composition** | narrative and letter of suasion scored for accuracy of verb morphology, prepositions, syntax | narrative and letter of suasion detailed ratings much as for oral discourse and global rating for coherence | formal request letter and informal note scored for ability to distinguish formal and informal register |

## TABLE 10–2.    Oral Proficiency Interview Scale

| LEVEL | DESCRIPTION |
|---|---|
| 0 | Unable to function in the spoken language |
| 0+ | Able to satisfy immediate needs using rehearsed utterances |
| I | Able to satisfy minimum courtesy requirements and maintain very simple face-to-face conversations on familiar topics |
| I+ | Can initiate and maintain predictable face-to-face conversations and satisfy limited social demands |
| 2 | Able to satisfy routine social demands and limited work requirements |
| 2+ | Able to satisfy most work requirements with language usage that is often, but not always, acceptable and effective |
| 3 | Able to speak the language with sufficient structural accuracy and vocabulary to participate effectively in most formal and informal conversations on practical, social, and professional topics |
| 3+ | Often able to use the language to satisfy professional needs in a wide range of sophisticated and demanding tasks |
| 4 | Able to use the language fluently and accurately on all levels normally pertinent to professional needs |
| 4+ | Speaking proficiency is regularly superior in all respects, usually equivalent to that of a well-educated highly articulate native speaker |
| 5 | Speaking proficiency is functionally equivalent to that of a highly articulate well-educated native speaker and reflects the cultural standards of the country where the language is natively spoken |

The OPI has come under harsh criticism in recent years from a large number of language testing specialists. Albert Valdman (1988:125) summed up the complaint:

From a Vygotskyan perspective, the OPI forces test takers into a closed system where, because the interviewer is endowed with full social control, they are unable to negotiate a social world. For example, they cannot nominate topics for discussion, they cannot switch formality levels, they cannot display a full range of stylistic maneuver. The total control the OPI interviewers possess is reflected by the parlance of the test methodology. . . . In short, the OPI can only inform us of how learners can deal with an artificial social *imposition* rather than enabling us to predict how they would be likely to manage authentic linguistic interactions with target-language native speakers.

Bachman (1988:149) also points out that the validity of the OPI simply cannot be demonstrated "because it confounds abilities with elicitation procedures in its design, and it provides only a single rating, which has no basis in either theory or research."

Meanwhile, a great deal of experimentation continues to be conducted to design better oral proficiency testing methods. Some bright hopes are in the making as researchers specify better methods of conducting and evaluating oral tests (Shohamy 1988, Douglas 1988, Van Lier 1989, Bachman 1991, Ross and Berwick 1992, and Stansfield and Kenyon 1992, among many others). With continued critical attention to issues of language testing in the years to come, we will most likely solve some of the thorny problems of how to specify the traits of communicative language proficiency and how to devise valid, reliable, and practical methods to measure those traits.

## In the Classroom: Steps To Creating Intrinsically Motivating Tests[1]

It is no easy task to create effective, valid, practical classroom tests. Often teachers dash off their tests and quizzes the night before they are administered, with too little time left to devote to (a) designing items that are appropriately calibrated for their students' proficiency level, (b) constructing a test that adequately samples the material covered, and (c) making sure it can be completed in the anticipated time frame. The result is that both teacher and students become frustrated over the inadequacy of the measurement device.

There are many different steps a teacher can take to create effective classroom tests, so many that a whole course in language testing is strongly urged, especially for novice teachers. In the meantime, just *one* among many considerations that you, as a teacher, might make in the design of classroom tests is to think of a test as a form of *intrinsically motivating feedback.* In other words, your tests are not just a necessary evil in classroom bureaucracy but rather are important means for building the competence, autonomy, and self-evaluation among your students. Consider, then, the following broad and widely generalized principles of intrinsic motivation that you can apply to your classroom tests.

1.  **The principle of giving students advance preparation.**

    This may sound simple, but much too often teachers do little to help students to prepare for a test. Tests, by their very nature, are anxiety-raising experiences. Students don't know what to expect. And they may not be aware of test-taking strategies that could help them. So, your first task in creating intrinsically motivating tests is to be an ally in the preparation process. You can do the following:

---

[1]An edited excerpt from H. Douglas Brown (1994), *Teaching by Principles: Interactive Language Teaching Methodology,* Regents Prentice Hall, Chapter 19.

- Provide information about the general format of a test.
- Provide information about types of items that will appear.
- Give students opportunities to practice certain item types.
- Encourage a thorough review of material to be covered.
- Offer advice on strategies for test preparation.
- Offer advice on strategies to use during the test itself.
- Give anxiety-lowering reassurance.

2. **The principle of face validity.**

Sometimes students don't know **what** is being tested when they tackle a test. Sometimes they feel, for a variety of possible reasons, that a test isn't testing what it is "supposed" to test. Face validity means that the students, as they perceive the test, feel that it is valid. You can help to foster that perception with:

- a carefully constructed, well thought-out format
- items that are clear and uncomplicated
- directions that are crystal clear
- tasks that are familiar and relate to their course work
- a difficulty level that is appropriate for your students
- test conditions that are **biased for best,** and therefore bring out students' best performance

3. **The principle of authenticity.**

Make sure that the language in your test is as natural and authentic as possible. Also, try to give language some **context** so that items aren't just a string of unrelated language samples. Thematic organization of items may help in this regard. Or, consider a story line that may run through your items.

Also, the tasks themselves need to be tasks that they have practiced and feel comfortable with. A classroom test is not the time to introduce brand new tasks because you won't know if student difficulty is a factor of the task itself or of the language you are testing.

4. **The principle of "washback."**

"Washback," as noted previously in this chapter, is the benefit that tests offer to learning. When students take a test, they should be able, within a reasonably short period of time, to utilize the information about their competence that test feedback offers. Formal tests must therefore be learning devices through which students can receive a diagnosis of areas of strength and weakness.

Their incorrect responses can become windows of insight about further work. Your **prompt** return of written tests with your feedback is therefore very important to intrinsic motivation.

One way to enhance washback is to provide **narrative evaluations** of test performance. Many teachers, in our overworked (and underpaid) lives, are in the habit of returning tests to students with a letter grade or a number score on it and considering our job done. In reality, letter grades and a score showing the number right or wrong give absolutely no information of intrinsic interest to the student whatsoever. Grades and scores reduce a mountain of linguistic and cognitive performance data to an absurd minimum. At best they give a **relative** indication of a formulaic judgment of performance as compared to others in the class—which fosters competitive learning, not cooperative learning.

So, when you return a written test, or even a data sheet from an oral production test, consider giving more than a number or grade or phrase as your feedback. Even if your evaluation is not a neat little paragraph appended to the test, at least you can respond to as many details throughout the test as time will permit. Give praise for strengths—the "good stuff"—as well as constructive criticism of weaknesses. Give strategic hints on how a student might improve certain elements of performance. In other words, take some time to make the test performance an intrinsically motivating experience through which a student will feel a sense of accomplishment and challenge.

Finally, washback also implies that students have ready access to you to discuss the feedback and evaluation you have given. I'm sure you have known teachers in your life with whom you wouldn't dare "argue" about a grade. In an interactive, cooperative, intrinsically motivating classroom, one could hardly promote such a tyrannical atmosphere. For learning to continue, learners need to have a chance to feed back on your feedback, to seek clarification of any issues that are fuzzy, and to set appropriate new goals for themselves for the days and weeks ahead.

These four principles are just a beginning, but they might help you to think primarily of the benefit to the student that your tests can provide. Once your orientation is toward the intrinsic motivation of the learner, you are at least attitudinally prepared to fine-tune the actual construction of the test itself.

## Suggested Readings

Language testing has become the focus of a great deal attention by a growing number of specialists in the field. An excellent review of research and issues is provided in two successive issues of *Language Teaching* by *Skehan* (1988, 1989b) and a little more recently by *Bachman* (1991).

Practical issues in classroom language testing are treated in such books as *Hughes* (1989) and *Madsen* (1983).

Sometimes the best way to understand how different kinds of tests vary is to examine them yourself. Check your closest library, language institute, or foreign languages department to see if tests are available for your perusal. You will find it enlightening to look through them.

Communicative language testing issues are the focus of a good portion of *Weir* (1988), *Bachman* (1990), *Lowe and Stansfield* (1988), and *Swain* (1990).

A good picture of the controversies surrounding oral proficiency testing can be gained by looking at the June 1988 issue of *Studies in Second Language Acquisition* (*Valdman* 1988). Seven articles deal with current research and problems.

## Topics and Questions for Study and Discussion

1. Give examples of informal tests that you can perform every day in a classroom or conversation group (questions, giving directions, and so forth). Do they fit the definition of a test?

2. Examine a readily available standardized or classroom test of language. Analyze it to discover what the *method* of *measurement* is, for *whom* the test is intended, what *competence* it purports to measure, and exactly what it *actually* measures.

3. For the same test, assess its practicality, reliability, and various forms of validity. On the basis of your evaluation, is it a "good" test?

4. Distinguish between content and construct validity. If content validity is absent, why does construct validity assume greater importance? Explain the statement (p. 255): "There is no final, absolute, and objective measure of validity." Why does validity ultimately go back to the rather subjective opinion of testers and theorists?

5. What is face validity? Aside from its importance to the learner, how might face validity be a factor of interest to the teacher and to the administrator?

6. What is language aptitude? Can it be sufficiently measured? If possible, examine the Modern Language Aptitude Test. Does it really test language aptitude? On the basis of the multiplicity of variables at play in the process of second language acquisition, what other factors would *you* include in a test of aptitude?

7. Review the arguments advanced both to support and refute the unitary trait hypothesis. Was Oller's initial support in favor of the hypothesis just wishful thinking? If not, from where did such hopes spring?

8. If you were able, in Question 2, to look at an existing language test, assess it again from the point of view of the various criteria for a *communicative* test discussed in this chapter.

9. Is there any way to resolve the dilemma of giving large-scale communicative tests while still maintaining a sense of practicality (the feasibility of scoring thousands of tests relatively quickly and cheaply)?

10. Why is oral proficiency testing so fraught with controversy? What is inadequate about a five-point scale to indicate oral proficiency? What contextual factors does the interview format fail to provide?

11. Think of a recent language test that you either gave or took. Evaluate that test on the basis of the principles of intrinsically motivating tests outlined in the vignette. How might that test have become more intrinsically motivating?

# Chapter 11

# THEORIES OF SECOND LANGUAGE ACQUISITION

The principal purpose of this book is to encourage teachers and future teachers to develop an integrated understanding of the principles underlying the learning and teaching of foreign languages. That purpose has necessarily involved *theoretical* considerations. A theory, as I noted in the first chapter, is an extended definition. We have examined essential components of an extended definition of second language acquisition. That is, we have attempted to answer the perplexing question "What is second language acquisition?" And we have seen that second language acquisition is, among other things, not totally unlike first language acquisition, is a subset of general human learning, involves cognitive variations, is closely related to one's personhood, is interwoven with second culture learning, involves interference, the creation of new linguistic systems, and the learning of discourse and communicative functions of language. All of these categories and the nearly infinite number of subcategories subsumed under them form the basis for structuring an integrated theory of second language acquisition.

Is there such a unified theory? Can we identify an "orthodoxy" in the field of second language acquisition—a standard model or theory to which large numbers of researchers and teachers predominantly subscribe? The answer, of course, is no. And as surely as competing theories are typical of all disciplines that attempt to give explanatory power to complex phenomena, so does this field have its fair share of models and hypotheses, each vying for credibility and validity. We can be quite content with this state of the art, for it is reflective of the intricacy of the acquisition process itself and the variability of individuals and contexts.

In this chapter we will critically examine a number of current models and theories of second language acquisition. It will no doubt be useful for you to consider each of these "opinions" and to glean from them some insights about how an overwhelming number of variables (which have been defined and discussed in this book) actually do mesh in a consistently patterned tapestry of factors. First, we will briefly look at what some of these factors are.

# Taxonomies, Hypotheses, and Models

To say that second language learning is a complex process is obviously trite. The pages of this book alone bear testimony to that complexity. But complexity means that there are so many separate but interrelated factors within one intricate entity that it is exceedingly difficult to bring order and simplicity into that entity. We can become easily discouraged at the enormity of the task before us. We must nevertheless pursue the task of theory building. (For an overview of second language acquisition theory-building, see Spolsky 1988 and Long 1990a.) Consider, for a few moments, some of the taxonomies, hypotheses, and models that begin to form grist for the theory builder's mill.

First, take a look at a taxonomy that was proposed some 20 years ago (Yorio 1976), represented in Figure 11–1. Many of the complexities of second language acquisition described then still apply.

In this book certain factors subsumed in the chapter topics are themselves a verbal outline of a theory of second language acquisition:

1.  A theory of second language acquisition includes an understanding, in general, of what language is, what learning is, and for classroom contexts, what teaching is.

2.  Knowledge of children's learning of their first language provides essential insights to an understanding of second language acquisition.

3.  However, a number of important differences between adult and child learning and between first and second language acquisition must be carefully accounted for.

4.  Second language learning is a part of and adheres to general principles of human learning and intelligence.

5.  There is tremendous variation across learners in cognitive style and within a learner in strategy choice.

6.  Personality, the way persons view themselves and reveal themselves in communication, will affect both the quantity and quality of second language learning.

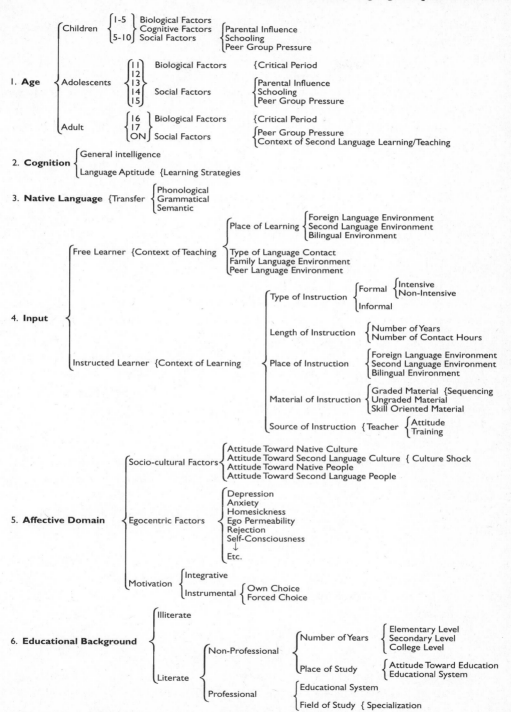

FIGURE 11–1.   Classification of learner variables (Yorio 1976:61)

7.  Learning a second culture in all its ramifications is often very much a part of learning a second language.

8.  The linguistic contrasts between the native and target language form one source of difficulty in learning a second language. But the creative process of forming an interlanguage system involves the learner in utilizing many facilitative sources and resources. Inevitable aspects of this process are errors, from which learners and teachers can gain further insight.

9.  Communicative competence, with all of its subcategories, is the ultimate goal of learners as they struggle with function, discourse, register, and nonverbal aspects of human interaction and linguistic negotiation.

10. Ultimately we cannot know whether our teaching or our research hypotheses are valid unless we can devise tests of language that tap into the learner's competence and provide us with meaningful, interpretable information.

11. Finally, a theory of second language acquisition must be comprehensive in including as many relevant factors as possible while at the same time it must have practical application in the real world.

However vague and general those 11 statements are, they constitute a framework for a theory of second language acquisition. That framework has had substance built into it in the course of each chapter of the book. The interrelationships within that framework have been dealt with. One cannot, for example, engage in contrastive analysis and draw implications from it without knowledge of the place of interference in human learning in general. In comparing and contrasting first and second language acquisition it is impossible to ignore affective and cultural variables and differences between adult and child cognition. Determining the source of a second language learner's error inevitably involves consideration of cognitive strategies and styles, group dynamics, and even the validity of data-gathering procedures. No single component of this "theory" is sufficient alone: the interaction and interdependence of the other components is necessary.

Another set of factors was provided by Lightbown (1985:176–180) in a summary of research findings of the previous decade in second language acquisition. In abbreviated form, her generalizations for adult second language acquisition were as follows:

1.  Adults and adolescents can "acquire" a second language.

2.  The learner creates a systematic interlanguage that is often characterized by the same systematic errors as [those of] the child learning the same language as the first language, as well as others that appear to be based on the learner's own native language.

3.  There are predictable sequences in acquisition so that certain struc-

tures have to be acquired before others can be integrated.

4.  Practice does not make perfect.

5.  Knowing a language rule does not mean one will be able to use it in communicative interaction.

6.  Isolated explicit error correction is usually ineffective in changing language behavior.

7.  For most adult learners, acquisition stops—"fossilizes"—before the learner has achieved nativelike mastery of the target language.

8.  One cannot achieve nativelike (or near nativelike) command of a second language in one hour a day.

9.  The learner's task is enormous because language is enormously complex.

10. A learner's ability to understand language in a meaningful context exceeds his or her ability to comprehend decontextualized language and to produce language of comparable complexity and accuracy.

Lightbown's list of generalizations is interesting and has some applications to classroom practices. The conclusions are carefully drawn out of research findings of the last decade. But, like the 11 previous items, the list is obviously "incomplete," and clearly some of the points need to be considerably refined and subdefined before we can start constructing a viable theory.

Perhaps a good look at some current theories and models will help you to engage in a process of integration and unification.

# Krashen's Input Hypothesis

One of the most controversial theoretical perspectives is found in a set of hypotheses about second language learning that were made by Stephen Krashen (1977, 1981, 1982, 1985) in a host of articles and books. Krashen's hypotheses have had a number of different names. In the earlier years the "Monitor Model" and the "Acquisition-Learning Hypothesis" were more popular terms; in recent years the *Input Hypothesis* has been a common term to refer to what are really a set of interrelated hypotheses.

In describing the Monitor Model, Krashen claimed that adult second language learners have two means for internalizing the target language. The first is "acquisition," a subconscious and intuitive process of constructing the system of a language, not unlike the process used by a child to "pick up" a language. The second means is a conscious "learning" process in which learners attend to form, figure out rules, and are generally aware of their own process. The "Monitor" is an aspect of this second process; it is a "device" for "watchdogging" one's output, for editing and making alterations or corrections as they are consciously perceived. Krashen claimed that "fluency in second language performance is due to what we have acquired, not what we have learned" (1981a:99). Adults should, therefore, do as much acquiring as possible in order to achieve communicative fluency; otherwise, they will get bogged down in rule learning and too much conscious attention to the forms of language and to watching their own progress. According to Krashen (1982), our conscious learning processes and our subconscious acquisition processes are mutually exclusive: learning cannot "become" acquisition. This claim of "no interface" between acquisition and learning is used to strengthen the argument for recommending large doses of acquisition activity in the classroom, with only a very minor role assigned to the Monitor. Once fluency is established, only then should an optimal amount of Monitoring, or editing, be employed by the learner (Krashen 1981a).

The Input Hypothesis, a major offshoot of the Monitor Model, claims that an important "condition for language acquisition to occur is that the acquirer *understand* (via hearing or reading) input language that contains structure 'a bit beyond' his or her current level of competence. . . . If an acquirer is at stage or level *i,* the input he or she understands should contain *i + 1*" (1981a:100). In other words, the language which learners are exposed to should be just far enough beyond their current competence that they can understand most of it but still be challenged to make progress. The corollary to this is that input should neither be so far beyond their reach that they are overwhelmed (this might be, say, *i + 2*), nor so close to their current stage that they are not challenged at all (*i + 0*). An important part of the Input Hypothesis is Krashen's recommendation that speaking not be taught directly or very soon in the language classroom. Speech will "emerge" once the acquirer has built up enough comprehensible input (*i + 1*), as we saw in Chapter Eight in a discussion of the Natural Approach. Krashen further claims that the best acquisition will occur in environments where anxiety is low and defensiveness absent, or, in Krashen's terms, in contexts where the "affective filter" is low.

Both the Monitor Model, with its distinction between acquisition and learning, and the Input Hypothesis have intuitive appeal to researchers and teachers in the field. Who can deny that we should have less "learning" in our classrooms than we have traditionally become accustomed to? Who in their right mind would refute the importance, in second language learning, of whatever it is that a child does ("acquisition") to be so successful in first language learning?

Unfortunately, second language acquisition is not as simply defined as Krashen would claim, and therefore, his assumptions have been hotly disputed (e.g., McLaughlin 1978, Gregg 1984, White 1987, Brumfit 1992, to name but a few) Psychologists like Barry McLaughlin (1978, 1990a) sharply criticized Krashen's rather fuzzy distinction between subconscious (acquisition) and conscious (learning) processes. Psychologists are still in wide disagreement in their definitions of "the notoriously slippery notion" (Odlin 1986:138) of consciousness. Recently, McLaughlin (1990a:627) commented:

> My own bias . . . is to avoid use of the terms conscious and unconscious in second language theory. I believe that these terms are too laden with surplus meaning and too difficult to define empirically to be useful theoretically. Hence, my critique of Krashen's distinction between learning and acquisition—a distinction that assumes that it is possible to differentiate what is conscious from what is unconscious.

He continues by noting that the literature in experimental psychology indicates that there is no long term learning (of new material) without *awareness,* an observation well documented by Richard Schmidt (1990) for second language learning in particular. We do well, therefore, to operate on the assumption that (a) no input becomes *intake* (see below) without what we loosely understand as conscious awareness, and that (b) language acquisition theories that appeal to conscious/subconscious distinctions are highly suspect.

A second criticism of Krashen's views arose out of the claim that there is no interface—no overlap—between acquisition and learning. We have already seen over and over again in this book that so-called dichotomies in human behavior always simply define the end-points of a continuum, and not mutually exclusive categories. As Gregg (1984:82) pointed out, "Krashen plays fast and loose with his definitions. . . . If unconscious knowledge is capable of being brought to consciousness, and if conscious knowledge is capable of becoming unconscious—and this seems to be a reasonable assumption—then there is no reason whatever to accept Krashen's claim, in the absence of evidence. And there is an absence of evidence." Second language learning clearly is a process in which varying degrees of learning and of acquisition can be beneficial depending upon the learner's own styles and strategies. Long (1983, 1988), Ellis (1990b), Doughty (1991), and Buczowska and Weist (1991) have all shown, in a number of empirical research studies, that instruction in conscious rule learning can indeed aid in the attainment of successful communicative competence in a second language.

A third difficulty in Krashen's Input Hypothesis is found in his explicit claim (1986:62) that "comprehensible input is the only causative variable in second language acquisition." In other words, success in a foreign language can be attributed to *input* alone. Such a theory ascribes little credit to learners and their own active engagement in the pursuit of language competence. First of all, it is important to distinguish between input and *intake.* The latter is the subset of all input that actually gets assigned to our long-term memory store. Just imagine, for example, reading a book, listening to a conversation, or watching a movie—in any language. This is your input. But your intake is what you take with you over a period of time and can later "remember." Second language learners are exposed to potentially large quantities of input, only a fraction of which becomes intake.

How does input convert to intake? Seliger (1983) offered a conceptualization of the process that has become widely accepted. Certain learners are what he called *High Input Generators* (HIG), people who are good at initiating and sustaining interaction, or, "generating" input from teachers, fellow learners, and others. *Low Input Generators* (LIG) are more passive learners who do little to stick their necks out to get input directed toward them. In two studies of second language learners, Seliger found that "learners who maintained high levels of interaction [HIGs] in the second language, both in the classroom and outside, progressed at a faster rate than learners who interacted little [LIGs] in the classroom." (p. 262) Such studies, coupled with a great deal of intuitive observation of successful learners, suggests that Krashen's comprehensible input must at the very least be complemented by an "output hypothesis" that gives extensive credit to the role of the learner's production.

Finally, it is important to note that the notion of *i* + 1 is nothing new. It is a reiteration of a general principle of learning that we have already discussed here (Chapter Four). Meaningfulness, or "subsumability" in Ausubel's terms, is that which is relatable to existing cognitive structures, neither too far beyond the structures (*i* + *2*), nor the existing structures themselves (*i* + *0*). But Krashen presents the *i* + *1* formula as if we are actually able to define *i* and *1*, and we are not, as Gregg (1984), White (1987), and others have so ably pointed out. Furthermore, the notion that speech will "emerge" in a context of comprehensible input sounds promising, and for some learners (bright, highly motivated, outgoing learners!), speech will emerge. But we are left with no significant  information from Krashen's theories on what to do about the other half of our language students for whom speech does not "emerge" and for whom the "silent period" might last forever.

Krashen's theories have had wide appeal to teachers who cry for something simple and concrete on which to base their methodology. It is easy to see how there is such appeal since the claims that are made do indeed reflect some important principles of second language acquisition. But in their oversimplicity, the claims have been exaggerated. Nevertheless, in the final analysis, oddly enough, I feel we owe a debt of gratitude to Krashen for his bold, if brash, insights. They have spurred many a researcher to look very carefully at what we do know, what the research evidence is, and then in the process of refutation to propose plausible alternatives. We continue now with several of these alternative theoretical perspectives.

# McLaughlin's Attention-Processing Model

It is quite tempting, with Krashen, to conceptualize second language acquisition in terms of conscious and subconscious processes. In explaining the difference between a child's and an adult's second language acquisition,

**TABLE 11–1.   Possible Second Language Performance as a Function of Information-Processing Procedures and Attention to Formal Properties of Language (McLaughlin et al. 1983)**

| ATTENTION TO FORMAL PROPERTIES OF LANGUAGE | INFORMATION PROCESSING | |
|---|---|---|
| | CONTROLLED | AUTOMATIC |
| Focal | (Cell A) Performance based on formal rule learning | (Cell B) Performance in a test situation |
| Peripheral | (Cell C) Performance based on implicit learning or analogic learning | (Cell D) Performance in communication situations |

our first appeal is to children's "knack" for "picking up" a language, which, in everyday terms, refers to what we think of as subconscious. We like to think that children are not "aware" of their language acquisition. But as both McLaughlin (1990a) and Schmidt (1990) agreed, "awareness" and "consciousness" are tricky terms; therefore, in order to form a sound theory of second language acquisition, we are better off not appealing to the conscious/ unconscious continuum.

A more sound heuristic for conceptualizing the language acquisition process, one that did indeed avoid any direct appeal to a consciousness continuum, was proposed by McLaughlin and his colleagues (McLaughlin, Rossman, and McLeod 1983; McLeod and McLaughlin 1986; McLaughlin 1987, 1990b). Their model juxtaposes processing mechanisms (*controlled* and *automatic*) and categories of *attention* to form four cells (see Table 11–1).

Controlled processes are "capacity limited and temporary" and automatic processes are "relatively permanent" (McLaughlin et al. 1983:142) We can think of controlled processing as typical of anyone learning a brand new skill in which only a very few elements of the skill can be retained. When you first learn to play tennis, for example, you can only "manage" the elements of, say, making contact between ball and racquet, getting the ball over the net, and hitting the ball into the green space on the other side of the net. Everything else about the game is far too complex for your capacity-limited ability.

Automatic processes, on the other hand, refer to processing in a more "accomplished" skill, where the "hard drive" (to borrow a computer analogy) of your brain can manage hundreds and thousands of bits of information simultaneously. The automatizing of this multiplicity of data is accomplished by a process of *restructuring* (McLeod and McLaughlin 1986; McLaughlin 1987, 1990b), in which "the components of a task are coordinated, integrated, or reorganized into new units, thereby allowing the . . . old components to be replaced by a more efficient procedure." (McLaughlin 1990b:118) Restructuring is conceptually synonymous with Ausubel's construct of subsumption discussed in Chapter Four.

Both ends of this continuum of processing can occur with either *focal* or *peripheral* attention to the task at hand; that is, focusing attention either centrally or simply on the periphery. It is easy to fall into the temptation of thinking of focal attention as "conscious" attention, but such a pitfall must be avoided. Both focal and peripheral attention to some task may be quite conscious (Hulstijn 1990). When you are driving a car, for example, your focal attention may center on cars directly in front of you as you move forward; but your peripheral attention to cars beside you and behind you, to potential hazards, and of course to the other thoughts "running through your mind," is all very much within your conscious awareness.

While most controlled processes are focal, some, like child first language learning or the learning of skills without any instruction, can be peripheral. Similarly, most automatic processes are peripheral, but some can be focal, as in the case of a pianist performing in a concert or a learner taking a test.

How does McLaughlin's model apply to practical aspects of learning a second language? I have attempted to "demystify" some of the rather complex constructs of the attention-processing model in Table 11–2. It is important to note that these cells are described in terms of one's processing of and attention to *language forms* (grammatical, phonological, discourse rules and categories, lexical choices, etc.). If, for example, peripheral attention is given to language forms in a more advanced language classroom, focal attention is no doubt being given to meaning, function, purpose, or person. Child second language learning may consist almost exclusively of peripheral (cells C and D) attention to language forms. Most adult second language learning of language forms in the classroom involves a movement from cell A through a combination of C and B, to D. Peripheral, automatic attention-processing of the "bits and pieces" of language is thus an ultimate communicative goal for language learners.

# Bialystok's Analysis/Automaticity Model

In 1978, Ellen Bialystok offered yet another means of conceptualizing the varied processes of second language learning. At the heart of her model (see Figure 11–2) of second language learning is a distinction between explicit and implicit linguistic knowledge. In the *explicit* category are the facts that a person knows about language and the ability to articulate those facts in some way. *Implicit* knowledge is information that is automatically and spontaneously

## TABLE 11-2.  Practical Applications of McLaughlin's Attention-Processing Model

|  | CONTROLLED: new skill, capacity limited | AUTOMATIC: well-trained, practiced skill capacity is relatively <u>un</u>limited |
|---|---|---|
| FOCAL intentional attention | A • grammatical explanation of a specific point<br>• word definition<br>• copy a written model<br>• the <u>first</u> stages of "memorizing" a dialog<br>• prefabricated patterns<br>• various discrete-point exercises | B • "keeping an eye out" for something<br>• advanced L2 learner focuses on modals, clause formation, etc.<br>• monitoring oneself while talking or writing<br>• scanning<br>• editing, peer-editing |
| PERIPHERAL incidental attention | C • simple greetings<br>• the <u>later</u> stages of "memorizing" a dialog<br>• TPR / Natural Approach<br>• new L2 learner successfully completes a <u>brief</u> conversation | D • open-ended group work<br>• rapid reading, skimming<br>• free writes<br>• normal conversational exchanges of some length |

used in language tasks. Processes (solid lines in the figure) are universal while strategies are optional and vary across individuals, as we have already defined earlier. The "R" is the response that a person makes to another person upon receiving some sort of linguistic message. Type I responses are spontaneous and Type II responses are time-delayed.

Several years after her 1978 publication, Bialystok began to modify her framework for conceptualizing second language acquisition (Bialystok 1982, 1985, 1990b; Bialystok and Bouchard-Ryan 1985). The modification consisted of hypothesizing a two-dimensional framework in which *analysis* and *automaticity* can interact, but her use of the latter term differs from McLaughlin's.

In her first factor—analysis—mental representations can be either unanalyzed or analyzed. "Unanalyzed knowledge is the general form in which we

**Input**

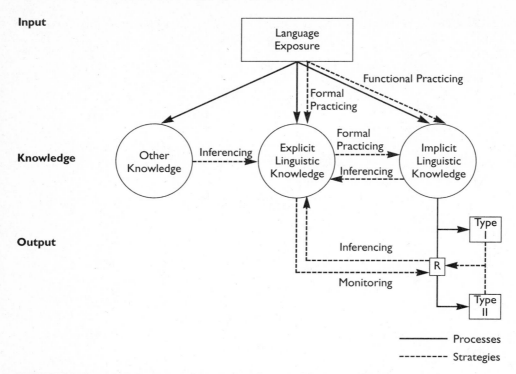

FIGURE 11–2.   Model of second language learning. (Bialystok 1978:71)

know most things without being aware of the structure of that knowledge"
(Bialystok 1982:183); on the other hand, learners are overtly aware of the structure of analyzed knowledge. For example, at the unanalyzed extreme of this
knowledge dimension, learners have little awareness of language rules, but at
the analyzed end, learners can verbalize complex rules governing language.

The distinction between automatic and non-automatic processing refers
to the relative access the learner has to the knowledge irrespective of its degree
of analysis. Knowledge that can be retrieved easily and quickly is automatic.
Knowledge that takes time and effort to retrieve is non-automatic. This continuum is akin to what were called Type I and Type II responses in her 1978
model. Bialystok later modified this continuum by referring to it as a factor of
*control*—our "ability to intentionally focus attention on relevant parts of a
problem to arrive at a solution." (Bialystok and Mitterer 1987:148) As was true
for the McLaughlin model, both forms of attention can be either analyzed or
unanalyzed.

Bialystok's model was recently criticized for stretching information-processing models beyond their limits, "thus giving the explanations a forced air."
(Hulstijn 1990:42) Bialystok countered with a response that, among other
things, reminded us that dichotomies are "seductive" (Bialystok 1990b:46) and

that her model does not present a dichotomy as much as a continuum of information-processing possibilities. As the critiques and interpretations continue, we can nevertheless garner some insights here about second language acquisition: learners are not only affected by their relative degree of being able to analyze language but also by the *time* it takes to process linguistic data.

# Variability Models

One of the most interesting, if not heated, current debates in second language acquisition theory centers on the extent to which the *variability* manifested in the interlanguage competence of learners can be systematically explained. The essence of the problem is that learners can and do exhibit a tremendous degree of variation in the way they speak (and write) second languages. Now, native speakers, of course, also exhibit variation. I might pronounce the word "garage" as /gərádj/ sometimes, and at other times /gəráž/. I might choose to say "bicycle" at times, and at others, "bike." Phrases and other discourse elements vary as well. Second language learners vary even more in their choice of output. Is that variation predictable? Can we explain it? Or do we dismiss it all as "free variation?"

A growing number of researchers are addressing the issue of interlanguage variation. Notable among these contributions are Elaine Tarone's (1988) "capability continuum paradigm" and Rod Ellis's (1986) "variable competence model," both of which have inspired a good deal of research on the issue (see Adamson 1988, Young 1988, Crookes 1989, for example).

Tarone (1988) granted that non-systematic free variation and individual variation do indeed exist but chose to focus her research on *contextual* variability, that is, the extent to which both linguistic and situational contexts may help to systematically describe what might otherwise appear simply as unexplained variation. The emphasis on context thus leads us to look carefully at the conditions under which certain linguistic forms vary. For example, if a learner at one point in time says

1. "He must paid for the insurance."

and at another time says

2. "He must pay the parking fee."

an examination of the linguistic (and conceptual) context might explain the variation. In this case, sentence (1) was uttered in the context of describing an event in the past and sentence (2) referred to the present moment.

One of the most fruitful areas of interlanguage research in recent years has focused on the variation that arises from the disparity between *classroom* contexts and *natural* situations outside language classes. As researchers have examined instructed second language acquisition (Ellis 1990b, Doughty 1991,

Buczowska and Weist 1991), not only has it become apparent that instruction makes a difference in learners' success rates but also that the classroom context itself explains a great deal of variability in learners' output.

Ellis (1986) drew a more "internal" picture of the learner in his variable competence model. Drawing on Bialystok's categories, Ellis hypothesized a storehouse of "variable interlanguage rules" (p. 269) depending on how automatic and how analyzed the rules are. He drew a sharp distinction between planned and unplanned discourse in order to examine variation. The former implies less automaticity, and therefore requires the learner to call upon a certain category of interlanguage rules, while the latter, more automatic production, predisposes the learner to dip into another set of interlanguage rules.

Both models have come under recent attack. Kevin Gregg (1990) quarreled with both Tarone's and Ellis's rejection of Chomsky's "homogeneous competence paradigm" (see the discussion in Chapter Two of this book about competence and performance). "Why should the fact that a learner's competence changes over time lead us to reject the standard concept of competence?" argued Gregg (1990:367). It would appear from Ellis's arguments that Chomsky's "performance variables" may be better thought of as part of one's "variable competence" and therefore not attributable to mere "slips" in performance. Such arguments and counter-arguments (see responses to Gregg by Ellis 1990a and Tarone 1990) will continue, but one lesson we are learning in all this is apparent: even the tiniest of the bits and pieces of learner language, however random or "variable" they may appear to be at first blush, may be quite "systematic" if we will only keep on looking. It is often tempting as a teacher or as a researcher to dismiss a good deal of learners' production as a mystery beyond our capacity to explain. Short of engaging in an absurd game of straining at gnats, we must guard against yielding to that temptation.

# The Believing and Doubting Games

Throughout this book, and especially in the theories just discussed, the concept of a *continuum* has been utilized to describe the variable nature of truth as it often hangs precariously between two polar opposites. We have seen from the beginning that truth is neither unitary nor unidimensional. We have seen that definitions and extended definitions are never simple. Just as a photographer captures many facets of the same mountain by circling around it, truth presents itself to us in many forms, and sometimes those forms seem to conflict.

This elusive nature of truth was addressed by Peter Elbow (1973) a number of years ago in an essay about the intellectual enterprise. Describing yet another continuum, Elbow noted that most scholarly traditions are too myopically involved in what he called the "doubting game" of truth seeking. "The doubting game seeks truth . . . by seeking error. . . . You must assume [an asser-tion] is untrue. . . . You make a special effort to extricate yourself from the assertions in question. . . . You must hold off to one side the self, its wishes, preconceptions, experiences, and commitments" (1973:148). Elbow felt that the doubting game has gained a monopoly on legitimacy in Western culture: ". . . To almost anyone in the academic or intellectual world, it seems as though when he plays the doubting game he is being rigorous, disciplined, rational, and tough-minded. And if for any reason he *refrains* from playing the doubting game, he feels he is being unintellectual, irrational, and sloppy" (p. 151).

Elbow contended that we need to turn such conceptions upside-down, to look at the other end of the continuum and recognize the importance of what he called the "believing game." In the believing game you refrain from doubt-ing the assertions: "you don't want them to fight each other" (p. 149). You try to find truths, not errors; you make acts of self-insertion and self-involvement, not self-extrication. "It helps to think of it as trying to get inside the head of someone who saw things this way. Perhaps even constructing such a person for yourself. Try to have the experience of someone who made this assertion" (p. 149).

Elbow eloquently demonstrated how language itself is a good case in point for the importance of the believing game. Meaning is not absolute and fixed. We use language to negotiate meaning. Remember the exchange between Alice and Humpty Dumpty in *Through the Looking Glass,* quoted in Chapter Two? Humpty concludes that he can *make* a word mean something if he chooses to. Meaning is fluid, dynamic, and subjective. In a behavior as com-plex as second language learning, we cannot doggedly play only the doubting game; we must temper our cautious doubts with a willingness to accept certain assertions until we can categorically rule them out. But Elbow is careful to conclude his essay with a note on the interdependence of the believing game and the doubting game. "The doubting game," he says, "is not in itself the vil-lain. . . . The two games  re interdependent. . . . The two games are only halves of a full cycle of thinking. Because human functioning is organic and develop-mental, because for example you cannot learn to be a cut-throat editor till you learn to be a prolific producer, so too people cannot learn to play well either the doubting game or the believing game till they also learn to play the other one well" (pp. 190–191).

If you were to try to unify or to integrate everything that every second lan-guage researcher concluded, or even everything listed in the previous section, you could not do so through the doubting game. But by balancing your per-spective with a believing attitude toward those elements that are not categori-cally ruled out, you can maintain a sense of perspective. Both Ochsner (1979) and Schumann (1982a) referred to this same apparent dilemma in second lan-guage acquisition research. Ochsner (1979) made a plea for a "poetics" of second language acquisition research in which we use two research traditions to draw conclusions. One tradition is a *nomothetic* tradition of empiricism, scientific methodology, and prediction; this is the behavioristic tradition referred to in Chapter One. On the other hand, a *hermeneutic* (or, in Chapter One, the cognitive/rationalistic) tradition provides us with a means for interpretation and understanding in which we do not look for absolute laws. "A poetics of second language acquisition lets us shift our perspectives," according to Ochsner (1979:71), who sounded very much like he had been reading Peter Elbow!

Schumann (1982a) adopted a similar point of view in recommending that we see both the "art" and the "science" of second language acquisition research. Nothing that Krashen and McLaughlin (see Chapter Nine) have had two different experiences themselves in learning a second language, Schumann suggests that "Krashen's and McLaughlin's views can co-exist as two different paintings of the language learning experience—as reality symbolized in two different ways" (p. 113). His concluding remarks, however, lean toward viewing our research as art, advantageous because such a view reduces the need of closure and allows us to see our work in a larger perspective with less dogmatism and ego involvement. In short, it frees us to play the believing game more ardently and more fruitfully.

# From Theory to Practice

The believing game and doubting game are poignantly illustrated in even a quick glance at the various approaches, syllabus designs, and procedures (in short, at various *methods*) that people have used in the last century or so of foreign language teaching. The cycles that are represented in the "in-the-classroom" vignettes throughout this book are the result of believing games and doubting games in continued interplay. We have moved in and out of paradigms (Kuhn 1970, Spolsky 1990) as inadequacies of the old ways of doing things are replaced by better ways. These trends in language teaching are partly the result of theories in practice. As research points the way toward more effective ways of teaching and learning, approaches and techniques are conceived and developed. The use of those approaches and techniques, in turn, continually provides essential data for the enlightening of further research, and the interdependent cycle goes on.

As we look back over the last 100 years of language teaching there are some revolutions apparent in that history. Gouin's Series Method, Berlitz's Direct Method, and the Oral-Aural or Audiolingual Method were revolutionary in their overthrow of previous ways of doing things. Since the 1960s we have made quantum leaps in our knowledge about the process of learning and teaching a second language. Our methodology has developed and grown with this increasing research. Some language specialists (Raimes 1983, for example) would dispute the claim that we have seen an actual revolution, but we have indeed experienced radical changes in our approaches to language teaching over the past three decades.

How might those approaches be described? First, they are cautiously eclectic. Tremendous variation among learners is recognized; human beings do not behave, each one, like the other, consistently and uniformly. Therefore, no single method suffices to answer all needs of all learners at all times. We are wary of jumping onto bandwagons. But there is no magic about eclecticism. It is easy to be an eclectic and dip haphazardly into every attractive aspect of every conceivable method or approach, and then jumble everything together. It is quite another task to practice "enlightened" eclecticism—that is, to engage in an intelligent use of selected approaches built upon and guided by an integrated and broadly based theory of second language acquisition.

Second, our current approaches do not look to the traditional disciplines—linguistics, psychology, education—for direct *applications,* but rather for *insights* into language, human behavior, and pedagogy that undergird language teaching practices. We have come to a point in our young history where we understand that those traditional disciplines are an important part of our research tradition but that our research must be directly focused on second language learning and teaching itself.

Third, current theories-in-practice are characterized by a substantial body of research on second language acquisition from which we can derive enlightened approaches to teaching (see Spolsky 1990, Schultz 1991). We must be firmly grounded in that important body of research and be able to understand the implications of research findings. At the same time, as we have already seen, we need to be able to fill in the empirical gaps with generous doses of artistic elements of the believing game.

Fourth, language learning and teaching are recognized as personal encounters. The affective domain has taken on primary importance as we recognize in human communication the building of interpersonal relationships through social interchange. We understand more convincingly than ever before that learners will achieve their fullest potential in language classes when they are intrinsically driven by their own personal need for gaining competence in a language. Part of that intrinsic set of motives involves learners in taking charge of their own destiny by understanding their own strengths and weaknesses and developing the strategic competence to capitalize on the former and to compensate for the latter.

Finally, and perhaps most importantly, our stockpile of research and practice has clearly demonstrated how crucial it is to focus on *communication* in the classroom. Natural, authentic, functional language is being taught and used in the classroom. By means of the development of content-centered, experiential learning in well-planned and efficiently managed communicative *tasks* (Nunan 1991a), language classrooms have done an aboutface from their counterparts of three decades ago.

Have we "arrived"? Surely not. But we may have moved from the stage of professional childhood—of looking for final, clear-cut answers, and of grasping at a method here and a technique there—to adolescence, if not adulthood. We are secure in our general understanding of the language acquisition process and of the importance of communication in language learning. But we are also prepared to face the complexity and unpredictability of human behavior and ready to convert momentary failures into new ventures in the search for better and better ways to enable second language learners to communicate effectively.

As you develop an enlightened approach to the language classroom, there are some important warning signals to attend to. Mark Clarke (1982) cautioned teachers to be aware of the various "bandwagons" that travel through our language teaching profession: the "latest word," the trendy, the fashionable methods, materials, and techniques with their carnival appeal. Bandwagons are usually extremist and authoritarian in nature, insisting that there is only one possible way of teaching a foreign language. They tend to claim an all encompassing theory that leaves nothing unexplained. They are dramatic and appealing with a flashy "bag of tricks" that is hard to resist. While bandwagons can sometimes stimulate you to rethink your current stance, there is a great temptation to jump onto a bandwagon and consider that your days of searching for classroom techniques are over. Clearly this is the last thing that should happen to a cautious, enlightened eclectic who understands the inherent ambiguity in second language theory and practice.

## Intuition: The Search for Relevance

Once you have found a way to form a healthy theoretical perspective within a wide variety of viewpoints, you may still be left with a feeling of "how does all this relate to the 'real world' of the classroom?" The search for the relevance of theory has taken teachers on many varied and circuitous paths. But there is, I believe, one principle that can help you to make intelligent choices in the use of methods and classroom techniques. That principle has to be seen through, yes, yet another continuum of possibilities—one not unlike the believing and doubting continuum: the principle of intuition.

Teachers generally want to "know" that a method is "right," that it will work successfully. We want finely tuned programs that map the pathways to successful teaching. In other words, we tend to be born doubters. But the believing game provides us with a contrasting principle, intuition. Psychological research on cognitive styles has shown us that people tend to favor either an *intuitive* approach or an *analytical* approach to a problem. Ewing (1977:69) noted that analytical or "systematic" thinkers "generally excel in problems that call for planning and organization, as when one set of numbers must be worked out before another can be analyzed." On the other hand, he goes on to say, ". . . intuitive thinkers are likely to excel if the problem is elusive and difficult to define. They keep coming up with different possibilities, follow their hunches, and don't commit themselves too soon." It is clear, however, that both styles are essential for efficient cognitive functioning. While people tend to favor one style or the other, it is the complementation of intuition and analysis that enables us to make good decisions, to solve problems, and to categorize the world around us. Sternberg and Davidson (1982) found that "insight"—making inductive leaps beyond the given data—is an indispensable factor of what we call "intelligence," much of which is traditionally defined in terms of analysis.

All this suggests that intuition forms an essential component of our total intellectual endeavor. Three decades ago, Bruner and Clinchy (1966:71) discussed the contrasting role of intuition and analysis in educational systems in general, "Intuition is less rigorous with respect to proof, more visual or 'ikonic,' more oriented to the whole problem than to particular parts, less verbalized with respect to justification, and based on a confidence in one's ability to operate with insufficient data." One of the important characteristics of intuition is its nonverbalizability; often, persons are not able to give much verbal explanation of why they have made a particular decision or solution. Baldwin (1966:87), in a companion article, cautioned against leading people to believe that all worthy solutions are verbalizable. "The person who refuses to use his intuition unless he can verbalize it is cutting himself off from one of his own abilities. It is this danger that perhaps underlies the demand for training intuition." The implications for teaching are clear. We daily face problems in language teaching that have no ready analysis, no available language or metalanguage to capture the essence of why a particular decision was made. Bruner and Baldwin are saying that we can and should be at ease in such situations.

Intuition involves a certain kind of risk-taking. As we saw in Chapter Six, language learners need to take risks willingly. Language teachers, too, must be willing to risk techniques or assessments that have their roots in a "gut feeling," a hunch, that they are right. Bruner and Clinchy (1966:74) noted that such intuitive risks can often lead to subsequent analysis: "Analysis in a well-trained problem-solver can be just as activating as intuition, but in many cases it takes a hunch to figure out first where the analytic tools should be applied. . . . It is often a first order approximation, a nonrigorous proof showing that one is in the right domain, that gives one the confidence to go on with exacting and sometimes tedious analytic procedures of proof. . . ." In a field such as second language teaching, we are daily faced with situations for which there is insufficient data for a full analysis. In our universe of complex theory, we still perceive vast black holes of unanswerable questions about how people best learn second languages. Intuition, "the making of good guesses in situations where one has neither an answer nor an algorithm for obtaining it" (Baldwin 1966:84), fills the void.

There is ample evidence that good language teachers have developed good intuition. In an informal study of cognitive styles among ESL learners a few years ago, I asked the teachers of the ESL learners to predict the TOEFL score that each of their students would attain when they sat for the TOEFL the following week. The teachers had been with their students for only one semester, yet their predicted scores and the actual TOEFL results yielded the highest (+.90) correlations in the whole study. Many good teachers cannot verbalize why they do what they do, in a specific and analytical way, yet they remain good teachers.

How do you "learn" intuition? There is no simple answer to this question, yet some ingredients of a rationale are apparent. First, you need to internalize essential theoretical foundations like those we have been grappling with throughout this book. Intuition is not developed in a vacuum. It is the product, in part, of a firm grounding in what is known, in analytical terms, about how people learn languages and why some people do not learn languages.

Second, there is no substitute for the experience of standing on your own two feet (or sitting down!) in the presence of real learners in the real world. Intuitions are formed at the crossroads of knowledge and experience. As you face those day-by- day, or even minute-by-minute, struggles of finding out who your learners are, deciding what to teach them, and designing ways to teach, you learn by trial, by error, and by success. You cannot be a master teacher the first time you teach a class. Your failures, near failures, partial successes, and successes all teach you intuition. They teach you to sense what will work and what will not work.

A third principle of intuition learning follows from the second. You must be a willing risk-taker yourself. Let the creative juices within you flow freely. The wildest and craziest ideas should be entertained openly and valued positively. In so doing, intuition will be allowed to germinate and to grow to full fruition.

Our search for relevance can become thwarted by overzealous attempts to find analytical solutions. We may be looking too hard to find the ultimate system. As Schumann (1982a) said, at times we need to feel, ironically, that our own ideas are *un*important. That way we avoid that panicky feeling that what we do today in class is somehow going to be permanently etched in the annals of foreign language history. The relevance of theory can be perceived by adopting an essential attitude of self-confidence in our ability to form hunches that will probably be "right." We teachers are human. We are not fail-safe, preprogrammed robots. We therefore need to become willing risk-takers.

# Out On A Limb: The Ecology of Language Acquistion

This final end-of-chapter vignette is not directed, as all the previous ten counterparts are, toward classroom methodology. Rather, it is simply the product of some of my right-brain musings as I have struggled over the years with the complexities of the kinds of models of second language acquisition that have been described in this chapter. Such models, in their graphic or flowchart form, always appear to be so mechanical. Some of them more closely resemble the wiring diagrams pasted on the back of electric stoves than what I like to imagine the human brain must "look" like. Or certainly than the way our *organic* world operates!

So, heeding my sometimes rebellious spirit, I was moved one day in a second language acquisition class I was teaching to create a different "picture" of language acquisition: one that responded not so much to rules of logic, mathematics, and physics, as to botany and ecology. The germination (pun intended) of my picture was the metaphor once used by Derek Bickerton in a lecture at the University of Hawaii about his contention that human beings are "bioprogrammed" for language (see Bickerton's [1981] *The Roots of Language*), perhaps not unlike the bioprogram of a flower seed, whose genetic makeup predisposes it to deliver, in successive stages, roots, stem, branches, leaves, and flowers. In a burst of wild artistic energy, I went out on a limb to extend the flower-seed metaphor to language acquisition. My picture of the "ecology" of language acquisition is in Figure 11–3.

At the risk of overstating what may already be obvious to you, I will nevertheless indulge in a few comments. The rainclouds of input stimulate seeds of predisposition (innate, genetically transmitted processes). But the potency of that input is dependent on the appropriate styles and strategies that a person puts into action (here represented as soil). Upon the germination of language abilities (notice not all the seeds of predisposition are effectively activated), networks of competence (which, like underground roots, cannot be observed from above the ground) build and grow stronger as the organism actively engages in comprehension and production of language. The resulting root system (inferred competence) is what we commonly call intake. Notice that several factors distinguish input from intake. Through the use of further strategies and affective abilities, coupled with the feedback we receive from others (note the tree trunk), we ultimately develop full-flowering communicative abilities. The fruit of our performance (or output) is of course conditioned by the climate of inumerable contextual variables.

At any point the horticulturist (teacher) can irrigate to create better input, apply fertilizers for richer soil, encourage the use of effective strategies and affective enhancers and, in the greenhouses of our classrooms, control the contextual climate for optimal growth!

No, this is not the kind of extended metaphor that one can "prove" or verify through empirical research. But, lest you scoff at such outlandish depictions, think about how many factors in second language acquisition theory are

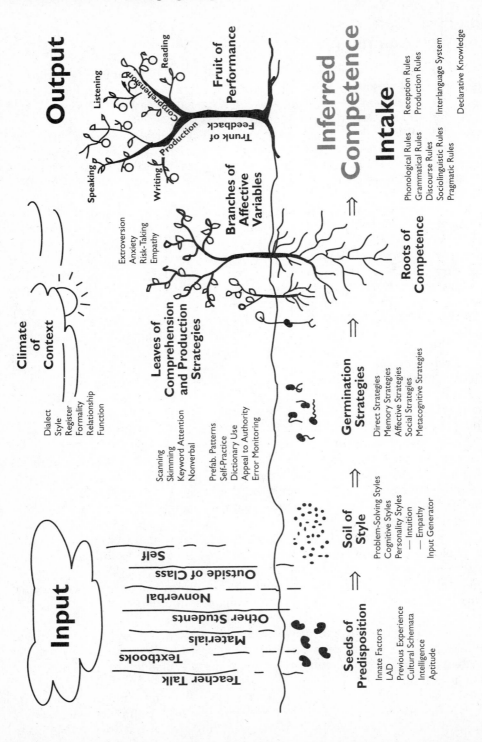

FIGURE 11–3.   The ecology of language acquisition (Brown 1991)

conceptualized and described metaphorically: language acquisition *device, pivot* and *open* words, Piaget's *equilibration, cognitive pruning,* Ausubel's *subsumption, transfer,* social *distance, global* and *local* errors, *monitoring,* affective *filter, automatic* and *controlled* processing. If a metaphor enables us to describe a phenomenon clearly and to apply it wisely, then we can surely entertain it—as long as we understand that these word-pictures are usually subject to certain breakdowns when logically entended too far.

So, while you might exercise a little caution in drawing a tight analogy between Earth's botanical cycles and language learning, you might just allow yourself to think of second language learners as budding flowers—as plants needing your nurture and care. When the scientific flowcharts and technical terminology of current second language research become excruciatingly painful to understand, try creating your own metaphors, perhaps! Play the believing game, and enjoy it.

## Suggested Readings

Many books and articles are available on second language acquisition theories and models. In order to probe more deeply into the work of people like Krashen, McLaughlin, Bialystok, Ellis, and Tarone, you should look at their original work, cited in the chapter. But for an overview of a number of theories, *McLaughlin*'s (1987) book is good source, along with Chapter 10 of *Ellis* (1986), and *Schultz* (1991).

Variability models are the subject of both *Tarone* (1988) and parts of *Ellis* (1986). An overview is provided by *Adamson* (1988). For a good sense of the controversy involved in variability models, see *Gregg*'s (1990) excellent critique, followed by *Tarone*'s and *Ellis*'s responses in the same issue.

The Winter, 1990 issue of *TESOL Quarterly* was entirely given over to the scope and form of theories of second language acquisition. Articles by leading theorists (McLaughlin, Bialystok, Long, Schumann, Spolsky, and others) provide a good sense of current issues in theory-making.

*Elbow*'s (1973) entertaining essay is stimulating reading, and gives you the point of view of a scholar who is not in the second language acquisition field. You might wish to follow that with a reading of *Ochsner* (1979) and *Schumann* (1982a), for a similar set of observations from two second language researchers.

## Topics and Questions for Study and Discussion

1. Go back to your definitions of language, learning, and teaching that you formulated at the beginning of this book. How might you revise those definitions now?

2. Can your own understanding of second language acquisition theory in general, or some particular subset of it, be represented in some

kind of diagram or flowchart? Share your thoughts with classmates or colleagues.

3. Review the tenets of Krashen's Input Hypothesis. Which ones are most plausible? Least plausible? How would you take the "best" of his theories and apply them in the classroom and yet still be mindful of the various problems inherent in his ideas about second language acquisition?

4. How does Seliger's concept of high and low input generators give more credit to the proactive role of language learners themselves than does Krashen's emphasis on comprehensible input? What is the role output in language learning? Why doesn't Krashen talk about output?

5. How does McLaughlin's "redefinition" avoid reference to consciousness? Does it succeed, in your mind? Give some further practical examples of language classroom activities that fall into each of the four cells.

6. Bialystok underscores, among other things, the importance of the amount of time that a learner takes to access stored information. Can learners be trained to be quicker in their retrieval of information? Speculate on some possibilities for such training.

7. It was noted that the classroom context itself can explain a good deal of learners' variability. Give some examples of classroom-induced variability in learner language.

8. Consider some of the controversies that have been discussed in this book: innateness, defining intelligence, the Whorfian hypothesis, the strong version of the Contrastive Analysis Hypothesis, Krashen's Input Hypothesis, discrete point and integrative testing, and others. Play the believing game with what might be labeled the unpopular side of the controversy. How does it feel? How does it help to put things into balance? In what way are both games necessary for ultimate understanding?

9. Review the five characteristics of the current language teaching "revolution." Do you find evidence of those characteristics in classes you have taken or observed? What further characteristics would you add?

10. Can you identify any "bandwagons" that have appeared in foreign language teaching in recent years? Or some methods that begin to take on a bandwagon image? If so, what is it that leads you to put them into that category?

11. Try to make a list of characteristics of a "successful language *teacher*." What steps do you think you could take to train yourself to

be more successful? That is, what are your weaknesses and strengths, and how might you work on those weaknesses from what you know so far about foreign language teaching?

12.  Just for the fun of it, get out your "crystal ball" and try to predict what language teaching approaches will emerge in the future. What will be some of the characteristics of those approaches?

# Bibliography

Abraham, Roberta G. 1981. The relationship of cognitive style to the use of grammatical rules by Spanish-speaking ESL students in editing written English. Unpublished doctoral dissertation, University of Illinois at Urbana-Champaign.

Abraham, Roberta G. 1985. Field independence-dependence and the teaching of grammar. TESOL Quarterly 19:689–702.

Acton, William. 1979. Second language learning and perception of difference in attitude. Unpublished doctoral dissertation, University of Michigan.

Adamson, H.D. 1988. Variation Theory and Second Language Acquisition. Washington DC: Georgetown University Press.

Adler, Peter S. 1972. Culture shock and the cross cultural learning experience. Readings in Intercultural Education, Volume 2. Pittsburgh: Intercultural Communication Network.

Alatis, James E. (Editor). 1990. Georgetown University Round Table on Languages and Linguistics 1990. Washington, DC: Georgetown University Press.

Alderson, J. Charles. 1991. Language testing in the 1990s: How far have we come? How much further do we have to go? In Anivan 1991.

Allwright, Richard L. 1975. Problems in the study of teachers' treatment of learner error. In Burt and Dulay 1975.

Allwright, Richard L. 1980. Turns, topics, and tasks: Patterns of participation in language learning and teaching. In Larsen-Freeman 1980.

Alpert, R. and Haber, R. 1960. Anxiety in academic achievement situations. Journal of Abnormal and Social Psychology 61:207–215.

Alptekin, C. and Atakan, S. 1990. Field dependence-independence and hemisphericity as variables in L2 achievement. Second Language Research 6:135–149.

American Council on the Teaching of Foreign Languages (ACTFL). 1982. ACTFL Provisional Proficiency Guidelines. Hastings-on-Hudson, NY: ACTFL.

Anderson, Neil J. 1991. Individual differences in strategy use in second language reading and testing. The Modern Language Journal 75:460–472.

Anderson, Richard C. and Ausubel, David A. (Editors). 1965. Readings in the Psychology of Cognition. New York: Holt, Rinehart & Winston.

Andersen, Roger W. 1978. An implicational model for second-language research. Language Learning 28:221–282.

Andersen, Roger W. 1979. Expanding Schumann's pidginization hypothesis. Language Learning 29:105–119.

Andersen, Roger W. (Editor). 1981. New Dimensions in Second Language Acquisition Research. Rowley, MA: Newbury House Publishers.

Andersen, Roger W. 1982. Determining the linguistic attributes of language attrition. In Lambert and Freed 1982.

Angelis, Paul and Henderson, Thelma. (Editors). 1989. Selected Papers from the Proceedings of the BAAL/AAAL Joint Seminar "Communicative Competence Revisited." Applied Linguistics 10 (June 1989).

Anivan, S. (Editor). 1991. Current Developments in Language Testing. Singapore: SEAMEO Regional Language Center.

Anthony, Edward M. 1963. Approach, method and technique. English Language Teaching 17:63–67.

Asher, James. 1977. Learning Another Language Through Actions: The Complete Teacher's Guidebook. Los Gatos, CA: Sky Oaks Productions.

Au, S.Y. 1988. A critical appraisal of Gardner's social-psychological theory of second language learning. Language Learning 38:75–100.

Augustine, St. 1838. Confessions. Translated by Edward B. Pusey. Oxford: J.C. Parker Company.

Austin, John L. 1962. How to Do Things with Words, Cambridge, MA: Harvard University Press.

Ausubel, David A. 1963. Cognitive structure and the facilitation of meaningful verbal learning. Journal of Teacher Education 14:217–221.

Ausubel, David A. 1964. Adults vs. children in second language learning: Psychological considerations. Modern Language Journal 48:420–424.

Ausubel, David A. 1965. Introduction to part one. In Anderson and Ausubel 1965.

Ausubel, David A. 1968. Educational Psychology: A Cognitive View. New York: Holt, Rinehart & Winston.

Bachman, Lyle F. 1982. The trait structure of cloze test scores. TESOL Quarterly 16:61–70.

Bachman, Lyle F. 1984. The TOEFL as a measure of communicative competence. Paper delivered at the Second TOEFL Invitational Conference, Educational Testing Service, Princeton, NJ, October, 1984.

Bachman, Lyle F. 1988. Problems in examining the validity of the ACTFL oral proficiency interview. Studies in Second Language Acquisition 10:149–164.

Bachman, Lyle F. 1990. Fundamental Considerations in Language Testing. New York: Oxford University Press.

Bachman, Lyle F. 1991. What does language testing have to offer? TESOL Quarterly 25:671–704.

Bachman, Lyle F. and Palmer, Adrian. 1981. The construct validation of the FSI oral interview. Language Learning 31:67–86.

Bachman, Lyle F. and Palmer, Adrian. 1982. The construct validation of some components of communicative proficiency. TESOL Quarterly 16:449–465.

Bacon, Susan M. 1992. The relationship between gender, comprehension, processing strategies, and cognitive and affective response in foreign language listening. Modern Language Journal 76:160–178.

Bailey, Kathleen M. 1983. Competitiveness and anxiety in adult second language learning: Looking at and through the diary studies. In Seliger and Long 1983.

Bailey, Kathleen M. 1985. Classroom-centered research on language teaching and learning. In Celce-Murcia 1985.

Bailey, Kathleen M. 1986. Class lecture, Spring 1986. Monterey Institute of International Studies.

Baldwin, Alfred. 1966. The development of intuition. In Bruner 1966.

Banathy, Bela, Trager, Edith C., and Waddle, Carl D. 1966. The use of contrastive data in foreign language course development. In Valdman 1966.

Bandura, Albert and Walters, Richard H. 1963. Social Learning and Personality Development. New York: Holt, Rinehart & Winston.

Bar Adon, A. and Leopold, Werner F. (Editors). 1971. Child Language: A Book of Readings. Englewood Cliffs, NJ: Prentice-Hall, Inc.

Bateson, Gregory. 1972. Steps to an Ecology of Mind. New York: Ballantine Books.

Beebe, Leslie M. 1983. Risk-taking and the language learner. In Seliger and Long 1983.

Beebe, Leslie M. (Editor). 1988. Issues in Second Language Acquisition: Multiple Perspectives. New York: Newbury House Publishers.

Bellugi, Ursula and Brown, Roger (Editors). 1964. The Acquisition of Language. Monographs of the Society for Research in Child Development, Number 29 (Serial Number 92).

Berko, Jean, 1958. The child's learning of English morphology. Word 14: 150–177.

Berko-Gleason, Jean. 1982. Insights from child acquisition for second language loss. In Lambert and Freed 1982.

Berko-Gleason, Jean, 1985. The Development of Language. New York: Charles E. Merrill Publishing Company.

Berko-Gleason, Jean. 1988. Language and Socialization. In Kessel 1988.

Berns, Margie S. 1984a. Functional approaches to language and language teaching: Another look. In Savignon and Berns 1984.

Berns, Margie S. 1984b. Review of Finocchiaro and Brumfit 1983. TESOL Quarterly 18:325–329.

Berns, Margie S. 1990. Contexts of Competence: Social and Cultural Considerations in Communicative Language Teaching. New York: Plenum Press.

Bialystok, Ellen, 1978. A theoretical model of second language learning. Language Learning 28:69–83.

Bialystok, Ellen. 1981. Some evidence for the integrity and interaction of two knowledge sources. In Andersen 1981.

Bialystok, Ellen. 1982. On the relationship between knowing and using linguistic forms. Applied Linguistics 3:123–139.

Bialystok, Ellen. 1983. Inferencing: Testing the "hypothesis testing" hypothesis. In Seliger and Long 1983.

Bialystok, Ellen. 1985. The compatibility of teaching and learning strategies. Applied Linguistics 6:255–262.

Bialystok, Ellen. 1990a. Communication Strategies. Cambridge, MA: Basil Blackwell.

Bialystok, Ellen. 1990b. The dangers of dichotomy: A reply to Hulstijn. Applied Linguistics 11:46–52.

Bialystok, Ellen and Bouchard-Ryan, E. 1985. A metacognitive framework for the development of first and second language skills. In Forrest-Pressley et al. 1985.

Bialystok, Ellen and Mitterer, J. 1987. Metalinguistic differences among three kinds of readers. Journal of Educational Psychology 79:147–153.

Bickerton, Derek. 1981. Roots of Language. Ann Arbor, MI: Karoma Publishers.

Bierce, Ambrose. 1967. The Devil's Dictionary. New York: Doubleday, Inc.

Blair, Robert W. (Editor). 1982. Innovative Approaches to Language Teaching. Rowley, MA: Newbury House Publishers.

Blatchford, Charles H. and Schachter, Jacqueline (Editors). 1978. On TESOL 78: EFL Policies, Programs, Practices. Washington DC: Teachers of English to Speakers of Other Languages.

Bley-Vroman, Robert. 1988. The fundamental character of foreign language learning. In Rutherford and Sharwood-Smith 1988.

Bloom, Lois. 1971. Why not pivot grammar? Journal of Speech and Hearing Disorders 36:40–50.

Bloom, Lois (Editor). 1978. Readings in Language Development. New York: John Wiley & Sons.

Bolinger, Dwight. 1975. Aspects of Language. Second Edition. New York: Harcourt Brace Jovanovich, Inc.

Bongaerts, Theo and Poulisse, Nanda. 1989. Communication strategies in L1 and L2: Same or different? Applied Linguistics 10:253–268.

Bowen, J. Donald. 1975. Patterns of English Pronunciation. Rowley, MA: Newbury House Publishers.

Bowen, J. Donald, Madsen, Harold, and Hilferty, Ann. 1985. TESOL Techniques and Procedures. Rowley, MA: Newbury House Publishers.

Braine, Martin D.S. 1965. On the basis of phrase structure: A reply to Bever, Fodor, and Weksel. Psychological Review 72:153–159.

Breen, Michael P. and Candlin, Christopher N. 1980. The essentials of a communicative curriculum in language teaching. Applied Linguistics 1:89–112.

Briere, Eugene J. and Hinofotis, Frances B. 1979. Concepts in Language Testing: Some Recent Studies. Washington, DC: Teachers of English to Speakers of Other Languages.

Brodkey, Dean and Shore, Howard. 1976. Student personality and success in an English language program. Language Learning 26:153–159.

Brown, H. Douglas. 1970. English relativization and sentence comprehension in child language. Unpublished doctoral dissertation, University of California, Los Angeles.

Brown, H. Douglas. 1971. Children's comprehension of relativized English sentences. Child Development 42:1923–1936.

Brown, H. Douglas. 1972. Cognitive pruning and second language acquisition. Modern Language Journal 56:218–222.

Brown, H. Douglas. 1973. Affective variables in second language acquisition. Language Learning 23:231–244.

Brown, H. Douglas (Editor). 1976a. Papers in Second Language Acquisition. (Language Learning Special Issue Number 4). Ann Arbor, MI: Research Club in Language Learning.

Brown, H. Douglas. 1976b. What is applied linguistics? In Wardhaugh and Brown 1976.

Brown, H. Douglas. 1977a. Cognitive and affective characteristics of good language learners. In Henning 1977.

Brown, H. Douglas. 1977b. Some limitations of C-L/CLL models of second language teaching. TESOL Quarterly 11:365–372.

Brown, H. Douglas. 1980. The optimal distance model of second language acquisition. TESOL Quarterly 14:157–164.

Brown, H. Douglas. 1989. A Practical Guide to Language Learning. New York: McGraw-Hill.

Brown, H. Douglas. 1990. M&Ms for language classrooms? Another look at motivation. In Alatis 1990.

Brown, H. Douglas. 1991. Breaking the Language Barrier. Yarmouth, ME: Intercultural Press.

Brown, H. Douglas. 1994. Teaching by Principles: Interactive Language Teaching Methodology. New York: Prentice Hall Regents.

Brown, H. Douglas, Yorio, Carlos A., and Crymes, Ruth H. (Editors). 1977. Teaching and Learning English as a Second Language: Trends in Research and Practice. On TESOL 77. Washington, DC: Teachers of English to Speakers of Other Languages.

Brown, James D. and Bailey, Kathleen M. 1984. A categorical instrument for scoring second language writing skills. Language Learning 34:21–42.

Brown, Roger. 1966. The "tip of the tongue" phenomenon. Journal of Verbal Learning and Verbal Behavior 5:325–337.

Brown, Roger, 1973. A First Language: The Early Stages. Cambridge, MA: Harvard University Press.

Brown, Roger and Bellugi, Ursula. 1964. Three processes in the child's acquisition of syntax. Harvard Educational Review 34:133–151.

Brown, Roger and Hanlon, C. 1970. Derivational complexity and order of acquisition in child speech. In Hayes 1970.

Brumfit, Christopher. 1992. Review of Stephen Krashen's Language Acquisition and Language Education (1989). Applied Linguistics 13:123–125.

Bruner, Jerome (Editor). 1966a. Learning About Learning. Washington, DC: United States Government Printing Office.

Bruner, Jerome S. 1966b. Toward a Theory of Instruction. New York: W. W. Norton & Company.

Bruner, Jerome and Clinchy, Blythe. 1966. Towards a disciplined intuition. In Bruner 1966a.

Bruner, Jerome S., Olver, Rose, and Greenfield, P. (Editors). 1966. Studies in Cognitive Growth. New York: John Wiley & Sons.

Buczowska, Ewa and Weist, Richard M. 1991. The effects of formal instruction on the second language acquisition of temporal location. Language Learning 41:535–554.

Burling, Robbins. 1970. Man's Many Voices. New York: Holt, Rinehart & Winston.

Burt, Marina K. 1975. Error analysis in the adult EFL classroom. TESOL Quarterly 9:53–63.

Burt, Marina K. and Dulay, Heidi. 1975. New Directions in Second Language Learning, Teaching, and Bilingual Education. On TESOL '75. Washington, DC: Teachers of English to Speakers of Other Languages.

Burt, Marina K. and Kiparsky, Carol. 1972. The Gooficon: A Repair Manual for English. Rowley, MA: Newbury House Publishers.

Burt, Marina K., Dulay, Heidi C., and Finocchiaro, Mary (Editors). 1977. Viewpoints on English as a Second Language. New York: Regents Publishing Company.

Busch, Deborah. 1982. Introversion-extraversion and the EFL proficiency of Japanese students. Language Learning 32:109–132.

Cairns, E. and Cammock, T. 1989. The 20-item matching familiar figures test: Technical data. Unpublished manuscript, University of Ulster Coleraine.

California State Department of Education. 1986. Schooling and Language Minority Students: A Theoretical Framework. Sacramento, CA: Department of Education.

Campbell, Russell. 1978. Notional-functional syllabuses 1978: Part I. In Blatchford and Schachter 1978.

Canale, Michael. 1983. From communicative competence to communicative language pedagogy. In Richards and Schmidt 1983.

Canale, Michael. 1984. Considerations in the testing of reading and listening proficiency. Foreign Language Annals 17:349–357.

Canale, Michael and Swain, Merrill. 1980. Theoretical bases of communicative approaches to second language teaching and testing. Applied Linguistics 1:1–47.

Carmichael, L., Hogan., H.P., and Walter, A.A. 1932. An experimental study of the effect of language on visually perceived form. Journal of Experimental Psychology 15:73–86.

Carrell, Patricia L. 1982. Cohesion is not coherence. TESOL Quarterly 16:479–488.

Carrell, Patricia L. 1986. A view of the written text as communicative interaction: Implications for reading in a second language. In Devine et al. 1986.

Carroll, John B. 1956. Language, Thought, and Reality: Selected Writings of Benjamin Lee Whorf. Cambridge, MA: M.I.T. Press.

Carroll, John B. 1961. Fundamental considerations in testing for English language proficiency of foreign students. Washington, DC: Center for Applied Linguistics.

Carroll, John B. and Sapon, Stanley M. 1958. Modern Language Aptitude Test. New York: The Psychological Corporation.

Carroll, Lewis. 1872. Through the Looking Glass. Boston: Lee & Shapard.

Carroll, Susanne and Meisel, Jurgen M. Universals and second language acquisition: Some comments on the state of current theory. Studies in Second Language Acquisition 12:201–208.

Cathcart, Ruth L. and Olsen, Judy E.W.B. 1976. Teachers' and students' preferences for correction of classroom conversation errors. In Fanselow and Crymes 1976.

Celce-Murcia, Marianne (Editor). 1985. Beyond Basics: Issues and Research in TESOL. Rowley, MA: Newbury House Publishers.

Celce-Murcia, Marianne (Editor). 1991. Teaching English as a Second or Foreign Language. Second Edition. New York: Newbury House Publishers.

Celce-Murcia, Marianne and Hawkins, Barbara. 1985. Contrastive analysis, error analysis, and interlanguage analysis. In Celce-Murcia 1985.

Celce-Murcia, Marianne and McIntosh, Lois. 1979. Teaching English as a Second or Foreign Language. Rowley, MA: Newbury House Publishers.

Chaika, Elaine. 1989. Language: The Social Mirror. New York: Newbury House Publishers.

Chamot, Anna U. and McKeon, Denise. 1984. Second language teaching. Rosslyn, VA: National Clearinghouse for Bilingual Education.

Chamot, Anna Uhl and O'Malley, Michael. 1986. A Cognitive Academic Language Learning Approach: An ESL Content-based Curriculum. Wheaton, MD: National Clearinghouse for Bilingual Education.

Chamot, Anna Uhl and O'Malley, Michael. 1987. The cognitive academic language learning approach: A bridge to the mainstream. TESOL Quarterly 21:227–249.

Chamot, Anna Uhl, O'Malley, Michael, and Kupper, Lisa. 1992. Building Bridges: Content and Learning Strategies for ESL. Books 1, 2, 3. New York: Heinle and Heinle, Publishers.

Chapelle, Carol A. 1983. The relationship between ambiguity tolerance and success in acquiring English as a second language in adult learners. Unpublished doctoral dissertation, University of Illinois.

Chapelle, Carol. 1992. Disembedding "disembedded figures in the landscape . . .": An appraisal of Griffiths and Sheen's "reappraisal of L2 research on field dependence/independence." 1992. Applied Linguistics 13:375–384.

Chapelle, Carol and Abraham, Roberta G. 1990. Cloze method: What difference does it make? Language Testing 7:121–146.

Chapelle, Carol and Green, Pat. 1992. Field independence/dependence in second language acquisition research. Language Learning 42:47–83.

Chapelle, Carol A. and Roberts, Cheryl. 1986. Ambiguity tolerance and field independence as predictors of proficiency in English as a second language. Language Learning 36:27–45.

Chesterfield, Ray and Chesterfield, Kathleen B. 1985. Natural order in children's use of second language learning strategies. Applied Linguistics 6:45–59.

Chihara, Tetsuro and Oller, John W. 1978. Attitudes and proficiency in EFL: A sociolinguistic study of adult Japanese speakers. Language Learning 28:55–68.

Chomsky, Noam. 1959. A review of B.F. Skinner's Verbal Behavior. Language 35:26–58.

Chomsky, Noam. 1964. Current issues in linguistic theory. In Fodor and Katz 1964.

Chomsky, Noam. 1965. Aspects of the Theory of Syntax. Cambridge, MA: M.I.T. Press.

Chomsky, Noam. 1966. Linguistic theory. In Mead 1966.

Chun, Ann E., Day, Richard R., Chenoweth, N. Ann, and Luppescu, Stuart. 1982. Types of errors corrected in native-nonnative conversations. TESOL Quarterly 16:537–547.

Clark, Herbert H. and Clark, Eve V. 1977. Psychology and Language: An Introduction to Psycholinguistics. New York: Harcourt Brace Jovanovich, Inc.

Clark, John L.D. 1983. Language testing: Past and current status—directions for the future. The Modern Language Journal 67:431–443.

Clarke, Mark A. 1976. Second language acquisition as a clash of consciousness. Language Learning 26:377–390.

Clarke, Mark A. 1982. On bandwagons, tyranny, and common sense. TESOL Quarterly 16:437–448.

Clarke, Mark A. and Handscombe, Jean. 1982. Pacific Perspectives on Language Learning and Teaching. On TESOL '82. Washington, DC: Teachers of English to Speakers of Other Languages.

Clarke, Mark, Losoff, Ann, McCracken, Margaret Dickenson, and Rood, David S. 1984. Linguistic relativity and sex/gender studies: Epistemological and methodological considerations. Language Learning 34:47–67.

Coffey, Margaret Pogemiller. 1983. Fitting In: A Functional/Notional Text for Learners of English. Englewood Cliffs, NJ: Prentice-Hall.

Cohen, Andrew D. and Aphek, Edna. 1981. Easifying second language learning. Studies in Second Language Acquisition 3:221–236.

Coleman, Algernon. 1929. The Teaching of Modern Foreign Languages in the United States: A Report Prepared for the Modern Language Study. New York: Macmillan Company.

Comrie, Bernard. 1990. Second language acquisition and language universals research. Studies in Second Language Acquisition 12:209–218.

Condon, E.C. 1973. Introduction to Cross Cultural Communication. New Jersey: Rutgers University.

Cook, Vivian. 1969. The analogy between first and second language learning. International Review of Applied Linguistics 7:207–216.

Cook, Vivian. 1973. Comparison of language development in native children and foreign adults. International Review of Applied Linguistics 11:13–28.

Coopersmith, Stanley. 1967. The Antecedents of Self-Esteem. San Francisco: W.H. Freeman & Company.

Corder, S. Pit. 1967. The significance of learners' errors. International Review of Applied Linguistics 5:161–170.

Corder S. Pit. 1971. Idiosyncratic dialects and error analysis. Internation Review of Applied Linguistics 9:147–159.

Corder, S. Pit. 1973. Introducing Applied Linguistics. Harmondsworth, UK: Penguin Books.

Croft, Kenneth (Editor). 1980. Readings on English as a Second Language, Second Edition. Cambridge, MA: Winthrop Publishers.

Crookes, Graham. 1989. Planning and interlanguage variation. Studies in Second Language Acquisition 11:367–384.

Crookes, Graham and Schmidt, Richard W. 1991. Motivation: Reopening the research agenda. Language Learning 41:469–512.

Cummins, James. 1979. Cognitive/academic language proficiency, linguistic interdependence, the optimal age question and some other matters. Working Papers on Bilingualism 19:197–205.

Cummins, James. 1980. The cross-lingual dimensions of language proficiency: Implications for bilingual education and the optimal age issue. TESOL Quarterly 14:175–187.

Cummins, James. 1981. The role of primary language development in promoting educational success for language minority students. Sacramento, CA: California State Department of Education, Office of Bilingual Bicultural Education.

Curran, Charles A. 1972. Counseling-Learning: A Whole Person Model for Education. New York: Grune & Stratton.

Curran, Charles A. 1976. Counseling-Learning in Second Languages. Apple River, IL: Apple River Press.

Curtiss, Susan. 1977. Genie: A Psycholinguistic Study of a Modern-Day "Wild Child." New York: Academic Press.

Cziko, Gary A. 1982. Improving the psychometric, criterion- referenced, and practical qualities of integrative language tests. TESOL Quarterly 16:367–379.

D'Amico-Reisner, Lynne. 1983. An analysis of the surface structure of disapproval exchanges. In Wolfson and Judd 1983.

Danesi, Marcel. 1988. Neurological bimodality and theories of language teaching. Studies in Second Language Acquisition 10:13–31.

Davidson, Fred, Hudson, Thom, and Lynch, Brian. 1985. Language testing: Operationalization in classroom measurement and L2 research. In Celce-Murcia 1985.

Davies, Alan. 1989. Is international English an interlanguage? TESOL Quarterly 23:447–467.

Davies, Alan. 1990. Principles of Language Testing. Oxford: Basil Blackwell.

Day, Cathy. 1982. The optimal distance model of acculturation and success in second language learning. Unpublished doctoral dissertation, University of Illinois, Urbana-Champaign.

Day, Richard R., Chenoweth, N. Ann, Chun, Ann E., and Luppescu, Stuart. 1984. Corrective feedback in native-nonnative discourse. Language Learning 34:19–45.

Deci, Edward L. 1975. Intrinsic Motivation. New York: Plenum Press.

De Vito, Joseph A. 1971. Psycholinguistics. Indianapolis, IN: The Bobbs-Merrill Company, Inc.

Devine, Joanne, Carrell, Patricia L., and Eskey, David E. (Editors). 1986. Research in Reading ESL. Washington, DC: Teachers of English to Speakers of Other Languages.

Dewey, John. 1910. How We Think. Boston: D.C. Heath Company.

Dieterich, Thomas G., Freeman, Cecilia, and Crandall, Jo Ann. 1979. A linguistic analysis of some English proficiency tests. TESOL Quarterly 13:535–550.

Diller, Karl C. 1978. The Language Teaching Controversy. Rowley, MA: Newbury House Publishers.

Diller, Karl C. (Editor). 1981. Individual Differences and Universals in Language Learning Aptitude. Rowley, MA: Newbury House Publishers.

Donahue, Meghan and Parsons, Adelaide Heyde. 1982. The use of roleplay to overcome cultural fatigue. TESOL Quarterly 16:359–365.

Donne, John. 1624. Devotions upon Emergent Occasions. (Edited with commentary by: Anthony Raspa. 1975. Montreal: McGill-Queen's University Press.)

Doron, Sandra. 1973. Reflectivity-impulsivity and their influence on reading for inference for adult students of ESL. Unpublished manuscript, University of Michigan.

Doughty, Catherine. 1991. Second language instruction does make a difference: Evidence from an empirical study of SL relativization. Studies in Second Language Acquisition 13:431–469.

Douglas, Dan. 1988. Testing listening comprehension in the context of the ACTFL proficiency guidelines. Studies in Second Language Acquisition 10:245–261.

Drach, K. 1969. The language of the parent: A pilot study. Working Paper Number 14, Language Behavior Research Laboratory, University of California, Berkeley.

Dulay, Heidi C. and Burt, Marina K. 1972. Goofing: An indicator of children's second language learning strategies. Language Learning 22:235–252.

Dulay, Heidi C. and Burt, Marina K. 1974a. Errors and strategies in child second language acquisition. TESOL Quarterly 8:129–136.

Dulay, Heidi C. and Burt, Marina K. 1974b. Natural sequences in child second language acquisition. Language Learning 24:37–53.

Dulay, Heidi C. and Burt, Marina K. 1976. Creative construction in second language learning and teaching. Language Learning, Special Issue Number 4:65–79.

Dulay, Heidi C., Burt, Marina K., and Hernandez-Ch., Eduardo. 1975. Bilingual Syntax Measure. New York: Harcourt Brace Jovanovich, Inc.

Dunn, Rita, Beaudry, Jeffrey S., and Klavas, Angela. 1989. Survey of research on learning styles. Educational Leadership 32:50–58.

Duran, Richard P. (with Canale, Michael, Penfield, Joyce, Stansfield, Charles W., and Liskin-Gasparro, Judith E.) 1985. TOEFL From a Communicative Viewpoint on Language Proficiency: A Working Paper. Princeton, NJ: Educational Testing Service.

Durkheim, Emile. 1897. Le suicide. Paris: F. Alcan.

Eckman, Fred R. 1977. Markedness and the contrastive analysis hypothesis. Language Learning 27:315–330.

Eckman, Fred R. 1981. On the naturalness of interlanguage phonological rules. Language Learning 31:195–216.

Eckman, Fred R. 1991. The structural conformity hypothesis and the acquisition of consonant clusters in the interlanguage of ESL learners. Studies in Second Language Acquisition 13:23–41.

Edwards, Betty. 1979. Drawing on the Right Side of the Brain. Los Angeles: J.P. Tarcher/St. Martins.

Ehrman, Madeline. 1989. Ants, grasshoppers, badgers, and butterflies: Qualitative and quantitative investigation of adult language learning styles and strategies. Unpublished doctoral dissertation, Union Institute.

Ehrman, Madeline. 1990. The role of personality type in adult language learning: An ongoing investigation. In Parry and Stansfield 1990.

Ehrman, Madeline E. 1993. Ego boundaries revisited: Toward a model of personality and learning. In Alatis, James E. (Ed.), Georgetown University Round Table on Languages and Linguistics 1993. Washington DC: Georgetown University Press.

Ehrman, Madeline and Oxford, Rebecca. 1989. Effects of sex differences, career choice, and psychological type on adult language learning strategies. Modern Language Journal 73:1–13.

Ehrman, Madeline and Oxford, Rebecca. 1990. Adult language learning styles and strategies in an intensive training setting. Modern Language Journal 74:311–327.

Elbow, Peter. 1973. Writing Without Teachers. New York: Oxford University Press. (Appendix Essay: "The doubting game and the believing game: An analysis of the intellectual enterprise").

Ellis, Gail and Sinclair, Barbara. 1989. Learning to Learn English: A Course in Learner Training. Cambridge: Cambridge University Press.

Ellis, Rod. 1986. Understanding Second Language Acquisition. Oxford: Oxford University Press.

Ellis, Rod. 1987. Second Language Acquisition in Context. New York: Prentice Hall.

Ellis, Rod. 1989. Sources of intra-learner variability in language use and their relationship to second language acquisition. In Gass et al. 1989.

Ellis, Rod. 1990a. A response to Gregg. Applied Linguistics 11:384–391.

Ellis, Rod. 1990b. Instructed Second Language Acquisition: Learning in the Classroom. Cambridge, MA: Basil Blackwell.

Ely, Christopher M. 1986. An analysis of discomfort, risktaking, sociability, and motivation in the L2 classroom. Language Learning 36:1–25.

Ervin-Tripp, Susan. 1974. Is second language learning like the first? TESOL Quarterly 8:111–127.

Ewing, David W. 1977. Discovering your problem solving style. Psychology Today 11:12:69–73.

Faerch, Claus and Kasper, Gabriele. 1983a. Plans and strategies in foreign language communication. In Faerch and Kasper 1983.

Faerch, Claus and Kasper, Gabriele. (Editors). 1983b. Strategies in Interlanguage Communication. London: Longman.

Faerch, Claus and Kasper, Gabrielle. 1984. Two ways of defining communication strategies. Language Learning 34:45–63.

Fanselow, John F. and Crymes, Ruth H. (Editors). 1976. On TESOL 76. Washington, DC: Teachers of English to Speakers of Other Languages.

Farhady, Hossein. 1979. The disjunctive fallacy between discrete-point and integrative tests. TESOL Quarterly 13:347–357.

Farhady, Hossein. 1982. Measures of language proficiency from the learner's perspective. TESOL Quarterly 16:43–59.

Fast, Julius. 1970. Body Language. New York: M. Evans Company.

Fersh, Seymour (Editor). 1974. Learning About People and Cultures. Evanston, IL: McDougal, Littel & Company.

Finocchiaro, Mary. 1964. English as a Second Language: From Theory to Practice. New York: Simon & Schuster.

Finocchiaro, Mary and Brumfit, Christopher. 1983. The Functional-Notional Approach: From Theory to Practice. New York: Oxford University Press.

Flege, James E. 1981. The phonological basis of foreign accent: A hypothesis. TESOL Quarterly 15:443–455.

Flege, James Emil. 1987. A critical period for learning to pronounce foreign languages? Applied Linguistics 8:162–177.

Flynn, Suzanne. 1987. Contrast and construction in a parameter-setting model of L2 acquisition. Language Learning 37:19–62.

Fodor, Jerry A. and Katz, Jerrold J. (Editors). 1964. The Structure of Language: Readings in the Philosophy of Language. Englewood Cliffs, NJ: Prentice-Hall, Inc.

Forrest-Pressley, D.L., MacKinnon, G.E., and Waller, T.G. (Editors). 1985. Metacognition, Cognition, and Human Performance. Volume 1. New York: Academic Press.

Foster, George M. 1962. Traditional Cultures. New York: Harper and Row.

Fotos, Sandra S. 1991. The close test as an integrative measure of EFL proficiency: A substitute for essays on college entrance examinations? Language Learning 41:313–336.

Freire, Paolo. 1970. Pedagogy of the Oppressed. New York: Seabury Press.

Freud, Sigmund. 1920. A General Introduction to Psychoanalysis. New York: Liveright.

Fries, Charles C. 1945. Teaching and Learning English as a Foreign Language. Ann Arbor, MI: University of Michigan Press.

Fries, Charles C. 1952. The Structure of English. New York: Harcourt, Brace, and World.

Gage, Nathan (Editor). 1964. Handbook of Research on Teaching. Chicago: Rand McNally & Company.

Gagné, Robert M. 1965. The Conditions of Learning. New York: Holt, Rinehart & Winston.

Gaies, Stephen J. 1983. Learner feedback: An exploratory study of its role in the second language classroom. In Seliger and Long 1983.

Gardner, Howard. 1983. Frames of Mind: The Theory of Multiple Intelligences. New York: Basic Books.

Gardner, Robert C. 1982. Social factors in language retention. In Lambert and Freed 1982.

Gardner, Robert C. 1985. Social Psychology and Second Language Learning: The Role of Attitudes and Motivation. London: Edward Arnold.

Gardner, Robert C., Day, J.B., and MacIntyre, Peter D. 1992. Integrative motivation, induced anxiety, and language learning in a controlled environment. Studies in Second Language Acquisition 14:197–214.

Gardner, Robert C. and Lambert, Wallace E. 1972. Attitudes and Motivation in Second Language Learning. Rowley, MA: Newbury House Publishers.

Gardner, Robert C. and MacIntyre, Peter D. 1991. An instrumental motivation in language study: Who says it isn't effective? Studies in Second Language Acquisition 13:57–72.

Gass, Susan, 1989. Language universals and second language acquisition. Language Learning 39:497–534.

Gass, Susan, Madden, Carolyn, Preston, Dennis, and Selinker, Larry (Editors). 1989. Variation in Second Language Acquisition: Psycholinguistic Issues. Clevedon, Avon: Multilingual Matters.

Gatbonton, Elisabeth. 1983. Patterned phonetic variability in second language speech: A gradual diffusion model. In Robinett and Schachter 1983.

Gathercole, Virginia C. 1988. Some myths you may have heard about first language acquisition. TESOL Quarterly 22:407–435.

Gattegno, Caleb. 1972. Teaching Foreign Languages in Schools: The Silent Way. Second Edition. New York: Educational Solutions.

Gattegno, Caleb. 1976. The Common Sense of Teaching Foreign Languages. New York: Educational Solutions.

Genesee, Fred. 1982. Experimental neuropsychological research on second language processing. TESOL Quarterly 16:315–322.

Geschwind, Norman. 1970. The organization of language and the brain. Science 170:940–944.

Gibbons, John. 1985. The silent period: An examination. Language Learning 35:255–267.

Gleason, Henry A. 1961. An Introduction to Descriptive Linguistics. Revised Edition. New York: Holt, Rinehart & Winston.

Gleitman, Lila R. and Wanner, Eric. 1982. Language acquisition: The state of the state of the art. In Wanner and Gleitman 1982.

Goodman, Kenneth S. 1970. Reading: A psycholinguistic guessing game. In Singer and Ruddell 1970.

Gouin, Francois. 1880. L'art d'enseigner et d'etudier les langues. Paris: Librairie Fischbacher.

Graham, C.R. 1984. Beyond integrative motivation: The development and influence of assimilative motivation. Paper presented at the TESOL Convention, Houston, TX, March, 1984.

Greenberg, Joseph H. (Editor). 1963. Universals of Language. Cambridge, MA: M.I.T. Press.

Greenberg, Joseph H. 1966. Language Universals. The Hague: Mouton Publishers.

Gregg, Kevin R. 1984. Krashen's monitor and Occam's razor. Applied Linguistics 5:79–100.

Gregg, Kevin R. 1990. The variable competence model of second language acquisition and why it isn't. Applied Linguistics 11:364–383.

Grice, H.P. 1967. Logic and conversation. Unpublished manuscript, University of California, Berkeley.

Griffiths, Roger and Sheen, Ronald. 1992. Disembedded figures in the landscape: A reappraisal of L2 research on field dependence-independence. Applied Linguistics 13:133–148.

Guidelines for the Preparation of Teachers of English to Speakers of Other Languages in the United States. 1975. Washington, DC: Teachers of English to Speakers of Other Languages.

Guiora, Alexander Z. 1981. Language, personality and culture or the Whorfian hypothesis revisited. In Hines and Rutherford 1981.

Guiora, Alexander Z., Acton, William R., Erard, Robert, and Strickland, Fred W. 1980. The effects of benzodiazepine (valium) on permeability of ego boundaries. Language Learning 30:351–363.

Guiora, Alexander Z., Beit-Hallami, Benjamin, Brannon, Robert C., Dull, Cecelia Y., and Scovel, Thomas. 1972a. The effects of experimentally induced changes in ego states on pronunciation ability in second language: An exploratory study. Comprehensive Psychiatry 13.

Guiora, Alexander, Z., Brannon, Robert C., and Dull, Cecilia Y. 1972b. Empathy and second language learning. Language Learning 22:111–130.

Hakuta, Kenji. 1974. Prefabricated patterns and the emergence of structure in second language acquisition. Language Learning 24:287–297.

Hakuta, Kenji. 1976. A case study of a Japanese child learning English as a second language. Language Learning 26:326–351.

Hall, Edward. 1959. The Silent Language. New York: Doubleday & Company.

Hall, Edward. 1966. The Hidden Dimension. New York: Doubleday & Company.

Hall, Edward. 1974. Making sense without words. In Fersh 1974.

Halliday, Michael. 1973. Explorations in the Functions of Language. London: Edward Arnold.

Hammerly, Hector. 1985. An Integrated Theory of Language Teaching. Blaine, WA: Second Language Publications.

Hansen, Jacqueline and Stansfield, Charles. 1981. The relationship of field dependent-independent cognitive styles to foreign language achievement. Language Learning 31:349–367.

Hansen, Lynne. 1984. Field dependence-independence and language testing: Evidence from six Pacific island cultures. TESOL Quarterly 18:311–324.

Hansen-Bede, Lynn. 1975. A child's creation of a second language. Working Papers on Bilingualism 6:103–126.

Harlow, Linda L. 1990. Do they mean what they say? Sociopragmatic competence and second language learners. Modern Language Journal 74:328–351.

Hartnett, Dayle D. 1985. Cognitive style and second language learning. In Celce-Murcia 1985.

Hatch, Evelyn. 1978a. Discourse analysis and second language acquisition. In Hatch 1978b.

Hatch, Evelyn (Editor). 1978b. Second Language Acquisition. Rowley, MA: Newbury House Publishers.

Hatch, Evelyn and Long, Michael H. 1980. Discourse analysis, what's that? In Larsen-Freeman 1980.

Hayes, J. (Editor). 1970. Cognition and the Development of Language. New York: John Wiley and Sons.

Hendrickson, James M. 1980. Error correction in foreign language teaching: Recent theory, research, and practice. In Croft 1980.

Henning, Carol A. (Editor). 1977. Proceedings of the Los Angeles Second Language Research Forum. Los Angeles: University of California at Los Angeles.

Heyde, Adelaide. 1979. The relationship between self-esteem and the oral production of a second language. Unpublished doctoral dissertation, University of Michigan.

Higgs, Theodore V. 1982. Curriculum, Competence, and the Foreign Language Teacher. ACTFL Foreign Language Education Series. Lincolnwood, IL: National Textbook Company.

Higgs, Theodore V. and Clifford, Ray. 1982. The push toward communication. In Higgs 1982.

Hilgard, Ernest. 1963. Motivation in learning theory. In Koch 1963.

Hill, Jane. 1970. Foreign accents, language acquisition, and cerebral dominance revisited. Language Learning 20:237–248.

Hill, Joseph. 1972. The Educational Sciences. Detroit: Oakland Community College.

Hines, Mary and Rutherford, William. 1981. On TESOL '81. Washington, DC: Teachers of English to Speakers of Other Languages.

Hladik, Ellen G. and Edwards, Harold T. 1984. A comparative analysis of mother-father speech in the naturalistic home environment. Journal of Psycholinguistic Research, 13:321–332.

Hofstede, Geert. 1986. Cultural differences in teaching and learning. International Journal of Intercultural Relations 10:301–320.

Hogan, Robert. 1969. Development of an empathy scale. Journal of Consulting and Clinical Psychology 33:307–316.

Holmes, Janet. 1989. Sex differences and apologies: one aspect of communicative competence. Applied Linguistics 10:194–213.

Holmes, Janet. 1991. Language and gender. Language Teaching 24:207–220.

Holmes, Janet and Brown, Dorothy F. 1987. Teachers and students learning about compliments. TESOL Quarterly 21:523–546.

Holzman, Mathilda. 1984. Evidence for a reciprocal model of language development. Journal of Psycholinguistic Research 13:119–146.

Horstein, N. and Lightfoot, D. (Editors). 1981. Explanations in Linguistics: The Logical Problem of Language Acquisition. New York: Longman.

Horwitz, E.K., Horwitz, M.B., and Cope, J. 1986. Foreign language classroom anxiety. The Modern Language Journal 70:125–132.

Huang, Xiao-hua and Van Naerssen, Margaret. 1987. Learning strategies for oral communication. Applied Linguistics 8:287–307.

Hughes, Arthur. 1989. Testing for Language Teachers. Cambridge: Cambridge University Press.

Hulstijn, Jan H. 1990. A comparison between the information-processing and the analysis/control approaches to language learning. Applied Linguistics 11:30–45.

Hymes, Dell. 1967. On communicative competence. Unpublished manuscript, University of Pennsylvania.

Hymes, Dell. 1972. On communicative competence. In Pride and Holmes 1972.

Hymes, Dell. 1974. Foundations in Sociolinguistics: An Ethnographic Approach. Philadelphia: University of Pennsylvania Press.

Jacobs, Bob. 1988. Neurological differentiation of primary and secondary language acquisition. Studies in Second Language Acquisition 10:303–337.

Jacobs, Bob and Schumann, John. 1992. Language acquisition and the neurosciences: Towards a more integrative perspective. Applied Linguistics 13:282–301.

Jakobovits, Leon. 1968. Implications of recent psycholinguistic developments for the teaching of a second language. Language Learning 18:89–109.

James, Carl. 1990. Learner language. Language Teaching 23:205–213.

James, William. 1890. The Principles of Psychology. Volume 1. New York: Henry Holt & Company (Dover Publications 1950).

Jamieson, Joan. 1992. The cognitive styles of reflection/impulsivity and field independence and ESL success. Modern Language Journal. In press.

Jamieson, Joan and Chapelle, Carol. 1987. Working styles on computers as evidence of second language learning strategies. Language Learning 37: 523–544.

Jenkins, James and Palermo, David. 1964. Mediation processes and the acquisition of linguistic structure. In Bellugi and Brown 1964.

Jesperson, Otto. 1904. How to Teach a Foreign Language. Translated by Sophia Yhlen-Olsen Bertelsen. London: Allen & Unwin.

Jesperson, Otto. 1933. Essentials of English Grammar. London: Allen & Unwin.

Johnson, Jacqueline S. 1992. Critical period effects in second language acquisition: The effect of written versus auditory materials on the assessment of grammatical competence. Language Learning 42:217–248.

Jonz, Jon. 1990. Another turn in the conversation: What does cloze measure? TESOL Quarterly 24:61–83.

Joos, Martin. 1967. The Five Clocks. New York: Harcourt, Brace and World, Inc.

Judd, Elliot. 1983. The problem of applying sociolinguistic findings to TESOL: The case of male/female language. In Wolfson and Judd 1983.

Jung, Carl. 1923. Psychological Types. New York: Harcourt Brace Company.

Kachru, Braj B. 1965. The Indianness in Indian English. Word 21:391–410.

Kachru, Braj B. 1976. Models of English for the third world: White man's linguistic burden or language pragmatics? TESOL Quarterly 10:221–239.

Kachru, Braj B. 1977. New Englishes and old models. English Language Forum, July.

Kachru, Braj B. 1985. Standards, codification, and sociolinguistic realism: The English language in the outer circle. In Quirk and Widdowson 1985.

Kachru, Braj B. 1992. World Englishes: Approaches, issues, and resources. Language Teaching 25:1–14.

Kagan, Jerome. 1965. Reflection-impulsivity and reading ability in primary grade children. Child Development 36:609–628.

Kagen, Jerome, Pearson, L., and Welch, Lois. 1966. Conceptual impulsivity and inductive reasoning. Child Development 37:583–594.

Kaplan, Robert, Jones, Randall L., and Tucker, G. Richard. 1981. Annual Review of Applied Linguistics. Rowley, MA: Newbury House Publishers.

Keefe, J.W. 1979. Student Learning Styles: Diagnosing and Prescribing Programs. Reston, VA: National Association of Secondary School Principals.

Keirsey, David and Bates, Marilyn. 1984. Please Understand Me: Character and Temperament Types. Del Mar, CA: Prometheus Nemesis Book Company.

Kellerman, Susan. 1992. "I see what you mean": The role of kinesic behaviour in listening, and implications for foreign and second language learning. Applied Linguistics 13:239–258.

Kessel, Frank S. 1988. The Development of Language and Language Researchers: Essays in Honor of Roger Brown. Hillsdale, NJ: Lawrence Erlbaum Associates Publishers.

Kimble, Gregory A. and Garmezy, Norman. 1963. Principles of General Psychology. Second Edition. New York: The Ronald Press Company.

Kitao, S. Kathleen. Linguistic pragmatics and English language learning. Cross Currents 17:15–22.

Kleinmann, Howard. 1977. Avoidance behavior in adult second language acquisition. Language Learning 27:93–107.

Koch, S. (Editor). 1963. Psychology: A Study of Science. Volume 5. New York: McGraw-Hill Book Company.

Kohls, Robert L. 1984. Survival Kit for Overseas Living. Yarmouth, ME: Intercultural Press.

Krasegnor, Norman A., Rumbaugh, Duane M., Schliefelbusch, Richard L., and Studdert-Kennedy, Michael (Editors). 1991. Biological and Behavioral Determinants of Language Development. Hillsdale, NJ: Lawrence Erlbaum Associates, Publishers.

Krashen, Stephen. 1973. Lateralization, language learning, and the critical period: Some new evidence. Language Learning 23:63–74.

Krashen, Stephen. 1976. Formal and informal linguistic environments in language acquisition and language learning. TESOL Quarterly 10:157–168.

Krashen, Stephen. 1977. The monitor model for adult second language performance. In Burt, Dulay and Finocchiaro 1977.

Krashen, Stephen. 1981. Second Language Acquisition and Second Language Learning. Oxford: Pergamon Press.

Krashen, Stephen. 1982. Principles and Practice in Second Language Acquisition. Oxford: Pergamon Press.

Krashen, Stephen. 1985. The Input Hypothesis. London: Longman.

Krashen, Stephen D. 1986. Bilingual education and second language acquisition theory. In California State Department of Education 1986.

Krashen, Stephen and Terrell, Tracy D. 1983. The Natural Approach: Language Acquisition in the Classroom. Oxford: Pergamon Press.

Krashen, Stephen, Seliger, Herbert, and Hartnett, Dayle. 1974. Two studies in adult second language learning. Kritikon Literarum 3:220–228.

Krathwohl, David R., Bloom, Benjamin, and Masia, Bertram B. 1964. Taxonomy of Educational Objectives. Handbook H: Affective Domain. New York: David McKay Company.

Kuczaj, Stan A. (Editor). 1984. Discourse Development: Progress in Cognitive Development Research. New York: Springer Verlag.

Kuhn, Thomas. 1970. The Structure of Scientific Revolutions. Chicago: University of Chicago Press.

Labov, William. 1970. The study of language in its social context. Studium Generale 23:30–87.

Lado, Robert. 1957. Linguistics Across Cultures. Ann Arbor, MI: University of Michigan Press.

Lado, Robert. 1961. Language Testing: The Construction and Use of Foreign Language Tests. London: Longman Group Limited.

LaForge, Paul. 1971. Community language learning: A pilot study. Language Learning 21:45–61.

Lakoff, Robin. 1975. Language and Woman's Place. New York: Harper Colophon.

Lakoff, Robin. 1976. Language and society. In Wardhaugh and Brown 1976.

Lambert, Richard D. and Freed, Barbara F. 1982. The Loss of Language Skills. Rowley, MA: Newbury House Publishers.

Lambert, Wallace E. 1963. Psychological approaches to the study of language. Modern Language Journal 47:51–62, 114–121.

Lambert, Wallace E. 1967. A social psychology of bilingualism. The Journal of Social Issues 23:91–109.

Lambert, Wallace E. 1972. Language, Psychology, and Culture: Essays by Wallace E. Lambert. Stanford, CA: Stanford University Press.

Landes, James. 1975. Speech addressed to children: Issues and characteristics of parental input. Language Learning 25:355–379.

Langacker, Ronald W. 1973. Language and Its Structure. Second Edition. New York: Harcourt Brace Jovanovich, Inc.

Lange, Dale and Lowe, Pardee. 1986. Testing the transfer of the ACTFL/ETS/ILR reading proficiency scales to academia. Paper presented at the TESOL Testing Colloquium, Monterey, CA, March, 1986.

Langi, Uinise T. 1984. The natural approach: Approach, design, and procedure. TESL Reporter 17:11–18.

Larsen-Freeman, Diane. 1976. An explanation for the morpheme acquisition order of second language learners. Language Learning 26:125–134.

Larsen-Freeman, Diane (Editor). 1980. Discourse Analysis in Second Language Research. Rowley, MA: Newbury House Publishers.

Larsen-Freeman, Diane. 1986. Techniques and Principles in Language Teaching. New York: Oxford University Press.

Larsen-Freeman, Diane. 1991. Teaching grammar. In Celce-Murcia 1991.

Larsen-Freeman, Diane and Long, Michael H. 1991. An Introduction to Second Language Acquisition Research. New York: Longman.

Larson, Donald N. and Smalley, William A. 1972. Becoming Bilingual: A Guide to Language Learning. New Canaan, CN: Practical Anthropology.

Lawrence, Gordon. 1984. People Types and Tiger Stripes: A Practical Guide to Learning Styles. Gainesville, FL: Center for Applications of Psychological Type.

Leech, Gregory and Svartvik, Jan. 1975. A Communicative Grammar of English. London: Longman Group, Ltd.

Lenneberg, Eric H. 1964. The capacity for language acquisition. In Fodor and Katz 1964.

Lenneberg, Eric H. 1967. The Biological Foundations of Language. New York: John Wiley & Sons.

Lennon, Paul. 1991. Error: Some problems of definition, identification, and distinction. Applied Linguistics 12:180–196.

Leopold, Werner F. 1949. Speech Development of a Bilingual Child: A Linguist's Record. Evanston, IL: Northwestern University Press.

Leopold, Werner F. 1954. A child's learning of two languages. Georgetown University Round Table on Language and Linguistics 7:19–30.

Lett, John A. and O'Mara, Francis E. 1990. Predictors of success in an intensive foreign language learning context: Correlates of language learning at the Defense Language Institute Foreign Language Center. In Parry and Stansfield 1990.

Levine, Deena R., Baxter, Jim, and McNulty, Piper. 1987. The Culture Puzzle. New York: Prentice Hall.

Lightbown, Patsy M. 1985. Great expectations: Second language acquisition research and classroom teaching. Applied Linguistics 6:173–189.

Lightbown, Patsy and Spada, Nina. 1990. Focus-on-form and corrective feedback in communicative language teaching: Effects on second language learning. Studies in Second Language Acquisition 12:429–448.

Littlewood, W.T. 1981. Language variation and second language acquisition theory. Applied Linguistics 2:150–158.

Lock, Andrew. 1991. The role of social interaction in early language development. In Krasegnor et al. 1991.

Loftus, Elizabeth F. 1976. Language memories in the judicial system. Paper presented at the NWAVE Conference, Georgetown University.

Long, Michael H. 1977. Teacher feedback on learner error: Mapping cognitions. In Brown, H.D., Yorio, and Crymes 1977.

Long, Michael H. 1983. Does second language instruction make a difference? A review of research. TESOL Quarterly 17:359–382.

Long, Michael H. 1988. Instructed interlanguage development. In Beebe 1988.

Long, Michael H. 1990a. The least a second language acquisition theory needs to explain. TESOL Quarterly 24:649–666.

Long, Michael H. 1990b. Maturational constraints on language development. Studies in Second Language Acquisition 12:251–285.

Long, Michael H. and Porter, Patricia. 1985. Group work, interlanguage talk, and second language acquisition. TESOL Quarterly 19:207–228.

Lowe, Pardee and Stansfield, Charles W. (Editors). 1988. Second Language Proficiency Assessment: Current Issues. Englewood Cliffs, NJ: Prentice Hall Regents.

Lowenberg, Peter (Editor). 1988. Georgetown University Round Table on Languages and Linguistics: 1987. Washington, DC: Georgetown University Press.

Lozanov, Georgi. 1979. Suggestology and Outlines of Suggestopedy. New York: Gordon and Breach Science Publishers.

Lukmani, Yasmeen. 1972. Motivation to learn and language proficiency. Language Learning 22:261–274.

MacCorquodale, Kenneth. 1970. On Chomsky's review of Skinner's Verbal Behavior. Journal of the Experimental Analysis of Behavior 13:83–99.

MacIntyre, Peter D. and Gardner, Robert C. 1988. The measurement of anxiety and applications to second language learning: An annotated bibliography. Research Bulletin #672. London, Ontario: The University of Western Ontario.

MacIntyre, Peter D. and Gardner, Robert C. 1989. Anxiety and second language learning: Toward a theoretical clarification. Language Learning 39:251–275.

MacIntyre, Peter D. and Gardner, Robert C. 1991a. Investigating language class anxiety using the focused essay technique. Modern Language Journal 75:296–304.

MacIntyre, Peter D. and Gardner, Robert C. 1991b. Language anxiety: Its relationship to other anxieties and to processing in native and second languages. Language Learning 41:513–534.

MacIntyre, Peter D. and Gardner, Robert C. 1991c. Methods and results in the study of anxiety and language learning: A review of the literature. Language Learning 41:85–117.

Maclay, Howard and Osgood, Charles E. 1959. Hesitation phenomena in spontaneous English speech. Word 15:19–44.

Macnamara, John. 1973. The cognitive strategies of language learning. In Oller and Richards 1973.

Macnamara, John. 1975. Comparison between first and second language learning. Working Papers on Bilingualism 7:71:94.

Madsen, Harold S. 1982. Determining the debilitative impact of test anxiety. Language Learning 32:133–143.

Madsen, Harold S. 1983. Techniques in Testing. New York: Oxford University Press.

Malinowski, Bronislaw. 1923. The problem of meaning in primitive languages. In Ogden and Richards 1923.

Maratsos, Michael. 1988. Crosslinguistic analysis, universals, and language acquisition. In Kessel 1988.

Marckwardt, Albert D. 1972. Changing winds and shifting sands. MST English Quarterly 21:3–11.

Marshall, Terry. 1989. The Whole World Guide to Language Learning. Yarmouth, ME: Intercultural Press.

Maslow, Abraham H. 1970. Motivation and Personality. Second Edition. New York: Harper & Row.

McGroarty, Mary. 1984. Some meanings of communicative competence for second language students. TESOL Quarterly 18:257–272.

McGroarty, Mary and Galvan, Jose L. 1985. Culture as an issue in second language teaching. In Celce-Murcia 1985.

McLaughlin, Barry. 1978. The monitor model: Some methodological considerations. Language Learning 28:309–332.

McLaughlin, Barry. 1987. Theories of Second Language Learning. London: Edward Arnold.

McLaughlin, Barry. 1990a. "Conscious" versus "unconscious" learning. TESOL Quarterly 24:617–634.

McLaughlin, Barry. 1990b. Restructuring. Applied Linguistics 11:113–128.

McLaughlin, Barry, Rossman, Tammi, and McLeod, Beverly. 1983. Second language learning: An information-processing perspective. Language Learning 33:135–158.

McLeod, Beverly and McLaughlin, Barry. 1986. Restructuring or automaticity? Reading in a second language. Language Learning 36:109–123.

McNeill, David. 1966. Developmental psycholinguistics. In Smith and Miller 1966.

McNeill, David. 1968. On the theories of language acquisition. In Dixon and Horton 1968.

McTear, Michael F. 1984. Structure and process in children's conversational development. In Kuczaj 1984.

Mead, Robert C. (Editor). 1966. Reports of the Working Committee. New York: Northeast Conference on the Teaching of Foreign Languages.

Menyuk, Paula. 1971. The Acquisition and Development of Language. Englewood Cliffs, NJ: Prentice-Hall, Inc.

Milhollan, Frank and Forisha, B.E. 1972. From Skinner to Rogers: Contrasting Approaches to Education. Lincoln, NE: Professional Educators Publications, Inc.

Miller, George A. 1956. The magical number seven, plus or minus two: Some limits on our capacity for processing information. Psychological Review 63:81–97.

Miller, W.R. 1963. The acquisition of formal features of language. American Journal of Orthopsychiatry 34:862–867.

Milon, J. 1974. The development of negation in English by a second language learner. TESOL Quarterly 8:137–143.

Minnis, Noel (Editor). 1971. Linguistics at Large. New York: The Viking Press.

Moerk, Ernst L. 1985. Analytic, synthetic, abstracting, and word-class defining aspects of verbal mother-child interactions. Journal of Psycholinguistic Research 14:263–287.

Montgomery, Carol and Eisenstein, Miriam. 1985. Real reality revisited: An experimental communicative course in ESL. TESOL Quarterly 19:317–334.

Moore, Frank W. 1961. Readings in Cross Cultures. New Haven, CN: HRAF Press.

Morley, Joan. 1986. Current Perspectives on Pronunciation: Practices Anchored in Theory. Washington, DC: Teachers of English to Speakers of Other Languages.

Morris, Beth S.K. and Gerstman, Louis J. 1986. Age contrasts in the learning of language-relevant materials: Some challenges to critical period hypotheses. Language Learning 36:311–352.

Murdock, George Peter. 1961. The cross-cultural survey. In Moore 1961.

Myers, Isabel. 1962. The Myers-Briggs Type Indicator. Palo Alto, CA: Consulting Psychologists Press.

Naiman, Neil, Frohlich, Maria, Stern, H.H., and Todesco, Angie. 1978. The Good Language Learner. Toronto: Ontario Institute for Studies in Education.

Natalicio, D.S. and Natalicio, L.F.S. 1971. A comparative study of English pluralization by native and non-native English speakers. Child Development 42:1302–1306.

Nattinger, James R. 1984. Communicative language teaching: A new metaphor. TESOL Quarterly 18:391–407.

Neapolitan, Denise M., Pepperberg, Irene M., and Schinke-Llano, Linda. 1988. Second language acquisition: Possible insights from studies on how birds acquire song. Studies in Second Language Acquisition 10:1–11.

Nemser, W. 1971. Approximative systems of foreign language learners. International Review of Applied Linguistics 9:115–123.

Neufeld, Gerald G. 1977. Language learning ability in adults: A study on the acquisition of prosodic and articulatory features. Working Papers on Bilingualism 12:45–60.

Neufeld, Gerald G. 1979. Towards a theory of language learning ability. Language Learning 29:227–241.

Neufeld, Gerald G. 1980. On the adult's ability to acquire phonology. TESOL Quarterly 14:285–298.

New Standard Encyclopedia. 1940. Edited by Frank Vizetelly. New York: Funk & Wagnalls.

Ney, James and Pearson, Bethyl A. 1990. Connectionism as a model of language learning: Parallels in foreign language teaching. Modern Language Journal 74:474–482.

Nilsen, Alleen Pace, Bosmajian, Haig, Gershuny, H. Lee, and Stanley, Julia P. 1977. Sexism and Language. Urbana, IL: National Council of Teachers of English.

Nunan, David. 1991a. Communicative tasks and the language curriculum. TESOL Quarterly 25:279–295.

Nunan, David. 1991b. Language Teaching Methodology: A Textbook for Teachers. New York: Prentice Hall.

Nuttall, Christine. 1982. Teaching Reading Skills in a Foreign Language. London: Heinemann Educational Books.

O'Grady, William, Dobrovolsky, Michael, and Aronoff, Michael. 1989. Contemporary Linguistics. New York: St. Martin's Press.

O'Malley, Michael and Chamot, Anna Uhl. 1990. Learning Strategies in Second Language Acquisition. New York: Cambridge University Press.

O'Malley, Michael, Chamot, Anna Uhl, and Kupper, Lisa. 1989. Listening comprehension strategies in second language acquisition. Applied Linguistics 10:418–437.

O'Malley, J. Michael, Chamot, Anna U., Stewner-Manzanares, Gloria, Kupper, Lisa, and Russo, Rocco P. 1985a. Learning strategies used by beginning and intermediate ESL students. Language Learning 35:21–46.

O'Malley, J. Michael, Chamot, Anna U., Stewner-Manzanares, Gloria, Russo, Rocco P., and Kupper, Lisa. 1985b. Learning strategy applications with students of English as a second language. TESOL Quarterly 19:557–584.

O'Malley, Michael, Chamot, Anna Uhl, and Walker, C. 1987. Some applications of cognitive theory to second language acquisition. Studies in Second Language Acquisition 9:287–306.

O'Malley, J. Michael, Russo, Rocco P., and Chamot, Anna U. 1983. A review of the literature on learning strategies in the acquisition of English as a second language: The potential for research applications. Rosslyn, VA: InterAmerica Research Associates.

Obler, Lorraine K. 1981. Right hemisphere participation in second language acquisition. In Diller 1981.

Obler, Lorraine K. 1982. Neurolinguistic aspects of language loss as they pertain to second language acquisition. In Lambert and Freed 1982.

Ochsner, Robert. 1970. A poetics of second language acquisition. Language Learning 29:53–80.

Odlin, Terence. 1986. On the nature and use of explicit knowledge. International Review of Applied Linguistics 24:123–144.

Ogden, Charles K. and Richards, I.A. (Editors). The Meaning of Meaning. London: Kegan Paul.

Ohio State University. 1991. Language Files. Columbus, OH: Ohio State University Press.

Oller, John W. 1976. A program for language testing research. Language Learning, Special Issue Number 4:141–165.

Oller, John W. 1979. Language Tests at School: A Pragmatic Approach. London: Longman Group Limited.

Oller, John W. 1981a. Language as intelligence? Language Learning 31:465–492.

Oller, John W. 1981b. Research on the measurement of affective variables: Some remaining questions. In Andersen 1981.

Oller, John W. 1982. Gardner on affect: A reply to Gardner. Language Learning 32:183–189.

Oller, John W. (Editor). 1983. Issues in Language Testing Research. Rowley, MA: Newbury House Publishers.

Oller, John W. and Perkins, Kyle (Editors). 1980. Research in Language Testing. Rowley, MA: Newbury House Publishers.

Oller, John W. and Richards, Jack C. (Editors). 1973. Focus on the Learner: Pragmatic Perspectives for the Language Teacher. Rowley, MA: Newbury House Publishers.

Oller, John W. and Streiff, Virginia. 1975. Dictation: A test of grammar based on expectancies. English Language Teaching 30:25–36.

Oller, John W. and Ziahosseiny, Seid M. 1970. The contrastive analysis hypothesis and spelling errors. Language Learning 20:183–189.

Oller, John W., Baca, Lori L., and Vigil, Alfredo. 1978. Attitudes and attained proficiency in ESL: A sociolinguistic study of Mexican-Americans in the Southwest. TESOL Quarterly 11:173–183.

Oller, John W., Hudson, A., and Liu, Phyllis F. 1977. Attitudes and attained proficiency in ESL: A sociolinguistic study of native speakers of Chinese in the United States. Language Learning 27:1–27.

Olshtain, Elite. 1989. Is second language attrition the reversal of second language acquisition? Studies in Second Language Acquisition 11:151–165.

Olshtain, Elite and Cohen, Andrew D. 1983. Apology: A speech-act set. In Wolfson and Judd 1983.

Omaggio, Alice C. 1981. Helping Learners Succeed: Activities for the Foreign Language Classroom. Washington, DC: Center for Applied Linguistics.

Osgood, Charles E. 1953. Method and Theory in Experimental Psychology. New York: Oxford University Press.

Osgood, Charles E. 1957. Contemporary Approaches to Cognition. Cambridge, MA: Harvard University Press.

Ostrander, Sheila and Schroeder, Lynn. 1979. Superlearning. New York: Dell Publishing Company.

Oxford, Rebecca. 1990a. Language Learning Strategies: What Every Teacher Should Know. New York: Newbury House Publishers.

Oxford, Rebecca. 1990b. Styles, strategies, and aptitude: Connections for language learning. In Parry and Stansfield 1990.

Oxford, Rebecca and Crookall, David. 1989. Research on language learning strategies: Methods, findings, and instructional issues. Modern Language Journal 73:404–419.

Oxford, Rebecca and Ehrman, Madeline. 1988. Psychological type and adult language learning strategies: A pilot study. Journal of Psychological Type 16: 22–32.

Paribakht, Tahereh. 1984. The relationship between the use of communication strategies and aspects of target language proficiencies: A study of ESL students. Quebec: International Center for Research on Bilingualism.

Paribakht, Tahereh. 1985. Strategic competence and language proficiency. Applied Linguistics 6:132–146.

Parry, Thomas and Child, James R. 1990. Preliminary investigation of the relationship between VORD, MLAT, and language proficiency. In Parry and Stansfield 1990.

Parry, Thomas S. and Stansfield, Charles W. (Editors). 1990. Language Aptitude Reconsidered. New York: Prentice Hall Regents.

Patkowski, Mark S. 1990. Age and accent in a second language: A reply to James Emil Flege. Applied Linguistics 11:73–89.

Paulston, Christina B. 1974. Linguistic and communicative competence. TESOL Quarterly 8:347–362.

Pei, Mario. 1966. Glossary of Linguistic Terminology. New York: Anchor Books.

Peters, Ann M. 1981. Language learning strategies: Does the whole equal the sum of the parts? In Diller 1981.

Phillips, Elaine M. 1992. The effects of language anxiety on students' oral test performance and attitudes. Modern Language Journal 76:14–26.

Phillipson, Robert. 1992. Linguistic Imperialism. London: Oxford University Press.

Pike, Kenneth. 1967. Language in Relation to a Unified Theory of the Structure of Human Behavior. The Hague: Mouton Publishers.

Pimsleur, Paul. 1966. Pimsleur Language Aptitude Battery. New York: Harcourt, Brace & World.

Prator, Clifford H. 1967. Hierarchy of difficulty. Unpublished classroom lecture, University of California, Los Angeles.

Prator, Clifford H. 1972. Manual of American English Pronunciation. Diagnostic Passage. New York: Holt, Rinehart & Winston.

Prator, Clifford H. and Celce-Murcia, Marianne. 1979. An outline of language teaching approaches. In Celce-Murcia and McIntosh 1979.

Pride, J.B. and Holmes, J. (Editors). 1972. Sociolinguistics. Harmondsworth, UK: Penguin Books.

Quirk, R. 1988. The question of standard in the international use of English. In Lowenberg 1988.

Quirk, R. and Widdowson, Henry. 1988. English in the World: Teaching and Learning the Language and Literatures. Cambridge: Cambridge University Press.

Raimes, Ann. 1983. Tradition and revolution in ESL teaching. TESOL Quarterly 17:535–552.

Ramage, Katherine. 1990. Motivational factors and persistence in foreign language study. Language Learning 40:189–219.

Random House Dictionary of the English Language. 1966. New York: Random House.

Ravem, Roar. 1968. Language acquisition in a second language environment. International Review of Applied Linguistics 6:175–185.

Reid, Joy M. 1987. The learning style preferences of ESL students. TESOL Quarterly 21:87–111.

Reynolds, Allan G. 1991. The cognitive consequences of bilingualism. ERIC/CLL News Bulletin 14:1–8.

Rice, M. 1980. Cognition to Language: Categories, Word Meanings, and Training. Baltimore: University Park Press.

Richards, Jack C. 1974. Error Analysis: Perspectives on Second Language Acquisition. London: Longman Group, Ltd.

Richards, Jack C. 1975. Simplification: A strategy in the adult acquisition of a foreign language: An example from Indonesian/Malay. Language Learning 25:115–126.

Richards, Jack C. 1976. Second language learning. In Wardhaugh and Brown 1976.

Richards, Jack C. 1979. Rhetorical styles and communicative styles in the new varieties of English. Language Learning 29:1–25.

Richards, Jack C. 1984. The secret life of methods. TESOL Quarterly 18:7–23.

Richards, Jack C. and Rodgers, Theodore S. 1982. Method: Approach, design, and procedure. TESOL Quarterly 16:153–168.

Richards, Jack C. and Rodgers, Theodore S. 1986. Approaches and Methods in Language Teaching. Cambridge: Cambridge University Press.

Richards, Jack C. and Schmidt, Richard (Editors). 1983. Language and Communication. London: Longman Group Ltd.

Rivers, Wilga M. 1964. The Psychologist and the Foreign Language Teacher. Chicago: University of Chicago Press.

Rivers, Wilga M. 1981. Teaching Foreign Language Skills. Second Edition. Chicago: University of Chicago Press.

Roberts, Cheryl. 1983. Field independence as a predictor of second language learning for adult ESL learners in the United States. Unpublished doctoral dissertation, University of Illinois.

Robinett, B.J. and Schachter, Jacquelyn (Editors). Second Language Learning: Contrastive Analysis, Error Analysis, and Related Aspects. Ann Arbor, MI: University of Michigan Press.

Rogers, Carl. 1951. Client Centered Therapy. Boston: Houghton Mifflin Company.

Rogers, Carl R. 1983. Freedom to Learn for the Eighties. Columbus, OH: Charles E. Merrill Publishing Company.

Rosansky, Ellen J. 1975. The critical period for the acquisition of language: Some cognitive developmental considerations. Working Papers on Bilingualism 6:92–102.

Rosansky, Ellen J. 1976. Methods and morphemes in second language acquisition research. Language Learning 26:409–425.

Ross, Steven and Berwick, Richard. 1992. The discourse of accommodation in oral proficiency interviews. Studies in Second Language Acquisition 14:159–176.

Rost, Michael and Ross, Steven. 1991. Learner use of strategies in interaction: Typology and predictability. Language Learning 41:235–273.

Rubin, Joan. 1975. What the "good language learner" can teach us. TESOL Quarterly 9:41–51.

Rubin, Joan. 1976. How to tell when someone is saying "no." Topics in Culture Learning, Volume 4, East-West Culture Learning Institute, Honolulu. Reprinted in Wolfson and Judd 1983.

Rubin, Joan and Thompson, Irene. 1982. How to Be a More Successful Language Learner. Boston: Heinle and Heinle Publishers.

Rutherford, William. 1982. Markedness in second language acquisition. Language Learning 32:85–108.

Rutherford, William and Sharwood-Smith, Michael (Editors). 1988. Grammar and Second Language Teaching: A Book of Readings. New York: Newbury House Publishers.

Saussure, Ferdinand de. 1916. Cours de linguistique générale. (Course in General Linguistics. Translated by Wade Baskin. New York: McGraw-Hill Book Company, 1959.)

Savignon, Sandra J. 1972. Communicative Competence: An Experiment in Foreign Language Teaching. Philadelphia: The Center for Curriculum Development, Inc.

Savignon, Sandra J. 1982. Dictation as a measure of communicative competence in French as a second language. Language Learning 32:33–51.

Savignon, Sandra J. 1983. Communicative Competence: Theory and Classroom Practice. Reading, MA: Addison-Wesley Publishing Company.

Savignon, Sandra J. and Berns, Margie S. 1984. Initiatives in Communicative Language Teaching: A Book of Readings. Reading, MA: Addison-Wesley Publishing Company.

Scarcella, Robin C., Andersen, Elaine S., and Krashen, Stephen D. (Editors). 1990. Developing Communicative Competence in a Second Language. New York: Newbury House Publishers.

Schachter, Jacqueline. 1974. An error in error analysis. Language Learning 24:205–214.

Schachter, Jacquelyn. 1988. Second language acquisition and its relationship to Universal Grammar. Applied Linguistics 9:219–235.

Schinke-Llano, Linda. 1989. Early childhood bilingualism. Studies in Second Language Acquisition 11:223–240.

Schmidt, Richard W. 1983. Interaction, acculturation, and the acquisition of communicative competence: A case study of an adult. In Wolfson and Judd 1983.

Schmidt, Richard W. 1990. The role of consciousness in second language learning. Applied Linguistics 11:129–158.

Schultz, Renate. 1991. Second language acquisition theories and teaching practice: How do they fit? Modern Language Journal 75:17–26.

Schumann, John H. 1975. Affective factors and the problem of age in second language acquisition. Language Learning 25:209–235.

Schumann, John H. 1976a. Second language acquisition: The pidginization hypothesis. Language Learning 26:391–408.

Schumann, John H. 1976b. Second language acquisition research: Getting a more global look at the learner. Language Learning, Special Issue Number 4:15–28.

Schumann, John H. 1976c. Social distance as a factor in second language acquisition. Language Learning 26:135–143.

Schumann, John H. 1978. The Pidginization Process: A Model for Second Language Acquisition. Rowley, MA: Newbury House Publishers.

Schumann, John H. 1982a. Art and science in second language acquisition research. In Clarke and Handscombe 1982.

Schumann, John H. 1982b. Simplification, transfer, and relexification as aspects of pidginization and early second language acquisition. Language Learning 32:337–366.

Schumann, John H. 1990. Extending the scope of the acculturation/pidginization model to include cognition. TESOL Quarterly 24:667–684.

Schumann, John H. and Stenson, Nancy (Editors). 1974. New Frontiers of Second Language Learning. Rowley, MA: Newbury House Publishers.

Schumann, John H., Holroyd, Jean, Campbell, Russell N., and Ward, Frederick A. 1978. Improvement of foreign language pronunciation under hypnosis: A preliminary study. Language Learning 28:143–148.

Schwartz, Joan. 1980. The negotiation for meaning: Repair in conversations between second language learners of English. In Larsen-Freeman 1980.

Sciarone, A.G. and Schoorl, J.J. 1989. The cloze test: Or why small isn't always beautiful. Language Learning 39:415–438.

Scovel, Thomas. 1969. Foreign accents, language acquisition, and cerebral dominance. Language Learning 19:245–254.

Scovel, Thomas. 1978. The effect of affect on foreign language learning: A review of the anxiety research. Language Learning 28:129–142.

Scovel, Thomas. 1979. Review of Suggestology and Outlines of Suggestopedy, by Georgi Lozanov. TESOL Quarterly 13:255–266.

Scovel, Thomas. 1982. Questions concerning the application of neurolinguistic research to second language learning/teaching. TESOL Quarterly 16:323–331.

Scovel, Thomas. 1984. A time to speak: Evidence for a biologically-based critical period for language acquisition. Paper presented at San Francisco State University, January 19, 1984.

Scovel, Thomas. 1988. A Time to Speak: A Psycholinguistic Inquiry into the Critical Period for Human Speech. New York: Newbury House Publishers.

Sebuktekin, Hikmet. 1975. An Outline of English-Turkish Contrastive Phonology: Segmental Phonemes. Istanbul: Bogazici University.

Seliger, Herbert W. 1982. On the possible role of the right hemisphere in second language acquisition. TESOL Quarterly 16:307–314.

Seliger, Herbert W. 1983. Learner interaction in the classroom and its effects on language acquisition. In Seliger and Long 1983.

Seliger, Herbert W. and Long, Michael H. 1983. Classroom Oriented Research in Second Language Acquisition. Rowley, MA: Newbury House Publishers.

Selinker, Larry. 1972. Interlanguage. International Review of Applied Linguistics 10:201–231.

Selinker, Larry and Lamendella, John. 1979. The role of extrinsic feedback in interlanguage fossilization: A discussion of "Rule fossilization: A tentative model." Language Learning 29:363–375.

Shatz, Marilyn and McCloskey, Laura. 1984. Answering appropriately: A developmental perspective on conversational knowledge. In Kuczaj 1984.

Shohamy, Elana. 1988. A proposed framework for testing the oral language of second/foreign language learners. Studies in Second Language Acquisition 10:165–180.

Sinclair, J.M. and Coulthard, R.M. 1975. Towards an Analysis of Discourse: The English Used by Teachers and Pupils. Oxford: Oxford University Press.

Singer, H. and Ruddell, R.B. (Editors). 1970. Theoretical Models and Processes of Reading. Newark, DE: International Reading Association.

Skehan, Peter. 1988. Language testing: Part I. Language Teaching 21: 211–221.

Skehan, Peter. 1989a. Individual Differences in Second Language Learning. London: Edward Arnold.

Skehan, Peter. 1989b. Language testing: Part II. Language Teaching 22: 1–13.

Skehan, Peter. 1991. Individual differences in second language learning. Studies in Second Language Acquisition 13:275–298.

Skinner, B.F. 1938. Behavior of Organisms: An Experimental Analysis. New York: Appleton-Century-Crofts.

Skinner, B.F. 1953. Science and Human Behavior. New York: Macmillan Company.

Skinner, B.F. 1957. Verbal Behavior. New York: Appleton-Century-Crofts.

Skinner, B.F. 1968. The Technology of Teaching. New York: Appleton-Century-Crofts.

Slobin, Dan I. 1971. Psycholinguistics. Glenview, IL: Scott, Foresman & Company.

Slobin, Dan I. (Editor). 1986. The Crosslinguistic Study of Language Acquisition. Volumes 1 & 2. Hillsdale, NJ: Lawrence Erlbaum Associates.

Slobin, Dan I. (Editor). 1992. The Crosslinguistic Study of Language Acquisition. Volume 3. Hillsdale, NJ: Lawrence Erlbaum Associates.

Smith, Frank. 1975. Comprehension and Learning: A Conceptual Framework for Teachers. New York: Holt, Rinehart & Winston.

Smith, Frank and Miller, George A. (Editors). 1966. The Genesis of Language: A Psycholinguistic Approach. Cambridge, MA: M.I.T. Press.

Smith, Stephen M. 1984. The Theater Arts and the Teaching of Second Languages. Reading, MA: Addison-Wesley Publishing Company.

Snow, Marguerite A. and Shapira, Rina G. 1985. The role of social-psychological factors in second language learning. In Celce-Murcia 1985.

Sokolik, M.E. 1990. Learning without rules: PDP and a resolution of the adult language learning paradox. TESOL Quarterly 24:685–696.

Sorenson, Arthur. 1967. Multilingualism in the Northwest Amazon. American Anthropologist 69:670–684.

Spolsky, Bernard. 1969. Attitudinal aspects of second language learning. Language Learning 19:271–283.

Spolsky, Bernard. 1970. Linguistics and language pedagogy—applications or implications. Monograph on Languages and Linguistics 22. Report of the 20th Annual Round Table Meeting, Georgetown University.

Spolsky, Bernard (Editor). 1978a. Approaches to Language Testing. Arlington, VA: Center for Applied Linguistics.

Spolsky, Bernard. 1978b. Linguists and language testers. In Spolsky 1978a.

Spolsky, Bernard. 1988. Bridging the gap: A general theory of second language learning. TESOL Quarterly 22:377–396.

Spolsky, Bernard. 1990. Introduction to a colloquium: The scope and form of a theory of second language learning. TESOL Quarterly 24:609–616.

Spolsky, Bernard. 1989. Communicative competence, language proficiency, and beyond. Applied Linguistics 10:138–156.

Stansfield, Charles and Hansen, Jacqueline. 1983. Field dependence-independence as a variable in second language cloze test performance. TESOL Quarterly 17:29–38.

Stansfield, Charles W. and Kenyon, Dorry Mann. 1992. The development and validation of a simulated oral proficiency interview. Modern Language Journal 76:129–141.

Stauble, Ann-Marie E. 1978. The process of decreolization: A model for second language development. Language Learning 28:29–54.

Stenson, Nancy. 1974. Induced errors. In Schumann and Stenson 1974.

Stern, H.H. 1970. Perspectives on Second Language Teaching. Toronto: Ontario Institute for Studies in Education.

Stern, H.H. 1975. What can we learn from the good language learner? The Canadian Modern Language Review 34:304–318. Reprinted in Croft 1980.

Sternberg, Robert J. 1985. Beyond IQ: A Triarchic Theory of Human Intelligence. New York: Cambridge University Press.

Sternberg, Robert J. 1988. The Triarchic Mind: A New Theory of Human Intelligence. New York: Viking Press.

Sternberg, Robert J. and Davidson, Janet E. 1982. The mind of the puzzler. Psychology Today 16:6:37–44.

Stevick, Earl. 1974. The meaning of drills and exercises. Language Learning 24:1–22.

Stevick, Earl. 1976a. Memory, Meaning and Method. Rowley, MA: Newbury House Publishers.

Stevick, Earl. 1976b. English as an alien language. In Fanselow and Crymes 1976.

Stevick, Earl. 1982. Teaching and Learning Languages. New York: Cambridge University Press.

Stevick, Earl W. 1989. Success With Foreign Languages: Seven Who Achieved It and What Worked for Them. New York: Prentice Hall.

Stockwell, Robert, Bowen, J. Donald, and Martin, John W. 1965. The Grammatical Structures of English and Spanish. Chicago: University of Chicago Press.

Sullivan, Edmund V. 1967. Piaget and the School Curriculum: A Critical Appraisal. Toronto: Ontario Institute for Studies in Education.

Svanes, Bjorg. 1987. Motivation and "cultural distance" in second language acquisition. Language Learning 37:341–359.

Svanes, Bjorg. 1988. Attitudes and "cultural distance" in second language acquisition. Applied Linguistics 9:357–371.

Swain, Merrill. 1977. Future directions in second language research. In Henning 1977.

Swain, Merrill. 1984. Large-scale communicative language testing. In Savignon and Berns 1984.

Swain, Merrill. 1990. The language of French immersion students: Implications for theory and practice. In Alatis 1990.

Tannen, Deborah. 1986. That's Not What I Meant! How Conversational Style Makes or Breaks Your Relations with Others. New York: William Morrow.

Tannen, Deborah. 1990. You Just Don't Understand: Women and Men in Conversation. New York: William Morrow.

Tarone, Elaine. 1979. Interlanguage as chameleon. Language Learning 29:181–191.

Tarone, Elaine. 1981. Some thoughts on the notion of communication strategy. TESOL Quarterly 15:285–295.

Tarone, Elaine. 1983. Some thoughts on the notion of "communication strategy." In Faerch and Kasper 1983.

Tarone, Elaine, 1988. Variation in Interlanguage. London: Edward Arnold.

Tarone, Elaine. 1990. On variation in interlanguage: A response to Gregg. Applied Linguistics 11:392–400.

Tarone, Elaine, Frauenfelder, Uli, and Selinker, Larry. 1976. Systematicity/variability and stability/instability in interlanguage systems. In H.D. Brown 1976a.

Tarone, Elaine and Parrish, B. 1988. Task related variation in interlanguage: The case of articles. Language Learning 38:21–44.

Taylor, Barry P. 1974. Toward a theory of language acquisition. Language Learning 24:23–35.

Taylor, Barry P. 1975. The use of overgeneralization and transfer learning strategies by elementary and intermediate students in ESL. Language Learning 25: 73–107.

Taylor, Barry P. 1983. Teaching ESL: Incorporating a communicative, student-centered component. TESOL Quarterly 17:69–88.

Taylor, David S. 1988. The meaning and use of the term "competence" in Linguistics and Applied Linguistics. Applied Linguistics 9:148–168.

Thompson, Irene. 1991. Foreign accents revisited: The English pronunciation of Russian immigrants. Language Learning 41:177–204.

Torrance, E. Paul. 1980. Your Style of Learning and Thinking, Forms B and C. Athens, GA: University of Georgia.

Trayer, Marie. 1991. Learning style differences: Gifted vs. regular language students. Foreign Language Annals 24:419–425.

Twaddell, Freeman. 1935. On Defining the Phoneme. Language Monograph Number 166.

Twain, Mark. 1869. The Innocents Abroad. Volume 1. New York: Harper and Brothers.

Twain, Mark. 1880. A Tramp Abroad. Hartford, CN: American Publishing Company.

Upshur, John A. 1976. Discussion of "A program for language testing research." Language Learning, Special Issue Number 4:167–174.

Upshur, John A. and Homburg, T.J. 1983. Some relations among language tests as successive ability levels. In Oller 1983.

Valdman, Albert (Editor). 1966. Trends in Language Teaching. New York: McGraw-Hill Book Company.

Valdman, Albert (Editor). 1988. The Assessment of Foreign Language Oral Proficiency. Studies in Second Language Acquisition 10 (June 1988).

Van Ek, J.A. and Alexander, L.G. 1975. Threshold Level English. Oxford: Pergamon Press.

Van Ek, J.A., Alexander, L.G., and Fitzpatrick, M.A. 1977. Waystage English. Oxford: Pergamon Press.

Van Lier, Leo. 1989. Reeling, writhing, drawling, and fainting in coils: Oral proficiency interviews as conversation. TESOL Quarterly 23:489–508.

Vann, Roberta J. and Abraham, Roberta G. 1990. Strategies of unsuccessful language learners. TESOL Quarterly 24:177–198.

Varadi, T. 1973. Strategies of target language learner communication: Message adjustment. Paper presented at the Sixth Conference of the Romanian-English Linguistics Project. (Later reprinted in the International Review of Applied Linguistics) 18:59–71 (1980).

Vigil, Neddy A. and Oller, John W. 1976. Rule fossilization: A tentative model. Language Learning 26:281–295.

Wagner-Gough, Judy. 1975. Comparative studies in second language learning. CAL-ERIC/CLL Series on Languages and Linguistics 26.

Walsh, Terence M. and Diller, Karl C. 1981. Neurolinguistic considerations on the optimum age for second language learning. In Diller 1981.

Wanner, Eric. and Gleitman, Lila R. 1982. Language Acquisition: The State of the Art. Cambridge: Cambridge University Press.

Wardhaugh, Ronald. 1970. The contrastive analysis hypothesis. TESOL Quarterly 4:123–130.

Wardhaugh, Ronald. 1971. Theories of language acquisition in relation to beginning reading instruction. Language Learning 21:1–26.

Wardhaugh, Ronald. 1972. Introduction to Linguistics. New York: McGraw-Hill Book Company.

Wardhaugh, Ronald. 1974. Topics in Applied Linguistics. Rowley, MA: Newbury House Publishers.

Wardhaugh, Ronald. 1976. The Contexts of Language. Rowley, MA: Newbury House Publishers.

Wardhaugh, Ronald. 1977. Introduction to Linguistics. Second Edition. Rowley, MA: Newbury House Publishers.

Wardhaugh, Ronald. 1992. An Introduction to Sociolinguistics. Second Edition. Cambridge, MA: Basil Blackwell.

Wardhaugh, Ronald and Brown, H. Douglas (Editors). 1976. A Survey of Applied Linguistics. Ann Arbor: University of Michigan Press.

Watkins, David, Biggs, John, and Regmi, Murari. 1991. Does confidence in the language of instruction influence a student's approach to learning? Instructional Science 20:331–339.

Watson, John B. 1913. Psychology as the behaviorist views it. Psychological Review 20:158–177.

Webster's New International Dictionary of the English Language. 1934. Edited by W.A. Neilson. Springfield, MA: G. and C. Merriam Company.

Weinreich, Uriel. 1953. Languages in Contact: Findings and Problems. New York: Publication Number 1 of the Linguistic Circle of New York.

Weir, Cyril J. 1988. Communicative Language Testing. New York: Prentice Hall.

Weir, Ruth H. 1962. Language in the Crib. The Hague: Mouton Publishers.

Weissenborn, Jurgen, Goodluck, Helen, and Roeper, Thomas. 1991. Theoretical Issues in Language Acquisition: Continuity and Change in Development. Hillsdale, NJ: Lawrence Erlbaum Associates.

Weltens, Burt. 1987. The attrition of foreign language skills: A literature review. Applied Linguistics 8:22–38.

Weltens, Bert and Cohen, Andrew D. 1989. Language attrition research: An introduction. Studies in Second Language Acquisition 11:127–133.

Wenden, Anita L. 1985. Learner strategies. TESOL Newsletter 19:1–7.

Wesche, Marjorie B. 1983. Communicative testing in a second language. The Modern Language Journal 67:41–55.

White, Lydia. 1987. Against comprehensible input: The input hypothesis and the development of second language competence. Applied Linguistics 8:95–110.

White, Lydia. 1990. Second language acquisition and universal grammar. Studies in Second Language Acquisition 12:121–133.

Whitman, Randal. 1970. Contrastive analysis: Problems and procedures. Language Learning 20:191–197.

Whitman, Randal and Jackson, Kenneth L. 1972. The unpredictability of contrastive analysis. Language Learning 22:29–41.

Whorf, Benjamin. 1956. Science and linguistics. In Carroll 1956.

Widdowson, Henry G. 1978a. Notional-functional syllabuses 1978: Part IV. In Blatchford and Schachter 1978.

Widdowson, Henry G. 1978b. Teaching Language as Communication. Oxford: Oxford University Press.

Wilkins, David A. 1976. Notional Syllabuses. London: Oxford University Press.

Witkin, Herman A., Oltman, Philip K., Raskin, Evelyn, and Karp, Stephen. 1971. Embedded Figures Test. Manual for the Embedded Figures Test. Palo Alto, CA: Consulting Psychologists Press, Inc.

Wolfson, Nessa. 1981. Compliments in cross-cultural perspective. TESOL Quarterly 15:117–124.

Wolfson, Nessa and Judd, Elliot (Editors). 1983. Sociolinguistics and Language Acquisition. Rowley, MA: Newbury House Publishers.

Wolfson, Nessa, D'Amico-Reisner, Lynne, and Huber, Lisa. 1983. How to arrange for social commitments in American English: The invitation. In Wolfson and Judd 1983.

Wong, Rita F. 1986. Instructional considerations in teaching pronunciation. In Morley 1986.

Wong, Rita F. 1987. Teaching Pronunciation: Focus on Rhythm and Intonation. Washington, DC: Center for Applied Linguistics.

Yorio, Carlos. 1976. Discussion of "Explaining sequence and variation in second language acquisition." Language Learning, Special Issue Number 4:59–63.

Young, Dolly Jesusita. 1991. Creating a low anxiety classroom environment: What does language anxiety research suggest? Modern Language Journal 75: 426–439.

Young, Richard. 1988. Variation and the interlanguage hypothesis. Studies in Second Language Acquisition 10:281–302.

Yule, George and Tarone, Elaine. 1990. Eliciting the performance of strategic competence. In Scarcella, Andersen, and Krashen 1990.

Zangwill, Oliver. 1971. The neurology of language. In Minnis 1971.

# Index

## Subjects